JAMES L. WISER

Loyola University of Chicago

Political Philosophy: A History of the Search for Order

PRENTICE-HALL, INC., Englewood Cliffs, New Jersey 07632

Library of Congress Cataloging in Publication Data

WISER, JAMES L.
   Political philosophy, a history of the search for
order.

   Includes bibliographies and index.
   1. Political science—History. I. Title.
JA81.W54 1983   320'.01'09   82–10152
ISBN 0–13–684845–1   AACR2

Editorial production supervision: *Edith Riker*
Cover design: *Ray Lundgren*
Manufacturing buyer: *Ron Chapman*

Printed in the United States of America

10 9 8 7 6 5 4 3 2

ISBN 0-13-684845-1

Prentice-Hall International, Inc., *London*
Prentice-Hall of Australia Pty. Limited, *Sydney*
Prentice-Hall Canada Inc., *Toronto*
Prentice-Hall of India Private Limited, *New Delhi*
Prentice-Hall of Japan, Inc., *Tokyo*
Prentice-Hall of Southeast Asia Pte. Ltd., *Singapore*
Whitehall Books Limited, *Wellington, New Zealand*

TO
BETH, STEVEN, AND MICHAEL

CONTENTS

PREFACE

In an essay published in 1838, John Stuart Mill wrote:

> But they were destined to renew a lesson given to mankind by every age, and always disregarded—to show that speculative philosophy, which to the superficial appears a thing so remote from the business of life and the outward interests of men, is in reality the thing on earth which most influences them, and in the long run overbears every other influence save those which it must itself obey.[1]

In this passage, Mill essentially repeated an argument that the classical-Greek philosophers had long maintained. To them it had been obvious that humanity cannot help but express by its actions its understanding of the nature of things. Typically, this understanding includes basic assumptions concerning the human condition, the purposes of society, the meaning of nature, the direction of history, and the structure of being itself.

---

[1] John Stuart Mill, "Bentham," in Mary Warnock, ed., *John Stuart Mill: Utilitarianism, On Liberty, Essay on Bentham* (New York: New American Library, n.d.), p. 78.

That these assumptions are not often the subjects of popular political debate, does not deny their importance for and centrality to the existence of society. This is the case because every society necessarily operates according to a set of given presuppositions. It takes them as the "self-evident truths" upon which it is founded. And in the most serious cases, it enforces them with the authority and power of the government. It is fair to say that these assumptions, beliefs, and mutual expectations actually join to form the social fabric that is essential for political existence.

One of the effects of the rapid growth in the historical and social sciences during the nineteenth and twentieth centuries has been an increasing awareness of the diversity among such fundamental beliefs. Thus, the once-popular assumption that there may be a common, or at least uniform, set of social customs among nations is constantly being challenged by the evidence taken from societies of another time and place. This challenge is especially dramatic if one moves outside of the area of Western civilization and confronts cultures as rich as, if not richer than, our own. Such a confrontation, in turn, forces one to reconsider one's own beliefs and to speculate on their relative merit and worth. Such speculation, in fact, is the very material of political philosophy.

To fully appreciate contemporary politics, we must expand our vision of the political in such a way as to include that context of beliefs, expectations, and commitments which constitute our symbolic universe. Yet, unless a contrast is provided, this attempt to focus upon the larger context is extremely difficult. Indeed an adequate understanding of our society requires both an appreciation of our differences and an awareness of the available alternatives. It is obvious that modern Western politics takes place within a specific set of philosophical and cultural assumptions. Inasmuch as these assumptions affirm certain beliefs, they represent at the same time a rejection of possible alternatives. Thus a satisfactory understanding of ourselves ultimately requires that we comprehend this total pattern of affirmations and negations.

A central theme of this book is that one of the most fruitful contrasts to modern Western political philosophy is that body of work created by the classical-Greek and Christian thinkers. Indeed, to a certain degree, modern Western political philosophy may be seen as the product of a sustained effort to free itself from what it perceived to be the restraints and limitations of its own past. In part, therefore, Western modernity is based upon a negation of Western antiquity. Whether a real negation is, in fact, possible remains to be seen. Yet, whether it is desirable is a judgment that is intrinsic to the very practice of political philosophy itself.

This book accepts the premise that an adequate comprehension of our society depends in part upon an adequate understanding of where we have been. Thus, it argues that the *terminus ad quem* of the modern movement becomes apparent only in terms of its *terminus a quo*. Similarly, the true meaning of our deepest affirmations becomes clearer only with an appreciation of the negations upon which they are founded.

This premise explains in turn the principle of selection that is used throughout this book. It is obvious that every Western political philosopher has not been included, nor has every theme of political importance been developed. Similarly, it is apparent that certain thinkers, for example, Bacon and Descartes, and certain intellectual developments, for example, modern science, are included even though some may consider them to be political only in the widest sense. Yet inasmuch as politics is an activity which takes place within a particular spiritual and cultural context, a true understanding of political philosophy requires that we take notice of those thinkers and ideas which contributed most directly to the formation and structure of that context. Indeed it is the author's judgment that the thinkers discussed in this book are among the most helpful in this effort.

ACKNOWLEDGMENTS

It is impossible to thank adequately all the people whose ideas, writings, or conversations have helped me develop the intellectual perspective which informs this work. However, I would like to acknowledge Professors Lyman Tower Sargent, University of Missouri, Morton Schoolman, SUNY-Albany, Sidney A. Pearson, Jr., Radford University, Stuart A. Lilie, University of Central Florida, and Richard W. Krouse, Williams College. Each has read the manuscript either in its entirety or in part and has made a number of useful comments. I have benefited from their suggestions and am indebted to them for their expertise.

Finally, I would like to thank Margaret Kranzfelder, Jeanne Huchthausen, and Mary Margaret Kelly for their essential support in the preparation of this manuscript. Their professional skills and patience provided invaluable aid throughout the many and various stages of this project.

J. L. W.

PART 1

The Classical Tradition

1

PLATO

The Hellenic civilization of the fifth and fourth centuries B.C. has had such an immense attraction for Western society that it is, at times, difficult to appreciate the tenuous and fragile nature of its accomplishments. Its heroes have become our heroes, and the list is impressive. Even a partial roster would have to include such seminal figures as Aeschylus, Sophocles, Euripides, Aristophanes, Socrates, Plato, Aristotle, Pericles, Pindar, Thucydides, Herodotus, Xenophanes, Parmenides, and Heraclitus. And this list could easily be expanded. If it were, it would form the basis for most of the important pillars of modern Western civilization. As George Grant has written:

> Greece lay behind Europeans as a first presence. . . . It was for them primal in the sense that in its perfected statements educated Europeans found the way that things are. The Greek writings bared a knowledge of the human and non-human things which could be grasped as firmness by the European for the making of their own lives and cities.[1]

[1] George Grant, *Technology and Empire* (Toronto: House of Anansi, 1969), p. 18.

The stability attributed to the Hellenic spiritual tradition, however, was not a feature of Greek political existence. Although we tend to focus upon such political accomplishments as Athenian democracy, we should not forget that they were but a brief moment in a general political history which was, in fact, determined by other forces. Specifically, Hellenic society existed, for a time, as a pragmatic alternative to imperial rule. Greece initially gained its independence through a struggle with the Persian empire; ultimately, however, it succumbed to the empires of Macedonia and Rome. And with that fall, the imperial forms of political society reasserted their dominance.

As one might expect in such a situation, Greek political theory is characterized by an awareness of the unique and fragile nature of the Hellenic experiment. As this fragility became more apparent, a certain pessimism emerged which seemed to acknowledge the impending end of a noble, but doomed, epoch. By the close of the sixth century B.C. Athens was the arena for an intense political debate—a debate which was the occasion for the birth of political philosophy.

The immediate background for the political tensions of that time was the failure of the aristocracy. This failure was not simply a matter of one or two inept policy decisions. Rather it involved the aristocracy's inability to persuade the new and developing classes of the legitimacy of its rule. All classes agreed that true leadership demanded a certain set of political skills. Traditionally the aristocracy had argued that the necessary skills of good political leadership resided in a preeminent fashion among its own kind, because they were held to be the special product of good breeding. Historically, aristocratic rule had long been founded upon the possession of landed property. Yet with the development of commerce and the creation of an exchange economy, wealth—and the power which accompanies it—was redistributed among the several classes of Greek society. In particular a new commercial class emerged in the city-states which began to seek the political power by which it could augment its social position.

In response, the aristocracy defended its claim to rule by appealing to certain aristocratic virtues. For example, it was argued that good political leadership required a certain *spiritual* nobility, a quality which, in turn, was the product of tradition, good friendships, and noble blood. Such arguments, as can be found in the poems of Theognis and Pindar, had the obvious effect of excluding the new classes from political rule. From their perspective, these arguments appeared to be nothing more than reactionary attempts to preserve traditional, unfounded privileges. In time, the aristocratic argument lost its historical force. With the further development of the Athenian city-state, rule by the middle class soon became a reality.

Having achieved power, the middle class was faced with the problem of using it wisely. If noble blood was not the source of political skills, then how could such skills be gained? The apparent answer was education. But such a solution immediately posed new and difficult problems. Specifically, who were to be the educators? Two groups in particular claimed this privileged role: the Sophists and the philosophers.

THE SOPHISTS

Generally, the Sophists were groups of professional educators who traveled from city-state to city-state offering to teach for a fee. Their students typically were the sons of the new emerging middle class that had established itself in the democratic order. The Sophists' art was an ancient one, but only recently had they been able to practice it openly. This was due, in part, to the fact that the citizens of Greek city-states had traditionally doubted the wisdom of allowing their youth to be educated by "foreigners," (that is, anyone not a native of their own city-state). Indeed, there was no reason to believe that the wide-traveling Sophists, would be particularly loyal to the customs and traditions of their host city. Lacking such loyalty themselves, it would be difficult for them to instill in the youth that sense of respect and piety which was deemed essential by their elders.

By the fifth century, however, the climate of opinion had changed. In part, this was a reaction to the extremely optimistic rationalism of the early Eleatic philosophers. For example, a certain scepticism regarding both the ability and scope of human reason now began to develop. In addition, speculation in philosophy increasingly tended to substitute natural for divine causation; this had the effect of encouraging the development of the empirical sciences. More important, however, was a general shift away from a concern with natural phenomena to a preoccupation with human affairs. This new humanism was stimulated in part by the increasing contact with other peoples through war, travel, and the establishment of colonies. In addition, the fifth century was a period of intense legislative activity, which culminated in efforts to codify and amend laws long based on unquestioned custom and tradition. Given this, it became increasingly difficult for citizens simply to accept laws solely on the authority of time-honored usage. As tradition's hold upon the citizen loosened, the need for instruction and education became increasingly apparent. Thus the Sophists began to serve an important social function.

The teachings of the Sophists were varied and do not constitute a uniform curriculum. Generally, however, certain themes are associated with their work. First, they argued for the recognition of a distinction between law (*nomos*) and nature (*physis*). Second, they considered rhetoric to be the preeminent science. And finally, they claimed to be able to teach political virtue (*arete*).

Our understanding of the Sophists is generally dependent upon the picture drawn of them by their greatest opponent, Plato. Indeed, in such dialogues as the *Gorgias*, *Protagoras*, and *Hippias*, he portrays the Sophists as teachers who were willing to change their arguments so as to better conform to the dictates and tastes of the market. There is, no doubt, an element of personal rivalry which colors Plato's view. Yet to treat his criticisms as the mere products of a clash of personalities would be to miss the point. As he writes in his *Republic*, Plato understood the Sophists primarily as representatives of Athenian culture at large. His criticisms of their teachings, therefore, must be understood primarily as a critique of Athens itself and the civilizational order upon which it was based.

The political claim of the Sophists is nowhere more apparent than in the Platonic dialogue, *Protagoras*. In responding to Socrates's question concerning the nature of his teachings, Socrates has Protagoras claim, "What is that subject? The proper care of his [an Athenian citizen] personal affairs, so that he may best manage his own household, and also of the state's affairs, so as to become a real power in the city, both as speaker and man of action."[2] The real promise of the Sophists, therefore, was to teach the art of politics and thereby make good citizens. Central to that art, so they argued, was the skill of rhetoric; for in a democracy persuasion is the means to power.

INFLUENCE OF SOCRATES

The historical alternative to sophistic education was philosophical education, and no one was ever a better representative of philosophy than Socrates. There are few figures in the history of Western civilization who have exerted as much influence as this man. Yet all our knowledge of him is second hand; for Socrates, himself, never wrote. He was born around 470 B.C., seven years after the Athenians defeated the Persian army at Plataea. Thus, he lived through the artistic and political accomplishments of the Periclean Age (460–430). He also lived to see the Peloponnesian War (431–404), which ended with the eventual defeat of Athens and the overthrow of its democratic regime by the oligarchy of the Thirty Tyrants (404). In 403 B.C. democracy was restored, and in 399 Socrates was tried and executed for impiety and the corruption of youth.

---

[2] Plato, *Protagoras*, in W.K.C. Guthrie, trans., *The Collected Dialogues of Plato*, eds. Edith Hamilton and Huntington Cairns (Princeton, New Jersey: Princeton University Press, 1961), p. 317.

The source of Socrates's influence over Western civilization is based more upon his personality and character than upon any particular dogma or discovery associated with his teachings. Yet our understanding of that character is mediated by what we learn of Socrates from the writings of others. For all practical purposes there are four primary sources: Aristophanes, Xenophon, Plato, and Aristotle. The Socratic image, however, is not clear—and for two reasons. First, there are significant differences among the various accounts—especially so in the case of Aristophanes, Xenophon, and Plato. Second, those Platonic dialogues which are structured around the personality of Socrates do not draw a clear distinction between arguments original to Plato and those more directly associated with Socrates himself. These ambiguities have led to what is referred to as the "Socratic problem." They do not, however, nullify all attempts to appreciate the Socratic personality.

In the history of philosophy certain positions have come to be identified with Socrates. Cicero, for example, credits him with redirecting thoughts from natural to ethical philosophy by having been the first to "[call] philosophy down from the heavens and set her in the cities of men and bring her also into their homes and compel her to ask questions about life and morality and things good and evil. . . ."[3] Aristotle, on the other hand, seeking to distinguish between Socrates and Plato, mentions two specific Socratic accomplishments: first, the development of inductive argumentation, and, secondly, the demand for general definitions.

It is important to realize, however, that Socrates' concern for precise speech was not motivated simply by a demand for methodological rigor. This becomes clear if one examines the so-called early dialogues. In each dialogue the concern is for a clear understanding of a specific virtue. Thus, in the *Laches* Socrates seeks an understanding of courage; in the *Charmides*, of moderation; and in the *Euthyphro*, of piety. Finally, in the *Protagoras* this line of inquiry reaches its logical conclusion. There Socrates undertakes a discussion of the nature of virtue as a whole. The direction of this overall movement serves to reveal the true motive behind Socratic inquiry. Throughout, Socrates is attempting to discover the right way to live. As an attempt, it is based upon his prior rejection of the relativism implicit in the arguments of the Sophists.

As expressed by Plato, the Socratic position is that the life of virtue consists, in effect, in the life of philosophy. Inasmuch as philosophy is the *search* for truth, it necessarily begins with an admission of ignorance. By admitting ignorance, Socrates was implicitly challenging the adequacy of the existing Athenian political order and its beliefs. Indeed, in his *Apology* he

---

[3] Cicero, *Tusculan Disputation*, rev. ed., trans. J. E. King (Cambridge: Harvard University Press, 1945), p. 435.

argues that one of the reasons he has been condemned by the Athenian court is that, through his probing and questioning, he has revealed the ignorance of the Athenian leaders as well. But more importantly, by identifying the virtuous life with the life of philosophy, Socrates is challenging the authority of the political life. Indeed, if he is correct, politics is not the highest calling, and therefore it cannot demand from humanity its deepest loyalties. Loyalty to the regime is surpassed by loyalty to truth, and the political virtues of courage, moderation, and reverence are superseded by the philosophical virtues of wisdom and prudence. At its very inception, therefore, Western political philosophy raised a challenge to the traditional assumptions of political existence.

PLATO'S PHILOSOPHY

His Life

Plato was the greatest of Socrates's disciples; yet we know relatively little about his life and activities. Several "Lives of Plato" have come down to us; the most famous being the one compiled by Diogenes Laertius for his *Lives of the Philosophers.* Yet none of these were written by actual contemporaries of Plato, and the earliest can only be traced back to the second century after Christ. Among the known writings of such contemporaries of Plato as Aristotle, Demosthenes, and Xenophon, or of near contemporaries such as Aristoxenus of Messene, we find only short and relatively uninformative anecdotes. The most important source of information, however, is contained among thirteen letters purportedly written by Plato himself. Several of these, especially the second, third, seventh, and eighth, contain a good deal of autobiographical material. Unfortunately, the authenticity of all these letters has not been firmly established. At the turn of the century, the weight of scholarly opinion seemed to regard the letters as apocryphal. Today, however, there appears to be a wider acceptance of at least the most important ones.

Given this situation, the following picture emerges. Plato was born in 427 B.C. to an aristocratic family during the Peloponnesian War. It appears that he originally intended to pursue a career in politics; but, after coming under the influence of Socrates, he turned to a life of philosophy. With Socrates' execution in 399, Plato left Athens and undertook several years of foreign travel. In his *Seventh Letter*, he writes of going to Sicily and visiting the court of Dionysius I, the tyrant of Syracuse. Other stories from secondary sources describing this particular visit disagree as to what actually happened. However, there does seem to be ample evidence that during this time Plato was exposed to some of the scientific and theological beliefs of both the Pythagorean and Orphic cults which were established in that region. Indeed, the influence of their religious traditions can be found in several of Plato's later dialogues.

According to Plato's letters, he returned to Syracuse twenty years later upon the death of Dionysius and at the invitation of the former tyrant's brother-in-law, Dion. The latter, an admirer of Plato's work, invited him to direct the education of the prince, Dionysius II, according to the tenets of Plato's *Republic*. In that dialogue, Plato had argued for the necessity of a philosopher-king, and the opportunity to put his theory into practice appeared to be at hand. Unfortunately, the events that followed did not go according to plan. Dionysius soon tired of the discipline which Plato had demanded of him and established himself as a tyrant after the example of his father.

Returning to Athens, Plato once again devoted himself to the affairs of the Academy, which he had founded twenty years earlier in 387 B.C.. The Academy was a permanent seat of learning modeled after a similar institution founded by Plato's rival, the rhetorician Isocrates. Within it he gathered students and continued both in the study of science and philosophy and in the writing of dialogues. Among his pupils were Speusippus, Xenocrates, and most importantly, Aristotle. At 81 Plato died in the year 346.

In 399 the event that is so important to understanding the development of Plato's political thought occurred: the trial and death of Socrates. Responding to this crisis, Plato wrote:

> At last I came to the conclusion that all existing states are badly governed and the condition of their laws practically incurable, without some miraculous remedy and the assistance of fortune; and I was forced to say, in praise of true philosophy, that from her height alone was it possible to discern what the nature of justice is, either in the state or in the individual, and that the ills of the human race would never end until either those who are sincerely and truly lovers of wisdom come into political power, or the rulers of our cities, by the grace of God, learn true philosophy.[4]

According to Plato, the Athenian condemnation of Socrates served as proof that the political turmoil of the times was based upon a profound spiritual disorder. For Plato, Socrates was the wisest and most just man of the age. Athen's inability to recognize this fact showed that it was ignorant of justice itself. Without a knowledge of justice, a political society could not be just. And inasmuch as Socrates the philosopher pursued such a knowledge, he was, Plato maintained, the greatest benefactor of his society. Yet the proper

---

[4] Plato, *Epistle VII*, in Glenn R. Morrow, trans., *Plato's Epistles* (Indianapolis: Bobbs-Merrill, 1962), p. 217.

and supportive relationship which should exist between philosophy and politics had in reality been destroyed by the citizens of Athens. Thus, in the execution of Socrates, they had declared that philosophy was an enemy of the political order. In response, Plato set for himself the task of reversing that judgment. To do so, he had to accomplish two things. First, he had to account for the reasons why the Athenians had made such a mistake; and secondly, he had to establish those arguments which supported his own position. The dialogues which served those purposes most directly were the *Gorgias* and the *Republic*.

The Gorgias

Plato's *Gorgias* is his first truly political work. Although it may initially appear to be a dialogue concerned primarily with educational theory, it is, in fact, an attempt to analyze the spiritual and political ignorance that allowed Athens to turn against the insights of Socratic philosophy.

On its first level, then, the *Gorgias* is a debate between educators. Two teachers, Socrates and Gorgias, are vying for the right to educate the next generation of Athenian political leaders. Each claims to represent a tradition of knowledge which is vital for the political order of Athens. Gorgias, the Sophist, can teach rhetoric; Socrates represents philosophy. Yet the issue of what constitutes a proper civic education depends to a great degree upon a prior understanding of the requirements of political life. Thus, at a second level, the *Gorgias* is a dialogue concerning politics. This constant interplay between the concerns of education and those of politics is a characteristic trait in Platonic political philosophy. The *Gorgias* is the first work in which Plato describes that system of political education which is implicit in his understanding of philosophy; and in so doing it sets the standards for the positive political reforms Plato would introduce in the *Republic* and *Laws*.

The dialogue begins with Gorgias's attempt to clarify exactly what it is he claims to teach. Rhetoric, he argues, is the power to persuade others regarding political affairs. Socrates, on the other hand, seeks to establish a distinction: persuasion can attempt to change another's belief, or it can attempt to change what one knows. If it attempts the latter, then rhetoricians, themselves, must have some knowledge about that which they speak. In the case of politics, therefore, they must know justice. And unless they can make that claim, their skill is simply a matter of the ignorant persuading the ignorant.

To illustrate his point, Socrates makes a distinction between an art and a knack. Examples of the former are medicine and gymnastics; examples of the latter are cookery and cosmetics. Medicine and gymnastics are arts (*techné*) precisely because they are skills concerned with the good of the object with which they work. In this case, both seek to promote the true health of the body. Cookery and cosmetics, on the other hand, are knacks because their concern is primarily with producing pleasure. Cookery seeks to make food pleasing without regard for its nutritive value; similarly cosmetics seeks only the appearance of good health rather than health itself. Employing this distinction, Socrates labels rhetoric a knack and philosophy an art. Politics, for Socrates, is concerned with the health of the soul. Thus, as in the case of medicine, caring for the soul requires a knowledge of its needs and an awareness of what is good for it. Such an awareness is precisely the concern of philosophy. Rhetoricians seek to win the approval of the people through pleasing speeches. Their ability to do this, however, does not imply that they have a knowledge of what is good. Their claim to rule, therefore, is no more legitimate than the claim of cooks to cure.

Socrates' defense of a philosophical education depends upon a number of assumptions. First, his distinction between philosophy and rhetoric depends upon the validity of his distinction between art and knack. This, in turn, assumes that there is a difference between pleasure and good. Is the "good" distinct from "pleasure," or is it simply another name people give to that which they like? Secondly, the Socratic understanding that politics is concerned with the good of the soul presupposes that human beings can know what this good is. In the case of politics, can anyone know what justice is, or is one's understanding of justice simply a matter of convention and the subsequent belief in its utility? In the dialogue, these two assumptions are directly questioned by Callicles, the politically ambitious student of Gorgias. Callicles, claiming to be a "realist," introduces the Sophistic distinction between nature and convention and argues that conventional norms of justice are simply creations by the weak designed to protect themselves from the ambitions of the stronger. Nature (*physis*), according to Callicles, actually favors the rule of the strong and encourages them to pursue their pleasure with no regard for the interests of the inferior. At this point, however, the focus of the argument has shifted. Indeed, Socrates can admit that nature intends humanity to be happy. The real question is what produces true happiness—the life of pleasure or the life of goodness and justice? If it is the latter, then Socrates has not only established the distinction between pleasure and good, but has shown that true justice is, indeed, natural.

Socrates argues for his position by examining the effects of the alternative life styles upon the soul. According to Socrates, the life of pleasure is a life ruled by passion and desire, two qualities which, being insatiable, cannot be satisfied. Thus the life of pleasure is a frantic one which can promise no rest or final satisfaction. It is chaotic, disordered, and ultimately irrational. The just life, on the contrary, is one characterized by harmony, order, and happiness. This is so because the life of justice is a life devoted to serving the needs of the soul.

For Plato, humankind's spiritual life is somewhat analogous to its physical life. Just as the body must satisfy certain needs so that it can perform its natural functions well, so too must the soul. According to Plato, the function of the soul is to seek reality even unto its transcendent ground. To do so, it must be radically open to all the various realms within which reality is present. In effect, one must learn to open the soul, and philosophy is the means by which this can be done. Plato understood philosophy as the love of wisdom. As a form of love, it seeks to encounter and enjoy the object of its desire. In the case of philosophy this object is wisdom. Thus for Plato the well-functioning soul is in a constant state of quest. As such it is continually facing the task of going beyond mere appearances so as to encounter the true reality which makes wisdom possible. To accomplish such a mission the soul must be in form. In particular it must be well-ordered, harmonious, and properly disciplined—the very qualities which are characteristic of Platonic justice. Consequently Plato's argument for the desirability of justice is established by the very needs of the soul itself. The life of pleasure may be attractive, but it is ultimately a distraction from a higher quest. And, as a distraction, it necessarily damages the soul's attempt to fulfill its natural function. If people are to fulfill the highest possibilities of their spiritual nature, they must become just.

The argument now returns to its original political theme. To be a true politician, the overriding concern must be to promote the quality of life enjoyed by one's subjects. Accordingly, the true politician will be responsible for the "engendering of justice in the souls of his fellow citizens and the eradication of injustice, the planting of self-control and the uprooting of uncontrol, the entrance of virtue and the exit of vice."[5]

If this task is not a politician's real concern, then he or she is self-exposed as a practitioner of a knack rather than as the possessor of an art. In seeking to please people rather than to aid them, such politicians demonstrate their fundamental ignorance of humanity's psychic needs. Just as the sick would not turn over the care of their bodies to one who is ignorant of the principles of medical health, so too should the Athenians avoid being ruled by those rhetoricians who do not possess the art of spiritual care.

Plato's analogy between politics and medicine serves a number of functions. First, it allows him to emphasize the fact that human beings have certain spiritual needs which must be satisfied if we are to live truly normal lives. We are not simply bodily creatures, and, therefore, it is not enough to simply satisfy our bodily desires. Humanity requires an art other than the medical. Second, by comparing the political art and the medical art Plato is

[5] Plato, *Gorgias*, trans. W. C. Hembold (Indianapolis: Bobbs-Merrill, 1952), p. 79.

able to introduce his case for the political role of philosophers. Doctors are the legitimate practitioners of medicine because they possess that knowledge (art) which makes it possible for them to promote the health of the body. Similarly, the only ones who can legitimately practice the political art would be those who possess that knowledge concerned with promoting the health of the soul. As we have seen, the soul's health emerges in the pursuit of wisdom, and it is the philosophers who by their very nature are concerned with such a pursuit. They, in effect, are the only legitimate political rulers. In the *Gorgias*, Plato has Socrates say:

> In my opinion I am one of the few Athenians (not to say the only one) who has attempted the true art of politics, and the only one alive to put it into practice.[6]

Throughout the *Gorgias*, Plato has been concerned with explaining why Athens executed Socrates. The answer is now apparent. According to Plato the Athenians were suffering from a disease—a spiritual disease. In rejecting Socrates, they acted out of an ignorance of the soul's true needs and capacities. Had they understood humanity's spiritual quest, they would not have murdered the man who embodied such a quest. Thus, the Athenian ignorance was not simply the result of a lack of information or data. For Plato, this ignorance can only be explained in terms of a deeper spiritual disorder. Before such ignorance can be overcome, therefore, a spiritual conversion is necessary. It was Plato's hope that his *Republic* might serve as the necessary therapy.

The Republic

Somewhat surprisingly for a book in political philosophy, the *Republic* both begins and ends with a discussion that is related to the theme of death. It is as if the political arguments of the dialogue are framed by the philosopher's concern for ultimate things. This situation does, in fact, reflect rather accurately Plato's approach to political theory. He is concerned with understanding the nature of political order, and, in attempting this, he necessarily moves beyond the material realm and toward the transcendent. For Plato a truly scientific political inquiry begins with and culminates in the effort to understand ultimate reality. At this point in Western thought there is no distinction between philosophy and science. Thus, serious political theory necessarily moves into the realm of metaphysics.

The question which begins the dialogue is the same one which preoccupied Plato in the *Gorgias:* What is justice? After listening to several attempts by others to define the concept, one of the participants, Glaucon,

---

[6] Plato, *Gorgias*, p. 100.

challenges Socrates to develop his own understanding. But first Glaucon goes on to recall the sophistic distinction between convention and nature. This distinction argued that injustice (as defined by convention) is actually good. It allows human beings the pleasures and delights they naturally want. Yet suffering from someone else's injustice is a greater evil. So people devise a set of rules and customs in order to protect themselves from such a situation. They promise neither to do injustice nor to suffer it. Consequently it would appear that people practice justice only because they cannot bear the results of someone else's injustice. Justice is not pursued for its own sake but rather for the benefits which accompany it. If one could enjoy the benefits of injustice without paying the consequences, it would be natural to do so. Given this sophistic argument, Glaucon wishes that Socrates not only develop his understanding of justice but do so in such a way as to demonstrate its intrinsic worth. If justice truly were a virtue, that is a quality which develops and perfects the nature of humanity, then it must be good for the soul. Consequently its actual presence rather than the benefits which follow from its mere appearance would be required for true happiness.

In short, Socrates is being asked to show that justice is good or desirable by its very nature. Glaucon has suggested that human beings naturally desire the pleasures of injustice but agree to forego such pleasures because of the hazards involved. According to this perspective, then, people agree to call justice good—that is, it is a good by convention—even though they naturally desire its opposite. Morality, then, becomes a set of artificial standards created for the sake of convenience. If human beings were true to their nature, however, they would reject such restraints and pursue their own pleasure.

The argument is complex and cannot be answered easily. Before Socrates can show that justice is naturally good, he must first establish what it is that human nature finds desirable. And before he can discuss human nature, he must first examine the structure of nature itself. Here as nowhere else in the history of political theory is the close tie which binds political theory both with the philosophy of humanity and with ontology so clearly demonstrated.

Socrates approaches this problem by suggesting that they first search for justice in the city; being a larger object, justice-in-the-city should be easier to observe. This can be done by examining the development of the *polis* from its earliest to its most mature form. Socrates begins, then, by discussing the functions and contributions of the various elements, or classes, which compose the *polis*.

Reconstructing the *polis's* development through an imaginative history, Socrates attempts to show how human beings come to serve their needs by a process of social cooperation. As individuals people cannot satisfy fully all their various physical and cultural needs. Thus they form societies so as to benefit from the natural division of labor and one another's expertise. Tracing this development from a rather primitive level to the more-advanced contemporary cities of his day, Socrates focuses upon what he considers to be natural class divisions. There are, on one hand, the artisans who produce the necessary goods and services. On the other, there are the guardians who, as a martial class, preserve and defend the city. Throughout the *Republic*, Plato devotes a great deal of attention to the education and training of this guardian class. It is an education which is designed to equip the guardians with those virtues and qualities necessary if they are to rule well. As such, it is primarily concerned with their spiritual development. If they are to rule well, they must first be good people. Specifically, they must be courageous, moderate, wise, and just. It was Plato's belief that this disposition could be achieved, in part, by an education which was based upon a "proper theology."

A proper theology for Plato was one which respected the dignity of the gods and argued on behalf of humanity's moral responsibility for its own actions. Historically such a theology represented a challenge to the traditional Homeric religion of Plato's own time. According to Plato, the Homeric myths presented a confused picture of the relationship between the gods and the human race. And in so doing, it underemphasized the degree to which human beings are morally responsible for their own thoughts and acts. For Plato, then, the mythical world view of Homer simply failed to account for the integrity of the human soul; and without such an appreciation, true political order would be impossible.

In addition to developing the personal virtues of the rulers, Platonic education was also concerned with ensuring that the guardians did not become a self-serving elite. In part, this could be avoided by relying upon their virtue. Yet such virtue could be strengthened by certain institutional reinforcements. In particular, the guardians would be deprived of both a family and private wealth. A perennial challenge to public spiritedness is nepotism and, historically, the Greek *polis* did suffer from its politicians' having abused their offices for the sake of their families. In order to avoid this, Plato's *Republic* argued that the guardians would share a community of women, children, and property. Thus, by blurring family lines, the guardians would be encouraged to associate their individual good with the common good of the city.

Some commentators have looked upon this feature as an early example of a communistic social order. One should be cautious, however, in drawing such conclusions. First, this arrangement is intended only for the guardians; it is not meant for the larger political order as a whole. Second, the purpose of this arrangement is primarily spiritual not material. Plato's "communism" seeks to produce an attitude of public spiritedness. It is not primarily concerned with the production and distribution of material goods. A comparison which overlooks these important differences is not theoretically useful.

As Plato's educational process continues, those guardians who fail to master the necessary skills are placed in a third class, called the "auxiliaries." The auxiliaries consititute an intermediary class between the more select guardians and the tradespeople. As such, they are chiefly concerned with assisting the guardians in their efforts to order society. Although the auxiliaries may lack the wisdom of the guardians, they are educated enough to appreciate its authority. Therefore, they devote themselves to fostering and preserving those true opinions which reflect such wisdom within the society at large.

It is obvious at this point that Plato's *Republic* is developing a city which is based upon a class society. Yet, for Plato, the classes of this city only reflect the natural classes which exist among human beings. This is the case inasmuch as Plato holds a hierarchical view of human nature. According to such a view, some persons have developed their nature to a level beyond that of others. For Plato, such a development occurs when one moves toward knowledge. Thus it is wisdom and virtue, not wealth or social status, which determines Plato's natural aristocracy. Given this assumption, it is important that the social hierarchy accurately reflects the natural hierarchy. For if the truly best do rule, all people benefit.

One of the first tasks of the guardians will be to regulate the economic affairs of the city so as to avoid the two extremes of wealth and poverty. Experience has shown that economic extremes tend to divide the population into antagonistic classes and thus undermine the harmony of the whole. More importantly, however, the guardians will concern themselves with overseeing the education of the citizenry. This duty is of such importance that it is fair to say that, for Plato, education is the most important task for the statesman. Where the citizens have been well-educated and consequently have developed an habitual concern for common decency, there is no need to impose a control over the affairs of everyday life. Basically such guidance can be provided by the commonsense application of the public morality. Where such basic decency is absent, however, no amount of legislation will remedy the situation. Corrupt citizens will always bend the law so as to break its spirit.

Assuming that the guardians' program of moral education is successful, the well-governed city would exhibit the following traits. First, it would be wise, inasmuch as it would receive good counsel regarding its affairs. After all, the claim of the guardians to rule is based upon their knowledge and expertise, not upon their status or wealth. Secondly, the good city would be courageous. Courage, in this context, refers to the ability of a people to preserve and defend their true beliefs and opinions. Thirdly, the good city would display moderation. This would be the result of an educational program which would teach citizens to master lower pleasures for the sake of higher ones. Those pleasures which are superior by nature should rule those which are inferior. For example, the satisfaction of the intellectual or aesthetic passions would have a certain priority over the satisfaction of bodily or sensual desires. Finally, the good city would be just. As seen from the *Gorgias*, Plato understands justice as a condition of harmony and order. In the case of the city, this harmony would be reflected in the relationship among the classes:

> . . . the money-making, auxiliary, and guardian classes doing what's appropriate, each of them minding its own business in a city—would be justice and would make the city just.[7]

At this point, it would be helpful to look a bit more closely at Plato's understanding of justice. First, it must be remembered that one's membership in a class is not determined by birth, wealth, or social status. Class membership is determined by natural affinity; those who are by nature wise and capable of benefiting from a philosophical education are placed in the guardian class regardless of their original rank in society. Secondly, there is mobility between classes. If a person's nature is unsuitable for philosophy, he or she will be removed from the guardian class even though born of guardian parents. (Plato's insistence upon personal quality as the only legitimate standard for determining class membership is so strict that he even breaks with standard Greek tradition and includes the possibility of women joining the guardian class.)

Granting these qualifications, however, it is still apparent that Plato's understanding of justice is not an egalitarian one. This is made particularly clear in his "Myth of the Metals." Challenged to explain how he will convince democratic Athens to accept the rule of the guardians, Plato suggests the use of a public myth which describes the story of humanity's creation by the gods. This myth will tell how, although all peoples share their origin in earth, some were made from a mixture of gold and earth, others from a mixture with silver, and finally others from iron and brass. On one hand, by emphasizing our common origin, the myth calls attention to our common humanity. Yet, on the other hand, by distinguishing among the metals, it also acknowledges the fact of a natural hierarchy among human beings. It is apparent to Plato that, for whatever reason, people in fact differ in the degree to which they actualize their potential as rational beings. Justice, in turn, demands that this difference be reflected in the political structure itself.

[7] Plato, *The Republic*, trans. Allan Bloom (New York: Basic Books, 1968), p. 113.

Plato's conception of justice as a harmonious yet differentiated order based upon a natural hierarchy among citizens has led some to see him as a dogmatic reactionary defending tyrannical rule. This is certainly a misreading. It is true that Plato is by no means a liberal democrat. He does not believe that liberty is the ultimate political value, nor does he absolutely trust in the processes of majoritarian democracy. Yet to associate this position with tyranny is to misconstrue Plato's intention. The state for Plato does not possess its own distinct interests which are opposed to those of its citizens. Nor is its unity the result of its supposedly organic character. On the contrary, the regime is designed to promote the moral health of its citizens—a goal which is to be approached through education and persuasion. The philosopher-king, therefore, is not a social engineer seeking to manipulate the people for purposes of self-reward. Rather the philosopher-king is an educator attempting to elicit and sustain a life of moral virtue—with the goal being to nurture, not exploit, humankind. Indeed for Plato the regime's interest and the interests of its citizens are essentially the same—happiness. And their happiness, in turn, consists of a similar achievement—justice:

> . . . no city nor individual can be happy except by living in company with wisdom under the guidance of justice . . . [8]

Plato's argument is based on his belief that the soul is a structured reality; it has definite needs and requires specific goods. Just as the material body requires the skills of an expert for its own good; so, too, does the soul require the skills of the philosopher. For Plato the true aim of statesmanship is to engender the love of virtue. That this can be done only by those who already possess such a love is, for him, a matter of common sense. Indeed, rather than being tyrannical, Plato's regime is characterized by its deep concern for the common good.

Perhaps this can be clarified by examining more closely Plato's conception of the soul. After having developed a description of the good city and its consequent virtues, Plato suggests that a certain analogy can be drawn between the city and the soul. The *polis* is a human being "writ large." Consequently, its virtues can be seen analogously as operating within the human psyche. The soul, like the city, is composed of various elements; each element has its appropriate virtue; and the composite whole has its appropriate order. In particular, the soul is composed of a rational part which loves truth, the spirited which desires honor, and the passions which seek pleasure. Wisdom is the appropriate virtue of the first element; courage, of the second; and moderation, of the third. Justice exists, in turn,

[8] Plato, *Epistle VII*, p. 230.

when a harmony is established among these elements which acknowledges both the overall rule of reason and the subordination of the passions to both reason and honor-loving spirit. A soul which possesses these four virtues is well-ordered, harmonious, and healthy. Such a condition, in turn, is the greatest happiness possible for humankind.

Plato's picture of the just soul is a view of the human being described as if it had actualized the full potential of its nature. Empirically, however, such actualization is relatively rare. People tend to lead lives devoted to the satisfaction of the passions rather than to the pursuit of wisdom. Thus the first challenge is to awaken humanity to the life of virtue, and this, in turn, is the task of the political leadership. More specifically, it is a task which requires the efforts of the philosopher-king. The philosopher-king is a dramatic symbol created by Plato to once again emphasize the need for philosophy to guide the affairs of the *polis*. Philosophers claim this role, not because of any particular facts or information they may happen to possess, but in terms of what they are—a philosopher is a lover of wisdom. As such, a philosopher's soul exhibits that "clear pattern" which can serve as the source for spiritual and political order.

In developing his understanding of the philosophic soul, Plato distinguishes between two types of people. There are the lovers of truth (philosophers) and the lovers of appearance (*philodoxers*). The former have knowledge; the latter, opinion. The true distinction between knowledge and opinion, however, is not simply in the degree of certainty which accompanies the two forms of consciousness. Rather it is a distinction based upon differences within reality itself.

Central to Plato's argument has been his insistence that there is a distinction between knowledge and opinion and that, consequently, the one who possesses philosophical knowledge should rule. This distinction has been the basis of both the *Gorgias* and the *Republic*. In Books V and VI of the *Republic* Plato introduces the metaphysical arguments to support this position. To begin with, he suggests that reality is structured; it has a number of levels and thus cannot be reduced to one simple component. The first distinction, then, is between the realities of the visible world and those of the purely intelligible. Human beings are aware of certain things because they enjoy sense perception. The faculties of sight, hearing, taste, touch, and smelling provide them with an awareness of a certain class of objects. The most real things, however, are outside of this realm. Ideas, for example, can only be known through thought, and reason is a quality of the soul, not the body. Thus the realm of the intelligible is a metaphysical one, and metaphysical reality, for Plato, is the object of our deepest knowledge. Having established this dichotomy, Plato suggests further distinctions.

Within the realm of the visible, there are two levels. First, that of images; second, that of things. For example, our senses allow us to perceive both representations of things and the things themselves. Awareness of the first, Plato terms imagination (*eikasia*); of the second, he terms trust (*pistis*). Both imagination and trust, however, are forms of opinion (*doxa*). Opinion, therefore, can best be understood as a form of awareness, yet it is the awareness of a relatively impoverished level of reality. Images and things are conditional; thus they lack the absolute stability of being itself. Belonging to the realm of the senses, images and things are susceptible to change. They are particular and limited by the concrete material of their existence. A life guided solely by opinion, therefore, is a life attuned to the unstable, the particular, and the limited.

Within the realm of the intelligible, Plato again distinguishes between two levels. The first is that of the Forms, and awareness of the Forms is termed thought (*dianoia*). The second is that of the good (*agathon*), and contact with that is called intellection or dialectic (*noesis*). Both thought and dialectic are elements of knowledge. The Forms are the essential reality of all things which we perceive when we perceive them correctly. They are the idea, the perfected expression of what is. Each thing in the visible world can be understood as a particular manifestation of its substantial Form. These manifestations embody the Forms but do not exhaust them. For example, every tree in the world is a concrete expression of the Form, tree. It is this sharing in the Form that establishes their common nature as trees. Yet, no single tree is a perfect tree as such. The Forms are the immutable, perfected expressions of reality. They are the ideas against which all particular concrete things are to be measured. For example, the Form of the soul exists as that perfected idea which is more or less manifested in each individual. The less one is attuned to the Form, the greater is that person's fall from reality.

The good exists as both the ground of the Forms and that which makes them apparent before the mind's eye. On one hand, it is the ultimate source of reality, and on the other, it is reality's proper goal. Full knowledge, accordingly, understands how all of reality is informed by and related to the force of the good.

From this discussion, it should be apparent that for Plato "knowledge" is not simply a matter of possessing facts, data, or information. Rather, it refers to the conscious penetration into being itself. The person of knowledge has transcended the conditional, the particular, and the insubstantial—has in fact encountered being itself and is informed by this contact with its ground. Thus for Plato acquiring knowledge is as much a psychological as an epistemological event. Through the process of philosophical penetration, we not only add to our awareness of reality but also experience a perfecting of the soul. For Plato the soul by its very nature seeks that which is. Gaining knowledge, therefore, satisfies the soul's fundamental need, evokes its development, and promotes its happiness. As a result the philosophical encounter with the good produces that state of harmony, order, and coherence which is characteristic of psychic health. Perhaps this can be illustrated by examining Plato's "Allegory of the Cave."

The cave allegory pictures an underground chamber within which people dwell under artificially limited conditions. The cave dwellers are fastened in such a way as to be facing the front wall of the cave and, so restricted, as to be unaware of their situation. Before them are shadows being projected onto the wall. Behind is a stage upon which puppets are held before a fire so as to cause the shadows. The inhabitants of the cave are unaware of the stage, fire, and puppets. Thus their experience suggests that the shadows which they perceive are, indeed, real. For some reason one of the cave dwellers is torn free from the confining bonds and dragged out of the cave into the sunlight. There this person is exposed to reality. The cave is seen for what it is—a realm of appearances. The puppets are simply modeled after the items of reality; the fire, a pale imitation of the sun. The richness and beauty of reality cause the cave dweller to desire to stay in the world; but the prisoner is forced back into the cave and there attempts to describe the experiences of the world above to the others. This constant effort to challenge what the cave dwellers see as commonsense reality proves an irritation, and the visionary is eventually executed.

Plato suggests that the person who has escaped the cave is the philosopher. And it is obvious that this person is modeled after Socrates. More importantly, however, is Plato's interpretation of this allegory in light of his earlier metaphysics. The shadows on the wall of the cave are equivalent to appearances; the puppets are things. Together they constitute the realm of the cave, and awareness of them is what Plato means by opinion. Outside the cave, the features of reality are the Forms and the sun is the good. Consciousness of these is knowledge. The philosopher is that person who has undergone a conversion experience. He or she has been turned away from the cave and placed before reality. This experience, in turn, evokes in the person's soul the distinguishing characteristic of its personality—the love of truth. Having turned towards being but returned to the cave, the philosopher finds himself/herself in the situation of existing at one level of reality (visible world) yet desiring to be at another (the intelligible). This life, therefore, is one of tension; the philosopher yearns to participate in and live by the most real; yet there is also the call to remain in the cave. This pull or yearning creates the philosopher's characteristic form; the philosopher is an existence-in-tension and, as such, possesses the fifth virtue of prudence.

The virtue of prudence is described by Plato as the virtue of correct sight. The philosopher acquires such a quality because the soul has turned away from the realm of that which-is-coming-into-being and toward the realm of that which-simply-is. It is precisely this ability to see reality which recommends the philosopher for political leadership. Seeing the real, that person alone can attune the order of his or her existence to reflect the order of being. Such an attunement, in turn, promotes that psychic harmony which is characteristic of true human happiness. Having achieved existence-in-tension, the philosopher is bound by justice to encourage others to undertake similar efforts. Consequently political education is pictured as ultimately concerned with promoting this conversion experience. Although such an experience cannot be compelled, it can be encouraged through the practice of philosophical dialectic.

In Book VIII of the *Republic*, Plato develops a system by which various political regimes can be classified. The regime of the philosopher-king has already been discussed. There are four additional types: timocracy, oligarchy, democracy, and tyranny. Of particular interest here is the general approach used by Plato in arriving at these classifications. Unlike modern efforts these terms are not associated with particular institutional arrangements. This should not be surprising. Plato understood politics as the caring for and education of the soul. From this perspective, then, the institutional environment within which this takes place is not nearly as important as the model according to which people are being educated. Education instructs the soul to become someone. Who this someone is, is the ultimate political question. Plato suggests that the true nature of a political society is clearly revealed in terms of who it is educating its citizens to become. The regime of the philosopher-king establishes as its model the philosopher, that is, the lover of wisdom. Timocracy supports the character of the timocrat, that is, the lover of honor. Oligarchy is characterized by the predominance of the lover of wealth.

It is also interesting to note that, unlike many modern attempts, Plato's categories are both descriptive and evaluative. The concept "timocracy" is not only a means of describing the character of a particular regime, but also serves as a device to indicate its merit. Each form of regime is characterized by the predominance of a particular personality. As we have seen in Plato's discussion of the soul, human beings can be distinguished from one another in terms of the quality of that reality which serves as the primary object of their love. Wisdom is superior to honor; thus, the lover of wisdom is superior to the lover of honor. This same insight can be applied to political regimes. Those which promote the love of wisdom are superior to those which promote the love of honor. Timocracies, in turn, are superior to those which promote the love of wealth.

In Book VIII, Plato pays particular attention to the two regimes of democracy and tyranny. One must be careful not to confuse Plato's notion of democracy with the modern usage. He is not referring to democratic institutions in the current sense but rather to a regime which is characterized by the social predominance of democratic citizens. For Plato, such a regime suffers from both a lack of moderation and the collapse of freedom into license. Democratic people are chaotic; lacking any defining order, they possess no true sense of self. They are in a most serious way people without qualities. Rather than focusing upon a dominant good as the object of their love, they frantically experiment with a variety of life styles, attempting to enjoy the pleasures of each. As a consequence, democratic citizens lose the ability to accurately judge their situation; they confuse virtue with vice and spurn education as a possible remedy. Politically, such confusion expresses itself as anarchy.

Plato understands tyranny as a response to the chaos of democracy. A tyrant poses as the savior of the mob. Although at first presenting the appearance of a populist leader, the tyrant's true concern slowly reveals itself—power exercised for selfish motives. The tyrant is pictured as one who is enslaved by personal desires. Willing to subordinate everything in the service of those passions, the tyrant is faithless, deceitful, and consequently without friends. Impoverished by endless efforts to satisfy continually increasing desires, the tyrant ultimately is entrapped in the irrational effort to quench insatiable passions. The tyrant is, for Plato, the most wretched of human beings.

At the beginning of the *Republic*, Plato was challenged to show that justice was good in and of itself. Having completed his analysis of regimes, he is now in the position to do so. The effects of justice can be demonstrated by comparing the just city and the just person with their opposites. The philosopher-king and the good city can be compared to the tyrant and life under a tyranny. The harmony, beauty, and desirability of one stands in sharp contrast to the chaos, corruption, and repulsiveness of the other. The difference, as the *Republic* has demonstrated, is the presence of justice in the former and its absence in the latter.

Thus, by such an argument, Plato has responded to Glaucon's original challenge. He has shown that justice is a good demanded by humanity's very nature and that human nature can only be understood in the context of a metaphysics which incorporates both the immanent and transcendent dimensions of reality. The result has been his description of a "city-in-speech" which reflects the larger dimensions of this philosophy. Yet it is apparent to Plato that existing historical cities do not resemble his city-in-speech. This difference does not imply, however, that the *Republic* is a utopia. Rather it reveals the imperfection and shortcomings of all historically existing regimes. The *Republic* exposes our societies for what they actually are: partial realizations of true political order. Thus if justice exists in the *Republic*, it exists only there.

The Statesman

Although exact dating is difficult, the *Statesman* (sometimes referred to as the *Politicus*) probably was written between 365 and 362 B.C. and thus is one of Plato's later works. It addresses a large number of themes including the presentation of a cosmological myth which seeks to explain the imperfection of the world while at the same time acknowledging its relation to the divine. In the text itself, however, Plato claims that the chief purpose of the dialogue is to teach the general art of the dialectic. Accordingly, much of the discussion is devoted to illustrating the technique of proper division, a logical method whereby objects are placed in appropriate categories which reflect "real cleavages between specific forms."

This emphasis upon argumentation and the fact that the dialogue is part of a larger trilogy (*Theaetetus*, *Sophist*, and *Statesman*) which deals primarily with the problems of knowledge and truth might lead one to believe that this is essentially an epistemological study. Yet to maintain this would force one to overlook certain arguments which represent an important development in Plato's political thinking. Starting already with the *Theaetetus*, the philosopher is pictured as beginning a withdrawal from political affairs. Where once philosophy and politics were united in the excellence of the philospher-king, Plato now begins to speak of the second-best regime—one characterized by the rule of law rather than by the rule of the philosopher. This is done, however, in full awareness of the fact that philosophy always will remain the one true political art. Consequently, there is a certain tone of sober pessimism that emerges in the *Statesman* and grows eventually to dominate the *Laws*.

Both the *Republic* and the *Gorgias* have argued that education is the most authentic form of statesmanship and thus that politics depends upon some sort of expert knowledge. It is not surprising, therefore, that Plato's *Statesman* begins with an attempt to define what is the particular expertise of the true statesman. Using the technique of division, Plato arrives at a first answer. He suggests that the science of the statesman is "the science of the collective rearing of men."[9] The statesman's function, therefore, appears as analogous to that of the shepherd. Yet upon further consideration this analogy exhibits certain weaknesses. The statesman is both like and unlike shepherds, and, until the distinctions are clear, the dialogue has not reached an adequate conclusion. Statesmen are like shepherds because they do, indeed, tend "noninterbreeding herd[s]." Yet, unlike shepherds, their claim to rule is challenged by others. Therefore, until Plato's understanding of such leaders includes an analysis of their unique excellence which will distinguish them from their rivals, it is not yet complete.

A reconsideration of the shepherd analogy leads Plato to conclude that the original comparison went amiss when the statesman's art was described crudely as the science of rearing herds. The rearing of herds is essentially a matter of caring for the herd's physical needs while, as has been shown, for Plato politics is preeminently concerned with humanity's spiritual condition. To avoid any confusion on this issue, therefore, Plato

[9] Plato, *Statesman*, trans. J. B. Skemp (Indianapolis: Bobbs-Merrill, 1957), p. 21.

suggests that the true statesman is characterized by a concern for the herd *and* that the exercise of this concern involves some knowledge of human nature and its deeper needs. Indeed, statecraft is concerned with providing that which is appropriate for and thereby due to citizens. The concept that there is a "due measure" of citizens' needs, however, implies the existence of a fixed norm against which such measurement can be made, and knowledge of this norm, in turn, constitutes the statesman's expertise. In short, the true statesman must be a philosopher.

A variety of skills and crafts contribute to human well-being—each in its own way. Statecraft is the "higher science," however, because it is in the position of deciding which of the lower sciences shall be learned. Indeed, it is the political regime which determines when and how the various trades may be applied, and it does so correctly only when the true statesman has knowledge of the "right and wrong moment," or, if you will, a sense of due measure. A sense of due measure implies knowledge of a standard, and, for Plato, the political standard is always the virtuous soul. Thus, the statesman's art is concerned with guiding society for the sake of forming or "weaving" good character. This, in turn, is primarily a matter of education:

> When there is implanted in the soul of men a right opinion concerning what is honorable, just, and good, and what is the opposite of these—an opinion based on absolute truth and settled as an unshakable conviction—I declare that such a conviction is a manifestation of the divine in a race which is of supernatural lineage.[10]

In developing his argument, Plato admits that the typical politician can not truthfully claim to have mastered the art of statecraft. The historical fact is that the philosopher is not king. This admission introduces the discussion of the second-best regime. The best regimes are those which are guided by the statesman's art (philosophy), and, inasmuch as this art is always and necessarily actualized in an act of judgment, statecraft is necessarily embodied in the statesmen themselves. They must be free to act as their informed judgments demand. Thus, for Plato the best regime is the one which is ruled by the wise ruler, not by laws. Laws are necessarily general, whereas political choice always concerns particulars. Laws are necessarily inflexible, whereas politics always confronts change. In the spirit of the *Republic*, Plato writes:

> But the best thing of all is not full authority for laws but rather full authority for a man who understands the art of kingship and has wisdom.[11]

---

[10] Plato, *Statesman*, p. 97.
[11] Plato, *Statesman*, p. 66.

In view of the absence of such leaders, however, citizens, seeking "to secure for themselves the most tolerable life they can,"[12] must choose the second-best regime: the rule of law. In acknowledging that the rule of law is the *second-best* regime, however, Plato does not mean to imply that it is without true merit.

Indeed, true laws can be understood as "written copies of scientific truth in the various departments of life they cover, copies based as far as possible on the instructions received from those who really possess the scientific truth on these matters."[13] True law, therefore, conforms to reason, and it is this feature which accounts for its moral authority. Given this, one can distinguish between lawful regimes (monarchy, aristocracy, and democracy) and their corrupted forms (tyranny, oligarchy, and lawless democracy). Lawful regimes, submitting to the rule of reason as manifested in general laws, are a fairly close copy of the best regime. Following justice they seek to promote the well-being of their citizens according to those principles of statecraft as expressed by their laws. Those corrupted regimes which disregard the law, however, fail to imitate the true constitution and, as such, are "not genuine and have no real existence."[14] Given the fact that a true master of statecraft does not arise in the natural course of events, the need to preserve a constitution which is based on law and moral custom becomes a political objective of paramount importance. This issue, in turn, is a central theme in Plato's last work: the *Laws*.

The Laws

The *Laws*, left unrevised at Plato's death in 346 B.C., is both the longest and at the same time one of the least dramatic of his dialogues. It is also the only piece from which Socrates is entirely absent. The body of the text is a discussion which takes place between three elderly men: an Athenian (assumed to be Plato), a Cretan, and a Spartan. Their discussion concerns the founding of Magnesia, a settlement being established in Crete and therefore requiring both a constitution and specific political institutions. The Athenian's participation in this project is requested, and Plato uses this opportunity to offer advice on a large number of issues. He speaks to such topics as natural environment, population, occupations, property, education, punishment, and family life.

Plato's detailed development of such particular issues and the time and effort he devotes to describing the needs and requirements of what is clearly a second-best regime have led some commentators to argue that the *Laws* represents a more mature and less idealistic version of Platonic

---

[12] Plato, *Statesman*, p. 81.

[13] Plato, *Statesman*, p. 77.

[14] Plato, *Statesman*, p. 65.

political theory. Some have argued that the utopian fervor and romance of the *Republic* had now been replaced by a more chastened and pragmatic tone—one produced in part by Plato's failures in Sicily. Although there is no doubt that the *Laws* does differ from the *Republic*, one must be careful in specifying the exact character of such differences. The *Laws* is, indeed, a description of the second-best regime; but that does not necessarily imply that Plato's *Republic* is therefore a utopia. To call the *Republic* utopian and the *Laws* realistic is to misunderstand both works. For Plato, reality was always found in the Idea and, as such, was either more or less fully embodied within historical existence. Thus the *polis* of the *Republic* was the best inasmuch as it embodied most fully the idea of the good political order. The difference between the *Republic* and the *Laws*, therefore, is not due to the fact that Plato had changed his mind regarding the good political order. What had changed was his assessment of the ability of historical reality to live up to the idea. Consequently, the *Laws* is not a rejection of the idea of the *Republic*. It is, rather, a reassessment necessitated by Plato's increased awareness of humanity's resistance to reality itself.

Plato's fundamental insight had not changed: "Knowledge is unsurpassed by any law or regulation; reason, if it is genuine and really enjoys its natural freedom, should have universal power. . . . "[15] What had changed, however, were Plato's expectations of his fellow citizens. In the *Republic*, the guardians were beings of gold; their existential superiority established a "clear pattern in their souls," and this allowed them to serve as the active sources for political and social order. In the *Laws*, on the contrary, there are no clearly superior people; each stands in constant need of guidance and support in the effort to acquire virtue. Humankind has, in effect, suffered a certain leveling. The *Republic's* myth of the metals is replaced by a new and more appropriate analogy:

> . . . let's imagine that each of us living beings is a puppet of the gods . . . we have these emotions in us, which act like cords or strings and tug us about; they work in opposition, and tug against each other to make us perform actions that are opposed correspondingly. . . . One of these dragging forces, according to our argument, demands our constant obedience, and this is the one we have to hang on to, come what may; the pull of the other cords we must resist. This cord which is golden and holy, transmits the power of "calculation," a power which in a state is called the public law. . . . The force exerted by law is excellent, and one should always cooperate with it, because although "calculation" is a noble thing, it is gentle, not violent, and its efforts need assistants, so that the gold in us may prevail over the other substances.[16]

[15] Plato, *The Laws*, trans. Trevor J. Saunders (Baltimore: Penguin Books, 1970), p. 395.
[16] Plato, *Laws*, pp. 74–75.

Here, as in the *Statesman*, true law has been assigned the task of forming society's moral character in the best way possible. Accordingly, the laws and institutions of Magnesia will be developed with this project in mind. Of the many suggestions offered by Plato, two are of particular importance at this time.

First, Magnesia will be a mixed regime. Many classes will share in the exercise of political power; but all power will be constrained by a legal code which is universally binding. As we have seen, justice in the *Republic* consisted of a harmony among the classes which was based upon a common recognition that the guardians should rule. Under the different assumptions which govern the *Laws*, however, Plato seeks to establish a political harmony which is based more on a balance of interests than on the power of virtue. The mixed regime of the *Laws* is designed to combine the diverse principles of differing interests in such a way that they offset one another and produce, thereby, a certain level of moderation. In the case of Magnesia, this balance is to be achieved by blending the monarchic principle of wisdom with its democratic counterpart of freedom. Both principles, in turn, are subject to the authority of the law. Hopefully, such a combination would avoid the disadvantages apparent in such extremes as the Persian monarchy on one hand and Athenian democracy on the other. At the same time, such an arrangement would recognize the interests of the various classes and thereby attempt to satisfy their legitimate demands by giving each a share in the exercise of political power.

A second important characteristic of Magnesia is that it was a political theocracy. On one hand this should not be a surprise. The argument that true human order depends upon humanity's attuning of itself to the transcendent ground of being has run throughout all of Plato's work. For Plato the soul by its nature seeks the divine. As such its excellence is established by its knowledge of that transcendent good which the philosophical search first makes possible. Yet at the same time it still cannot be denied that the spirit of the *Laws* is markedly different from that of the *Republic*. Specifically in the *Laws* Platonic philosophy begins to acquire a dogmatic form.

Whereas in the *Republic* it was the mystical vision of the *agathon* which sustained the order of the human soul, in the *Laws* that order is now made to depend upon the public acceptance of a dogmatic creed. This creed, in turn, was designed to prevent three possible misunderstandings: " . . . (1) the gods do not exist, or (2) that they exist but take no thought for the human race, or (3) that they are influenced by sacrifices and supplications and can easily be won over." [17]

For Plato disbelief in the gods was, in fact, symptomatic of a deeper

---

[17] Plato, *Laws*, p. 411.

psychic illness. Hopefully, persuasion and reason could cure such a condition; yet persuasion only works for those who are willing to listen. Where such willingness does not exist, Plato counsels the use of coercion and entrusts the enforcement of Magnesia's civil religion to a Nocturnal Council.

This willingness to use violence in the support of spiritual values reflects the pessimism which is characteristic of Plato's later writings. His original hope that humanity would respond to the philosopher's appeal has all but vanished. Yet at the same time his commitment to the philosophical demanded that its truths be preserved. By systematizing the teachings of philosophic reason the civil religion of the *Laws* succeeded in preserving at least the form of the philosophical life. The danger, of course, was that others would soon confuse form and substance, and thus it became the obligation of Plato's students to preserve this vital distinction. Of these students, the most important was Aristotle.

BIBLIOGRAPHY

BARKER, ERNEST. *Greek Political Theory: Plato and His Predecessors.* London: Methuen & Co., 1918.

CUSHMAN, ROBERT. *Therapeia: Plato's Conception of Philosophy.* Chapel Hill: University of North Carolina Press, 1958.

FRIEDLANDER, PAUL. *Plato* 3 vols. Translated by Hans Meyerhoff. Princeton: Princeton University Press, 1969.

GRENE, DAVID. *Greek Political Theory.* Chicago: University of Chicago Press, 1950.

JAEGER, WERNER. *Paideia: The Ideals of Greek Culture* 3 vols. Translated by Gilbert Highet. Oxford: Oxford University Press, 1945.

KOYRE, ALEXANDRE. *Discovering Plato.* Translated by Leonora Rosenfield. New York: Columbia University Press, 1945.

RANDALL, JOHN HERMAN. *Plato: Dramatist of the Life of Reason.* New York: Columbia University Press, 1970.

STRAUSS, LEO. *The Argument and Action of Plato's Laws.* Chicago: University of Chicago Press, 1975.

STRAUSS, LEO. *The City and Man.* Chicago: Rand McNally, 1964.

TAYLOR, A. E. *Socrates: The Man and His Thought.* Garden City: Doubleday, 1953.

TAYLOR, A. E. *The Mind of Plato.* Ann Arbor: University of Michigan Press, 1960.

VOEGELIN, ERIC. *Plato and Aristotle.* Baton Rouge: Louisiana State University Press, 1957.

VOEGELIN, ERIC. *The World of the Polis.* Baton Rouge: Louisiana State University Press, 1957.

2

ARISTOTLE

LIFE AND WORKS

Aristotle was born in 384 B.C. in the small town of Stagira on the Chalcidic peninsula. His father, Nicomachus, was the court physician to Amyntas III, king of Macedonia. The fact that he spent his early years in this environment may account both for Aristotle's interest in biology and the natural sciences and for his deep dislike of the manners of courtly life. As a youth of seventeen he was sent to Athens for his education and there entered Plato's Academy. He remained there for twenty years until Plato's death in 347 B.C. After having been passed over in favor of Speusippus as the next leader of the Academy, Aristotle left Athens for Assos. This move began a five-year period in which Aristotle traveled to various centers in Asia Minor and Macedonia. During that time he was able to pursue his scientific interests and to pay special attention to marine biology.

From 347 to 343 B.C. Aristotle stayed with his friend and fellow student Hermias who had recently become the king of Atarneus and was engaged in a valiant effort to resist the forces of an expanding Persian empire.

During that time, Aristotle met and married Hermias' niece, Pythias. With Hermias' assassination by Persian forces in 343, Aristotle left Assos for Lesbos and in 342 B.C. accepted the invitation of Philip of Macedonia to become the tutor of the fourteen-year-old crown-prince Alexander.

The relationship between Aristotle and Alexander is a subject which has promoted a variety of fanciful stories. Realistically speaking, however, Aristotle's influence seems to have been minimal. Alexander's political ambitions actually ran counter to Aristotle's own preferences. Neither Alexander's replacing the city-state by a world empire nor his bringing together both Greek and non-Greek peoples within the imperial order would have pleased his former teacher. With the murder of Philip in 336 B.C. Alexander assumed the Macedonian throne, and Aristotle consequently returned to Athens.

Passed over once again in the selection of the Academy's leader after the death of Speusippus, Aristotle founded his own school in the Lyceum in 335. There for the next twelve years he taught and directed the research and speculation of a number of students. Whereas the Platonists of the Academy tended to emphasize the study of mathematics, the Lyceum under Aristotle focused upon the more empirical sciences such as biology and history. Typical of this empirical approach was the collecting and recording of 158 constitutions as a basis for Aristotle's discussion of regime theory in his *Politics*. Of this collection there remains today only the treatise, "The Athenian Constitution." Written sometime between 328 and 325, it is essentially a constitutional history of the Athenian city-state which culminates in a description of the actual constitution at the time of the treatise's composition.

With the death of Alexander in 323 B.C. a wave of anti-Macedonian feeling erupted in Athens. Because of both his earlier relationship with Alexander and his contemporary friendship with the Macedonian leader, Antipater, Aristotle became an obvious target for such emotions. Like Socrates before him, he was condemned to death on charges of impiety. "Saving Athens from sinning twice against philosophy," Aristotle withdrew with his disciples to Chalcis. In the following year he died at the age of sixty-two.

Aristotle's writings generally fall into two major groups—the "exoteric" or literary works, and the treatises. At one time it was argued that the exoteric works were literary compositions which were intended for a general audience, and, therefore, purposely contained false propositions. The treatises, on the other hand, were understood to contain Aristotle's true teachings and thus were seen as intended only for his closest associates. Today, however, this particular interpretation is no longer widely held. The differences between the exoteric works and the more formal treatises appear to be essentially a matter of literary technique and the degree of specialization required by the audience.

The literary works, many of which were written in dialogue form, were intended for a larger general audience and thus were consequently less technical in style and argument. None of these works are extant in complete form today. The portions we have are contained in fragments which appear as quotations in the works of other authors. As such, they are not a particularly useful resource in the effort to reconstruct Aristotle's theoretical development. Although fragments from such works as *Eudemus* or *On the Soul*, *Gryllus* or *On Rhetoric*, and Iamblichus's *Protrepticus* clearly indicate Plato's influence on the young Aristotle, one should be most cautious in assuming the authenticity of any particular passage or statement.

Most of what we know of Aristotle's teaching is contained in the treatises. Generally they represent notes used for Aristotle's lectures in the Lyceum and range over a number of topics such as metaphysics, physics, logic, rhetoric, meteorology, anatomy, psychology, physiology, aesthetics, politics, and ethics. The arrangement of the texts, their division into books, and the joining of books into treatises was the work of a first-century-B.C. scholar, Andronicus of Rhodes. Prior to Andronicus's discovery of the manuscripts and his subsequent publication of the treatises, Aristotle was chiefly known for his dialogues. The fact that the treatises were essentially unknown for three hundred years raises certain questions as to the authenticity of certain books and passages. However, even if he did not write every word himself, it is generally believed that, as a whole, the treatises accurately reflect Aristotle's essential teachings.

The manner in which the books were edited and the fact that the treatises were originally either Aristotle's own lecture notes or student summaries of his presentations explain to a large degree the style and tone of much of his writings. The treatises tend to be cryptic, disorganized, repetitious, and in some places contradictory. On the whole, however, they serve as an example of a powerful and inquisitive mind following wherever his philosophical search required. That such a search did not produce a perfectly organized logical system should not be surprising; for, although he tended to be more systematic than his teacher Plato, Aristotle never lost an appreciation of the fact that the philosopher's true attitude is one of wonder.

INFLUENCE OF PLATO

The question of Aristotle's relationship with Plato has provoked an intense scholarly debate. Some have argued that after an initial period of apprenticeship Aristotle gradually moved away from Plato and developed his own distinct philosophical approach. Others have suggested that Aristotle's work represents more of a refinement than a rejection of Platonic philosophizing. In either case there is no doubt that Aristotle, himself, was careful to point out where he disagreed with the teachings of his master. For example, in his *Metaphysics* Aristotle clearly rejects the Platonic theory of Forms; while in his *Categories* and *Physics* he introduces the concepts of substance and causation as alternative doctrines by which to explain the phenomena of change and movement. Whether these differences do, in fact, represent a fundamental critique of the experiences which form the core of Platonic philosophy is a larger question which will continue to be debated.

Similarly, in his ethical and political writings Aristotle often developed his own arguments by distinguishing them from certain propositions which he associated with Plato. For example, he devotes a whole chapter of his *Nichomachean Ethics* to a discussion of the inadequacies of Plato's concept of the good; and in his *Politics* he critically reviews certain features of both Plato's *Republic* and his *Laws*. These differences, along with Aristotle's concern for historical particulars, have led some commentators to suggest that whereas Plato may have been the first political philosopher, Aristotle was the first political scientist. Although there is something to this distinction, one must be careful not to impose modern meanings where they do not properly belong.

The contemporary distinction between Plato as a philosopher and Aristotle as a political scientist often carries with it certain highly questionable assumptions. For example, some see the difference between the two resting on the fact that Plato was an idealist while Aristotle was an empiricist. This distinction, however, is altogether inappropriate. First, as we have seen, Plato is not an idealist. The Ideas for him are real; they are not ideals in the modern sense of preferred values. Secondly, although Aristotle is concerned with beginning his investigation with a careful examination of "concrete particulars," he is not an empiricist in the modern sense. On the contrary, Aristotle's concrete particulars are not restricted to the realm of observed facts. Rather they also include such items as commonly held opinions (that which is thought about a subject in general) and even certain implications concerning terminology and usage. Finally, although Aristotle disagreed with Plato as to how we can gain knowledge of the Form, like Plato, he believed that it is the universal which is truly knowable.

A second modern assumption that is often associated with the difference between Aristotle and Plato is that the latter approached politics in a moralistic fashion while the former was much more neutral in his attitude. Aristotle's frequently quoted advice to a tyrant concerning the ways by which he could preserve his rule is often given as an example of his ethical neutrality. Such neutrality, in turn, is assumed to be a characteristic typical of the scientific attitude in general. Here again, however, the categories do not fit the case. First, the assumption that science requires a neutral or passive posture on the part of the investigator is both a modern presupposition and a highly questionable one. More importantly, however, is the valid argument that Aristotle, like Plato, was not simply a disinterested seeker after facts. His ethical and political works are replete with examples of his advocacy on behalf of particular preferences. Indeed, his *Ethics* and *Politics* were, in fact, originally parts of the same treatise. Similarly, just as his teleological view of the universe carries with it many important ethical consequences, so too do the categories which he employs in his political analysis. For example, in Book III of his *Politics*, Aristotle introduces a conceptual scheme for the classification of various constitutional systems. Part of the scheme is based upon a distinction between those regimes that consider the common interest of its citizens, as judged by the standard of absolute justice, and those that do not. Accordingly, when Aristotle distinguishes between a monarchy and a tyranny, his argument is based on the moral distinction between a "right" constitution and its "perverted" form. Such judgments, which are built into the very categories of Aristotle's descriptive political analysis, obviously belie any attempt to classify him as a neutral observer of political phenomena.

If it is inappropriate to distinguish Aristotle from Plato in terms of the former's "empiricism" or "neutrality," in what sense, then, is it permissible to speak of him as the first political scientist? Although Plato and Aristotle share a substantially similar understanding of god, humankind, nature, and society—and thus it is possible to speak of the classical-Greek tradition as a whole—it is, nonetheless, true that Aristotle approaches the study of political reality in a way in which Plato does not. Specifically, Aristotle is much more willing to consider the political realm as a distinct reality which can be studied primarily in its own terms. Unlike Plato, he does not feel the need to repeatedly locate the political within the order of the cosmos as a whole. Rather he is content to focus directly upon it and examine its internal structure.

This difference is manifested in a number of ways. Plato's *Republic* had presented a view of humankind which allowed for only one form of human excellence—the philosophical. Accordingly, human beings achieved excellence only when they became philosophers. Indeed, even the politician had to become a philosopher in order to be a true statesman; for according to Plato, philosophical excellence was the only true political art. In effect, then, for Plato there was no rigid distinction between the realm of the political and that of the philosophical. Both realms culminated in the same achievement—the emergence of the philosopher-king. The virtues of the philosopher had become the defining virtues for all human types. To do anything well meant to do it as the philosopher would do it. Thus the consideration of any particular human activity necessarily implied a consideration of the philosopher's activity, and such a consideration eventually led to the actual doing of philosophy itself. Plato's *Republic* is a good example of this approach. What begins as a discussion of justice soon expands (and necessarily so) into a consideration of philosophical anthropology, ontology, and theology.

Aristotle's political theorizing is quite different. His concern, as a political scientist, is with the distinctively political. That such a distinction can be made legitimately is central to Aristotle's approach, and he attempts to illustrate this possibility by establishing the following dichotomies. Unlike Plato, who saw only one form of human excellence, Aristotle saw two. In addition to the excellence of the person of theory (the philosopher), there is also the excellence of the person of practice (the *Spoudaios* or mature man). Each is excellent in his or her own way, and each has an exclusive arena within which to demonstrate that excellence. The person of theory is excellent due to possession of the intellectual virtues, and the appropriate realm for this type of excellence is the *school*. The person of practice, on the other hand, is excellent due to possession of the moral virtues, and this person's realm is that of the *city*. Although Aristotle does not totally separate these two realms, and although he argues for the ultimate superiority of the life of theory, it is obvious, nonetheless, that he has created a particular segment within reality that can be studied in its own terms. According to Aristotle, the political realm has its own peculiar excellence (the moral virtues), its own particular participant (the *Spoudaios*), and its own defining purpose (practical action). Accordingly, these elements can be understood in their own terms without constantly examining the needs and achievements of the theoretical order. In Aristotle, then, we have the first major separation between theory and practice, and it is on the basis of this distinction that the claim that he is the first *political* scientist can legitimately rest.

This "carving out" of a political realm has certain interesting methodological consequences. Inasmuch as the concerns of the realm of practice are different from the concerns of theory, the role of knowledge in each area is different. According to Aristotle, the political person needs to know only for the sake of action. The concern here is to act rightly, and the need to know is limited by that concern. For Plato, on the other hand, the true statesman was the philosopher. In this case the need to know was unbounded inasmuch as the philosopher's desire to know was understood to transcend all limits.

This distinction emerges rather clearly in a comparison of Plato's *Republic* and Aristotle's *Ethics*. The major effort of the *Republic* was Plato's attempt to prove that justice was naturally good. Only with this knowledge could one teach justice and consequently practice the art of politics. Aristotle's *Ethics*, on the other hand, begins with a rather interesting warning.

Aristotle addresses his students and tells them that his discussion will "start with what is known to us" and, thus, that only those students who have enjoyed a proper moral upbringing will be permitted to participate in these deliberations. Having a proper moral upbringing means that the students have acquired correct opinions about moral concerns. Using these opinions as a basis for argument, there will be no further need to ask why it is so.

Aristotle's difference with Plato is striking. Rather than proving the adequacy of certain opinions, Aristotle begins with them as a basis for further discussion. Whereas Plato spends the *Republic* proving that justice is good, Aristotle is concerned with addressing only those students who already believe that this is the case. This, in turn, enables him to move on to a discussion of acting justly. It is important to realize, through all of this, that Aristotle is quite certain that an opinion such as justice is good could be proven. Yet such a proof is the concern of the philosopher. As far as politics is concerned, all that is really necessary, according to Aristotle, is that the political leaders *believe* that it is good to be just and act accordingly. If they were to do so, they would be excellent politicians. Their inability to undertake a theoretical examination of justice itself, therefore, does not detract from their excellence as political actors. In short, for Aristotle, political excellence does not require the direct and immediate presence of philosophical virtue. Because of this, political excellence can be studied on its own terms, and this is the task of political science.

THE THEORETICAL, PRODUCTIVE, AND PRACTICAL SCIENCES

By distinguishing between theory and practice, the school and the city, the intellectual and the moral virtues, and the philosopher and the *Spoudaios*, Aristotle attempted to focus upon that which is distinctly political and to create, thereby, a distinctly appropriate science for the investigation of the political. Although in Aristotle's scheme philosophy is no longer an immediate requirement for the creation of political order, some form of knowledge is. And in his effort to demonstrate what is required, Aristotle introduced his distinction among the theoretical, productive, and practical sciences.

In his *Metaphysics*, Aristotle attempts to explain those criteria by which it is possible to distinguish among the three forms of rational inquiry. Each form or type can be characterized both by the nature of the object it investigates and by the investigator's concern or intention while undertaking the inquiry. For example, the theoretical sciences study unchanging principles. As such, the realities structured by these principles exist independently of humanity and are thus beyond its control.

Aristotle lists mathematics, physics, and metaphysics as examples of *theoretical* science. In each case, its investigators are concerned with understanding principles over which they have no influence. According to Aristotle, for example, both *physical nature* and *being* as such are the kinds of substance which have the principle of their movement and their rest present within themselves. Inasmuch as human beings cannot hope to alter the fundamental structure of nature or of being, their motive for engaging in purely theoretical inquiry is esentially that of intellectual interest. The theoretical sciences seek knowledge for its own sake. They arise out of a sense of wonder and culminate in a moment of understanding. Although the theoretical sciences do not present us with "results" in a pragmatic sense, they do allow humanity to share in an activity which is ultimately divine in nature. As such, theoretical inquiry represents the highest and most noble form of human endeavor.

The *productive* sciences are quite different. They are, in effect, all those skills, crafts, and arts which people employ in the self-conscious making of things. Thus their character is primarily technological. Unlike the theoretical sciences, the productive sciences deal with those objects over which humans do exercise some control. Generally this control is guided by the artisan's concern for utility. For example, carpenters work with wood in order to make it usable as a desk, a boat, or a house. In each case, they are taking the material at hand and forming it in such a way as to meet their own purposes. It is as if they are imposing a form upon the material and, in so doing, are using the object for a purpose which they bring to it. This is so inasmuch as it is a carpenter who ultimately decides if a particular piece of wood will become a desk, a chair, or a house. Whereas the theoretical sciences emerge from a sense of wonder, the productive sciences are born out of need. And, whereas the theoretical sciences seek wisdom, the productive sciences are concerned with efficiency. In short, they are the arts which guide one in the human action of making.

The *practical* sciences are in some respects similar to the productive sciences. Aristotle emphasizes this similarity by treating them both as forms of calculation, which is knowledge guided by a concern for action. That is, like the productive sciences, the practical sciences deal with realities over which humans exercise some control. Yet, unlike the productive sciences, the practical sciences are not concerned with the activity of making; rather they seek to inform human doing. They reflect, therefore, the differences between making and doing. Or in other terms—the differences between fabrication and nurture.

Perhaps this distinction can best be illustrated by examining Aristotle's two major examples of practical science: ethics and politics. For purposes of illustration, ethics can be understood as that practical science concerned with the direction of one's personal life. As such it deals with a reality over which people have some control; for each person determines to an extent who he or she will become. Ethical knowledge, accordingly, is concerned with the problems of living. It is, in effect, an applied science. Yet even though it is an applied science, it is different than the productive sciences. This difference is rooted in the fact that, unlike the productive sciences, the reality governed by ethics already carries with it its own purposes. Thus, rather than attempting to impose a purpose on human life, ethics is concerned with nurturing and developing that purpose which is already given in the structure of human nature itself. For Aristotle people are not free to make of themselves anything they wish. Rather they are to do those things appropriate to their human nature. Unlike the artisans who bend their material to fit their own design, ethical actors seek to fulfill the potential of their humanity by conforming to those principles inherent within human nature as such. Consequently, the science of ethics is concerned with teaching people how to act in light of a sufficient understanding of such principles. Its goal is happiness, not efficiency.

Politics is another example of a practical science. As such, it is concerned with guiding society in such a way as to allow it to fulfill the natural purpose of political existence. As we will see, Aristotle believes that there is a proper purpose implied by the very structure of a political association itself. Accordingly, regimes are not free to use society for any purpose whatsoever. Rather societies which are true to their nature must seek the common good. Political science, in turn, is that practical science concerned precisely with such matters. Like ethics, it seeks happiness, and, inasmuch as Aristotle associates happiness with action, it goes beyond a concern for knowledge simply for its own sake.

Aristotle's distinction among the theoretical, productive, and practical sciences should not be interpreted simply as an attempt to achieve an academic division of labor. Rather these distinctions, made at the level of rational inquiry, reflect, in turn, deeper distinctions within Aristotle's understanding of the human soul. The various types of science actually represent various forms of excellence within the human psyche. They are not dry epistemological categories but rather the means by which various elements of the soul articulate their proper and peculiar function. To *do* science, then, is to *be* human. For example, a life concerned with theoretical science achieves the fundamental excellence of humanity's godlike nature. Similarly, the doing of practical science attests to the psychic excellence of the person of moral virtue (*Spoudaios*). Thus our discussion of Aristotle's understanding of science will not be complete until it incorporates his analysis of the human soul and its particular needs. Such an analysis is a central concern of both his *Ethics* and *Politics*.

Of the three separate ethical treatises within Aristotle's work (*Magna Moralia, Eudemian Ethics,* and *Nicomachean Ethics*), the *Nicomachean Ethics* is regarded as his most mature effort. It represents a summary of his lectures as prepared by his son, Nicomachus, at the death of his father. In terms of both argument and structure it forms the introductory section of a larger work whose final portion has come to us as the *Politics.* The structure of the *Ethics* is relatively simple. Book I introduces the general subject and defines the problem of the treatise. Books II to V deal with moral virtue both in general and specific terms. Book VI is concerned with the intellectual virtues, while Book VII speaks of moral weaknesses. Books VIII and IX are devoted to a discussion of friendship, and Book X closes the treatise with an examination of pleasure and a discussion of happiness.

Throughout the *Ethics,* it is evident that Aristotle is interested in distinguishing his work from certain doctrines associated primarily with his teacher, Plato. For example, he devotes several passages to a critique of Plato's Form of the good. Yet the real difference between the two is more a matter of style than of any particular doctrine. Unlike Plato, who often contrasted the mere opinions of the average person to the knowledge of the philosopher, Aristotle continually refers to popular opinions as both a guide to and a check upon his own speculations. He finds in the most common and reasonable opinions a certain prudential wisdom which is a product more of experience than of schooling. His method in general, then, is to weigh what common opinion has to say and to borrow from it those elements that seem to stand up under the scrutiny of careful examination. That such a technique is not designed to produce a clear-cut ethical system was not a problem for Aristotle. Indeed, to expect precise and exact knowledge about ethical and political affairs is to misunderstand the very nature of the subject matter itself:

> Our discussion will be adequate if it achieves clarity within the limits of the subject matter. . . . Problems of what is noble and just, which politics examines, present so much variety and irregularity that some people believe that they exist only by convention and not by nature. . . . Therefore . . . we must be satisfied to indicate the truth with a rough and general sketch: when the subject and basis of a discussion consist of matters that hold good only as a general rule, but not always, the conclusions reached must be of the same order.[1]

The theme of Book I is a discussion of the good. Aristotle contends that all things aim at the good, and that for humans such a good is generally

[1] Aristotle, *Nicomachean Ethics,* trans. Martin Ostwald (Indianapolis: Bobbs-Merrill, 1962), p. 5.

referred to as happiness. Yet, although all people wish to be "happy," all do not agree as to the precise meaning of the term itself. In reality, the concept is used to refer to a variety of things. For example, some believe that the life of pleasure produces happiness; others, the life of honor; and others, the life of contemplation. The challenge is to determine which of these opinions is the most adequate, and to do so Aristotle turns to an examination of human nature.

Aristotle's approach to this problem is dictated by his belief that happiness is a condition which necessarily accompanies human activity. We are happy as humans when we are acting in a certain manner. More precisely, we are happy when we are living well. Yet in order to understand what it means to live well, one must understand the potential of human life as such. Such an understanding, in turn, can only be gained by an examination of the human soul.

For Aristotle the study of the human soul begins with an analysis of that variety of functions and actions which it makes possible. Thus, as the source of life, the soul's precise structure is revealed by the type of life which it is capable of generating. In the case of human beings, Aristotle speaks of three types: the life of nutrition and growth, the life of sense perception, and the life of reason. It is as if humans are capable of three levels of living, each with its own purpose, and each with its own standard of excellence.

Humankind shares the life of nutrition and growth with both the animal and vegetative world. Thus, although it is an important component of human life and, consequently, its needs and rules cannot be disregarded altogether, this first "life" does not constitute a peculiar excellence proper to people alone. Similarly the life of sense perception is shared by both humans and animals. Both are capable of experiencing pleasure and pain, and both act accordingly. Although it is true that an animal's response to pleasure and pain is more or less dictated by its instincts whereas a human's may be mediated by consciousness, it still is the case that life at this level does not constitute humankind's proper and peculiar function. Thus it is that Aristotle turns to the life of reason as being the distinctively human form of existence within the world. The human being is a rational animal, and only by living as such can it fulfill the full potential of its nature. Unlike the vegetative and animal realms, therefore, the human sphere includes the possibility of a level of excellence which goes beyond that of health and pleasure. Given this, the greatest happiness possible for human beings will be found at the level of the rational life:

> . . . we reach the conclusion that the good of man is an activity . . . in conformity with excellence or virtue, and if there are several virtues, in conformity with the best and most complete.[2]

---

[2] Aristotle, *Nicomachean Ethics*, p. 17.

Having examined the true meaning of happiness and having chosen the life of contemplation over both the life of pleasure and of honor, Aristotle then raises the question of how happiness can be achieved. Inasmuch as happiness accompanies acting well, and inasmuch as acting well presupposes certain virtues and accomplishments, it is obvious that humans are not born happy. Rather they are born with the potential of becoming happy, and thus the human challenge becomes that of actualizing this potential for happiness. Indeed such a challenge is the very concern of politics and, thereby, provides the relationship between Aristotle's ethical and political thought:

> Our results also tally with what we said at the outset: for we stated that the end of politics is the best of ends; and the main concern of politics is to engender a certain character in the citizens and to make them good and disposed to perform noble actions.[3]

Like Plato, Aristotle understands politics primarily in ethical terms. For him then, the problem of gaining happiness is equivalent to the problem of acquiring virtue. Virtue, in this sense, is any characteristic which allows the soul to perform its functions well. For the purpose of this discussion, however, Aristotle is concerned only with the soul's appetitive and rational elements.

Like the animals, humans experience both pleasure and pain and thus are moved by their appetites. They choose that which gives them pleasure and, freed from the strict discipline of animal instincts, they are faced with the problem of choosing well. They must learn to take pleasure in the right things, at the right times, and in the right manner. To succeed in this they must acquire the moral virtues; for according to Aristotle, these virtues are the very qualities which will allow citizens to choose well.

Books II to V are devoted to an analysis of the moral virtues. In them Aristotle offers a detailed discussion of selected examples. It would be a mistake, however, to interpret this listing as if it were a dogmatic ethical system. Aristotle is not concerned with defining moral absolutes. Indeed his sometimes tedious discussion of particulars is intended primarily as an illustration of certain general principles—the correct application of which always depends upon an act of judgment and refinement. Nonetheless, certain elements of this discussion are particularly noteworthy.

First, the moral virtues are acquired by habituation. For example, if we wish to become courageous, we become so by continually acting as a courageous person would act until such actions themselves become ha-

---

[3] Aristotle, *Nicomachean Ethics*, p. 23.

bitual. Strictly speaking, then, the moral virtues are not taught. They are acquired through a process of imitation. As such, moral education depends upon the presence of good models and the encouragement of appropriate habits. This, in turn, depends upon good legislation, inasmuch as a society establishes its pattern of shared expectations, preferred behavior, and favored habits through its laws. Thus without good laws the inculcation of moral virtue is impossible:

> Accordingly, if, as we have said, a man must receive a good up-bringing and discipline in order to be good, and must subsequently lead the same kind of life, pursuing what is good and never involun-tarily or voluntarily doing anything base, this can be effected by living under the guidance of a kind of intelligence and right order which can be enforced. Now, a father's command does not have the power to enforce or to compel, nor does, in general, the command of a single man, unless he is a king or someone in a similar position. But law does have the power or capacity to compel, being the rule of reason derived from some sort of practical wisdom and in-telligence.[4]

A second feature of Aristotle's discussion of the moral virtues in-volves the concept of moderation. Inasmuch as the appetites are concerned with pleasure and pain, excess and deficiency are the two extremes to be avoided. A life which has either too much or too little of either is ignoble and base. Choosing well, therefore, means avoiding these two extremes; the hu-man pursuit of pleasure consequently should be a moderate one. Yet the concept of moderation, itself, requires some clarification, and Aristotle is aware of this. He distinguishes, therefore, between the "mean of an entity" and "the mean relative to us." Ethical moderation is not equivalent to the mean of an entity, for such a mean is simply an arithmetical average. For ex-ample, the arithmetical mean of 2 and 10 is 6. And if one were to apply this mean absolutely it would lead to obviously inappropriate results. For exam-ple, if donations to some cause were accepted between $2 and $10, the vir-tue of generosity, calculated arithmetically, would require that each person donate $6. Yet $6 for a poor person may be too much to give, while $6 for a wealthy individual may be too little.

Thus it is that Aristotle associates moderation with "the mean rela-tive to us." Accordingly, in calculating what is moderate, each person must consider his own particular situation. Then each must seek to avoid both excess and deficiency from within that situation. For example, an extremely poor person may discover that any donation larger than $1 is excessive given the situation. Generosity in that case would require no more than $1. At

---

4 Aristotle, *Nicomachean Ethics*, p. 297.

first glance, Aristotle's attempt to avoid a rigid or mathematically absolute moral system may appear to encourage moral relativism. If the mean is relative to us, does this not free our actions from all binding external control? Although some may see this in Aristotle, it is clear that this is not his intention. Although ethical control can not be provided by an absolute moral rule, it is provided by the presence of practical reason. That is to say, in calculating what is moderate within a given situation we are to make our judgments as if we were ethically mature persons, that is, as if we were *Spoudaioi*. Accordingly, ethical control is exercised by imitating the person of moral excellence. Thus it is the presence of practical wisdom as embodied in the choices of the good person that provides the living rule of conduct:

> We may thus conclude that virtue or excellence is a characteristic involving choice, and that it consists in observing the mean relative to us, a mean which is defined by a rational principle, such as a man of practical wisdom would use to determine it.[5]

To return to our example of the donation, the poor person should ask, "What would the *Spoudaioi* do in this situation if they were I?" The answer to that question is equivalent to what the moral virtue of generosity would demand of that person according to the "mean relative to us."

Aristotle's discussion of moral virtue rejects the simplistic belief that we can relieve ourselves of the dilemma of choice by obediently submitting to certain mechanical rules. His, therefore, is an ethics which relies more upon existential strength than upon the power of dogmatic codes. This reference to existential strength, in turn, points forward to Aristotle's discussion of the intellectual virtues.

The human pursuit of pleasure need not be instinctual. When it is done in a human way, it is the result of deliberation and choice. As such, reason is necessarily involved in the direction and development of the appetites. Although the faculty of reason is not within the appetites, the appetitive element does respond to the influence of reason. In this sense, then, Aristotle sometimes refers to the appetites as belonging to the rational element.

The rational part of the soul, so Aristotle maintains, provides us with our distinctly human features. Only we as humans seek to attain truth, and in order to do so we must acquire the intellectual virtues; for they are the essential qualities which are necessary if the search for truth is to be successful. Unlike the moral virtues, which are acquired by habituation, the intellectual virtues arise from teaching and thus require experience and

---

[5] Aristotle, *Nicomachean Ethics*, p. 43.

time. In his analysis of the rational element of the soul, Aristotle distinguishes between scientific reason and calculative reason. As we saw earlier, it is this distinction within the soul of humans which supported Aristotle's earlier attempt to distinguish between theory and practice, the school and the city, and the philosopher and the *Spoudaios*.

Scientific reason is concerned with apprehending the unchanging principles of necessary realities. It is the concern of the school, and it expresses the excellence of the philosopher. In order for scientific reason to function as it should, it requires three intellectual virtues. Rational intuition (*nous*) allows us to correctly apprehend those first principles which cannot be logically demonstrated. Scientific knowledge (*episteme*) is the capacity to demonstrate the connections between things and begins from those principles made available by rational intuition. Theoretical wisdom (*sophia*) is that quality present when both rational intuition and scientific knowledge are present and concerned with the highest realities. Indeed, it is theoretical wisdom which represents the highest achievement of reason, and, as such, its functioning is the proper and peculiar activity which Aristotle associates with the greatest human happiness. The philosopher's life of contemplation is, for Aristotle, the greatest human good.

The second part of the rational element of the soul is calculative reason. Calculative reason is concerned with knowledge for the sake of action. It is the concern of the city, and the *Spoudaios* embodies its highest excellence. In order for calculative reason to function well, it requires two intellectual virtues. The first, art (*techné*), is the capacity for *making* well; while the second, practical wisdom (*phronesis*), is the quality necessary for *doing* well. The distinction here, of course, duplicates that between the productive and practical sciences. Accordingly, it is not necessary to repeat our analysis.

Of particular importance, however, is the relationship between practical wisdom and moral virtue. Practical wisdom is that form of right reason which enables citizens to decide correctly the requirements of moral virtue:

> Our discussion, then, has made it clear that it is impossible to be good in the full sense of the word without practical wisdom or to be a man of practical wisdom without moral excellence or virtue.[6]

It is clear from the above, then, that while Aristotle introduces certain distinctions between the realms of the intellectual and the moral, he does not separate them altogether. Thus, although he rejects the Socratic unity of

---

[6] Aristotle, *Nicomachean Ethics*, p. 172.

knowledge and virtue, he does not intend to make the latter totally independent of the former. That development is reserved for more modern times.

The question as to the proper relationship between the intellectual and the moral realm is raised once again in Book X of the *Ethics*. There Aristotle reintroduces the theme of Book I, that is, happiness. As has been shown, the happy life for Aristotle is one which is in conformity with virtue. His analysis of the soul, however, has established that there are two forms of human virtue; the moral and the intellectual. Moral virtue is associated with the exercise of practical wisdom, while theoretical virtue is expressed in the excellence of theoretical wisdom. In those cases where there is more than one virtue, Aristotle has argued that true happiness is to be found in a life in conformity with the highest virtue. As his analysis of reason has shown, Aristotle considers the intellectual virtues to be superior in kind. The life which they make possible (*bios theoretikos*) is the most continuous, the most self-sufficient, the most pleasurable, and concerned with the highest objects of knowledge. In effect, then, the good for humankind is the life of contemplation:

> . . . it follows that the activity of our intelligence constitutes the complete happiness of man, provided that it encompasses a complete span of life; for nothing connected with happiness must be incomplete. However, such a life would be more than human. A man who would live it would do so not insofar as he is human, but because there is a divine element within him. . . . So if it is true that intelligence is divine in comparison with man, then a life guided by intelligence is divine in comparison with human life. . . . We should try to become immortal as far as that is possible and do our utmost to live in accordance with what is highest in us.[7]

As this statement makes clear, Aristotle shares with Plato that understanding of philosophy which sees it as a human effort to encounter the divine. It is an encounter made possible by the "divine element within us" and it is directed toward that which is necessarily beyond our mere humanity.

Aristotle's argument that the life of contemplation is the best does not imply, however, that the life of practical action is lacking in its own excellence. The moral virtues are still virtues, and, although it is not the highest form of wisdom, practical wisdom is a feature required for the good functioning of the soul. Thus the realm of action is also a realm for human excellence. As the school is the place for contemplation, so, too, is the city the locus of moral virtue.

Aristotle's ranking of the school over the city and the philosopher

[7] Aristotle, *Nicomachean Ethics*, pp. 290–1.

over the *Spoudaios* has several interesting consequences. First, although the political has its own appropriate place, it does, nonetheless, point to a realm of excellence beyond itself. The political sphere is not enough. If humans are to be truly happy, they must move beyond the political and into the philosophical. According to this argument, then, to be a good person requires more than simply being a good citizen. It is no longer sufficient simply to obey the law, for now one must respond to the divine within oneself.

Second, inasmuch as humans have loyalties to a realm other than the simply political, the political realm, itself, can no longer claim to be an absolute. No longer an absolute, the city can no longer demand the citizen's absolute obedience. A tension, therefore, is established between the dual obligations of human beings. As citizens, they are obligated to their regime. As humans, each is obligated to the good.

This emphasis upon the tension between the good individual and the good citizen raises certain questions as to the contribution of philosophy to politics. As we have seen, both Plato and Aristotle emphasize the importance of philosophy and tend, thereby, to subordinate the political realm to the philosophical. In a certain sense, then, the political becomes valuable to the degree to which it supports and sustains the philosophical. What, however, does philosophy contribute to politics? Why should the statesman allow it to be practiced? For Plato, philosophy's contribution is both immediate and necessary. In his *Republic* he argued that only philosophers can establish a truly just regime. In effect, then, the purpose of political life, justice, can only be achieved with the direct aid of philosophy. Aristotle's answer to this same question, however, is more indirect.

In Book VIII Aristotle begins an analysis of friendship. Indeed, at first glance such a topic may appear inappropriate within a political work. Yet if we remember that Aristotle is drawing from his experience with the relatively small Greek city-state, we may at least see the significance of this topic for his argument. Whereas modern thinkers tend to treat friendship as a private or personal concern, Aristotle sees it as indispensable for political life:

> Friendship also seems to hold states together, and lawgivers apparently devote more attention to it than to justice. . . . When people are friends, they have no need of justice, but when they are just, they need friendship in addition. In fact, the just in the fullest sense is regarded as constituting an element of friendship. Friendship is noble as well as necessary. . . . [8]

From this account it would appear that, according to Aristotle, it is vital for the health of the political community that there be concord and

---

[8] Aristotle, *Nicomachean Ethics*, p. 215.

harmony among its citizens. Such a condition will exist if citizens are bound together by a common affection for a particular object. In analyzing such objects, Aristotle distinguishes among three: the useful, the pleasant, and the good. That is to say, people form friendships for the sake of gaining something from the relationship. For example, two people may form a friendship because it is useful to each or for the pleasure that they hope to get out of it. In such cases, however, the friendship is neither deep nor secure. The partners do not feel affection for one another *per se* but rather only in terms of the personal advantage each foresees. In such cases, the friendship tends to be short-lived; for once the partners gain the advantage they seek, the original motive for the friendship disappears.

This is not the case, however, when people become friends for the sake of one another's goodness:

> The perfect form of friendship is that between good men who are alike in excellence or virtue. For these friends wish alike for one another's good because they are good men and they are good *per se.* . . . Those who wish for their friends' good for their friends' sake are friends in the truest sense, since their attitude is determined by what their friends are and not by incidental considerations. . . . That such a friendship is lasting stands to reason. . . . [9]

According to this analysis, then, it would appear that rulers would want to foster goodness among their citizens not only for the citizens' sake and happiness but also for the sake of the regime. A well-ordered political society requires harmony and concord. This condition, in turn, is the result, in part, of those bonds formed within friendship, and friendship is most secure and enduring when it is among persons who are good. The philosopher's contribution to this task is obvious. First the philosophers, themselves, are good precisely to the extent that they develop their own appropriate intellectual and moral virtues. More importantly, however, the philosophers make a fundamental contribution toward the regime's program of civic education.

As we have seen, Artistole points to the *Spoudaios* as the politician of excellence. Yet part of the *Spoudaios's* excellence is due to the fact that this political being listens to the philosopher. The *Spoudaios* is, in effect, an example of the second-best "man" found in Hesiod's *Works and Days* as quoted by Aristotle:

> The man is all-best who himself works out every problem. . . .
> That man, too, is admirable who follows one who
> speaks well.

[9] Aristotle, *Nicomachean Ethics*, pp. 219–20.

He who cannot see the truth for himself, nor,
hearing it from others,
store it away in his mind, that man is
utterly useless.[10]

The *Spoudaios* is the citizen who is able to act according to the dictates of practical reason. Practical reason, in turn, is concerned with determining the appropriateness of certain acts vis-à-vis selected standards of conduct. Yet it is only theoretical wisdom which is capable of justifying the correctness of the original standards themselves. For example, all *Spoudaioi* act justly because they have been taught that justice is good. It is only philosophers, however, who are capable of demonstrating this original teaching. Thus it is that any regime's concern for the moral excellence of its citizens requires the presence—if only indirectly—of philosophers. They, or their laws, must teach the *Spoudaioi;* and, in doing so, the philosophers are contributing toward the vitality of the societies which support them.

THE ANALYSIS OF POLITICS

Unlike the *Ethics*, Aristotle's *Politics* lacks a clear and orderly structure. Rather than being a single unified treatise, it appears more as a collection of essays ranging over a variety of subjects. Book I primarily deals with the proper organization of the household and several economic issues which are associated with it. Book II is an examination of certain model states and selected theories concerning the best regime. Book III focuses upon constitutional theory, while Books IV and V deal with the problems of establishing and maintaining particular constitutional arrangements. Somewhat repetitiously, Book VI concentrates upon oligarchies and democracies, while its argument as a whole is concerned with discussing those measures required for ensuring their stability. Finally Books VII and VIII analyze the elements of the best regime and examine those educational programs which are necessary to sustain it. Throughout the treatise as a whole, however, Aristotle is consistent in his attempt to base his arguments upon historical examples and concrete particulars. As in the *Ethics*, he prefers to begin his analysis from those instances which are closest at hand.

Aristotle's empirical approach has both its advantages and disadvantages. One of the more important disadvantages is that it tends to bind Aristotle to the Greek city-state (*polis*). It is as if Aristotelian politics is limited to the particular form it assumed in the Greek experience. In those cases where Aristotle cannot transcend that form, his arguments tend to be

---

[10] Aristole, *Nicomachean Ethics*, pp. 7–8.

of little interest today. However, the interest that his work has evoked throughout the ages clearly demonstrates that such occasions are relatively infrequent. A second consequence of Aristotle's preoccupation with the *polis* is that it distracted him from examining one of the most important political events of his age, that is, the collapse of the *polis* and its replacement by an imperial form of political organization. Within Aristotle's lifetime the autonomous Greek city-state was to disappear forever. Yet if one simply read the *Politics*, one would have no indication that such an event ever took place.

Book I of the *Politics* begins with Aristotle's effort to establish the precise nature of a political association. In particular he wishes to distinguish it from several other forms of human association. Failing to do so, it would be impossible to understand both the specific purpose of political existence and the appropriate characteristics of the good regime. Accordingly Aristotle suggests that the political association is the natural termination of a series of earlier unions. First there is the union of male and female and that of master and slave. These together form the Greek household. The union of several households becomes the village, and finally several villages associate to form the city-state.

Typically each "association" has its own specific purpose and consequently its own appropriate structures. For example, according to Aristotle, the union of male and female is for the purpose of procreation, while that of the household is for the satisfaction of daily recurring needs. Similarly the political association, which is the most sovereign and inclusive union, exists for the sake of the good life. Thus, although it may grow for the sake of mere life, its purpose is that of the good life.

This distinction between the good life and mere living has already been established in Aristotle's *Ethics*. The good life is that which seeks the highest human happiness, that is, the life of virtue. To emphasize this point, Aristotle once again recalls the distinction between the life of sense perception, which is shared with the animals, and the life of reason:

> The reason why man is a being meant for political association, in a higher degree than bees or other gregarious animals can ever associate, is evident. . . . The mere making of sounds serves to indicate pleasure and pain, and is thus a faculty that belongs to animals in general. . . . But language serves to declare what is advantageous and what is the reverse, and it therefore serves to declare what is just and what is unjust. It is the peculiarity of man, in comparison with the rest of the animal world, that he alone possesses a perception of good and evil, of the just and unjust, and of other similar qualities; and it is association in [a common perception of] these things which makes a family and a *polis*.[11]

---

[11] Aristotle, *The Politics*, trans. Ernest Barker (New York: Oxford University Press, 1958), pp. 5–6.

It is evident from this statement that Aristotle considers humanity's political nature as an attribute of its rational nature. Inasmuch as we seek pleasure we are social animals. Yet more importantly, it is our rational nature and its needs that determine our political existence. We are political animals because we require the services of the city-state and its good laws if we are to acquire the necessary moral and intellectual virtues which make the good life—or the life of reason—possible. This need, in turn, serves to establish both the purpose of political society and the standard by which all regimes can be judged.

The rest of Book I is devoted to an examination of the household, its relationships, and its purpose. Therein Aristotle discusses such themes as the relationship of husband to wife, parent to child, master to slave and the art of acquisition. Perhaps two themes within this discussion should be noted at this time. First, in discussing the acquisition of property, Aristotle insists that it is not proper to accumulate wealth simply for wealth's sake. It is natural, he allows, to acquire enough wealth so as to support one in the pursuit of the good life. Yet since the amount necessary for such a pursuit is limited, it is a perversion when one seeks to accumulate unlimited wealth and property. With such an argument Aristotle is imposing political and moral restraints upon economic activity. In doing this, he is typical of the premodern attitude in general. For the classical thinkers economics was understood to be a necessary but subordinate form of human activity. As such, it was limited and placed in the service of higher values. The actual freeing of the economic realm from both political and moral restraints did not occur until the development of capitalism in the late Middle Ages.

A second noteworthy feature of Aristotle's discussion of the household is his analysis of slavery. According to Aristotle some among humanity are slaves by their very nature. They lack reason and thus are incapable of governing themselves. Although they are higher than animals because they, at least, can acknowledge reason in others, they are, nonetheless, intended by nature to be ruled by masters. Such a rule should not be arbitrary and, indeed, may even allow for friendship between master and slave; but it is still servitude. This feature of Aristotle's philosophy is unacceptable to a civilization that has adopted the Christian belief that all human beings have an inherent worth and dignity as children of God. Yet without justifying this doctrine, it is important to note that, according to Aristotle, slavery is legitimate only when it is based in nature. That form of slavery which is the result of either superior power or legal sanction is unjustifiable. Thus given this distinction, Aristotle's doctrine of natural slavery actually served as a criticism of most forms of slavery typically practiced in his time. In this way, then, it was an improvement upon the common Greek custom.

In preparing for his own theorizing, Aristotle devoted Book II of the *Politics* to a review of selected theories, constitutions, and legislators. In his review of political theory, he looked at such thinkers as Plato, Phaleas of Chalcedon, and Hippodamus of Miletus. In each case, he proceeded by summarizing certain of their arguments and then critically commenting on their appropriateness. For example, in his review of Plato he examined both the *Republic* and the *Laws* and criticized certain features of each. Concerning the *Republic* in particular, he argued against such institutions as the community of women and property. Not only are they impractical according to Aristotle, but they also attest to Plato's overemphasis of unity. Aristotle contends that as an aggregate of both numbers and kind, the city-state cannot be expected to exhibit the same degree of unity as does an individual.

Using the same method of analysis, Aristotle examined the constitutions of Sparta, Crete, and Carthage and the practices of such legislators as Solon, Philolaus, and Charondas. Throughout, his concern is to learn from experience and to borrow those techniques and practices which appear to be appropriate.

In Book III of the *Politics* he attempted to establish some fundamental definitions and analytical concepts with which a constitutional theory can be constructed. Accordingly, Book III defines such terms as "citizen," "*polis*," and "constitution." The substance of these concepts, however, was obviously borrowed from the immediate Greek context and thus cannot easily be transferred to other situations.

Of more lasting importance, however, is the typology by which Aristotle attempted to classify various constitutional systems. According to this scheme, the great variety of historical regimes can be reduced to six essential types. These types, in turn, can be differentiated according to both qualitative and quantitative standards. The fundamental qualitative consideration (already mentioned briefly in passing) is between a "right" constitution and a "perverted" constitution. A right constitution is one in which the regime considers the common good as judged by the standard of absolute justice. A perverted regime, on the other hand, considers only the personal interest of the rulers. The quantitative standard refers to the number who rule. Accordingly, a society may be ruled by either the one, the few, or the many. Rule by one on behalf of the common good is called *monarchy;* its perverted form is *tyranny*. Rule by the few on behalf of the common good is *aristocracy*, while its perverted form is *oligarchy*. Rule by the many on behalf of the common good is referred to as *polity;* its perverted form is *democracy*.

What is particularly interesting about this typology is the fact that it includes both a normative and a descriptive component. In his attempt to classify the various regimes, Aristotle was not satisfied with simply listing certain empirical traits. Rather, he attempted at the same time to understand the moral worth of the society under review. For him the important difference is not between the one, the few, and the many. Rather, inasmuch as the purpose of political association is the good life, the important difference is that which distinguishes the true from the perverted. This distinction, in turn, raises the question of justice.

At one level, there appears to be an overall consensus regarding the general nature of justice. As Aristotle writes:

> The good in the sphere of politics is justice; and justice consists in what tends to promote the common interest. General opinion makes it consist in some sort of equality.[12]

However, this apparent consensus quickly disappears when one attempts to specify the meaning of equality in more precise terms. Adopting the dominant Greek distinction of his day, Aristotle focused upon two particular interpretations of equality: the democratic and the oligarchic. For the democrat, the fact that all citizens are equal because of their free birth implies that they are equal in all things and, thus, that political offices should be distributed equally. The oligarchs, on the other hand, assume that superiority of wealth implies superiority in all things and, thus, that political offices should be distributed in such a way as to favor the rich. This problem is not simply one of definition. Indeed in Book V Aristotle argued that this disagreement as to the principle of justice and equality is the greatest single cause of turmoil and sedition.

According to Aristotle, both the democratic and oligarchic conceptions exhibit similar weaknesses. Inasmuch as each side is judging in its own case, both succeed in arriving at only a partial understanding of the full range of true justice. Specifically neither argument considers who are the persons to whom their principles properly apply nor what is the nature of the true political end. If they would do so, they would see that politics is concerned with the good life and that the good life is one of happiness and virtue. Accordingly those who contribute most to this end should, in justice, receive most.

Yet at the same time, Aristotle acknowledged that both arguments have a certain merit. The people at large do make a contribution to the common good because the collective worth of the many may at times surpass the worth of the few best. Similarly, the wealthy make a contribution to the city-state in terms of both the land they provide and their reliability in upholding contracts. Neither side, however, has considered the full case. According to Aristotle, the democratic demand for equality is appropriate if one demands equality only for those who are, in fact, equals. Likewise the

---

[12] Aristotle, *The Politics*, p. 129.

oligarchic demand for inequality is legitimate only if inequality is for the truly unequal.

Given the weaknesses and strengths of each position, what can be done? In Book V Aristotle suggested that both principles be incorporated into the constitution. Consequently a viable political regime will apply the democratic concept of equality in some instances and the oligarchic in others. How this can be done in particular may vary from society to society. However, in his *Nicomachean Ethics*, Aristotle suggested his own preferred arrangement.

The problem of justice is discussed in Book V of the *Ethics*. For Aristotle, justice is one of the moral virtues. As such, it is concerned with the general issue of pleasure. In particular, it is concerned with the pleasure one receives from profit. Just citizens are those who feel the right amount of pleasure, at the right time, and in the right manner when they acquire that profit which is their due. The question is, of course, how does one determine what is one's due. Does each have an equal claim to all and, if not, how are different claims to be legitimated? As one would expect, Aristotle begins with a discussion of equality. For Aristotle, justice demands that equals be treated equally. Yet there are two types of equality: proportionate and numerical; and each type has its own appropriate role to play. Justice demands that proportionate equality govern the distribution of the city-state's common goods. That is to say, in distributing honors, offices, and goods among its citizens the regime should give more to those who have given more to the city. If one citizen's contribution to the welfare of the society is twice that of another's, then the first should receive twice as much in return. Equality in this case applies to the ratio (2:1), not the individual. Thus it is the proportion (2:1 = 2:1) which must be equal, not the amount.

In those civil transactions concerning exchanges among citizens, justice demands numerical equality. After an exchange, each partner should have gained or lost equally. In such a case, then, justice is a corrective between gain or loss. It seeks to maintain an equilibrium and treats each of the partners as an equal. In the case where a particular transaction has allowed an individual to profit twice as much from the action as another, just rectification demands that the amount be redistributed in such a way so that each profits equally. In such cases, the parties are to be treated as equals regardless of the merits or excellence of the individuals involved.

Aristotle's distinction between distribution and rectification on one hand and proportionate and numerical equality on the other serves to incorporate both the oligarchic and democratic conceptions of justice. As such, it could serve as the basis for the mixed regime which is favored in the *Politics*.

This discussion of justice offers an interesting contrast to both the Platonic understanding and those more typical of the modern age. In his *Republic*, Plato equated justice with harmony. This harmony, however, was the result of the society's common acknowledgement of and submission to the excellence of the philosopher. For Plato the citizens recognized their place within the social order because of their appreciation of the philosopher's psychic order. Aristotle, on the other hand, neither relied upon nor expected such a natural harmony. For him, justice will best be served by balancing the interests of the various classes. If such a balance can be strengthened by a spirit of civic friendship, then political harmony will emerge. Unlike Plato's, therefore, Aristotle's harmony would be one which accepts the particular claims of the various classes and seeks to order them by achieving a balance rather than by a rank subordination. In this sense, the thinking of Aristotle is much closer to the Plato of the *Laws* than it is to the Plato of the *Republic*.

A second interesting contrast is that which can be found between Aristotelian justice and the more common modern forms. Typically modern arguments about justice concentrate upon the competing claims of individuals. Whether the approach is that of entitlement (natural-right theories) or need (welfare theories), the issue normally concerns an adjudication between competing individual claims. Aristotle, on the other hand, was much more aware of the common needs of the community. The just distribution of goods does not depend solely upon a comparison of autonomous individual claims. Rather for Aristotle justice requires that a citizen's contribution to the common interest be included within the calculation of benefits. Thus, the common interest enters as a factor in determining what is due to an individual citizen, and the needs of society as a whole become a consideration in all cases involving individual claims.

After having discussed the differences between a true and a perverted constitution, Aristotle then considered the general question of who should rule: the one, the few, or the many. He concretized these options by suggesting that we focus upon the following five forms of rule: the people at large, the wealthy, the best citizens, the one best citizen, or a tyrant. Each particular option has its own specific limitations and disadvantages. Given this, he considered the rule of law to be the best in general. Even though it may be true that in an ideal state the rule of the outstanding individual may be best, generally speaking the rule of law in accordance with the true constitution is to be preferred. As Aristotle writes:

> He who commands that law should rule may thus be regarded as commanding that God and reason alone should rule; he who commands that a man should rule adds the character of a beast. . . . Law (as the pure voice of God and reason) may thus be defined as 'Reason free from all passion.'[13]

[13] Aristotle, *The Politics*, p. 146.

The final pages of Book III and all of Book IV develop Aristotle's analysis of the various regimes. Generally speaking, there is no one perfect form. That which is best for a particular society will depend upon such factors as climate, size, traditions, and population. In order to accommodate these differences it is not only necessary to choose among the general forms themselves but also to acknowledge that each form has a variety of types which can be adjusted according to the local circumstances. For example, Aristotle distinguished five varieties of democracy, four types of oligarchy, and three forms of tyranny. However, if Aristotle does have a preferred regime in general, it would be a regime of law based upon a large middle class which possesses an adequate but moderate amount of property. Such a regime would be characterized by moderation and, hopefully, would avoid the extreme actions typical of those societies dominated either by the very wealthy or the very poor.

Book V of the *Politics* examines the causes of change within society both in general and in particular. The question is why do societies change their constitutions and what can be done to preserve their stability. As we have seen, seditious change is generally brought about because of a disagreement concerning equality. It is the passion for either equality or inequality regarding profit and honor that moves citizens to rebel. In view of this, the regime should take certain precautions, and Aristotle developed a number of possibilities.

In addition to such general causes common to all regimes, Aristotle also discussed those causes which are unique to particular forms of society. For example, democracies tend to be vulnerable to demagogues while aristocracies are threatened by feuds within the governing class itself. As before, Aristotle offered advice to each regime depending upon its particular form.

Books VII and VIII return to a general discussion of those qualities and characteristics required for good political order. As such, they reintroduce many of the themes first mentioned in Aristotle's *Ethics*. The central concern is and remains the good life:

> The best way of life, for individuals severally as well as for states collectively, is the life of goodness duly equipped with such a store of requisites . . . as makes it possible to share in the activities of goodness.[14]

Aristotle's charge is quite clear. The purpose of politics is to form a society which will allow both the contemplative person (philosopher) and the practical citizen (*Spoudaios*) to be at their best and thus to live happily. To show

[14] Aristotle, *The Politics*, p. 282.

how this can be done, Aristotle presented the central features of an "ideal state." Although he considered such issues as population, territory, class structure, property claims, and the planning of cities, his most important concern was that of education. Like Plato, Aristotle understood that education is the statesman's most important task.

Education, for Aristotle, is not the mere passing along of information and data. Rather, like Plato, he saw education as a moral and spiritual undertaking; the educator's task is to make people good—both as citizens and as human beings. Civic education, therefore, is concerned with teaching people how to rule and be ruled. General education, in turn, is concerned with the development of the moral and intellectual virtues. As such, it seeks to establish certain priorities: peace over war, leisure over action, and the good over the necessary or useful. Quite appropriately for a student of Plato, Aristotle ends both his analysis of education and his *Politics* with a discussion of music. It is, after all, the art of harmony.

BIBLIOGRAPHY

BARKER, ERNEST.   *The Political Thought of Plato and Aristotle.* New York: Dover Publications, 1959.

GRENE, MARJORIE.   *A Portrait of Aristotle.* Chicago: University of Chicago Press, 1963.

JAEGER, WERNER.   *Aristotle: Fundamentals of the History of His Development.* Translated by Richard Robinson. Oxford: Oxford University Press, 1934.

LLOYD, G. E. R.   *Aristotle: The Growth & Structure of His Thought.* Cambridge: Cambridge University Press, 1968.

MULGAN, R. G.   *Aristotle's Political Theory.* Oxford: Oxford University Press, 1977.

RANDALL, JOHN HERMAN.   *Aristotle.* New York: Columbia University Press, 1960.

STRAUSS, LEO.   *The City and Man.* Chicago: Rand McNally, 1964.

TAYLOR, A. E.   *Aristotle.* New York: Dover, 1955.

VOEGELIN, ERIC.   *Plato and Aristotle.* Baton Rouge: Louisiana State University Press, 1957.

3

THE HELLENISTIC AGE

THE CONQUEST OF ALEXANDER THE GREAT

It is ironic that for a period of six years Aristotle left Greece in order to serve as the tutor for the young Alexander of Macedonia. In this meeting of teacher and student the representatives of two distinct political eras confronted one another in mutual incomprehension. Aristotle, secure in the traditions of the Athenian order, could not possibly foresee the features of that world order which Alexander would be instrumental in creating. For Aristotle the Greek city-state represented the natural end and perfection of social and political evolution. As the family pointed toward the village, so, too, did the village point toward the *polis*. With each step, the adequate satisfaction of human needs seemed to require the development of a higher form of social organization. However, with the creation of the *polis* no further transitions seemed necessary. For Aristotle the self-sufficient Greek city-state appeared to be all that was required for the successful pursuit of the good life. Thus having achieved the possible satisfaction of all legitimate

59

human needs, nature, in effect, signaled an end to political evolution. Given this interpretation, Aristotle could find no compelling reason to go beyond the Hellenic form of political organization. At the same time, given his acceptance of the *polis* as natural, it is not surprising that Aristotle also assumed the naturalness of those major social distinctions upon which the *polis* was based. Consequently, the superiority of Greek to non-Greek, man to woman, parent to child, and master to slave were understood to be distinctions found in nature itself.

For Alexander, on the other hand, such assumptions could hardly appear as self-evident. Although ethnically related, the Macedonians shared neither the language nor the culture of the Greeks. Politically, Macedonia was a monarchy and thus maintained a form of political rule which had become mostly extinct within Greece proper. The Macedonians in addition had refused to participate in the confederation of Greek city-states that was based in Corinth. More to the point, Aristotle's faith in the naturalness and efficacy of the *polis* could not prevent its destruction by the armies of Alexander. Thus with the expansion of the Macedonian empire, the Greek city-state was eventually reduced to being a mere element within the imperial order. In most cases, it simply was transformed into an administrative unit whose functions were defined by the overall needs of the territorial monarchy. Similarly, Aristotle's argument concerning the natural distinction between Greek and non-Greek was, in fact, denied by the creation of a single political system which incorporated both Greek and barbarian alike. Thus as Alexander's empire expanded, it served to bring together such diverse races as the Greek, Persian, Egyptian, and Indian.

The conditions which were to support Alexander's ambitions had already been established by his father, Philip II. By reorganizing the cavalry and introducing modern military tactics, Philip was able to unify the Macedonian homeland and, thereby, to increase the resources at his disposal. With Philip's assassination in 336 B.C., Alexander assumed control of a powerful and well-organized military society. With it he began a campaign of conquest which would eventually succeed in substituting European for Asiatic rule throughout much of the Near East. At his death in 323 B.C., Alexander had introduced Macedonian rule into Greece, Egypt, Iran, Phoenicia, Babylon, Lydia, and several states in the Punjab region of India. Inasmuch as the empire's administrators were drawn primarily from the aristocracies of the Greek city-states, its development had the effect of extending Greek culture throughout its domain. A simplified version of the Attic dialect became the common language of the realm, and Greek civilization spread from India on one side to Carthage and Rome on the other. The period from Alexander's death in 323 B.C. to the conquest of Egypt by Rome in 30 B.C. is typically referred to as the Hellenistic Age. It acquires its character from the dominance and essential uniformity of Hellenistic culture among the upper classes. The Greek term *hellenizein* meant, "to act like a Greek," and such behavior became the accepted standard of the time.

Alexander died in 323 B.C. at the age of thirty-two. Although his plans are not known, it is clear that he had not accomplished all that he wished. It is possible, for example, that he intended to return from the East to the West and extend his control over the entire Mediterranean. With his death, however, his successors (the Diadochi) eventually gave up such ambitions of extended domination and involved themselves in a long series of wars to determine who would inherit the ruler's mantle. From this struggle there finally emerged three great family powers, each of which established itself in a particular section of the former empire. The Antigonids received Macedonia. The Seleucids acquired the Eastern provinces, and the Ptolemies ruled Egypt. In addition to consolidating their rule at home, the three successful dynasties attempted to achieve a certain balance of power among themselves. It was, however, a balance which was continually being tested, especially in certain "unclaimed" areas of Greece, Syria, and Asia Minor. As a consequence, the Rule of the Diadochi was never established securely within the former empire, and political order would eventually be imposed only from without.

From the beginning of the second century B.C., the Hellenistic world was exposed to increasing pressures from Rome. Through a series of conquests the Roman state was able to absorb one Hellenistic power after another. Finally in 30 B.C. this process reached its conclusion with the defeat of Egypt. Having destroyed one of the most powerful of the Hellenistic states, Rome was now in the position of establishing its own ecumenic empire that, by the imposition of a Latin administration, would bring political stability to the troubled Mediterranean.

The Rise of Divine Kingship

During the 300 years of the Hellenistic Age, monarchy was the dominant form of rule. Yet, unlike earlier forms of monarchy in the West, the Hellenistic king was often assumed to have certain divine qualities. Thus, for example, Alexander's campaign historian, Callisthenes, reported a revelation in which god had declared Alexander to be his son. Moreover, a number of popular legends concerning Alexander's conception by a serpent-god became quite common and thereby promoted this tendency to deify a truly exceptional person. Although the Greeks had already developed an intricate set of heroes, and in a few remote cases even granted divine honors to some, the god-king of the Hellenistic Age was a recent innovation. Contemporary scholarship suggests that the Hellenistic theories of divine-kingship emerged only after the Greek world had come into contact with various oriental cultures. This influence gained in strength after the death of Alexander and was apparently transmitted by the teachings and the traditions of the Neo-Pythagoreans.

Generally, the Hellenistic king governed as an absolute ruler. Freed from any legal restrictions, the king normally ruled by edict. In addition, he viewed both the people and the land as his own personal property. It was possible for him, therefore, to bequeath both his state and its people to another ruler. Succession was in the male line and was secured by an elaborate cult of ruler worship. For example, kings took such secondary names as "savior," "god," or "god-manifest" and were regularly worshiped in public festivals arranged by the state.

As the embodied law, the Hellenistic king was seen as the source of an active power which could help to stabilize the chaotic conditions of the age. Because the Hellenistic states were a mixture of races, civilizations, and traditions formed by the accidents of war and the efficacies of power, they were neither cohesive nor united. The territorial monarchies looked, therefore, to their king as a source of order and security. The king, in turn, acquired his power by imitating the serene authority of the gods. By becoming as self-sufficient and godlike as possible, the Hellenistic king was to function as the savior of his people. God's order would flow through him and, in so doing, establish the structure of society.

THE HISTORIES OF POLYBIUS

The Hellenistic Age was one of fundamental social and personal dislocation. The conquests of Alexander had succeeded in breaking the limits of the city-state; yet these limits had served as the moorings for the Greek way of life. With their destruction, the individual Greeks felt themselves cut adrift. Whereas earlier Greek citizens could locate themselves precisely in terms of the concrete traditions, practices, and legends of their particular city, with the creation of the Hellenistic monarchies, they were now simply an element within a vast field whose horizons opened to include peoples and civilizations about which they knew nothing. Whereas earlier the customs of the traditional city-state provided the practical examples which informed the Greek citizen's moral code, now they appeared to be simply the parochial expressions of a particular society within an open and complex world. In describing this situation, historian Edwyn Bevan has written:

> In the markets and courts and armies [of the new Hellenic world] Greeks from a multitude of different city-states were indiscriminately mixed together, not a stable society with fixed traditions, but a crowd of individuals, each out for his own profit in the great scramble. A world of unrest, the Greek citizen *déraciné*, un-

rooted, with no end in life but to get wealth, to get sensation, to get power—disorder and giddy chance in the place of the regular activities, amenities, and duties of the old city-state, a society demoralized as all societies must be in which there are continual dramatic vicissitudes of fortune, the same man now on the pinnacle of power and riches, now flung down into the mud. There was no sense or principle or order in the course of things, it was just a huge haphazard play of chance, of luck, *"Tyche"*, the only deity to be discovered in the world.[1]

The collapse of Greece and the rise of Hellenistic monarchies served to underscore the fluid and arbitrary nature of historical change. Politics as an attempt to create and maintain order appeared futile. Just as Macedonia had replaced Greece, so, too, was Rome challenging the newly achieved balance of power among the Diodachi. Historical change rather than political continuity appeared to be the dominant law. One of the clearest expressions of this experience is found in the histories of Polybius. Polybius was born at Megapolis around 200 B.C. Although a Greek by birth, he was brought to Rome in 168 B.C. after the Romans defeated Macedonia at Pydna. Once there he soon became the close friend of the young Roman, Scipio Aemilianus. Through his friendship with Scipio, Polybius met many of the leading Roman politicians of the day and eventually joined in Scipio's circle of acquaintances which had become the center of Roman culture during the third quarter of the second century. Although active in politics, Polybius's major interest was in the study of Roman history. Specifically, he was interested in discovering the reasons for Rome's recent political successes. Indeed within a period of only fifty years Rome had succeeded in extending its dominion throughout and beyond the Mediterranean area. In attempting to account for this success, Polybius focused upon the Roman political system. It appeared to him that the Roman regime contained certain features which accounted for the stability and vitality which were essential for Rome's growth and prosperity.

Paying particular attention to the Roman state during the Second Punic War (218–201 B.C.), Polybius examined the political, military, and religious conditions of Rome's success. Politically, Rome's essential strength was based on the form of its constitution. Rather than being a pure monarchy, aristocracy, or democracy, the Roman constitution had evolved in such a way as to contain elements of each. It was, therefore, a mixed regime. The monarchical element was represented by the office of the consuls; the senate represented the aristocracy; and the tribal assembly was characterized as democratic. Thus the Roman constitution not only gave representa-

---

[1] Edwyn Bevan, "Hellenistic Popular Philosophy," in J. B. Bury, ed., *The Hellenistic Age* (New York: W. W. Norton & Co., 1970), p. 80.

tion to the interests of the various social classes, but at the same time it contained a series of checks and balances which prevented any one particular group from exercising undue influence.

Although Polybius's discussion of the mixed regime may have influenced such subsequent thinkers as Montesquieu or the framers of the U.S. Constitution, it should not be divorced from its original context. Thus it is important to remember that his examination of the Roman state was essentially part of a larger inquiry. This larger study, in turn, was concerned with nothing less than the movement of history itself. Rome had succeeded where the Persians and Macedonians had failed. Yet Polybius was equally sensitive to the fact that Rome, too, would eventually fail. History promised no final victories, and the events of the Hellenistic Age simply reinforced this awareness. Change, instability, and purposelessness seemed to be the only constants. It was as if history were simply the plaything of Fate. In his *Histories*, Polybius recalls a passage attributed to Demetrius of Phalerum written in 317 B.C.:

> For if you consider not countless years or many generations, but merely these last fifty years, you will read in them the cruelty of Fortune. I ask you, do you think that fifty years ago either the Persians and the Persian king or the Macedonians and the king of Macedon, if some god had foretold the future to them, would ever have believed that at the time when we live, the very name of the Persians would have perished utterly—the Persians who were masters of almost the whole world—and that the Macedonians, whose name was formerly almost unknown, would now be the lords of it all? But nevertheless this Fortune, who never compacts with life, who always defeats our reckoning by some novel stroke; she who ever demonstrates her power by foiling our expectations, now also, as it seems to me, makes it clear to all men, by endowing the Macedonians with the whole wealth of Persia, that she has but lent them these blessings until she decides to deal differently with them.[2]

Nine books later in the same *Histories*, Polybius again reports that after his victory over Carthage Scipio feared that just as Fortune had destroyed Troy, the Assyrians, the Medians, the Persians, the Macedonians, and now Carthage, so, too, would it destroy Rome.

Given the extent of such destruction, and lacking the knowledge of any apparent purpose which was being served by it, the question arises as to the meaning of such historical events. Is there any pattern or form to his-

---

[2] Polybius, *The Histories*, trans. W. R. Paton (London: William Heinemann, 1927), VI, pp. 77–9.

torical change? Are there any standards according to which human beings (or society) can evaluate the significance of such events? For Polybius, the answer to such questions could only be found in an analysis of historical and political cycles.

Borrowing from Plato and Aristotle, Polybius distinguished between three legitimate and three corrupted forms of government. The legitimate forms were *kingship, aristocracy,* and *democracy;* their corrupted counterparts were *tyranny, oligarchy,* and *ochlocracy* or mob rule. Whereas for Plato and Aristotle these concepts were used in an attempt to distinguish the character or moral quality of a society's preponderant class, in Polybius they are primarily used to describe the particular moments of a grand historical cycle. Thus these forms are seen to appear in an established temporal sequence beginning with kingship. According to Polybius, government initially emerges as a response to chaos. Natural calamities, such as floods or drought, threaten the very possibility of social existence. In response the strongest (would-be kings) take it upon themselves to impose their will upon others. In doing so, they create a certain social order and in the process make life tolerable. With time, however, monarchies tend to degenerate into their corrupted form. Rejecting the demands of justice, monarchs inevitably become tyrants. However, as the abuses of tyranny become increasingly insufferable, the best members of such societies rise up, overthrow their tyrants, and establish an aristocracy in their place. For a while, then, society is characterized by the rule of the wise. In time, however, corruption once again enters such regimes and the aristocracies degenerate into oligarchies wherein the pursuit of wealth becomes the overriding concern of the leadership. As this abuse of privilege continues, the people, themselves, eventually rise up and establish democracies which are dedicated to the pursuit of freedom and the enjoyment of equality. Yet, as in the previous cases, democracies are an intrinsically unstable form of government and consequently tend to evolve toward their own corrupted form. In this case, mob rule results as the masses move to prevent the wealthy from reasserting their previous dominance. Violence and rioting produce chaos, and with the emergence of chaos the entire cycle begins once again.

In writing his history, Polybius displays an obviously pragmatic intention. In distinguishing his writings from other popular histories, Polybius emphasized the practical lessons that could be learned from his work. Such a teaching was possible in turn because Polybius had examined history with a view to the whole. Rather than simply describing a particular society, he attempted to analyze specifics in terms of a knowledge of the entire historical order. Knowing the order of the whole, Polybius's reader would then be in the position to act with this knowledge in mind. One could, in effect, predict what would happen and plan accordingly.

One of the obvious lessons to be learned from Polybius's history is that every pure form of government tends to degenerate into its corrupted alternative. Given this, one can expect political change; yet, at the same time, the rate of change is not necessarily constant. Although it is true that no society can endure forever, some may be able to postpone their fate longer than others. For Polybius, the secret of such resistance was found in the mixed constitution. By mixing the various elements of monarchy, aristocracy, and democracy it was possible to achieve a relatively stable society over time. This could be done inasmuch as the corruption of one element would be partially checked by the presence of the others.

Polybius's political teaching was clear. The Roman Republic was successful because it had achieved that constitutional mixture best designed to postpone the inevitable changes of history. In effect, then, Rome succeeded because of its privileged position within the historical cycle. That it had managed to achieve its constitutional balance while others, notably Carthage, were advancing into their corrupted forms, suggested that Rome's rule was truly fated. At that time in history it had become the regime of destiny. Yet at the same time, Polybius was deeply aware of the fact that Rome would eventually fall. Fortune dictated as much, and already Polybius could note certain symptoms pointing to Rome's decline. Yet, unlike his predecessors Plato and Aristotle, Polybius refused to analyze those symptoms. As an historian of power he had apparently lost sight of those philosophical principles which would have made such an analysis possible. As a result, his history ends on a theoretically ambiguous note.

THE PHILOSOPHIES OF SELF-SUFFICIENCY

Polybius's sense of awe in light of the rapid social and political changes during the Hellenistic Age is not surprising. In part, his effort to comprehend the cyclical movement of history can be interpreted as a creative response to the apparent senselessness of the public order. By seeking a pattern amidst change he was, in fact, resisting the absolute primacy of the chaotic. Yet such an act of resistance was not the only alternative available at that time. Rather than resisting, one could withdraw. By turning inward one could attempt to establish a meaningful life which was independent of the public order. If this tactic were chosen, then self-sufficiency rather than participation became the appropriate form of human behavior. As Edwyn Bevan has described it:

> If the movement of the world, in which the individual finds himself involved, has no perceivable purpose, if there is no cause larger

than himself which he may hope to see go forward, and go forward in some degree by his own devotion and efforts—then for certain men there comes, sooner or later, an imperious desire to escape from the current, to find rest for the soul in some firm standing-place outside the turmoil.[3]

Indeed, this "imperious desire to escape" is a feature which was characteristic of most of the major philosophical schools of the Hellenistic period. As a consequence it is not surprising to discover the popularity of both the Cynics and the Epicureans. Each school, in its own way promised to free people from those interests which served to entangle them in the affairs of a senseless world.

Cynics

During the third century B.C., the teachings of the Cynics were promulgated in the Hellenistic and Roman world through the sermons of such popular spokespersons as Teles and Bion of Borysthenes. The founders of the school—Antisthenes and Diogenes—were, however, contemporaries of Plato and Aristotle. And, as such, both men claimed to be the true followers of the Socratic way. For them Socrates, as the gadfly of Athens, was essentially an irreverent intellectual who delighted in exposing the inadequacies of the popular beliefs of his day. Ignoring Socrates' positive moral intentions, the Cynics emphasized only his relentless questioning of conventional opinion. For them the practice of philosophy could, in large part, be reduced to the imitation of the Socratic way. Yet in imitating Socrates the Cynics exaggerated, and therefore eventually distorted, his most important qualities. Whereas Socrates taught that a person should attain self-knowledge, the Cynics argued that one who did achieve such self-knowledge became thereby self-sufficient. For the Cynics, then, the wise Hellenic, having achieved inward self-sufficiency, no longer required the services of the political community. On the contrary, the state and its demands were pictured as obstacles which actually hindered the wise person's development. As a consequence, for the Cynics politics became a matter of indifference.

In criticizing the general Greek commitment to the political community, the Cynics emphasized the traditional distinction between nature and custom. Formed by mass opinion, the laws of society were understood to be simply the products of custom. To live according to them therefore was to live hypocritically. Nature, on the other hand, was understood to be structured by universal laws. Inasmuch as the truly virtuous person was the one who lived according to nature, the Cynics argued on behalf of the sim-

[3] Bevan, "Hellenistic Popular Philosophy," pp. 82–3.

ple and primitive life as an alternative to the decadence of the city. Nature, in short, was understood as the negation of civilization. For example, Antisthenes argued that since animals live closer to nature than humankind does, the virtuous person would be the one who best approximated the life of the animals. Similarly, Diogenes suggested that the behavior of dogs should serve as the model for human actions.

From the Cynic's view, being truly self-sufficient, wise Greeks or Hellenics lived according to the laws of nature rather than by the rules of the city. As such their only true social relations would be those which they formed with other wise souls. In doing so they would, in fact, be constituting a single universal community of the wise. Thus in rejecting one's historical citizenship, the Cynic chose to become a citizen of the world. It was as if the wise belonged to a single universal human society; a society within which the distinction between Greek and barbarian, rich and poor, or free and slave disappeared. This doctrine of a universal society of humankind which transcends the orders and distinctions of historical societies is referred to as *cosmopolitanism*. As such, it is an idea which will receive further develoment in the evolutions of both Stoicism and Christianity. However, because it was already present among the Cynics, it is important to realize its particular function within their system. Cynicism was an essentially individualistic philosophy; its model was the self-sufficient individual. Thus in the thinking of the Cynics, cosmopolitanism played a fundamentally negative rather than a positive role. It was not a call to a higher or dual citizenship. Rather, it was essentially a device that argued against the concrete traditions of particular historical communities. By claiming to be citizens of the world, the Cynics were, in fact, denying the claims of their native cities. In this sense then, cosmopolitanism was an expression of withdrawal.

The Cynics' withdrawal from the political community was only one aspect of their overall attempt to withdraw from the external world in general. In seeking self-sufficiency, people had to free themselves from those entanglements which bound them to the outside world. Generally, those entanglements took the form of "interests." A person's interest in reputation, wealth, or family was, in effect, an attachment to realities upon which one could become dependent. As a consequence, true independence demanded the giving up of interests. Freedom, in turn, implied indifference. The wise person was one who defeated the desire for wealth, property, marriage, family, or social esteem. In a dialogue attributed to Lucian, entitled *The Cynic*, the following statement summarizes rather clearly both the Cynics' attitude toward possessions and their respect for the model provided by animal nature:

> I pray that I may have feet no different from horses' hooves, as they say were those of Chiron, and that I myself may not need bed-

clothes any more than do the lions, nor expensive fare any more than do the dogs. But may I have for bed to meet my needs the whole earth, may I consider the universe my house, and choose for food that which is easiest to procure. Gold and silver may I not need, neither I nor any of my friends. For from the desire for these grow up all men's ills—civic strife, wars, conspiracies, and murders. All these have as their fountainhead the desire for more. But may this desire be far from us, and never may I reach out for more than my share, but be able to put up with less than my share.[4]

Epicureans

A similar example of aestheticism can be found in the teachings of the Epicureans. Epicureans were members of an Athenian school which was established by Epicurus around 307 B.C. Although he was extremely popular and apparently quite prolific, little of Epicurus's original work is extant today. Apart from selected fragments and letters, his ideas are most systematically represented in the poetry of his distinguished disciple Lucretius (94–55 B.C.). Together they were the chief representatives of ancient materialism.

In general, materialism argues that all of reality is reducible to simple matter or matter-in-motion. In particular, Epicurean materialism was based upon the atomistic theories of Democritus which were originally developed in the fifth century B.C. Democritus had argued that all of reality was composed of little seeds or atoms of homogeneous matter. The only characteristics which could be attributed to those atoms were size, shape, and inherent motion. As a consequence all other qualities, such as color, sound, and taste, were understood as being derivative and resulting from the impact of the atom's motion upon the senses. Endowed with eternal motion, atoms moved about in empty space and formed conglomerations which produced the objects of everyday experience. Reality, therefore, was simply the result of a series of accidental collisions. As such, it exhibited neither purpose nor meaning. Given this, nature appeared to be without design and thus was incapable of providing any standards for the creation of order—be it personal, political, or historical.

Democritus's materialistic world-view logically implied a materialistic view of human nature. Accordingly, Epicurus upheld the position that the human being was, in fact, nothing but a collection of physical sensations. This human locus of vibrating atoms not only experienced their impact passively but at the same time reciprocated by directing his or her own actions outward against the forces of the environment. From such a per-

---

[4] Lucian, "The Cynic," in M. D. Macleod, trans., *Lucian* Cambridge: Harvard University Press, 1967), VIII, pp. 403–05.

spective, life appeared as an ongoing exchange of motion between a human being and the environment. The fortunate individual would be the one who could manage this exchange in such a way as to provide for the maximum degree of personal pleasure.

Although such a view may be depressing to one who accepts the existence of a spiritual reality, Epicurus himself understood materialism as a truly liberating doctrine. According to Epicurus, if his teachings were accepted, they would free humankind from that ignorance which was the traditional cause of fear and worry. First, the fear of death would disappear because death would be seen as nothing but the cessation of physical motion. As such, it was neither unknown nor fearful. Secondly, the fear of the torments of hell would disappear because, given the atomist view of reality, there could be no spiritual life after death. With the death of the body, a human would simply cease to exist. Finally, humankind's fear of the gods would disappear because, even though the gods may exist, they are neither interested in nor would they interfere with the affairs of the world. Liberated from such fears and informed by the truths of materialism, the wise could achieve that state of serenity and peace which was most conducive to their own happiness.

Epicurus's positive moral teaching was typical of hedonism in general: pleasure was the only moral good and pain was clearly evil. Yet, unlike certain sensualist versions, Epicurus's hedonism cannot be reduced to mere licentiousness. First, he distinguished between natural and unnatural desires. The former were characterized by the fact that they were limited and thus relatively easy to satisfy. Examples would be the desires for food and sleep. Generally, Epicurus recommended that we limit our desires to the natural ones. Secondly, he distinguished between intellectual and bodily pleasures and argued for the superiority of the former over the latter. Thus Epicurean hedonism contained a distinctively aesthetic quality which rejected the pursuit of worldly interests for the sake of study and contemplation. Finally, Epicurus's philosophy was based upon a wholly negative understanding of pleasure: pleasure was simply the logical opposite of pain, and the pursuit of pleasure became, therefore, the avoidance of pain. Given this understanding, the wise person could best avoid pain by disciplining appetites and curtailing desires. In a world of scarcity, the least painful life would be the one that required the least to satisfy its needs:

> Thus when I say that pleasure is the goal of living I do not mean the pleasures of libertines or the pleasures inherent in positive enjoyment . . . I mean, on the contrary, the pleasure that consists in freedom from bodily pain and mental agitation. The pleasant life is not the product of one drinking party after another or of sexual intercourse with women and boys or of the sea food and other

delicacies afforded by a luxurious table. On the contrary, it is the result of sober thinking. . . . [5]

Epicurus's desire for serenity and peace seemed to necessitate a withdrawal from worldly concerns. Accordingly society was pictured as a source of distraction, and political participation was seen as potentially disturbing. The wise would refrain from active political involvement. Much like Epicurus himself, they might retreat to the company of their friends, within the quiet confines of house and garden. Generally all hedonistic philosophies assume a sense of individualism, inasmuch as only the individual can actually experience pleasure and pain. This individualistic perspective is evident throughout Epicurus's writings. He is primarily concerned with consoling the wise follower, not with constructing the good society. Similarly his political thinking begins from a decidedly individualistic premise. Society is not natural. Rather it is the result of a contract among individuals who agree to set up certain rules of conduct so that each person may be insured against the infliction of pain and the intrusion of worldly forces. Justice therefore is simply a matter of convention, and laws are to be obeyed only inasmuch as they allow for public order and personal security. Consequently, in all instances political values were reduced to a calculation which began with the primacy of personal, individual needs.

The Gnostic Religions

Cynicism and Epicureanism can be understood in part as an intellectual response to the social and political developments within the Hellenistic Age. The pointless destruction of traditional cultures, the imposition of foreign rule, and the blending of Eastern and Western civilizations promoted a certain weariness which sought its relief through the individual's withdrawal from the public realm. During periods of severe dislocation, however, the spirit of withdrawal can easily become one of rejection. A good example of such a transformation can be found in the popularity of the various gnostic religions throughout the early and late Hellenistic periods.

Originally scholars understood Gnosticism to be a peculiarly Christian aberration, and consequently it was generally associated with the teachings of such early Christian heretics as the Egyptian Valentinus. However, recent scholarship has established as fact that gnostic beliefs emerged within a great variety of religious traditions and, thus, that Gnosticism itself was not essentially dependent upon the doctrines of Christian revelation. Indeed, it is now possible to distinguish among Christian, Jewish, Hellenistic pagan, and Eastern varieties of Gnosticism. Common to all, how-

[5] Epicurus, "Letter to Menoeceus," in George Strodach, ed., *The Philosophy of Epicurus* (Evanston: Northwestern University Press, 1963), pp. 183–4.

ever, was a fundamental rejection of the world and the individual's place within it.

The gnostic rejection of the world was based upon a radically dualistic theology. On one hand, there was a god who, being absolutely transmundane, neither created the world nor shared in its nature. On the other hand, there was the material world, which was both created and ruled by powerful evil forces which sought to enslave humankind, and in so doing, to obstruct its awareness of god's true nature. The human being as a composite of body and spirit was caught in between. Human spirit was, in fact, a portion of the divine substance. However, through creation it had fallen into the material world and was held captive there with the human body. Immersed within flesh, the spirit was unaware of its true self. Ignorant, it was benumbed by the powers of evil. Liberation, therefore, required that the spirit be freed from its ignorance by gaining both a knowledge (*gnosis*) of its true self and, at the same time, an awareness of its critical condition. Accordingly, god sent a messenger who imparted this necessary knowledge and, thereby, allowed human beings to prepare for their future ascent out of the material realm of darkness. In death, the spirit was stripped of its material elements and eventually rose to be reunited with the original divine substance.

As all religions do, Gnosticism necessarily implied a specific morality. For gnostics, the world was evil, and thus they were contemptuous of all mundane interests. Being hostile toward the world, gnostics understood themselves as freed from any obligations to adhere to its customs, laws, or practices. This attitude, in turn, produced two strikingly contrary conclusions. Given the corruption of the world, certain gnostic religions argued for a radically ascetic morality. Awaiting death, the individual was to avoid any further contamination by the world and thus was to reduce contacts with it to an absolute minimum. The libertine gnostics, on the other hand, interpreted their rejection of the world to imply a radical freedom from its restraints and orders. Being the realm of darkness, the world and its laws had no authority over enlightened gnostics. Consequently they could do as they wished, inasmuch as their personal salvation had already been assured by their possession of the secret gnostic teachings. In either case, however, the antipolitical implications of Hellenistic Gnosticism were obvious to all.

The quest for the origin and sources of this outbreak of gnostic speculation during the Hellenistic Age has led in many directions. Some scholars have attempted to trace Gnosticism to certain elements within Greek philosophy; others look to Judaism; and still others emphasize the oriental influences introduced by Alexander's expansion into the East. Perhaps the most plausible explanation, however, is that offered by the philosopher, Hans Jonas. Rather than attributing the variety of gnostic doctrines to a common intellectual source, Jonas suggests that Gnosticism is better understood as a response to certain social and personal conditions. As the territorial monarchies replaced the classical city-states, individual citizens could no longer identify closely with their society. Having become private persons, these dwellers in the new Hellenic world felt increasingly estranged from their surroundings. This alienation, in turn, produced the gnostic's desire to escape. Describing this experience, Jonas writes:

> In this three-term configuration—man, world, god—man and god belong together in contraposition to the world, but are, in spite of this essential belonging-together, in fact separated precisely by the world. To the Gnostic, this fact is the subject of revealed knowledge, and it determines gnostic eschatology: *we* may see in it the projection of his basic experience, which thus created for itself its own revelatory truth. Primary would then be the feeling of an absolute rift between man and that in which he finds himself lodged—the world.[6]

STOICISM

Of all the responses to the dislocations of the Hellenistic period, perhaps the most positive was that of Stoicism. Yet for several reasons it is difficult to give a systematic account of this school. First, the writings of its founders are extant only as fragments, and, second, many of its major teachings underwent frequent revision. Whereas at the beginning, Stoicism contained an element of idealism which demanded such perfection that its application to the affairs of human beings was almost impossible, in its mature form it was reduced to the ideological justification for common Roman practice. Given this evolution, therefore, it is necessary to distinguish among the Early, Middle, and Late Stoics.

The Early Stoics

The Early Stoics were consciously responding to the same political and existential conditions that produced the Cynics, the Epicureans, and the variety of gnostic religious movements. Indeed the founder of the Stoics, Zeno, was originally a disciple of Crates the Cynic. Born in Cyprus around 336 B.C., Zeno traveled to Athens and eventually founded his own school. The school's name was derived from the steps or open porch (*stoa*) from

[6] Hans Jonas, *The Gnostic Religion*, 2nd ed. (Boston: Beacon Press, 1963), pp. 326–7.

which Zeno taught. Typically the most important contributors to Stoicism were the early heads of the school, and they include Zeno (300–263), Cleanthes (263–232), Chrysippus (232–207), Zeno of Tarsus and Diogenes the Babylonian (together 207–150), and Antipater of Tarsus (150–129).

In general the early Stoics shared a sensualist view of knowledge. Breaking from both the Platonic and the Aristotelian notion of form, they believed that all of human knowledge was derived ultimately from sense perception. Accordingly the impression of physical objects was understood to produce a set of corresponding concepts in the mind. Nature, in turn, was understood to be a precisely ordered cosmos. It emerged from a primeval fire and periodically was reabsorbed back into it through a worldwide conflagration. Thus, although Stoicism seemed to be suggesting a materialistic cosmology, it was a materialism of a particular sort. For the Stoics this primal fire possessed a divine nature. Thus, because all of reality shared in this fundamental matter, the world was, in fact, an embodied spiritual force. As a result the materialism of the Stoics can best be understood as a pantheistic monism. The universe was god. Its passive qualities constituted the natural elements of earth and water; whereas its active quality, fire, existed as soul. Thus although the soul was principally rooted in heaven, it actually pervaded all of nature and thus gave the world those qualities of regularity and order which the Stoics found to be typical of the cosmos. According to them the universe was governed by unalterable laws, the rationality of which reflected the presence of god in nature. Order, constituted by divine reason, pervaded all.

The Stoics' belief in the rational design of nature's plan supported, in turn, their conception of fate and duty. Whereas for the Greeks, duty had been defined in terms of the concrete needs of the city-state, for the Stoics duty required that each person attune their behavior to the harmony of cosmic reason. Thus the anarchistic tendencies associated with the collapse of local cultures were successfully checked by the Stoic sense of a natural order. The cosmos was an ordered hierarchy of law, and human behavior was appropriate only to the extent it fit the providential plan of events. Every human being was assigned a role to play, and the primary obligation of each was to play that role as well as possible. Yet inasmuch as the eventual results of such efforts were beyond human control, the Stoic ethic emphasized intent rather than results. Duty demanded that one should *intend* to play one's role, and to the degree expected. The consequences, however, were a matter of indifference. Accordingly duty to one's assigned task, not glory, success, or wealth, was the key theme of Stoic morality. For example in Cicero's *Republic*, Scipio says:

> Such a man [the wise individual] considers our military commands and civil magistracies among necessary, not among desirable

things, to be undertaken only as a public duty, not to be sought for the sake of glory and reward.[7]

The Stoic conception of nature as an equivalent to divine reason had important implications for the Stoic theory of humanity. Whereas the Cynics argued that to live naturally was to live as a beast, the Stoics understood the natural life as that which was most attuned to the dictates of reason. The human goal was to achieve perfect reason, and to do this individuals had to attain a level of self-control which would allow them to successfully suppress their desires and emotions. Inasmuch as the rational soul was to be undisturbed in its pursuit of the divine, Stoic apathy required not only the repression of such emotions as fear or revenge but also the control of such feelings as love and pity. Concentrating upon the demands of divine reason, the Stoic found all other values to be indifferent. Honor, success, and station in life were all equally unimportant. Such qualities, which historically functioned to differentiate some people from others, paled to insignificance in light of the brilliance created by the divine spark in the souls of all humankind. Thus central to the Stoic understanding of human nature was a belief in the fundamental equality of all people irrespective of their position within society. Indeed, for the Stoics, nature was ruled by one law, the law of reason, and it spoke to all humankind with equal force. Moral persons, in turn, were obligated to obey nature's law—an obligation which necessarily superseded their obligations to the traditions and practices of the local community.

Unlike the Sophists of the fifth century, the Stoics believed that justice and law existed in nature and thus that they could not be reduced to purely cultural preferences. Nature's order, established by divine reason, served as a standard for right and wrong. Its principles were eternal and binding upon all people. In a famous passage within his *Republic*, Cicero summarized the Stoic understanding of "true law"; it was, however, a conception that can be traced back to such early thinkers as Chrysippus and Zeno:

> There is in fact a true law—namely right reason—which is in accordance with nature, applies to all men, and is unchangeable and eternal. By its commands this law summons men to the performance of their duties; by its prohibitions it restrains them from doing wrong. Its commands and prohibitions always influence good men, but are without effect upon the bad. To invalidate this law by human legislation is never morally right, nor is it permissible ever to restrict its operation, and to annul it wholly is impossi-

---

[7] Cicero, *On the Commonwealth*, trans. George Sabine and Stanley Smith (New York: The Liberal Arts Press, Inc., n.d.), p. 122.

ble. . . . But there will be one law, eternal and unchangeable, binding at all times upon all peoples; and there will be, as it were, one common master and ruler of men, namely God, who is the author of this law, its interpreter, and its sponsor.[8]

In general a specific political community is demarcated by the extent of its authority and the reach of its laws. Consequently, by arguing that god ruled over all people and that the laws of nature extended throughout time and space, the Stoics were suggesting that there is a universal community of humankind. Earlier the Cynics had developed a similar theory of cosmopolitanism as a device by which to destroy local loyalties. For the Stoics, however, the cosmopolis had become a positive moral ideal. The wise, bound in obedience to reason, existed in a natural harmony with one another. This harmony, in turn, created the bonds of their transcendent community and established, thereby, their citizenship.

The early Stoics never fully resolved a tension found within their system. On one hand, they emphasized the universal community of humankind and the fundamental equality of all people. Yet, on the other hand, they retained the Cynic's sharp distinction between the wise person and the rest of humanity. It appears that, for the early Stoics, the cosmopolis belonged to the wise and, consequently, that human equality presupposed the prior perfection of the human soul. In effect, then, a sharp dichotomy was established. On one hand there was the ideal, and on the other, the reality. Inasmuch as there was no middle ground between the two, the wise few tended to be set apart from the rest of humanity. Similarly by arguing that the rational cosmopolis was the only true state, the early Stoics tended to be indifferent towards the problems and experiences of existing societies. If Stoicism was to exert any practical influence, it would have to overcome these difficulties. The attempt to do so characterized the efforts of the so-called Middle Stoics.

The Middle Stoics

Traditionally, the most important spokespersons of the Middle Stoics are considered to be Panaetius of Rhodes (185–109 B.C.) and Posidonius (135–50 B.C.). Each in his own way attempted to accommodate the teachings of Stoicism to Roman practice by underplaying the perfectionism of the earlier writers. Although such efforts may have been necessary, in some cases they threatened to transform Stoic philosophy into a mere rationalization for Roman imperial ambition. For example, Posidonius apparently equated the Stoic vision of the cosmopolis with Rome's efforts to establish a world empire. As such, Roman expansion was portrayed

---

[8] Cicero, *On the Commonwealth*, pp. 215–6.

as part of a divine plan, and the moral citizen appeared duty bound to contribute to its actualization. Similarly, in his *Republic*, Cicero argued that the Stoic ideal of the mixed state was never so fully realized as it was in the Roman Republic.

But despite Posidonius's wide influence, Panaetius of Rhodes was perhaps the most important Middle Stoic of all. As a teacher he succeeded in popularizing Stoic doctrine among the Roman nobility and joined with Polybius in contributing to the influential Scipionic Circle. His most important disciple was Cicero, and it is chiefly through the latter's works that the teachings of Panaetius are known today. Panaetius modified the earlier Stoic teachings by introducing a large measure of eclecticism. Breaking from the highly systematized thought of Chrysippus, he turned to a variety of sources for his ideas and was especially interested in the works of Plato and Aristotle. In particular, he appropriated Plato's understanding of the soul as containing both a rational and an irrational element. In so doing, he forced the Stoics to reconsider their original idea of perfect apathy. In accepting the irrational as a legitimate element of the soul, Panaetius allowed for a certain display of emotion and desire. Thus rather than attempting to destroy the passions, he sought to regulate them according to the needs of human reason. As a consequence, his view of human nature was more realistic, and it had the effect of reducing that distance between the ideal and the real which was characteristic of traditional Stoic thought.

Similarly, in his political theory Panaetius argued that the ideal cosmopolis was not simply restricted to the perfectly wise few who somehow had risen above the rest of humanity. On the contrary, he taught that reason was the law for all people regardless of their obvious differences in character and endowment. Thus in Panaetius's work the egalitarian aspect of Stoicism received major emphasis, while the traditional distinction between the few and the many receded somewhat into the background. Accompanying this was Panaetius's insistence that the laws of nature were not simply the sources of harmony for the wise. Rather inasmuch as the natural law was more or less implicit within the practices of existing states, it could also serve as a real standard for the actual practices of concrete societies. As a consequence, reason was understood to be not only capable of providing guidance for those individuals who were seeking an inner peace but also as establishing those general principles to which all governments should conform. Indeed, avoiding unjust acts was not enough. Rather each state was obligated to actively pursue justice in order to achieve that harmony which was necessary for its continued existence. Thus, like Polybius, Panaetius favored a mixed constitution which would contain selected elements of monarchy, aristocracy, and democracy. His theory was particularly popular during the later stages of the Roman Republic and found one of its strongest advocates in Cicero.

Among the Late Stoics the most important were the Spaniard Seneca (4 B.C.–A.D. 65), the slave Epictetus (A.D. 55–135), and the Roman emperor Marcus Aurelius (A.D.120–180). By their time Stoicism had become a popular Roman tradition. Yet, as a political theory, it had ceased to develop further. For example, Seneca's famed celebration of the pleasures of a far-removed Golden Age was intended as a rigorous critique of contemporary Roman civilization and its materialistic life style. Thus rather than attempting to organize political society for action in history, Seneca's Stoicism actually expressed a form of social exhaustion. Similarly, both Epictetus and Marcus Aurelius were almost entirely preoccupied with their private quest for a personal ethics. In particular, they were interested in Stoicism as a possible source of individual guidance and comfort. Thus for them it had become primarily a means of consolation by which the individual could escape from the horrors of worldly existence through an act of will. Perhaps the best example of this tendency can be found in the writings of Marcus Aurelius. As the emperor of Rome he sat at the pinnacle of worldly power. Yet, for him, life appeared to lack any intrinsic importance; it was simply a point in time located between the past and the future:

> Of human life the time is a point, and the substance is in a flux, and the perception dull, and the composition of the whole body subject to putrefacation, and the soul a whirl, and fortune hard to divine, and fame a thing devoid of judgment. And, to say all in a word, everything which belongs to the body is a stream, and what belongs to the soul is a dream and vapour, and life is a warfare and a stranger's sojourn, and after-fame is oblivion.[9]

Although the Roman Empire would continue for several hundred more years, one already notices in this statement a lack of purpose and confidence in worldly affairs. As such, it foreshadowed not only the collapse of the Roman Empire but also Western civilization's growing receptivity to a renewed spiritualism implicit within the Christian message.

ROMAN LAW

The influence of the Roman Law tradition upon Western political theory was due, in part, to its contribution to the Catholic Church's system of canon law. More importantly, however, was its role in the development of the modern nation-state. During the twelfth century, as the Holy Roman

---

[9] Marcus Aurelius, "Meditations," in George Long, trans., *Marcus Aurelius Meditations: Epictetus Enchiridion*, ed. Russell Kirk (Chicago: Henry Regnery Co., 1956), pp. 18–19.

Empire was in the process of dissolution, the emerging nation-states were increasingly in need of a secular legal tradition. Feuds between imperial and papal forces, growing trade among the towns, and an expanding civil bureaucracy combined to create the need for a more sophisticated system of civil and criminal law. The obvious available resource was that which was provided by the Roman tradition. Thus beginning in the twelfth century, and centered at the University of Bologna, a revival in the study of Roman law provided the basis for almost all the legal systems of Europe and Latin America.

Central to the Roman Law tradition was its distinction among *jus civile, jus gentium,* and *jus naturale. Jus civile* was the civil law and, as such, referred to the customs and practices of the various cities as they faced their particular and differing situations. For example, the *jus civile* of Rome was first codified around 450 B.C. Known as the Twelve Tables, it formed the basic statement of the customary and binding practices of that society. Eventually, praetors were elected and charged with the responsibility of interpreting the Twelve Tables according to the requirements of equity and fairness.

As Rome began to expand its rule and consequently came into increasing contact with differing civil systems, it became necessary to find a means for adjudicating differences among the various traditions. Even though such thinkers as Cicero had tended to equate Roman practice with the Stoic conception of a universal world law, it was apparent that Roman customs were, in fact, but one set among a variety of tribal traditions. *Jus gentium,* or the law of the tribes, developed as a response to this situation. At first it was simply the product of Rome's increasing contacts with foreigners. As such it dealt basically with commercial practices and emerged from judicial decisions which attempted to blend the various customs according to the dictates of common sense. In time these decisions were recorded, promulgated, and grew to become the *jus gentium.* By the end of the Republic, the *jus gentium* had expanded beyond its original scope and soon became a symbol for those legal traditions which were understood to be common to all nations. Whereas the *jus civile* referred to the particular laws of any one nation, the *jus gentium* appeared as a higher law which transcended and thereby included the common practices of all. As such, it was widely interpreted as a manifestation of the natural reason which was shared by all humankind.

At first, the *jus gentium* was equated with the Stoic concept of natural law. For example, the famous Roman jurist Gaius (A.D. 110–180) wrote in his *Institutes:*

> All nations which are governed by statutes and customs make use partly of law which is peculiar to the respective nations, and partly of such as is common to all mankind. Whatever law any nation has

established for itself is peculiar to the particular state (*civitas*), and is called civil law, as being the peculiar law of that state, but law which natural reason has laid down for mankind in general is maintained equally by all men, and is called *jus gentium*, as being the law which all nations use.[10]

In time, however, a certain distinction was introduced. According to the Stoic conception, natural law was an expression of divine reason and, as a consequence, could contain no imperfections. Yet, on the other hand, it was obvious that the practices of nations were far from ideal. The case in point was the issue of slavery. While slavery was an institution of the *jus gentium*, it nonetheless violated the fact that all people are free by nature. Thus in order to preserve the Stoic conception of law, there had to exist a higher order of reason which was free from the imperfections of the actual *jus gentium*. That higher order was referred to as the *jus naturale*. Among the Roman jurists the most important spokesperson for this higher tradition was the Syrian commentator Ulpian (A.D. 170–228), who offered this explication of the two laws: "It is easy to understand that this law [*jus gentium*] differs from the natural [*jus naturale*] because it is common only between men, while the former is common between all living creatures." By including animals within the scope of the natural law, Ulpian was able to distinguish between common human practices and the universal dictates of reason itself. According to this thinking, human conventions may reflect the higher order of nature, but they are not necessarily identical with it. For example, such duties as caring for one's offspring or repelling acts of violence are natural obligations for both humans and animals. The practice of slavery, however, is a uniquely human institution. Thus although slavery was established by usage, it was not required by a law of nature.

With its rediscovery in the twelfth century, the Roman distinction between *jus civile*, *jus gentium*, and *jus naturale* effectively entered into the mainstream of Western political thought. The *jus gentium* eventually became the basis for the modern concept of international law. And the *jus naturale* was incorporated into Christianity by identifying the Stoic conception of reason (*logos*) with the divine word (*logos*) of Christ. With the developed natural-law tradition, it was argued that a discrepancy between the higher law and a particular conventional or positive law required that the latter be corrected. As a consequence, the natural law became a means of granting or denying legitimacy to various political decisions. On one hand, those policies which agreed with the dictates of the natural law assumed an immediate authority, and in some cases were presented as divine ordinances. On the other hand, the existence of a standard above and

---

[10] Gaius, "Institutes," in Paul Sigmond, ed., *Natural Law in Political Thought* (Cambridge: Winthrop Publishers, 1971), pp. 33–34.

superior to the positive law allowed for an exercise of individual judgment and in some cases justified selected acts of disobedience and resistance.

BIBLIOGRAPHY

ADCOCK, F. E. *Roman Political Ideas and Practice.* Ann Arbor: University of Michigan Press, 1964.

BURY, J. B., et al. *The Hellenistic Age: Aspects of Hellenistic Civilization.* New York: W. W. Norton & Co., 1970.

EHRENBERG, VICTOR. *Man, State, and Deity.* London: Methuen & Co., 1974.

HADAS, MOSES. *Hellenistic Culture: Fusion and Diffusion.* New York: W. W. Norton & Co., 1972.

JONAS, HANS. *The Gnostic Religion.* Boston: Beacon Press, 1963.

RIST, J. M. *Stoic Philosophy.* Cambridge: Cambridge University Press, 1969.

ROSTOVTZEFF, M. *The Social and Economic History of the Hellenistic World.* 3 vols. Oxford: Oxford University Press, 1941.

SYME, R. *The Roman Revolution.* Oxford: Oxford University Press, 1960.

TARN, W. W. *Alexander the Great.* 2 vols. Cambridge: Cambridge University Press, 1948.

VOEGELIN, ERIC. *The Ecumenic Age.* Baton Rouge: L.S.U. Press, 1974.

PART II

The Christian Tradition

4

AUGUSTINE AND EARLY CHRISTIANITY

ROME: THE HOLLOW EMPIRE

Rome's military success and its subsequent rapid expansion throughout the Mediterranean created a distinct set of challenges for its republican institutions. The problem of maintaining a growing imperial army and the ambitions of certain party leaders brought about a series of events which slowly but steadily transformed the Roman Republic into an imperial monarchy. This process culminated in 27 B.C. when Octavius Caesar was granted extraordinary powers at the command of the senate. Thus, although an effort was made to preserve the appearances of traditional republicanism, Rome in actuality had become a monarchy. As the Roman historian Dio Cassius (A.D. 155–235) wrote:

> So then the whole power of people and senate was transferred to Augustus, and, thenceforward Rome was literally a monarchy; even if later two or three persons held power simultaneously the term monarchy is still accurate. The name "monarchy," to be sure,

the Romans so detested that they did not call their emperors dictators or kings or anything similar; but since absolute authority over the state rested upon them, they could only be kings.[1]

In granting Octavius his extraordinary powers, the Senate conferred upon him the title of "Augustus." Inasmuch as the Romans referred to sacred objects as "augusta," the term was intended to denote a divine or superhuman quality. Indeed, in Virgil's (70–19 B.C.) *Aeneid*, Augustus Caesar was portrayed as being of divine lineage if not a god himself. This tendency to divinize the Roman emperors was indicative of the increasing influence of the Hellenistic East upon Roman culture. The Egyptian cult of Isis and the Persian religion of Mithra had infiltrated Roman practice and encouraged, thereby, the further unification of secular and sacred experience. Indeed, within two generations after Augustus both the emperors Caligula (A.D. 37–41) and Nero (A.D. 57–68) had insisted upon their personal divinity.

As Roman power expanded throughout the region it effectively destroyed the remnants of once-flourishing local civilizations. Yet having overwhelmed such indigenous cultures, it was then faced with the task of replacing them with some alternative set of social and cultural practices. That challenge was not easily met. A conservative attempt to revivify local customs made little sense in view of the traditional society's reduced stature vis-à-vis the new imperial order. On the other hand, a progressive attempt to create a new imperial civilization was extremely difficult, since the empire itself was basically an external order imposed upon the people and thus essentially unrelated to their shared experiences and traditional life styles. As a result, the Roman Empire faced a critical situation. As a form of political and military organization, it was extremely efficient and thus successful in terms of its practical interests. Yet, as a substantive society, it was hollow and meaningless. Thus the spread of the empire was due more to its organizational efficiency than to its social vitality. As Eric Voegelin writes:

> The new empires originated, not in a ferocious will to conquer, but in the fatality of a power vacuum that attracted and even sucked into itself, unused organizational force from the outside; it originated in circumstances beyond control rather than in deliberate planning.[2]

Consequently unlike most traditional empires, the Roman Empire did not represent the particular beliefs, customs, and practices of a single concrete

---

[1] As quoted in *A History of Rome*, ed. Moses Hadas (Garden City: Doubleday, 1956), p. 91.

[2] Eric Voegelin, *The Ecumenic Age* (Baton Rouge: Louisiana State University Press, 1974), pp. 117–18.

society. It was, instead, a multicivilizational empire. It exhibited a universal form, but it did not represent a universal civilization. Thus, similar to Alexander's Macedonian empire, its pragmatic success did not imply a spiritual meaning which could inspire its citizens. As it extended throughout the Mediterranean, it appeared to have no purpose other than its own further expansion. With no content of a particular civilization to carry forward, the empire appeared to be a power in the service of no particular cause except the needs of power itself. Again, in the words of Eric Voegelin:

> . . . it was a graveyard of societies, including those of the conquerors, rather than a society in its own right.[3]

As we have seen, one possible response to such an apparently meaningless historical development was that of spiritual withdrawal. The Cynics, Stoics, and Epicureans turned inwards in an effort to turn away. Another alternative to such a situation, however, would be to create a context within which the apparent chaos of pragmatic history could be shown to yield a higher meaning. In other words, the world empire seemed to require a world religion. Thus while the Italian upper classes adopted either a Stoic pantheism or a Pythagorean mysticism, the lower classes returned to the traditional worship of local cult deities. At the same time there emerged a number of Eastern religions which attempted to expand beyond their original locations through a program of vigorous missionary activity. They attempted, in effect, to convert the empire. Surveying their activity, Michael Rostovtzeff writes:

> I have referred already to the fact that certain of these local Eastern cults became prominent, spread beyond the limits of a single country and people, and created religious societies and local churches of their own, till they became cosmopolitan and set forth to propagate their doctrine over the world. . . . The earliest of these proselytizing religions were Egyptian and Anatolian: the Graeco-Egyptian worship of the trinity including Serapis, Isis, and Harpocrates came from Egypt; and Asia Minor exported the worship of the Great Mother in a Hellenized form. These were followed by cults of other deities—the Syrian sky-god and the Syrian sun-god, worshipped in various shapes; Mithras, the warrior god of the sun, saviour and champion of man and man's civilization; and Sabazius, the mystical deity of Thracians and Anatolians. Each of these religions, with a view to its diffusion over the world, constructed a definite theology, definite mystical rites, and a definite priestly hierarchy.[4]

[3] Voegelin, *The Ecumenic Age,* p. 134.

[4] Michael Rostovtzeff, *Rome,* trans. J. D. Duff (Oxford: Oxford University Press, 1960), p. 296.

Of all these newly expanding Eastern religions, unquestionably the most important for the West was Christianity.

CHRISTIANITY

Christianity was a particularly appropriate response to the Roman situation because it exhibited the same universal characteristics as found in the empire itself. Just as the empire brought together diverse ethnic and geographical groups by imposing a common organization upon them, so, too, did Christianity claim to unite all humanity in a common spiritual community. Although rooted in Galilee, the Christian religion claimed to represent the universal teachings of a world-transcendent god. As such, its god was not to be identified with the history or customs of a particular locality. Similarly, its teachings were not intended to separate one group from another by establishing distinctive practices or cults but rather were meant to unite all people under the one law of divine love. As a consequence, Christians were not necessarily members of a particular tribe or ethnic group. They were, instead, participants in an open spiritual community which extended throughout time for all humankind. The preeminent expression of this belief in a universal community of humankind is found in the Christian concept of the mystical body. For Christians, the mystical body was the true community of humanity. It was composed of all of those who shared in the spirit of Christ. Thus, living or dead, Jew or Gentile, all people belonged together in that common order effected by the soul's submission to God. Expressing this element of universalism, St. Paul wrote to the Ephesians:

> I, therefore, a prisoner for the Lord, beg you to lead a life worthy of the calling to which you have been called, with all lowliness and meekness, with patience, forbearing one another in love, eager to maintain the unity of the Spirit in the bond of peace. There is one body and one Spirit, just as you were called to the one hope that belongs to your call, one Lord, one faith, one baptism, one God and Father of us all, who is above all and through all and in all.[5]

As a universal spiritual community, Christianity existed alongside of the universal pragmatic community of the Roman Empire. Soon the relationship between these two "universal" communities created a series of problems for those who were responsible for the administration of each. Even though religious persecution was not a traditional Roman practice,

[5] Wayne A. Meeks, ed., *The Writings of St. Paul* (New York: W. W. Norton & Co., 1972), p. 128.

the Emperor Trajan (A.D. 98–117) passed a law which allowed for such persecutions if necessary. Although his reasons for doing so are not entirely clear, he may have acted because of the Christian refusal to participate in the practice of ruler-worship. Throughout the second century, most rulers simply ignored the Christian sects. During the third century, however, Christianity became increasingly popular among the empire's soldiery, and the emperors came to fear that it would eventually undermine the loyalty of the military to the state itself. In response they began a campaign of ruthless persecutions. The result, however, was only to further damage the prestige of the empire. The historian Rostovtzeff writes:

> When the state emerged from the convulsions of the third century [military insurgency, foreign invasions, demands from the serfs for social changes, and a declining economy] almost entirely deprived of moral authority and relying upon force alone, it was confronted by the Christian Church fully armed in the organization which had been voluntarily accepted by her adherents. The moral authority which the civil power had lost was her (the Church) sole but sufficient support. . . . The Church had proved herself stronger than her adversary.[6]

Thus by the beginning of the fourth century imperial rule was bowing to reality; the Roman emperors were finally forced to accept the Christian church, and the coregents Constantine and Licinius announced a policy of religious toleration in A.D. 313. Almost eighty years later, in 391, Emperor Theodosius banned paganism from Rome and, in so doing, attempted to unite the hitherto separate communities of church and state into a single ecumenical order which would uphold established Christianity as the official civil religion of the empire. Such an attempt, however, was bound to fail in time. Theoretically, the spirit of Christian universalism could not tolerate such an intimate identification with any particular regime.

Any account of Christianity that was limited to its cultural and political function within the Roman Empire would be partial at best. Although it played a vital role in the later development of the West, Christianity was not intended to be primarily a political or social doctrine. On the contrary, as a religious system its essential concern was with humanity's relationship to god. This feature of Christianity is expressed clearly in a passage from *The Confessions of Saint Augustine*. Referring to a time before his conversion and addressing himself to God, Augustine wrote:

> So I set about finding a way to gain the strength that was necessary for enjoying You. And I could not find it until I embraced the *Medi-*

---

[6] Rostovtzeff, *Rome*, pp. 303–308.

*ator between God and man, the man Christ Jesus, who is over all
things, God blessed forever,* who was calling unto me and saying: *I
am the Way, the Truth, and the Life;* and who brought into union
with our nature that Food which I lacked the strength to take: for
the Word was made flesh that your Wisdom, by which You created
all things, might give suck to our souls' infancy. For I was not yet
lowly enough to hold the lowly Jesus as my God, nor did I know
what lesson His embracing of our weakness was to teach. For your
Word, the eternal Truth, towering above the highest parts of Your
creation, lifts up to himself those that were cast down. He built for
Himself here below a lowly house of our clay, that by it He might
bring down from themselves and bring up to Himself those who
were to be made subject, healing the swollenness of their pride and
fostering their love: so that their self-confidence might grow no further but rather diminish, seeing the deity at their feet, humbled by
the assumption of our coat of human nature: to the end that weary
at last they might cast themselves down upon His humanity and rise
again in its rising.[7]

Several features of Augustine's narrative prayer require elaboration. First, it forcefully illustrates the importance of Christ to the believing
Christian. Accordingly it would appear that the essential feature of Christianity is to be found in the personality of Jesus Christ. As a god-human, He
created the Christian community by extending his power out to and
through his believers. Thus in the words of the Catholic doxology, it is
"Through him [Christ], with him, and in him in the unity of the Holy Spirit
all glory and honor is yours almighty Father, forever and ever." Given this
understanding of the role and meaning of Christ's personality, it is obvious
that the appearance of Christ forces Christians to rethink their understanding of human history. The fact that Christ lived becomes the central
historical happening, and all other events will be significant only insofar as
they are related to this essential occurrence.

A second characteristic of the Christian experience as expressed by
Augustine is found in his emphasis upon humanity's radical need for God's
saving action. According to Augustine, human beings are both weak and
sinful. In need of healing and swollen with pride, they are saved only
through God's action upon them. As a consequence any excellence or virtue
of which humans are capable is necessarily insufficient. Only when the
Christian has been totally exhausted by his or her own efforts is he or she
ready to be lifted up by God Himself. Augustine's emphasis upon
humanity's radical dependency is both typical of Christianity and at the
same time represents a certain break with the classical Greek tradition.

---

[7] F. J. Sheed, ed., *The Confessions of Saint Augustine*, Books I–X, (New York: Sheed & Ward,
1942), p. 122.

This may be illustrated by comparing Augustine's understanding of human nature with that of Aristotle. Like Augustine, Aristotle understood humankind's nature to be defined by its particular relationship with the divine. For him the philosopher was the most human of all people precisely because the philosopher participated in the sacred transcendent through the life of reason. Yet, for Aristotle, human relationship with the divine was decidedly one-dimensional. Participation in the transcendent was primarily the result of one's own virtuous effort. Although god may have exerted a certain attraction as the final cause, the straining and seeking to make contact was essentially that of the human actor alone. God, on the other hand, was the unmoved mover. Indeed in his *Nicomachean Ethics*, Aristotle argued that humans and god could not even enjoy a true friendship because of their radical inequality. Given this emphasis upon the human effort required to create a sacred relationship, it is not surprising that so much of Aristotle's thought was devoted to an examination of virtue and education. Indeed intellectual and moral education became the necessary means for developing those possibilities implicit within human nature itself. The good life was a goal to be achieved, and the necessary means for its actualization rested with the person.

For Christianity, on the other hand, the relationship between God and humanity contained both a first and second dimension. Not only did Christians, like the Greeks, experience a longing in their soul for the sacred, but at the same time, they understood the Incarnation to be a sign that God also longed for and sought after humanity. In philosophical terms, Christianity was based upon an appreciation of the fact that the human experience of questing and seeking was reciprocated by God Himself. Accordingly both God and humanity sought to encounter one another, and the striving of humanity to participate in the transcendent was complemented by the desire of transcendence itself to enter into history. For all Christians, therefore, the relationship between God and the human went beyond that of Aristotle's impossible friendship and actually became a relationship of love. The soul was no longer simply the source of that energy by which the worshiper could reach out to God, but rather at the same time it became the receptacle of that divine energy by which God had reached out to His people. In this sense, then, the Christian experience built upon rather than negated the Greek understanding of human nature. Like the Greeks, the Christians accredited the experience of the human being's rational openness toward the transcendent. Yet beyond that, they claimed to have experienced the complementary spiritual process of God's opening toward humanity. The soul was what the Greeks believed, but more, and its additional quality was the unique content of Christian revelation.

Christianity's emphasis on God's movement towards humanity carried with it the necessity of reconsidering Aristotle's understanding of virtue. For the Christian all human action, even the most virtuous, was incapable of bringing anyone to God. Although men and women sought God, it was God's seeking of them that brought about the full actualization of the human potential. Thus not only did God act upon the human race, but His actions were the necessary conditions for human satisfaction. For the Christian, therefore, grace, not virtue, merited salvation. Given this, the traditional Aristotelian intellectual and moral education no longer retained its original function. It was valuable inasmuch as it helped produce the excellent person; but human excellence, alone, was no longer the condition for human happiness. Thus the Christian experience of the Incarnation implied a new understanding of what was required for human happiness. In short, it altered the classical definition of the good life.

Politics is an attempt by human beings to order their society in such a way as to establish the historical conditions which support the good life. To the extent that Christianity suggested both a new understanding of history and a new conception of the good life, it necessarily implied a new approach to the problems of political order. One of the first attempts to systematically present the new Christian approach is found in *The City of God* by St. Augustine. It was an effort, in turn, which proved to be an authoritative account of Christian doctrine throughout the Middle Ages and into the present. Referring to this, the political scientist Herbert Deane writes:

> The limited role of the state, its primary concern with maintaining external peace and order among men rather than with molding human aspirations and values, the accent on the inadequacies and imperfections of the peace and justice that it manages to preserve, and its preoccupation with law and punishment instead of education and moral therapy—all these themes which emerge in Christian political thought and are brought together by Augustine are the characteristic features of most Western political thought in the centuries which intervene between him and us.[8]

LIFE OF AUGUSTINE

Born in A.D. 354 in Tagaste, a city in the African province of Numidia, Augustine was originally raised as a Christian by his mother, Monica. Upon moving to Carthage in 370, however, in order to pursue the study of rhetoric, Augustine soon broke with the moral and intellectual teachings of the church and began to read deeply in the literature of paganism. After an

---

[8] Herbert Deane, "Classical and Christian Political Thought," *Political Theory*, 1 (1973), p. 425.

initial exposure to Stoicism, especially as formulated in the works of Cicero, Augustine became acquainted with Manicheism and eventually adopted its religious teachings. During the fourth century, Manicheism had grown to become Christianity's chief rival in the field of ethics. As a system, it was based upon the teachings of the Persian ascetic Manes (born around A.D. 215). As a mixture of Persian Zoroastrianism and Ebionite gnosticism, Manicheism postulated a fundamental duality between the forces of light and the forces of darkness. The principle of light was associated with god and moral goodness, while the forces of darkness included Satan and moral evil. As two fundamental principles, these forces existed from the very beginning of time and consequently were engaged in a continual and eternal conflict with one another. Eventually, during this battle, it happened that various fragments of light had become entrapped within the world of darkness. Specifically, the human soul, which was composed of light, had become encased in the darkness of the human body. Manes taught that a process of liberation was required that would allow the fragments of light to escape from their darkness and return to their heavenly home. Generally, this liberation was based upon a series of ascetic practices by which practitioners reduced their involvement with the material world.

From a strictly theological perspective Manicheism would appear to have had minimal attraction to a Christian. First, it challenged the omnipotent nature of a loving creator-god, and, second, it denied the unique status of Jesus Christ. For the Manicheans, Christ was simply one of the prophets and thus stood among such others as Adam, Noah, Buddha, and most importantly Manes, himself. For Augustine, however, the appeal of Manicheism was of a decidedly intellectual nature. First, Manichean dualism appeared as a logical explanation for the reality of evil. For Augustine, the traditional Christian explanation was paradoxical. On one hand, it acknowledged the reality of evil, and yet on the other hand, it claimed that God had created the whole world and that He was good. Secondly, Manicheism treated the principles of light and darkness as material forces. Thus the soul was understood to be a fragment, and god, itself, was a material being. Such a materialism appealed to Augustine because he had not yet accepted the possibility of an immaterial reality which could exist beyond the realm of the senses.

In 384 Augustine was appointed Milan's municipal professor of rhetoric. There he began a spiritual transformation which would culminate in his eventual return to Christianity in 386 and in his ordination to the priesthood in 391. This conversion was facilitated by Augustine's growing disenchantment with Manicheism: the grounds upon which the Manicheans attempted to demonstrate the certitude of their truth remained unclear to him; and Manicheism's reasons for believing that the struggle between good and evil was necessarily eternal and without end still failed to convince him unshakeably. In an attempt to resolve these difficulties, he met with a preeminent Manichean bishop but left discouraged over the possibility of any true reconciliation.

Moreover, during his stay in Milan Augustine began to read certain neo-Platonic treatises. Claiming to interpret the teachings of Plato, the neo-Platonic school was represented in Rome by the philosophers Plotinus (A.D. 205–270) and Porphyry (233–300). Plotinus's lectures had been published as the *Enneads*, and it was most probably a Latin translation of these notes which Augustine first read. According to Plotinus, the major errors of his day were those of materialism, scepticism, and dualism. Plotinus taught the antidote to this relativism: that reality was spiritual, knowable, and single. In general Plotinus argued that by a process of spiritual intuition, seekers could learn to transcend the imperfections of the material world and achieve thereby an ecstatic union with god. As a result of this encounter with neo-Platonism, Augustine eventually rejected the materialism of his youth. At the same time he came to understand that evil could be explained as a privation rather than as a creation. Thus being essentially the absence of good, it did not require a positive explanation.

Having thus resolved the intellectual difficulties which first drove him from Christianity and toward Manicheism, Augustine once again began to reconsider the church's teachings. Under the influence of Ambrose, the bishop of Milan, he read the Scriptures and was particularly impressed with the epistles of Paul. Indeed it was during a reading of Paul's letter to the Romans that he finally decided to rejoin the church of his mother.

Upon his conversion to Christianity, Augustine left teaching and returned to Africa in order to establish a monastic community. After his ordination (391), he went to the city of Hippo, and in 396 he became its bishop. Once there he began a career both as a church administrator and as an apologist for Christian doctrines. As an apologist, his writings were voluminous and ranged over a wide variety of topics. Generally they were drafted as responses to the concrete challenges and issues that confronted his administration at any given time. As a consequence they lack the systematic character which can be found in more disinterested works. However, the diffuse nature of Augustine's theological writings can only be partially explained in terms of the circumstances within which they were produced. Just as important was the fact that Augustine was not primarily interested in building a strictly intellectual system. In short, he did not write to create dogma but rather to convert people. Referring to this quality, the philosopher Frederick Copleston has said:

> Reason has its part to play in bringing a man to faith, and, once a man has the faith, reason has its part to play in penetrating the data of faith; but it is the total relation of the soul to God which primar-

ily interests Augustine. . . . [Augustine] emphasized the fact that knowledge of the truth is to be sought, not for purely academic purposes, but as bringing true happiness, true beatitude . . . he sees knowledge in function of an end, beatitude.[9]

Augustine remained in Hippo until his death in A.D. 430. He died as the city, once a Roman protectorate, was being besieged by the Vandals.

ANALYSIS OF *THE CITY OF GOD*

Begun in 413 and completed in 426, *The City of God* is generally considered to be both Augustine's most important writing and the greatest apologetical work of early Christianity. As was the case in most of his writings, Augustine intended the book as a response to specific challenges facing the church of his day. In particular with the fall of Rome in 410, certain critics began to question the very efficacy of the Christian religion. They argued, in effect, that Rome's political decline had begun only after it had rejected its traditional pagan deities. Thus its fall could be seen as a proof of the inferiority of Christianity itself. According to Augustine, a full response to this charge required nothing less than a total critique of the pagan world-view. And the first ten books of *The City of God* were written with this purpose in mind:

> And therefore, in these ten books . . . I have . . . satisfied the desire of certain persons, by refuting the objections of the ungodly, who prefer their own gods to the Founder of the holy city, about which we undertook to speak. Of these ten books, the first five were directed against those who think we should worship the gods for the sake of the blessings of this life, and the second five against those who think we should worship them for the sake of the life which is to be after death.[10]

During the time in which Augustine was writing his defense of Christian efficacy, he was actively engaged in the apostolic mission of his office. As a bishop he was concerned with promoting the faith and gaining converts. In 412 he began to correspond with a Roman official in Africa by the name of Volusian. Volusian was interested in the Christian faith but bothered by serious doubts concerning the doctrine of the Incarnation. The frequency and degree of such scepticism convinced Augustine that Christianity's development would require a systematic and positive statement of

[9] Frederick Copleston, S. J., *A History of Philosophy* (Garden City: Doubleday, 1962), II, pp. 64–66.
[10] Augustine, *The City of God*, trans. Marcus Dods (New York: Random House, 1950), p. 344.

its major teachings. This, in turn, became the purpose of the final twelve books of his manuscript. As he wrote in his *Retractations* of 427:

> But lest anyone charge that we have only argued against the beliefs of others, and have not stated our own, it is just this that the second part of this work [*The City of God*] . . . accomplishes. . . . The first four of the following twelve books, then, deal with the origin of the two cities, one which is of God, the other of this world; the next four books treat of their growth and progress; but the third four books, which are also the last, deal with their destined ends. And so, although the entire 22 books were written about both cities, yet they have taken their title from the better one, and consequently are called, *On the City of God*.[11]

Thus as its completion Augustine's *The City of God* was intended to represent the authoritative statement of the Christian position during its early years.

As the above statement by Augustine makes clear, the argument of *The City of God* is structured on the concept of the two cities. Prior to Augustine, the idea of the two cities can be found in the writings of such Stoics as Cicero, Seneca, and Marcus Aurelius and in the works of such neo-Platonists as Plotinus and Porphyry. Augustine, however, most probably was influenced by the concept's frequent appearance in Scripture. For Augustine the two cities are the city of God and the earthly city. Both are essentially spiritual communities, and membership in each, therefore, is determined by the spiritual disposition of its respective citizens:

> Accordingly, two cities have been formed by two loves: the earthly by the love of self, even to the contempt of God; the heavenly by the love of God, even to the contempt of self. The former, in a word, glories in itself, the latter in the Lord. . . . And therefore the wise men of the one city, living according to man, have sought for profit to their own bodies or souls, or both. . . . But in the other city there is no human wisdom, but only godliness. . . .[12]

According to Augustine, therefore, all people may be defined in terms of that object whose love dominates their soul. The soul which is formed by the love of God (*amor dei*) is radically opened toward the transcendent and sacred object of its desire. The soul which is formed by the love of self (*amor sui*) is closed around itself and thus denied the openness of that relationship formed in God. As a closed soul, it suffers from pride, and, for Augustine, pride is the source of all sin.

[11] Augustine, *Retractations*, trans. Mary Bogan (Washington, D.C.: Catholic University of America Press, 1968), p. 210.
[12] Augustine, *The City of God*, p. 477.

To this point, Augustine's theory is similar to St. Paul's conception of the mystical body. For Paul all people come to share in the mystical body by opening themselves to the power of Christ. Inasmuch as each is offered the opportunity of responding to Christ's evocation, those who refuse have to assume the responsibility of their decision. In Augustine, however, the emphasis moves away from human freedom and toward God's sovereignty. In his doctrine of predestination, Augustine argues that God has already selected those who will be graced with the power of *amor dei* and those who won't. Thus although he had written that the free choice of the individual's will is the sole source of evil, Augustine, nonetheless, continued to emphasize the ultimate power of God's grace. According to Augustine all people are weakened by original sin and thus must be empowered to will correctly by the grace of God. Although such willing is done freely, it, nonetheless, presupposes the enabling quality of gratuitous grace. Yet inasmuch as such grace is truly gratuitous, it is never really earned. Thus God, alone, must ultimately decide who will benefit from the free gift of His grace. In his *Retractations*, Augustine wrote:

> For it is precisely the will by which one sins and lives rightly. . . . Unless this will, then, is freed by the grace of God from the servitude by which it has been made a "servant of sin" and unless it is aided to overcome its vices, mortal men cannot live rightly and devoutly. And if this divine beneficence by which the will is freed had not preceded it, it would be given according to its merits and would not be grace, which is certainly given gratuitously.[13]

Focusing primarily upon the political implications of Augustine's theory of the two cities, it is obvious that this doctrine involves a radical reconsideration of one's social orientation. The two cities are essentially spiritual communities. Although at times Augustine wrote in such a way as to suggest that he identified the city of God with the institutional church or equated the earthly city with the Assyrians or Roman Empire, it is clear that no such identification is strictly intended. The citizens of the two cities are intermixed, and they will not be separated until the day of final judgment. Until then only God knows who they are. Inasmuch as one's true citizenship is determined solely by the disposition of one's soul, any historical or institutional affiliation is of a decidedly secondary importance. For example, one may be a member of the hierarchy of the church and still belong to the earthly city. Or one could be an officer of the state and truly belong to the city of God. The effect of this Augustinian doctrine was to loosen the individual's ties to his or her political community. Being a Roman citizen or achieving a certain social rank became, in effect, unimportant. Indeed, the

---

[13] Augustine, *Retractations*, pp. 35–36.

only important society was that spiritual community formed by those in the past, present, and future who truly loved God. That city was understood to include both humans and angels and thus exhibited an obviously nonterrestrial quality. Indeed, by transcending nature the city of God also transcended history. And in doing so, it implied both a new understanding of history and a new attitude toward historical society.

Although recent scholarship has shown that Christianity was not unique in its rejection of the cyclical conceptions of history which were typical of pagan antiquity, its particular understanding has, nonetheless, played a unique role in Western thought. In general, Christianity differed from other contemporary philosophies in its claim to have found a meaning within history itself. As we have seen, the ancient Greek philosophers looked to nature rather than to history as a source for their knowledge. Indeed Plato shared with such philosophers as Heraclitus a general distrust of the historical realm because it appeared to be constantly changing and thus lacking that stable form which true knowledge necessarily presupposed. Even the historian Polybius, who had discovered a certain pattern to historical events, finally despaired of ever finding the real meaning which was implicit in the rise and fall of historical civilizations. With the Christian belief in the Incarnation, however, history finally appeared to achieve a stable moment of universal significance. For the Christian the events of Christ's birth, death, and resurrection created a point of meaning within history which could give direction to the structure of time itself. All events could be seen as either leading to or moving away from this central point, and, as a consequence, it became possible to see history as a line with a definite beginning, middle, and end. Such a structured progression contained the promise of a meaningful story. Inasmuch as the Christian understanding of history presupposed the Christian experience of faith, the meaning which was discovered in history emerged only in view of specific Christian assumptions concerning sin and salvation. Strictly speaking, for Christianity there is a meaning *in* history, but it is not the meaning *of* history. God, not history, is the source of meaning, and therefore history became meaningful only because God had chosen to enter into it.

In his effort to express this Christian view Augustine organized the second, or positive, section of his book according to historical categories. In it he claimed to tell of the origin, progress, and destiny of the two cities. Thus the very meaning of Christian revelation was presented in historical terms. Since Augustine had argued that the only significant question in one's life is the question of membership in the city of God, and since he believed that such a question could be resolved only through the grace of God, it is not surprising that for him the meaning of history became apparent precisely in those moments during which God erupted into time so as to form the community of His believers. Indeed meaningful history for

Augustine is sacred history, and it is composed of those events which constitute the history of the city of God. All other temporal phenomena are profane in nature and consequently bear no immediate relationship to the meaning of history itself.

Given this perspective, Augustine reviewed the major events of the Old and New Testaments. Using an analogy based upon the Book of Genesis's account of the six days of creation, he organized the history of the city of God into six periods: from Adam to Noah, from Noah to Abraham, from Abraham to David, from David to the exile, from the exile to Christ, and from Christ to the end of the world. With the appearance of Christ, however, God's historical action has been essentially completed. The sixth age, therefore, was an indefinite period of waiting for the end of the world. With the Incarnation, God's promise of salvation had been fulfilled, and all that remained was to await His second coming so that promised salvation could be effected. For Augustine, history was at an end and its meaning was clear: properly understood, it told the story of humanity's estrangement from and ultimate reconciliation with God. The task of each person, therefore, was to participate in this sacred drama and to live his or her historical destiny accordingly. All other concerns were unimportant. As a consequence, for Augustine neither mundane history nor political action contained any promise of potential meaning. By finding meaning in a sacred history Augustine effectively removed it from the mundane world. In the words of the philosopher Karl Loewith:

> What really begins with the appearance of Jesus Christ is not a new epoch of secular history, called "Christian," but the beginning of an end. The Christian times are Christian only in so far as they are the last time. . . . The "meaning" of the history of this world is fulfilled against itself because the story of salvation, as embodied in Jesus Christ, redeems and dismantles, as it were, the hopeless history of the world.[14]

Having denied an intrinsic meaning to secular history, and having transferred all of humankind's loyalties to the spiritual community of the city of God, it is apparent that Augustine's theory radically undermined the importance and dignity of the state. This, in turn, is evident both in his description of its genesis and in his analysis of its fundamental character.

For Augustine the state is necessary only because of human sin. If humankind had not sinned, the state would not be required. Yet because of sin humans need to be controlled, and the state is the best instrument for that purpose. Thus like the practice of slavery and the institution of private property, the state is legitimate only inasmuch as it is a necessary response to

[14] Karl Loewith, *Meaning in History* (Chicago: University of Chicago Press, 1957), p. 197.

humanity's depraved condition. According to Augustine the state, slavery, and private property are at the same time both the consequences of and partial remedies for human sinfulness. In Augustine's view, God originally gave human beings dominion only over the animals. With sin, however, that dominion has been extended to include humans themselves. Thus, desirous of power, sinful people have acted so as to gain control over others. As a consequence, the state appears to have originated in vice and not, as the Greeks believed, in virtue:

> Justice being taken away, then, what are kingdoms but great robberies? For what are robberies themselves, but little kingdoms? The band itself is made up of men; it is ruled by the authority of a prince, it is knit together by the pact of the confederacy; the booty is divided by the law agreed on. If, by the admittance of abandoned men, this evil increases to such a degree that it holds places, fixes abodes, takes possession of cities, and subdues peoples, it assumes the more plainly the name of a kingdom, because the reality is now manifestly conferred on it, not by the removal of covetousness, but by the addition of impunity. Indeed, that was an apt and true reply which was given to Alexander the Great by a pirate who had been seized. For when the king had asked the man what he meant by keeping hostile possession of the sea, he answered with bold pride, "What thou meanest by seizing the whole earth; but because I do it with a petty ship, I am called a robber, whilst thou who dost it with a great fleet art styled emperor."[15]

Yet even though the state originates in vice, it also may serve as a practical remedy for the effects of sin. Given humanity's sinful condition and its desire to control others, the state prevents its citizens from destroying one another by imposing its authoritative order upon them. Without such an imposition, humans would soon destroy one another, and peace would be altogether impossible.

Like the Greeks, Augustine developed a eudaemonistic ethical system because he argued that the true purpose of all human action was happiness. Yet, according to Augustine, the Greeks had only partially realized the full significance of this truth. Whereas they understood that happiness consisted in attaining a desired object, they could not appreciate the revealed truth that true happiness ultimately required a loving union with God himself. Given this, Augustine's ethical system was essentially an ethics of love, and it was totally concerned with achieving a mystical union of the human will with that of God. This achievement, in turn, became the standard by which all virtues were to be measured. For example, justice, as a

[15] Augustine, *The City of God*, pp. 112–13.

principle of distribution, means giving to each his or her due. Yet from the perspective of the mystic, everything belongs to and, thus, is due to God. Consequently true justice would require that all be given to God, and theoretically such a condition could exist only in the city of God.

Augustine's emphasis upon the transcendent dimension of all virtue and his view that the state is, in fact, a necessary evil required that he reconsider both its nature and its function. First, in analyzing the state it was necessary to comprehend its specific quality. In particular, it was necessary to question the simplistic identification of one's political regime with the good order itself. This tendency to equate a particular historical state with the ideal regime was most apparent in the work of Cicero. As we have seen, Cicero appeared to treat the Roman Republic as if it were equivalent to the ideal Stoic cosmopolis. Such equations, however, not only failed to appreciate the radically transcendent quality of the good order but, at the same time, actually distorted the very nature of the political community itself. Thus Augustine challenged Cicero's contention that the state was a community bound by its agreement with respect to justice and asserted instead that

> . . . a people is an assemblage of reasonable beings bound together by a common agreement as to the objects of their love; then, in order to discover the character of any people, we have only to observe what they love. Yet whatever it loves, if only it is an assemblage of reasonable beings and not of beasts, and is bound together by an agreement as to the objects of love, it is reasonably called a people; and it will be a superior people in proportion as it is bound together by higher interests, inferior in proportion as it is bound together by lower.[16]

Thus in a manner somewhat similar to Plato's, Augustine classified the quality of various regimes according to the quality of those things to which they were dedicated. Consequently although a certain hierarchy among the states could be established, none could reach so high as to be considered just. Implicit in this doctrine, therefore, is Augustine's fundamental teaching that no citizen owed an unqualified loyalty to his political community. As Christians all people are pilgrims who are simply passing through the world and, as such, cannot be absolutely bound by the demands of actual states.

Augustine's analysis of the origin and character of political society did not imply, however, that it was totally without value. Inasmuch as one person's coercive authority over another is evil, all political societies are evil. Yet, given the reality of human sinfulness, they are at the same time

[16] Augustine, *The City of God*, p. 706.

necessary evils. Thus, just as Augustine did not equate the city of God with the church, so, too, did he refuse to identify the earthly city with the state. While the earthly city lacked all righteousness, the state actually maintained a certain degree of order and consequently benefited the members of the city of God during their earthly pilgrimage. Thus as a source of order and authority the state serves definite human needs; the most important one being humanity's need for peace.

According to Augustine, all of creation is naturally ordered by its need for peace. Indeed the supreme good can actually be defined as "peace in eternity," for as the union of the human and divine will ultimately bring eternal life, so, too, does it grant peace. Yet inasmuch as the whole is ordered towards peace, so too, then are all of its parts. Thus for Augustine it is possible to trace the regulative principle of peace throughout all the orders of nature, beginning with the harmony of the material world and ending with the tranquility of the city of God:

> The peace of the body then consists in the duly proportioned arrangement of its parts. The peace of the irrational soul is the harmonious repose of the appetites, and that of the rational soul the harmony of knowledge and action. The peace of body and soul is the well-ordered and harmonious life and health of the living creature. Peace between man and God is the well-ordered obedience of faith to eternal law. Peace between man and man is well-ordered concord. Domestic peace is the well-ordered concord between those of the family who rule and those who obey. Civil peace is a similar concord among the citizens. The peace of the celestial city is the perfectly ordered and harmonious enjoyment of God, and of one another in God.[17]

From this account, it is evident that civil society has a role to play in actualizing the universal law of nature. Through the imposition of its rule the state is able to create a harmonious order among its citizens. Thus, because political power serves a legitimate end, all citizens, including Christians, are obligated to obey. It is only on those occasions when the state attempts to interfere with any of God's commandments that a Christian may legitimately disobey, and even then such disobedience does not imply the right to revolt.

By distinguishing among regimes according to the quality of their concerns, Augustine attempted to differentiate between the higher and lower orders. No regime is just, but all are not equally bad. Thus although it is impossible to perfect a political society, it is, nonetheless, possible to improve it. Such improvement, in turn, could best be achieved through an application of Christian principles. In Book V Augustine created the picture of

---

[17] Augustine, *The City of God*, p. 690.

ideal rulers and described the happiness of these ideal Christian princes in the following terms:

> But we say that they are happy if they rule justly; if they are not lifted up amid the praises of those who pay them sublime honours, and the obsequiousness of those who salute them with an excessive humility, but remember that they are men; if they make their power the handmaid of His majesty by using it for the greatest possible extension of His worship; if they fear, love, worship God; if more than their own they love that kingdom in which they are not afraid to have partners; if they are slow to punish, ready to pardon; if they apply that punishment as necessary to government and defence of the republic, and not in order to gratify their own enmity; if they grant pardon, not that iniquity may go unpunished, but with the hope that the transgressor may amend his ways; if they compensate with the lenity of mercy and the liberality of benevolence for whatever severity they may be compelled to decree; if their luxury is as much restrained as it might have been unrestrained; if they prefer to govern depraved desires rather than any nation whatever; and if they do all these things, not through ardent desire of empty glory, but through love of eternal felicity . . . [18]

It is apparent that for Augustine the application of Christian principles would necessarily improve the quality of political society. At the same time, although the church could not be equated with the city of God, it was for Augustine its representative. Thus the promulgation of Christian principles necessarily implied a socially activist church. By regarding the church as a higher society (inasmuch as it loved higher things), and by arguing for the political relevancy of Christian principles, Augustine seemed to suggest that the institutions of the church were above those of the state. In doing so he implicitly raised the question of the proper relationship between the temporal and spiritual powers. This question, in turn, would become one of the major issues throughout the Middle Ages. And, indeed, only with the privatization of religion in the seventeenth century would it begin to disappear.

BIBLIOGRAPHY

COCHRANE, CHARLES. *Christianity and Classical Culture.* Oxford: Oxford University Press, 1957.

COPLESTON, FREDERICK. *A History of Philosophy: Medieval Philosophy.* New York: Doubleday, 1962.

[18] Augustine, *The City of God*, p. 178.

D'ARCY, M. C., et al.   *Saint Augustine*. New York: Meridian Books, 1957.

DEANE, HERBERT A.   *The Political and Social Ideas of St. Augustine*. New York: Columbia University Press, 1963.

DODDS, E. R.   *Pagan & Christian in an Age of Anxiety*. New York: W. W. Norton & Co., 1970.

FIGGIS, J. N.   *The Political Aspects of St. Augustine's "The City of God."* London: Longmans, Green & Co., 1921.

JAEGER, WERNER.   *Early Christianity and Greek Paideia*. Oxford: Oxford University Press, 1969.

MARKUS, R. A.   *Augustine: A Collection of Critical Essays*. New York: Doubleday, 1972.

VOEGELIN, ERIC.   *The Ecumenic Age*. Baton Rouge: L.S.U. Press, 1974.

WAND, J.W.C.   *A History of the Early Church to* A.D. *500*. London: Methuen & Co., 1937.

5

THOMAS AQUINAS AND MEDIEVAL CHRISTIANITY

SACRUM ET IMPERIUM

When the Roman Empire finally adopted Christianity as its official state religion, it was immediately faced with the problem of establishing a proper harmony between the empire's temporal and spiritual powers. Indeed beginning already with Constantine, the Eastern empire's solution pointed towards a form of caesaropapism wherein the emperor assumed certain major ecclesiastical functions. Acting as both prince and bishop Constantine believed that his responsibility as emperor necessarily implied his involvement in religious affairs. Consequently as emperor he both appointed and deposed church patriarchs, set the boundaries for ecclesiastical jurisdictions, and oversaw the relations among clerics, monks, and the various church institutions. At the same time considering himself to be the vice-regent of God, he was concerned with the conversion of non-Christians and, as a consequence, involved himself in dogmatic and doctrinal matters.

According to the principles of caesaropapism, the Eastern emperors were understood to be ruling with God at their side. Thus the emperors too, became sacred, and their earthly kingdom consequently was enjoined with that of heaven. For example, in instructing his son, Romanos II (A.D. 959–963), about the emperor's special status, Constantine VII (913–959) wrote:

> And the Almighty shall cover thee with His shield. . . . Thy throne shall be as the sun before Him, and His eyes shall be looking towards thee, and naught of harm shall touch thee, for He hath chosen thee and set thee apart from thy mother's womb, and hath given unto thee His rule as unto one excellent above all men, and hath set thee as a refuge upon a hill and a statue of gold upon a high place, and as a city upon a mountain hath He raised thee up, that the nations may bring to thee their gifts and thou mayest be adored of them that dwell upon the earth.[1]

Having been selected by God, His emperors were charged with aiding in the completion of the divine plan for the world. As a consequence, their foremost duty was to lead their subjects to God by carefully preserving the truths of the Christian faith.

Not surprisingly, the western solution to the problem of coordinating the spiritual and temporal powers of the empire evolved in its own distinctive way. On one hand, this evolution was determined by the collapse of Byzantine (Eastern Roman) power in Italy, while on the other it was the result of the Papacy's strong reaction to imperial religious policy. Beginning in the fifth century and continuing for over three hundred years, the Latin (Western) church gradually began to distance itself from the Eastern empire. On theological matters the Western popes increasingly resented the Byzantine emperors' intrusion into what they considered to be strictly spiritual concerns. Situated in the East and therefore sensitive to the demands of Greek and Egyptian Christians, the Byzantine emperors had attempted on several occasions to strike a compromise between the monophysite heresies of the East and the orthodox doctrines preferred by the Latin hierarchy. In response, the popes insisted upon establishing a more rigid distinction between temporal and spiritual jurisdictions. Thus by denying the Byzantine emperors a role which they had traditionally claimed, the popes further weakened the ties between Rome and Constantinople.

The papal doctrine of separate spiritual and temporal powers received its classic expression in the writings of Pope Gelasius I (492–496). Referred to as the doctrine of the two swords, it established the Western alternative to Byzantine caesaropapism:

---

[1] As quoted in Harry Magoulias, *Byzantine Christianity: Emperor, Church and the West* (Chicago: Rand McNally, 1970), p. 8.

Admittedly, before the advent of Christ there actually existed—though in a prefigurative sense—men who were concurrently kings and priests; sacred history records that such a one was Saint Melchizedek [Gen. 14]. This the Devil, who always tyrannically arrogates to himself what is proper to divine worship, has imitated, so that pagan emperors caused themselves to be called supreme pontiffs. But when the One came who was truly King and Pontiff, then no emperor accepted the name of pontiff and no pontiff claimed the supreme dignity of king. Indeed, parts of Him—of the true King and Pontiff—splendidly obtained of either, in participation of His nature, so that there continue both a kingly and a priestly class. Christ, however, mindful of human frailty, has, by a marvelous dispensation, regulated what would serve the salvation of His own and has separated the offices of the two powers [*officia utriumque potestatis*] by means of distinctive functions and dignity, intending that His own should be saved by salutary humility and not be carried away by human pride. Hence, Christian emperors are in need of pontiffs for their eternal life, and pontiffs must make use of imperial regulations for temporal necessities.[2]

Papal resistance to the emperors was successful, in part, because of the fact that imperial power was actually declining within Italy itself. After the division of the empire and with the fall of Rome, the Byzantine emperors found it more and more difficult to exert their influence within the Western provinces. The presence of Germanic tribes, which had invaded the West, served at the same time to cut it off from the East. Thus by the sixth century, the Byzantine administration of Rome had collapsed, and the city was forced to turn to the organization of Pope Gregory (590–604) for its defense. Later during the Lombardian invasion of the Italian peninsula, it became apparent to everyone that the then-reigning Byzantine emperor was no longer able to defend his Western subjects. Accordingly, the pope faced with the need for protection was forced to seek a new alliance with another temporal power. Fortunately by that time the Kingdom of the Franks had emerged as a viable and willing alternative.

The Franks were one of the Germanic tribes that had swept across Europe during the period of the great migrations from A.D. 376 to 568. Typically upon settling down these tribes established kingdoms. Thus there was a Vandal kingdom in Africa, a Visigoth kingdom at Toulouse, and a Herulian kingdom in Italy. Generally, however, these societies were short-lived, and most were absorbed by larger movements after a brief period of self-rule. The one exception to this pattern, however, was the Kingdom of

---

[2] As quoted in Francis Dvornik, *Early Christian and Byzantine Political Philosophy: Origins and Background* (Washington, D.C.: The Dumbarton Oaks Center for Byzantine Studies, 1966), II, p. 807.

the Franks. They settled in the Roman province of Gaul and, being somewhat removed from Central Europe, avoided much of the destruction which characterized the general history of the migration period. By 739 the Franks had achieved such stability and power that Pope Gregory III wrote to their king, Charles Martel, to request aid against the Lombards. On Christmas day in the year 800 the pope crowned another Frankish king, Charlemagne, as the Holy Roman Emperor. With this event the break with Byzantium was finalized, and the Western solution to the problem of temporal and spiritual power was now able to evolve within the context of Gelasius's original doctrine of two swords.

Most commentators have typically treated the doctrine of the two swords as Gelasius's attempt to settle the relationship between the church and state. Yet, strictly speaking, the problem of church-state relationships was not the issue in the early Middle Ages. Indeed the terms "church" and "state" themselves, are inappropriate for that particular time. First, the modern concept of "state" implies a secular institution. Accordingly, in modern political thought the state is understood to be concerned with regulating its citizens' public behavior. Not immediately involved with the problems of their spiritual life, it relegates those concerns to such private institutions as the church or family. Second, the contemporary debate on church-state relationships is one whose primary interest lies in regulating the affairs of two separate societies—each seen as having its own particular purposes and distinct memberships. At the time of Gelasius, however, neither of these conditions existed. In practice, medieval politics was not a secular activity. In this aspect, at least, it continued the Platonic tradition by defining politics as that activity concerned with the health of the soul. In theory, then, medieval Europe was not composed of two societies, one secular and the other sacred. Rather Europe was the single society of Christendom. As a consequence any discussion of temporal and spiritual offices was, in fact, a discussion concerned with ordering the various ranks of its members within the single sphere of the Christian community. In this respect, then, Gelasius's doctrine of the two swords presupposed the integrity of the Christian mystical body. Thus as a single society constituted by the spiritual power of Christ, early medieval Europe transcended such modern dichotomies as church-state, secular-spiritual, or public-private. Indeed the distinction between the spiritual and temporal orders was a distinction which was, in itself, based upon the oneness of the Christian faith. As the historian Walter Ullmann has put it:

> Whilst the early and high Middle Ages did not distinguish between religious, political, moral (etc.) norms, but considered only the faithful, there was, nevertheless, a crucial distinction between the members of the Church, that is, the clergy and the laity. . . . Since

both constituted the Church, the problem of the relations between the two formed an essential topic in the Middle Ages. Clergy and laity were epitomized in priests and kings and focalized as priesthood (*sacerdotium*) and kingship (*regnum*).[3]

However, almost from the very foundation of the Holy Roman Empire, the Gelasian doctrine faced a series of challenges. On one hand because of local conditions within Italy, the Papacy, in violation of the Gelasian principle, soon acquired the characteristics of a temporal principality. On the other hand the Frankish monarchy acted at times in a theocratic manner and, thereby, implicitly challenged the jurisdictional distinctions which were at the base of the medieval order. In time these disputes became more intense, and ultimately by the twelfth century they signaled the end of the medieval Christian form of society.

Of the various disputes which arose within medieval Christendom, perhaps the most important began during the Papacy of Gregory VII. When Gregory assumed the papal throne in 1073, he began a series of reforms which were designed to purify the practices of the clergy and protect the church from the undue influence of temporal leaders. In particular, he wished to abolish the practice of simony whereby the clergy were able to purchase their ecclesiastical offices from temporal feudal lords. This practice not only resulted in the promotion of unworthy bishops but at the same time it limited the pope's influence over his own church officers. In 1075, therefore, the pope prohibited lay investiture and thereby effectively removed temporal rulers from the ecclesiastical selection process. Having prohibited simony, however, it became necessary to develop a series of sanctions which the pope could use against those princes who continued the forbidden practice in spite of the papal injunction. Thus the question of papal sanctions against temporal princes raised once again the issue of spiritual and temporal jurisdiction. When Emperor Henry IV appointed the bishop of Milan, Gregory reacted strongly. Henry, in turn, convened a council of nobles and bishops which acted to support his position and moved towards deposing the pope. Gregory responded by excommunicating the emperor and absolving all of his vassals from their oaths of loyalty to him. This conflict continued even after the deaths of the two men and was eventually resolved only in 1122 at the Diet of Worms. The so-called compromise at Worms was, in fact, a victory for the papal forces. The kings lost their semi-ecclesiastical functions and some of their control over church appointments, while the church was able to separate itself from the temporal authorities and thereby gain for itself a position of independent leadership within European society. Although both sides to this dispute acknowledged

[3] Walter Ullmann, *A History of Political Thought: The Middle Ages* (Baltimore: Penguin Books, 1965), p. 17.

the Gelasian principle and therefore addressed their arguments to what they believed should be the correct ranking of powers within the unity of Christendom, the fact of unity, itself, became increasingly difficult to maintain. Indeed, as time went on, both the *sacerdotium* and *regnum* evolved in a similar manner. On one hand, the sacred power hardened into an ecclesiastical organization that became increasingly preoccupied with the problems of institutional self-government and its legal relationships with the rest of society. On the other hand, the temporal power withdrew into its own autonomous realm and established thereby the grounds for the modern secular nation-state.

Although the tension between the temporal and spiritual powers was the most important factor contributing to the eventual dissolution of the Christian Empire, other forces also came into play. Theologically the idea of a single Christianity was challenged by the frequent appearance of various heretical movements throughout the Middle Ages. By their very nature heresies necessarily constituted a radical denial of the one Christian faith. For example, religious dualism which posited that satan and not God had created the world established a strong foothold in the Cathar churches of Italy and France. Similarly in the eleventh and first half of the twelfth centuries, a variety of millenial movements emerged throughout much of Western Europe. Generally the millenarians looked forward to a future age in which humankind would be both perfectly good and perfectly happy. In some of their more extreme versions, such as that developed by the Italian abbot Joachim of Fiore (1145–1202), the millenarians advocated an armed struggle against the forces of the pope, who was portrayed as being the antichrist as foretold in the Book of Daniel. Such movements obviously represented a theological diversification which denied the fact of there being only one church.

At the same time the empire was facing a similar process of political fragmentation. On its fringe, new national political units were emerging. Thus in England, Sicily, and France national regimes began the process of consolidating their rule by distancing themselves from both the pope and the Holy Roman emperor. Ultimately, with the development of the autonomous French and English monarchies, the empire was in fact reduced to its Germanic core. Consequently, it is possible to argue that by the thirteenth century, the dissolution of the Holy Roman Empire was essentially completed. Its dissolution, in turn, implied the beginnings of the modern nation-state. As Joseph Strayer writes:

> Thus in the centuries between 1000 and 1300 some of the essential elements of the modern state began to appear. Political entities, each with its own basic core of people and lands, gained legitimacy by enduring through generations. Permanent institutions for financial and judicial business were established. Groups of profes-

sional administrators were developed. A central coordinating agency, the chancery, had emerged with a staff of highly trained clerks. . . . These basic elements of the state appeared almost everywhere in Western Europe during the twelfth and thirteenth centuries. But while they appeared everywhere, their rate of growth was uneven. The rate was most rapid in England, France, and the Spanish Kingdoms; much less rapid in Germany; rapid but distorted in Italy.[4]

Ironically, it was during this period of dissolution and fragmentation that medieval Christianity produced its greatest intellectual and spiritual representative.

THE EARLY WORK OF THOMAS AQUINAS

Born near Naples around 1225, Thomas Aquinas was sent to the Benedictine abbey of Monte Casino at the age of five. As the son of an Italian noble he was expected to become a monk and thereby assume his rightful place within feudal society. When the monastery was closed by the troops of Emperor Frederick II, Aquinas went to the University of Naples and there began his study of the traditional liberal arts. In reading logic and astronomy he was introduced to the study of philosophy proper. In particular under the guidance of Peter of Ireland he read the logical, scientific, and cosmological works of Aristotle. In 1244 Thomas shocked his family by announcing that he had decided to become a Dominican friar. Unlike the Benedictines the Dominicans were not part of the established social order. Rather as itinerant preachers they lived among the urban poor and sustained themselves by begging. In a fit of rage his parents arranged for Thomas to be kidnapped and held prisoner for more than a year at the family castle. Once it became apparent that he would not change his mind, however, Thomas was released and sent by his order to Cologne so as to study under the tutelage of the learned Dominican friar, Albert the Great (1206–1280). Albert was a man of enormous curiosity and wide learning. Under his direction Thomas was soon exposed to the full range of Aristotle's thought, which had only recently become available in Latin translation.

In 1252 Albert decided that Thomas was ready for advanced study and sent him to Paris to pursue a Mastership in theology. There as part of his apprenticeship Thomas was required to deliver a series of lectures on the *Sentences* of Peter Lombard. As an anthology and commentary upon selected patristic and ecclesiastical texts Lombard's *Sentences* served as the standard textbook for the study of dogmatic theology. Consequently, at this

[4] Joseph R. Strayer, *On the Medieval Origins of the Modern State* (Princeton: Princeton University Press, 1970), pp. 34–35.

time, Thomas was concerned almost entirely with the study of the Bible. Nonetheless, he did manage to write two short manuals which were designed to introduce a beginning student to the terminology of Aristotelian physics and metaphysics. In 1256 Thomas finished his Mastership and assumed the Dominican chair of theology at the University of Paris. During the three years in which he held this position Thomas's principal duty was to lecture on the Bible. At the same time, however, he began but did not finish a commentary on Boethius and presided over a series of twenty-nine disputations which were later published as *Disputed Questions on Truth.*

In 1259 Thomas was called to serve at the papal court in Italy, where he spent his next six years teaching in Rome, Orvieto, and Viterbo. In addition to his instructional responsibilities Thomas served as an advisor to and consultant for the popes. In particular Pope Urban IV was interested in opposing the teachings of certain Greek theologians. He instructed Thomas to familiarize himself with both the writings of the Greek theologians and the teachings of the Eastern councils. The result of this effort was Aquinas's *Against the Errors of the Greeks.* Similarly at the pope's request, Thomas also wrote his *Catena Aurea* as a patristic commentary on the Gospels. From the philosophical perspective, however, the most important product of this Italian period was the encyclopedic *Summa contra Gentiles.*

The *Summa contra Gentiles* is important not only as the only complete summary of Christian doctrine that Thomas ever wrote but also as an example of his efforts to reconcile the apparently competing claims of reason and faith. Thomas originally wrote the four books of his *Summa contra Gentiles* at the request of a Dominican missionary who felt the need for a theological manual to instruct him during his efforts to gain converts among the non-Christians of Spain and North Africa. Among those who were being evangelized were Jews, pagans, and Moslems. Given this, Thomas had to draft his arguments in such a way as to appeal to the various groups involved. In particular in dealing with pagans and Moslems Thomas could not rely upon the authority of Scripture. As he wrote in the first chapter of Book I:

> . . . It is difficult because some of them, such as the Mohammedans and the pagans, do not agree with us in accepting the authority of any Scripture, by which they may be convinced of their error. Thus, against the Jews we are able to argue by means of the Old Testament, while against heretics we are able to argue by means of the New Testament. But the Mohammedans and the pagans accept neither the one nor the other. We must, therefore, have recourse to the natural reason, to which all men are forced to give their assent.[5]

[5] Thomas Aquinas, *Summa contra Gentiles*, trans. Anton Pegis (Garden City: Doubleday, 1955), I, p. 62.

It is clear from the above that for Thomas natural reason could be used in the service of Christianity. Rather than seeing reason as contradicting the true faith, he understood it to serve as its complement. The reason for this was contained in Thomas's acceptance of Aristotle's proposition that

> . . . the principles of eternal things are of necessity always the most true; for they are true not merely sometimes, nor is there anything which is the cause of their existence, but they are the cause of the existence of the other things accordingly, as each thing is related to its existence, so is it related to its truth.[6]

For Aristotle, then, truth was to be found in the cause of things and, in particular, in the first cause. For Thomas, inasmuch as God was the cause of everything, He was at the same time the source of all truth. Reason's search for the truth was, in fact, a search for God, and philosophy, as the search for the first principle, became the art of guiding people towards their proper end. As rational creatures humans seek the good of reason. Yet, inasmuch as the good of reason is truth, and inasmuch as God is the truth, humanity's natural rational end is God Himself. For Aquinas, then, reason is the means by which humans are oriented towards the transcendent. As the power by which humans participate in the order of being, reason necessarily refers humanity to the God who is both the cause and end of creation. Thus to rationally describe the world is to describe the truth of God, and to be wise is to live as one who is dedicated to the principles of spiritual order.

Because Thomas understood the world to be infused by the power of divine intelligence, for him the rational description of reality became a primary means by which humankind gained knowledge of the divine order itself. Thus in seeking to explain God to the pagans, Thomas believed that it was possible to appeal to the teachings of natural reason. In a sense, then, all people were naturally called to God, and by examining the principles of that calling as they operated through reason it would be possible to bring each to a recognition of his divine goal. According to Thomas, then, reason as science and philosophy was capable of reaching certain truths about the divine order, and in the first three books of his *Summa contra Gentiles* he sought to demonstrate those principles without the aid of revelation. Thus in Book I he attempted to rationally prove various truths about God's nature. For Thomas unaided reason could demonstrate that God existed, that He was eternal, unchanging, and immaterial, and that He was free from all composition. In Book II Thomas focused upon God's relationship with the world and discussed such themes as creation, hierarchy, and the human

---

[6] Aristotle, *Metaphysics*, trans. Hippocrates G. Apostle (Bloomington: Indiana University Press, 1973), p. 36.

soul. Book III was essentially a discussion of good and evil. It included a treatment of human happiness, divine providence, sexual ethics, and a consideration of rewards and punishments. What each of the first three books has in common, however, is its strict reliance upon arguments which were based solely upon the principles of natural reason. Yet as powerful as these arguments were for Thomas, they were necessarily imperfect; for, inasmuch as they were based solely upon human reasoning, they were incapable of grasping the richer and fuller truth of God Himself. For this higher knowledge human beings were dependent upon divine revelation, and, for Thomas, that revelation was the core of the Christian teaching:

> That there are certain truths about God that totally surpass man's ability appears with the greatest evidence . . . the human intellect is not able to reach a comprehension of the divine substance through its natural power. . . . Yet beginning with sensible things, our intellect is led to the point of knowing about God that He exists, and other such characteristics that must be attributed to the First Principle. There are, consequently, some intelligible truths about God that are open to the human reason; but there are others that absolutely surpass its power.[7]

Given this understanding, Thomas saw revelation as a suprarational rather than as an irrational power. The teachings of revealed Christianity went beyond reason but did not contradict it; for, inasmuch as reason was correct, it, too, was informed by that same divine truth which was revealed in the person of Christ. Thus in Book IV Thomas introduced those supplemental teachings which were available to humanity only because God had chosen to reveal His nature. For example, although reason could demonstrate God's existence, only revelation could establish His trinitarian nature. And although reason could specify several aspects of God's relationship with the world, only revelation could teach the truth of the Incarnation. Finally, although reason could establish a natural ethics which directed humans towards happiness, only Christian revelation could attest to the believer's resurrection after death and final happiness in the presence of God Himself. In each case, then, revelation introduced a higher supernatural truth which complemented the natural needs of rational minds. The intellect necessarily led to Christian results, Thomas maintained, and it was this fact which accounted for his faith in the possibility of spreading the Christian message to all the world.

Thomas achieved his synthesis between philosophy and religion by bringing together the teachings of Christian theology and classical Greek philosophy. Although he drew upon such writers as St. Augustine, the

[7] Aquinas, *Summa contra Gentiles*, I, pp. 63–64.

Pseudo-Dionysius, Maimonides, and selected Arabian philosophers, his primary source for this task was Aristotle. When the emperor Justinian closed the schools of philosophy in Athens in 529 Aristotelian scholarship entered into a long period of decline. Although some of the logical works were known from the commentaries and translations of Boethius (480–525), it was only in the twelfth century that Aristotle's works once again achieved a wide circulation. The primary reason for this renewed interest was due to the influence of Latin translations of Arabic texts and commentaries which reached Europe through Spain. Among the Arabic commentators the most important was Averroes (1126–1198), and in many cases it was Averroes' interpretation of Aristotle which established the "official" version of Aristotelianism. Although Aristotle's logic had been accepted and studied in Western universities for a number of years, certain of his physical and metaphysical doctrines were seen as a challenge to Christian orthodoxy. In 1210 the council of Paris forbade the study of his natural philosophy, and in 1231 and 1263 papal bulls were issued which reinforced this original decree.

For his part, Thomas sought to accommodate Aristotelianism to Christianity. Thus in developing his position he attempted to correct some of the misinterpretations of the Averroists which in their radical form appeared to contradict Christian teachings. Two issues were of primary importance. First, the Averroist interpretation of Aristotle's understanding of the active and the receptive intellect appeared to challenge the Christian belief in personal immortality. In response, Aquinas wrote his *On the Unity of the Intellect*. As a detailed exegesis of Aristotle's *De Anima* it demonstrated the errors of the Averroist interpretation and thereby reduced the distance between the Aristotelian and Christian positions. The second contested issue was concerned with the eternity of the world. The Averroists taught that Aristotle had demonstrated the eternity of the world; the church's position, on the other hand, stated that reason was capable of proving that God had existed before the world was created and thus that it could not be eternal. For his part, Thomas sought a middle way. In his *On the Eternity of the World*, he argued that neither position could be established solely by reason and, as a consequence, that the doctrine of creation in time had to be accepted in faith as a revealed truth. In so arguing, he defended Aristotle against the charge that he had contradicted himself but, at the same time, accepted the ultimate truth of the Church's position.

In his effort to defend a moderate Aristotelianism, Aquinas undertook the task of writing a series of commentaries based upon the philosopher's original works. Using a Latin translation from the original Greek Thomas wrote detailed commentaries on Aristotle's *De Anima, Physics, De Interpretatione, Posterior Analytics, Nicomachean Ethics*, and *Metaphysics*. In addition at his death he left six other unfinished commentaries;

one of which was on Aristotle's *Politics*. Attesting to the eventual success of Thomas's efforts to incorporate Aristotelianism into Catholic doctrine is the fact that by the nineteenth and twentieth centuries Thomistic philosophy had achieved a unique authority among the church's teachings: he had become in some respects Catholicism's "official philosopher."

With the death of Pope Urban IV in 1265, Thomas left the papal court in order to set up a Dominican house of studies in Rome while teaching theology at one of the city's local churches. While teaching the younger theologians Aquinas decided to write his own introductory textbook as a replacement for the traditional *Sentences* of Peter Lombard. This project, in turn, resulted in the eventual publication of his theological masterpiece, the *Summa Theologica*. Containing three parts, Thomas's text was intended primarily for Catholic students of theology. Consequently in drafting his arguments Aquinas was able to draw from both reason and revelation. He did so, however, without abandoning the fundamental distinctions which he first developed in the *Summa contra Gentiles*. Thomas's *Summa Theologica* is generally considered to be his most mature and developed work.

The first part of the *Summa Theologica* covers much of the same ground as Books I and II of the earlier work. Thus it develops such topics as the existence and nature of God, humanity's knowledge of God, the creation, and problems in cosmogony. The lengthy second part is, in effect, a Christian treatise on ethics and, as such, corresponds to the third book of the earlier *Summa contra Gentiles*. It, in turn, is divided into two sections. The first, modeled after Aristotle's *Nicomachean Ethics*, begins with a discussion of human happiness and develops the relative contributions of the intellectual and moral virtues to the good life. In addition, it considers the role of the theological virtues of faith, hope, and charity and concludes with a discussion of law and grace. The second section of the second part is Thomas's detailed examination of individual moral topics in which the various virtues are contrasted with their corresponding sins. Here, for example, he discusses such concepts as prudence, justice, courage, and temperance. The third and final part of the *Summa Theologica* is concerned strictly with theological topics. Beginning with an examination of the Incarnation it includes a discussion of the Virgin Mary and the life of Christ and finishes with an analysis of the sacraments of baptism, confirmation, the eucharist, and penance. Although Thomas did not live to complete this book, it is considered to be his greatest work, with wide-ranging impact in fields beyond theology itself. Political theorists have been particularly interested in the arguments of the second part; for it is these arguments which provide the context for his specifically political teachings.

In 1268 Thomas returned to France to assume once again the Dominican chair in theology at the University of Paris. During the next four years, he worked on the second part of his *Summa Theologica* and continued in his defense of Aristotelian philosophy. In 1272 he left Paris again in order to establish a Dominican house of theology in Naples. There, on December 6, 1273, while saying Mass, Thomas experienced a vision which he interpreted as signaling the end of his scholarly activity. Thus despite repeated pleas from various church leaders, he refused to write anything more from that day forward, and, on March 7, 1274, he died while on his way to a general council of the church. In 1323 Pope John XXII declared Thomas to be a saint of the Roman Catholic Church.

AQUINAS'S POLITICAL WRITINGS

Aquinas's essential political teachings are contained in a small manuscript entitled *On the Governance of Rulers (De Regimine Principum)* which was begun during Thomas's second stay in Rome, probably around 1265. The treatise was dedicated to the King of Cyprus, most probably Hugo II, and was left unfinished when the student-king died at the age of 17 in 1267. Thomas himself completed all of the first book and the first four chapters of the second before abandoning the project. Thus it was left to his pupil, Ptolemy of Lucca, to finish the remaining sections. In his dedication, Thomas stated his purpose to be:

> . . . [to] write a book on government, in which . . . I should care-fully expound according to the authority of Holy Writ and the teachings of the philosophers as well as the practice of worthy princes, both the origin of government and the things which per-tain to the office of a ruler . . . [8]

In structuring his arguments, Thomas followed rather closely the model provided by Aristotle's *Politics.* Thus in Book I he followed Aristotle's lead by examining the nature of political life, the various forms of govern-ment, and the relationship of politics to virtue and human happiness. Similarly the extant chapters of Book II discuss various items which must be considered in both the selection of sites for and the foundation of new regimes. Thus in some ways Book II represents a close and subsequently out-dated imitation of Book VII of Aristotle's *Politics.*

In returning to the Aristotelian tradition with its concern for the naturalness of political life, Thomas necessarily broke with several of Augustine's political teachings. As has been shown, Augustine believed that political society was the direct result of the corruption of human nature through sin. Aquinas, on the other hand, believed that political existence

---

[8] Thomas Aquinas, *On the Governance of Rulers,* trans. Gerald Phelan (New York: Sheed & Ward, 1938), p. 29.

was a natural condition and thus that political society would have existed even if humankind had never sinned. Even in the state of innocence the relationship of ruler to ruled would have existed by necessity. Given this, Aquinas acknowledged that the political relationship within a state of innocence would be somewhat different from the political relationship that actually existed among citizens as they are. For example, prior to sin political authority would not require the exercise of coercion. Similarly the ruler would not have to be concerned with guaranteeing the conditions for material existence nor with securing the means for the citizens' moral and civic betterment. Nonetheless, even among perfectly good citizens, political authority would be required so that the wisest of the good could serve as guides for the others.

According to Aquinas humanity's natural need for authority can be traced back to its rational nature. In order for human reason to develop, individuals must collaborate and thereby, through the division of labor, gain as a species that knowledge which is impossible for each to acquire alone. As rational creatures, human beings are political precisely because they, unlike the animals, are rational:

> Moreover, all other animals are able to discern by inborn skill what is useful and what is injurious; just as the sheep naturally regards the wolf as his enemy. . . . Man, however, has a natural knowledge of the things which are essential for his life only in a general fashion, inasmuch as he has power of attaining knowledge of the particular things necessary for human life by reasoning from universal principles. But it is not possible for one man to arrive at a knowledge of all things by his own individual reason. It is, therefore, necessary for man to live in a group so that each one may assist his fellows, and different men may be occupied in seeking by their reason to make different discoveries, one, for example, in medicine, one in this and another in that.[9]

For Aquinas human reason, untainted by sin, implied both the division of labor and the power of speech. Thus humankind's rationality, itself, seemed to require that society exist. Society, in turn, comes into existence only when a number of individuals are brought together in a united effort to achieve a common end. This, in turn, requires coordination—not because people are sinful but because of the legitimate differences between the individual and the whole:

> If, therefore, it is natural for man to live in the society of many, it is necessary that there exist among men some means by which the group may be governed. For where there are many men together,

[9] Aquinas, *On the Governance of Rulers*, pp. 34–35.

and each one is looking after his own interest, the group would be broken up and scattered unless there were also someone to take care of what appertains to the common weal. . . . Indeed it is reasonable that this happen, for what is proper and what is common are not identical. Things differ by what is proper to each; they are united by what they have in common. For, diversity of effects is due to diversity of causes. Consequently there must exist something which impels towards the common good of the many, over and above that which impels towards the private good of each individual.[10]

Thus for Aquinas, even within a state of innocence humanity's very nature implied its sociality and its sociality, in turn, required the coordinating power of a hierarchical authority. The state, as a consequence, was not seen primarily as a necessary evil but as an actual and positive good. Summarizing Aquinas's teachings on this point, Professor Dino Bigongiari remarks:

> A state according to St. Thomas is a part of the universal empire of which God is the maker and ruler. Its laws are, or can be made to be, particular determinations of this empire's eternal code; and the authority which enforces these laws is a power whose origin is also in God. Its goal and justification is to offer man satisfactory material conditions of life as a basis for a moral and intellectual education which, in turn, must be such as to lend itself to the spiritual edification of the Christian man.[11]

Even though Aquinas returned to the political tradition of Aristotle, he did so as a Christian. Thus although he understood political society to be natural, he was at the same time deeply aware of the human race's sinful condition. In the state of innocence those in authority could rely upon the spontaneous obedience of their subjects; but after humanity's fall coercion became necessary so as to assure proper compliance with the law. Thus because of human sin, God grants political authorities the dual power of making laws and enforcing their observance through the threat of punishment. Such power is legitimate, in turn, if it is acquired rightly, exercised justly, and used for the common good:

> If, therefore, a group of free men is governed by their ruler for the common good of the group, that government will be right and just, as is suitable to free men. If, however, the government is organized, not for the common good of the group but for the private interest of the ruler, it will be an unjust and perverted government.[12]

---

[10] Aquinas, *On the Governance of Rulers*, pp. 35–36.

[11] Dino Bigongiari, *The Political Ideas of St. Thomas Aquinas* (New York: Hafner Publishing Co., 1953), p. vii.

[12] Aquinas, *On the Governance of Rulers*, p. 37.

This distinction, of course, was borrowed from Aristotle, and like Aristotle Thomas used it to establish a scheme according to which various regimes could be classified. Those regimes pursuing the common good could be classified as kingships, aristocracies, and timocracies depending upon whether they were ruled by the one, the few, or the many. Their corrupted counterparts, on the other hand, were tyranny, oligarchy, and democracy. Unlike Aristotle, however, Thomas did not accept the doctrine of natural slavery; for him the truly natural human was the free and spiritually mature Christian.

Having distinguished among the six types of regimes, Thomas argued that in general political monarchy was the best possible form. Theoretically, regimes ruled justly by one prudent king or queen would be better able to preserve that fundamental social unity which was required for peace and security. In addition, the relationship of monarchs to their people would be natural inasmuch as it would be analogous to God's relationship with His creation and the soul's relationship with its body. Yet, just as monarchy is the best possible regime, so, too, is its opposite, tyranny, the worst. Thus every precaution must be taken in order to prevent monarchs from becoming tyrants. On one hand, candidates for kingship should be carefully screened so that only the virtuous are chosen. Yet, on the other hand, the reality of human sinfulness requires that certain limits on the kingly power be established by the imposition of constitutional institutions. Drawing upon the teachings of Aristotle, the Roman constitution, and the Old Testament discussion of kingship and democracy, Thomas argued that a constitution which involved the various classes of society in some form of mixed rule would prove to be both the most stable and the most satisfying. Its stability would prevent the chaos out of which tyrannies emerged, and its openness to the major classes would allow people to satisfy their natural desire to participate in political life. If these precautions failed, however, and a tyranny did develop, Thomas refused to allow for the practice of tyrannicide. Rather than killing the tyrant, a people should tolerate the evils of such rule for the sake of ensuring stability. If the tyranny becomes extreme, however, the society may legally resist the tyrant by either deposing the oppressor or appealing to a higher authority.

Following Aristotle, Thomas argued that the purpose of society was to pursue the good life. The good life, in turn, was that which promoted human happiness, and human happiness essentially consisted in living the life of virtue. Thus it was that this goal established the primary duties of kings. In order that virtue be fostered and preserved, citizens require both a sufficiency of material goods and the development of proper moral habits. Good rulers are those who guide society in such a manner as to provide both the economic and educational basis for moral well-being.

To this point, Aquinas had followed Aristotle rather closely. Like

Aristotle, he based his political theory upon a eudaemonistic and teleological ethical system. Accordingly human nature was understood to require that people live in a certain way, and it was the fulfillment of that requirement which produced the condition of happiness. For Aristotle such a condition was actualized when citizens engaged in the life of philosophical contemplation. Thus for him the philosopher was the truly happy person. Aquinas, however, was a Christian and, as a Christian, he experienced the action of God upon humanity in history. Thus although the virtuous life of philosophy represented a certain human excellence, the highest human happiness necessarily resulted from an act of God upon humans. Salvation rather than contemplation was the specific prerequisite for full human happiness, and salvation was a gift from God bestowed upon humanity because of God's love for His people. For Aquinas, therefore, it was the saint and not the philosopher who was the truly happy person. Thus whereas the philosopher's contemplation of God represented a certain natural excellence, the saint's enjoyment of the beatific vision was actually a supernatural accomplishment made possible by the grace of God.

By subordinating contemplation to salvation, Aquinas necessarily limited the goals and functions of political society. Inasmuch as the pursuit of the moral life was no longer the final end for humankind, political authority could no longer claim to be the final authority. As a result, society's goal, moral and intellectual virtue, retained its value but was now subordinated to the higher and ultimate end of spiritual perfection. In pointing to an end beyond itself, political society was transformed into being a necessary but insufficient condition for ultimate human happiness:

> Therefore, since man, by living virtuously is ordained to a higher end, which consists of the enjoyment of God. . . then human society must have the same end as the individual man. Therefore, it is not the ultimate end of an assembled multitude to live virtuously, but through virtuous living to attain to the possession of God.[13]

For Aquinas, the good political society served an important but ultimately instrumental role. Kings were to order those things which were within their domains but they, in turn, were to be ordered by those who were charged with caring for human spiritual perfection. In short, for Thomas the kings were to be subject to priests in general and to the Roman pope in particular:

> Furthermore if it could attain this end [possession of God] by the power of human nature, then the duty of a king would have to include the direction of men to this end. . . . But, because a man does

---

[13] Aquinas, *On the Governance of Rulers*, pp. 97–98.

not attain his end which is the possession of God, by human power, but by Divine power . . . therefore the task of leading him to that end does not pertain to human government but to divine.[14]

Thomas's understanding of the proper relationship between the church and the state was based ultimately on his understanding of the hierarchy among human ends. For Aquinas humanity has both a natural and a supernatural goal. Thus the superiority of the supernatural over the natural implied the superiority of the church over the state. Yet inasmuch as the supernatural does not negate but rather supplements the order of nature, the church had no reason to interfere with the state as long as the temporal government exercised its own proper functions correctly. As a consequence the church's political authority was understood to operate indirectly, and church sovereignty was thereby delegated to the officers of the state.

AQUINAS AND THE NATURAL-LAW TRADITION

Thomas's greatest contribution to legal theory is not found in his *On the Governance of Rulers* but rather in a segment within the first part of the second section of his *Summa Theologica*. This placement is important because it indicates Thomas's understanding of the function and purpose of law itself. According to Thomas's theology God is the external principle who draws all people towards Himself in two distinct but complementary ways. First, He aids humanity by granting it the gift of grace; second, He instructs it through the teachings of the law. Thus for Thomas law functions within a specifically theological context: its purpose, to instruct humankind by motivating it to act in such a way as to fulfill God's original design. In this perspective, the law is not primarily a set of restrictions but rather a positive means for the attainment of human beatitude. Its authority, in turn, is ultimately derived from the fact that it is based upon that divine order which determines the rational structure of the universe.

By associating the moral authority of the law with its basis in divine rationality, Thomas's arguments represent both a continuation and a development of the natural-law tradition. As has been shown, this tradition found its earliest formal expression in Stoicism. For example, in Cicero, nature manifested both a material and moral order. Thus through the use of right reason, humanity was able to discover certain natural laws which could serve as standards for the determination of right and wrong. As

[14] Aquinas, *On the Governance of Rulers*, p. 98.

precepts of nature rather than of humankind, these laws were understood to be universally valid and thus functioned to bind all people together in a community of reason under God.

The Stoic understanding of natural law was modified and developed by several generations of Roman jurists. For example, the commentaries of Gaius and Ulpian, with the latter's emphasis upon human freedom and equality, were preserved in extracts collected during the preparation of Justinian's *Corpus of Civil Law* which was originally published around A.D. 533. Indeed, with the reemergence of interest in Roman Law during the twelfth and thirteenth centuries Justinian's code became a major source for the transmission of the natural-law tradition into medieval Europe. Although the early Christians were generally suspicious of pagan thought, the natural-law doctrine of the Stoics found an extremely receptive audience among Christian thinkers. This sympathetic reception may be explained, in part, by three features of medieval Christendom. First, Christian moral theory could easily accommodate specific Stoic teachings. Second, the Christian view of nature supported a positive interpretation of the natural order. And finally, specific doctrines within the church's own canon law contained elements of an undifferentiated natural-law theory.

An example of the compatibility between Christian and Stoic morality can be found in the ethical teachings of St. Paul. On several occasions, Paul referred to the symbol of the mystical body of Christ. As such, he spoke of one, universal humankind which was formed as a single community through the transforming power of the spirit of Christ. With this emphasis upon the universal family of humankind and its common spiritual heritage, the Christian concept of the mystical body was obviously a symbolic equivalent to the older Stoic conception of the cosmopolis. More specifically, in his *Epistle to the Romans,* Paul spoke of a moral law written in the hearts of the Gentiles which instructed them in their duties toward God and his people. Although this reference to the human conscience suggested an intuitional rather than a rationalistic mode, it is not difficult to see its similarity with the traditional Stoic doctrine of natural reason.

In granting a moral authority to the principles of nature, the natural-law tradition assumed that nature was capable of serving as a model for humanity. This assumption concerning the character of nature itself found support in the Christian attitude towards the world. For the Christians the material world was good because it was created by a good God. After describing the days of creation, chapter one of the *Book of Genesis* concluded by claiming, "And it was so. And God saw everything that He had made, and behold it was very good." [15] Inasmuch as nature carried God's imprint, it necessarily manifested a certain dignity and value. As

[15] *The Holy Bible*, Revised Standard Version (Cleveland: World Publishing Co., 1962), p. 2.

a consequence, nature, especially in its uncorrupted form before the human race's fall, was understood to be an expression of God's original intention for humankind. As such, it could serve as a standard or norm to which all people should aspire.

A final feature which helps explain the medieval adoption of the natural-law tradition can be found in the juristic writings of the canon lawyers. By the twelfth century the church had become aware of its need to collect and codify its laws and pronouncements. Accordingly, in 1139 the Bolognese monk, Gratian, published his *Concordantia Discordantium Canonum*, also referred to as the *Decretum*. As a collection of church law, the *Decretum* was intended to serve as a textbook for those who were studying canon law in the universities. Influenced by both the early church teachers and the ancient Roman jurists, Gratian referred in his work to the doctrine of natural law and seemed to equate it with the divine law of Scripture:

> The human race is ruled in two ways: by natural law and by custom. Natural law is what is contained in the Old and New Testaments which commands every man to do unto another what he would have done unto himself and forbids him to do unto another what he would not have done unto himself.[16]

This seeming identification of natural law with divine law was characteristic of most canon lawyers. Although this association led to a certain theoretical ambiguity, there is no doubt that the canon jurists played a major role in preserving the natural-law tradition throughout Christian Europe. As the political scientist Paul Sigmund writes:

> The canon law was an important influence in transmitting patristic conceptions of natural law to medieval Europe, in particular the belief in freedom and communal ownership as the original and natural state of man. What it added was the assertion that a conflict between natural law and an existing legal provision was grounds for annulment of the positive law. . . . The canon lawyers did little, however, to develop the concepts taken over from the Roman writers. The creative thinking was done by the theologians, and especially by the greatest of the medieval writers on theology, St. Thomas Aquinas.[17]

As this statement indicates, Thomas is typically considered to be medieval Europe's greatest natural-law theoretician.

[16] As quoted in Paul Sigmund, *Natural Law in Political Thought* (Cambridge: Winthrop Publishers, 1971), p. 48.
[17] Sigmund, *Natural Law in Political Thought*, pp. 38–39.

Aquinas's discussion of natural law is situated within his general examination of law as such. As has been shown, Thomas understood the law to be a form of instruction concerning humanity's pursuit of the common good. Thus he defines law as, "an ordinance of reason for the common good made by him who has care of the community, and promulgated."[18] Several features of this definition deserve further comment. First, according to Thomas's understanding, unless a rule is both rational and at the same time concerned for the common good, it is not a true law. Thus in order for a rule to be a true law, it must meet certain substantive criteria. In short, morality is made the basis of legality, and those who are empowered to legislate are at the same time bound by the limits of the moral order. Thus for Thomas it is right reason and not the will of the sovereign which is the source of that obligation imposed by all true law.

Second, Thomas's definition of law describes its general function. Inasmuch as this function can be accomplished in several different ways, this definition is applicable, in turn, to several different types of law. Indeed, in his *Summa Theologica*, Thomas wished to distinguish among four types in particular, each of which, however, functioned in the manner described above. The first type of law is the eternal law, and according to Thomas it is "the Divine Reason's conception of things."[19] As such, the eternal law is that dictate of practical reason by which God governs the universe. As God's creation, the universe is imprinted with the order of divine reason and to that degree can be said to partake of the eternal law. Human beings, however, as rational creatures participate more directly in the eternal law because they partially share in that divine *ratio* which is its source. This participation by humanity in the eternal law is called natural law, and Thomas describes it as follows:

> Now among all others, the rational creature is subject to Divine providence in the most excellent way, in so far as it partakes of a share of providence, by being provident both for itself and for others. Wherefore it has a share of the Eternal Reason, whereby it has a natural inclination to its proper act and end: and this participation of the eternal law in the rational creature is called the natural law.[20]

For Thomas the natural law is the means by which Christians are able to partially discern God's plan for themselves and the world. Operating according to a direct moral intuition, it provides them with a standard by

[18] Thomas Aquinas, *Treatise on Law*, ed. Stanley Parry (Chicago: Henry Regnery Co., n.d.) pp. 10–11.

[19] Aquinas, *Treatise on Law*, p. 15.

[20] Aquinas, *Treatise on Law*, p. 15.

which they can discern good from evil. Thus by examining its natural inclinations humanity is able to arrive at a limited understanding of what it is that God wishes it to accomplish. Having been created with a given nature humanity is required to satisfy specific needs. The natural law, in turn, instructs humankind concerning this project. Yet, given the limits of human nature, such instruction is necessarily restricted to the most general of principles. For example, inasmuch as people are living creatures, the natural law requires that they be concerned with their self-preservation and the preservation of the species through procreation and education. Similarly inasmuch as people are also rational creatures, the natural law requires that they preserve their rational nature by seeking a knowledge of God and by participating in the civilizing processes of society.

These tenets of the natural law are obviously general and imprecise. Although at several places within his *Summa* Thomas specifies certain particular practices as "unnatural," for example, adultery, usury, and gluttony, the natural law is by its very nature both universal and nonparticular. Given this its teachings must be adapted and applied to the specific conditions of particular situations. To do so, people create human laws which both specify the general teachings of natural reason and add to this the power of compulsion as a means of enforcing the laws' moral claims. From Thomas's perspective, therefore, the laws of various societies are different inasmuch as they must acknowledge and reflect the differing conditions particular to each. However, although circumstances may require that laws differ from one another, they all nonetheless acquire their authority as law precisely because they share in the rule of right reason.

If humans were purely natural beings, fulfilling the natural law would be a sufficient guarantee of their excellence. Yet, as has been shown, Thomas as a Christian understood humankind to have both a natural and a supernatural destiny. This second or transcendental purpose, in turn, requires special instruction, and for Thomas that was available in the unique revelations of the Old and New Testaments. Thus a fourth and final type of law was to be found in divine law, which consisted of those revelations to the faithful that permitted them to share more perfectly in the dictates of the eternal law. As faith complemented reason, so, too, did the divine law complement and expand the teachings of nature.

To a large extent, Thomas's importance in Western political thought can be explained in terms of his ability to synthesize the major intellectual forces of his day. He not only attempted to harmonize the teachings of pagan antiquity with those of medieval Christianity, but, at the same time, he sought to express this harmony in a language that was appropriate within an increasingly modern environment. In doing so, he managed to create a viable intellectual and cultural framework for his day. Thus as the historian Henry Adams wrote:

> Compared with it [Thomism] all modern systems are complex and chaotic, crowded with self-contradictions, anomalies, impractible functions and outworn inheritances; but beyond all their practical short-comings is their fragmentary character. An economic civilization troubles itself about the universe much as a hive of honeybees troubles itself about the ocean, only as a region to be avoided. The hive of St. Thomas sheltered God and man, mind and matter, the universe and the atom, the one and the multiple, within the walls of an harmonious home.[21]

Thomas's harmonious home was not the result of his attempt to build a dogmatic system. Indeed at the center of his thought was the denial that such a system was possible. For Thomas, knowledge of ultimate reality was characterized by its negative quality. Thus rather than knowing what God was, a person could, at best, only know what He was not. Such knowledge, in turn, was incapable of producing a dogmatic system. Thus rather than claiming positive certitude, it could only rely upon the use of creative analogies. As such, the harmonizing skills of Thomas can not be attributed to the discipline required of a dogmatist. Rather they were the result of the intense spirituality of his personality. As a saint Thomas focused his whole existence upon God, and it was this single focus, in turn, which gave an order and structure to all that he wrote.

BIBLIOGRAPHY

COPLESTON, FREDERICK.   *Aquinas.* Baltimore: Penguin, 1955.

COPLESTON, FREDERICK.   *Medieval Philosophy.* New York: Harper & Row, 1961.

GIERKE, OTTO.   *Political Theories of the Middle Age.* Translated by Frederic William Maitland. Boston: Beacon Press, 1958.

GILSON, ETIENNE.   *Reason and Revelation in the Middle Ages.* New York: Charles Scribner's Sons, 1938.

HEARNSHAW, F.J.C., ed.   *Medieval Contributions to Modern Civilization.* New York: Barnes & Noble, 1967.

HEARNSHAW, F.J.C., ed.   *The Social and Political Ideas of Some Great Medieval Thinkers.* New York: Barnes & Noble, 1967.

JAFFA, HARRY.   *Thomism and Aristotelianism.* Chicago: University of Chicago Press, 1952.

KENNY, ANTHONY.   *Aquinas.* New York: Hill and Wang, 1980.

KENNY, ANTHONY.   *Aquinas: A Collection of Critical Essays.* London: Macmillan, 1969.

---

[21] As quoted in Albert William Levi, *Philosophy as Social Expression* (Chicago: University of Chicago Press, 1974), p. 162.

MARITAIN, JACQUES. *St. Thomas Aquinas.* New York: Sleed and Ward, 1946.

ROMMEN, HEINRICH. *The State in Catholic Thought.* St. Louis: B. Herder, 1945.

STRAYER, JOSEPH R. *On the Medieval Origins of the Modern State.* Princeton: Princeton University Press, 1970.

ULLMANN, WALTER. *A History of Political Thought: The Middle Ages.* Baltimore: Penguin, 1965.

WEISHEIPL, JAMES. *Friar Thomas d'Aquino.* London: Blackwell, 1974.

Birth of Modernity: In Search of a New Order

6

MACHIAVELLI

RISE OF THE NATION-STATE AND ITALIAN POLITICS

With the victory of the Roman Catholic church over the Holy Roman emperor in the investiture conflict, the empire could no longer realistically claim to be the dominant source of political order for Western Europe. Yet this particular struggle was only one of the many indications that new forces were sweeping Europe. Indeed between 1000 and 1300 many of the essential features of the modern nation-state system began to appear. They arose, however, against a background formed by the waning of feudalism.

Feudalism was essentially a system of reciprocal rights and obligations based upon a hierarchical organization of personal and legal relationships. Inasmuch as there was no strict separation between the public and private system, the distinction between political authority and personal rights was imprecise. One's deepest loyalties were to such local units as family, lord, community, or church. Consequently there were few permanent institutions which could organize people for large-scale social projects.

Power was diffuse rather than concentrated, and economic production was regulated both according to the needs of the producer and the values of Christianity.

Beginning in 1000 Europe entered into a period of increasing stability and prosperity. The population grew, argicultural production increased, commercial trade expanded, and a relatively large educated class began to develop. Typically these changes placed a certain strain on the feudal system. For example, with the development of significant commercial activity a new merchant class emerged and quickly gained in both power and importance. This class bought goods not to consume them but in order to trade and sell them. Socially the new income created by this activity soon produced a challenge to the principles and position of those who benefited from the traditional land-based form of wealth. Economically the customary feudal restraints on production were increasingly perceived by the commercial classes as unacceptable restrictions upon their economic activity and trade.

Feudalism typically had dispersed political power among a large number of local organizations. Feudal estates, free city-states, and bishops' jurisdictions tended to check one another and thereby served as the basis for medieval constitutionalism. In addition the monarchs generally found themselves limited by national parliaments which were securely in the hands of the landed nobility.

Large-scale commercial trading, however, required territorial integrity. Travel would have to be safe, uniform standards of weights and measures would have to be regulated, permanent institutions to oversee financial and judicial affairs would have to be created, and general systems of taxation would have to be introduced.

In addition to creating and financing standing military armies in order to secure territorial integrity, societies found that new public bureaucracies and trained labor were necessary to support the diverse activity of nation-state building. In many cases, this process was welcomed by politically ambitious national monarchs who saw the centralized and efficient nation-state as a practical means by which to consolidate their rule. The first societies in Europe to adjust to the new forces were France and England.

During the Hundred Years' War (1339–1453) the feudal institutions of both societies collapsed under the strain of prolonged military engagement. As a consequence both monarchies took action to consolidate their rule. In England the Tudors secured royal power for themselves with victory in the War of the Roses in 1485. In France Louis XI established an absolute monarchy by decree in 1469. With the defeat of the Anjou in 1480 this arrangement was further secured. A similar process was underway in

Spain—although at a slower rate. The marriage of Ferdinand and Isabella united the territories of Aragon and Castile, and with the victory over the Moors at Granada in 1492 the Spanish monarchy cemented its hold on national power. Yet while England and France were evolving as nation-states, both Italy and Germany failed to participate in this development. Indeed, the Italian failure was the immediate occasion for Machiavelli's political writings.

As France, England, and Spain developed highly centralized monarchies and fielded the large armies that such consolidation made possible, Italy continued in a feudal arrangement. The peninsula was largely divided among five political forces: The Papal States (which were, in fact, a collection of semiautonomous fiefdoms acknowledging some sort of theoretical tie to the pope); Florence; Milan; Venice; and the Kingdom of Naples. A fragile stability was maintained by a balance of power among the five. Groups of city-states would form temporary coalitions which provided an uneasy working arrangement and, at the same time, prevented any one from gaining inordinate power. Although the Papal States under Alexander and Julius II entertained the idea of unifying all of Italy under its leadership, generally speaking, none of the five commanded sufficient forces to impose its design upon the others.

This weakness led to the practice of inviting in foreign troops in an effort to accomplish regional aims. A secret alliance between Naples and Florence led Ludovico Sforza of Milan to invite in the French troops of Charles VIII in 1494. Although the French did not accomplish their immediate goal of conquering Naples, the ease of their advance through Italy was apparent to all. In 1499 the French were back, and their renewed success encouraged the Spanish to undertake similar adventures.

To protect themselves against such invasions, the Italian city-states began to hire mercenaries; this, in turn, exposed the country to roving bands of Swiss, Germans, Albanians, and Croatians who plundered the countryside and exploited their employers. In short, Italy had become helpless, and the city-states appeared to be incapable of reacting appropriately. In 1527 Rome was sacked by German mercenaries and the pope had to pay a large ransom to escape.

Machiavelli's Florence was deeply affected by these tragic events. In 1494—the same year that Charles VIII undertook the first French invasion—the city of Florence expelled Pietro di Medici. For the greater part of the fifteenth century the Medicis had ruled the wealthy city-state; with the expulsion of Pietro, however, Florence returned to its republican tradition. In 1502 the Florentines elected Pietro Soderini to the city's highest office. At 29 years of age, Machiavelli joined Soderini's staff and for the next ten years served ably in the diplomatic corps of the Republic. In 1512 the Medicis in an alliance with both the Papacy and the Spanish monarchy returned to Florence and overthrew the Republic. Implicated in a counterplot, Machiavelli was forced into exile.

As an exile Machiavelli turned to farming and writing. He maintained a vigorous correspondence with a number of officials and briefly in 1525 engaged in a limited amount of semiofficial diplomatic activity. His major efforts, however, were of a literary nature. His most famous works were *The Prince*, (1513); *Discourses on the First Ten Books of Titus Livius* (1519); the *Art of War* (1520); *Life of Castruccio Castracani* (1520); *History of Florence*, (1525); and a number of plays, of which the most famous is the comedy, *La Mandragola*.

ANALYSIS OF *THE PRINCE*

The Prince as originally written in 1513 was dedicated to Giuliano di Medici. But with Medici's death in 1516, Machiavelli rededicated the work to Lorenzo di Medici, duke of Urbino. The manuscript was first circulated privately. It was not to be published until 1532, five years after Machiavelli's death. In 1559 Pope Paul IV placed the book on the Index of Prohibited Books compiled by the Roman Catholic Inquisition.

The Prince begins with a dedication to the ruler Lorenzo di Medici. In it Machiavelli admits that he wished to "gain the favour of a prince" and hopes that the prince "will recognize the great and unmerited sufferings inflicted on me by a cruel fate." [1] Such admissions have led some to see Machiavelli as essentially an unprincipled office-seeker courting the favor of those in power. Indeed Machiavelli's desire to return to office was well known. Yet there is more in this dedication than simply Machiavelli's own personal ambition. His gift to the prince was an offer of knowledge. More importantly, it was an offer of a specific kind of knowledge, "knowledge of the deeds of great men." [2] From Machiavelli's viewpoint, "it is necessary to be a prince to know thoroughly the nature of the people, and one of the populace to know the nature of princes." [3] Machiavelli, in turn, presented himself as that "one of the populace" who could best educate the ruler.

The very fact that Machiavelli felt the need for a new political science indicates one of the essential features of his thinking. Traditionally, philosophy had presented itself as the appropriate wisdom for the ruler. Thus, for example, the Dutch humanist and contemporary of Machiavelli,

[1] Nicolo Machiavelli, *The Prince and the Discourses*, ed. Max Lerner (New York: Random House, 1950), p. 3. Reprinted by permission of Oxford University Press.

[2] Machiavelli, *The Prince*, p. 3.

[3] Machiavelli, *The Prince*, p. 4.

Desiderius Erasmus (1466–1536) published his *Education of a Christian Prince* in 1516. Following the traditional approach Erasmus argued that the personal virtue of the prince was his most important attribute as a ruler and that such virtue was best secured through a rigorous philosophical education. Machiavelli, on the other hand, maintained that traditional political philosophy was, in fact, incapable of providing the guidance which a prince actually required and that consequently a new beginning was necessary.

Indeed in his *Discourses*, he refers to his work as an effort "to open a new route, which has not yet been followed by anyone. . . ."[4]

Machiavelli's boast on behalf of his own novelty, however, must be weighed carefully. First, his *Prince* was essentially an example of a literary genré which had already been developed during the late Middle Ages. Referred to as a "mirror for princes," this form of literature provided a collection of maxims and rules which were intended to instruct the prince in the art of governance. Second, although Machiavelli emphasized the pragmatic realism of his own writings, the realistic or secular study of political life had already earned an audience in Italy as early as 1400 with the publication of Caluccio Salutati's *The Tyrant*. Since then a commitment to political "realism" was continued in the numerous writings of the humanistic historiographers which included Machiavelli's younger contemporary, Guiccardini.

Yet at the same time there is something to Machiavelli's claim. Whereas his style and approach may have been shared by others, his writings are nonetheless characterized by his rejection of certain elements within the tradition of Western political thought. In particular he rejected those elements which he believed were based upon "imagined republics and principalities which have never been seen or known to exist in reality."[5] His teachings, on the other hand, would "go to the real truth of the matter." The advantage of his approach, according to Machiavelli, was that it could provide "something of use to those who understand," whereas the alternative would "rather . . . bring about [the prince's] own ruin than his preservation." This was the case because a "man who wishes to make a profession of goodness in everything must necessarily come to grief among so many who are not good."

The above statements from chapter 15 of *The Prince* are often cited as evidence of Machiavelli's realism. Yet this term is too imprecise. There is no doubt that Machiavelli was breaking with the classical form of political philosophy. For the classical thinkers a fundamental task of political philosophy was to present an analysis of the best regime, and this was done with

[4] Machiavelli, *Discourses*, p. 103.

[5] The following quotations are drawn from Machiavelli, *The Prince*, p. 56.

a clear awareness that the best regime was not in fact actualized in any given society. Does this, however, mean that the best regime exists only in one's imagination? Given Machiavelli's assumptions, yes. But those were not the assumptions of the classical theorists.

As we have seen, classical political theory began with a particular set of metaphysical assumptions which guided each of the theorists during their investigations of reality. Plato and Aristotle, for example, were concerned with examining the nature of political life; yet from their perspective that could best be done by examining politics in its most perfected form. Thus just as the true nature and potential of an acorn is visible only when it becomes a developed oak tree, so too is the true nature of a political society most clearly seen only in the outlines of the best regime. By knowing the completed potential of political life classical theorists believed that they had achieved thereby a full understanding of its nature. The obvious fact that existing historical societies never fully realized the principles of their development only meant that each was in some way imperfect. This imperfection, in turn, was not interpreted as constituting a denial of the validity of those principles against which the particular societies were being measured. Inasmuch as those principles were true, they were not the products of the theorist's imagination. Thus from the classical perspective the inability of a society to achieve its natural form in the best regime represented a condemnation of that society and not an attack upon the veracity of the theorist's understanding.

Given this, then, it is apparent that Machiavelli's rejection of classical theory as offering us only "imagined republics" was, itself, based upon a more fundamental rejection of those metaphysical assumptions which supported the classical world-view. For Machiavelli traditional political theory was useless because it presupposed a mistaken view of reality. Consequently what for the classics appeared to be "knowledge of the best" was for Machiavelli "imagination of what ought to be."

From Machiavelli's perspective the nature of reality was not to be discovered in the visions of metaphysicians. Instead nature revealed itself through its history, and thus the real was to be found in that which had been. Thus Machiavelli wrote in the *Discourses*, it is a mistake to believe " . . . heaven, the sun, the elements, and men had changed the order of their motions and power and were different from what they were in ancient times."[6] Given this, then, it followed that an adequate understanding of history provided the only reliable guide for the present, and the useful political scientist, therefore, would be the one who could draw the appropriate lessons from the past. Specifically the knowledge that could be offered the prince would be that which was gained by the study of the deeds of

---

[6] Machiavelli, *Discourses*, p. 105.

great historical figures. By imitating the success of others the prince could hope to achieve the same for himself. In short, Machiavelli's new science of politics was the science of exemplary actions.

The twenty-six chapters of *The Prince* may be organized into the following sections. The first section, chapters 1 through 11, presents a typology of regimes. In it Machiavelli distinguishes among the various types of political regimes and analyzes the particular strengths and weaknesses of each. Accordingly he begins with the most general division, that is, between republics and monarchies, and then proceeds to an examination of the various types of monarchies, distinguishing between those which are hereditary and those which have been acquired recently. Of the recently acquired, Machiavelli separates the entirely new from those annexed to hereditary regimes. These, in turn, are either identified as being accustomed to monarchies or as being originally free states. The process of annexation, in turn, can be accomplished by force of arms, good fortune, special ability, villainy, or the favor of one's fellow citizens. In each case, however, special concerns arise, and Machiavelli attempts to discuss each in its turn. This first section of *The Prince* finally ends with a discussion of ecclesiastical principalities.

The second section (chapters 12 through 25) is a discussion of those general methods for ruling which according to Machiavelli have proven useful in all circumstances. It begins with Machiavelli's attempt to establish the foundations upon which all regimes must rest. For him there are two: good laws and good arms. Of these, the former presupposes the latter, so Machiavelli devoted chapters 12 to 14 to a discussion of military affairs.

Chapters 15 through 25 present an outline of those general principles of conduct by which the prince should regulate his affairs. This third section more than anything else Machiavelli wrote has contributed to his image as a ruthless and immoral practitioner of power politics. Several quotations may indicate the tone of his discussion:

> Therefore it is necessary for a prince who wishes to maintain himself to learn how not to be good.[7]

> The reply is, that one ought to be both feared and loved, but as it is difficult for the two to go together, it is much safer to be feared than loved. . . .[8]

> . . . and in the actions of men, and especially princes from which there is no appeal, the end justifies the means. Let the prince, therefore, aim at conquering and maintaining the state, and the means will always be judged honourable and praised by every one. . . .[9]

[7] Machiavelli, *The Prince*, p. 56.

[8] Machiavelli, *The Prince*, p. 61.

[9] Machiavelli, *The Prince*, p. 66.

Such statements as these and Machiavelli's repeated praise of such ruthless politicans as Caesare Borgia have led many to decry his immoral opportunism. Yet one should be clear as to what is involved. There is no doubt that Machiavelli's prescriptions violate some of the major tenets of Christian morality. But is a rejection of Christian morality equivalent to a rejection of morality *per se?* Several arguments should be considered.

Throughout *The Prince*, Machiavelli reminds his readers that they ought to study the actions of eminent people so as to imitate them when possible. In particular he recommends Moses, Cyrus, Romulus, and Theseus. Each of these historical figures was successful in creating a form of political order for a people who were otherwise disbanded, oppressed, or disorganized. In doing so, they both ennobled their country and augmented its fortune. As a contrast to these, Machiavelli presents the stories of Agothocles of Sicily and Oliverotto da Fermo. Both men became princes by "some nefarious or villainous means" so that, although their cruelties allowed them to gain power, they will, nonetheless, prevent them from achieving glory.[10] In writing of Agothocles, Machiavelli says:

> Nevertheless his barbarous cruelty and inhumanity together with his countless atrocities do not permit of his being named among the most famous men. We cannot attribute to fortune or virtue that which he achieved without either.[11]

Machiavelli's attempt to distinguish such admirable leaders as Moses and Cyrus from such as Agothocles and Oliverotto provides an important clue to the quality of his thinking. On one hand like Polybius before him, Machiavelli acknowledged the undeniable role of power in political life. Thus he accepted the fact that historical and cultural accomplishments presupposed the existence of a certain degree of civilizational order and that such order, in turn, was often the result of an exercise of sheer brute power. As such it appeared that the best in human behavior often was possible only because of those conditions which were the results of humanity's worst actions. Similarly as an historian, Machiavelli was aware of the disturbing fact that at times truly superior civilizations are destroyed by those which are inferior yet more energetic. Thus as a "realist" Machiavelli acknowledged the primacy of political power. Yet unlike other realists of his day, such as Guicciardini, he did not allow the reality of mere power to prevent him from distinguishing between its appropriate and inappropriate use. Indeed the essential difference between Moses and Agothocles depended upon this point. Agothocles succeeded because of his cruelty, whereas Moses suc-

---

[10] Machiavelli, *The Prince*, p. 31.
[11] Machiavelli, *The Prince*, p. 32.

ceeded because of his virtue (*virtu*). This, in turn, implies that whereas Moses deserves to be honored and imitated, Agothocles is to be condemned and forgotten.

This fundamental distinction between the honorable and the cruel suggests that the concept of *virtu* played an important role in Machiavelli's understanding of political reality. The meaning of this concept, in turn, is most clearly developed within the context of his discussion of fortune (*Fortuna*). Although the concept of fortune is not used consistently throughout all of his work, it is in part employed as a secularized equivalent for the Christian symbol of providence. Christianity argued that the events of history were not simply an arbitrary collection of meaningless happenings. Rather God exercised a loving care which directed the events of history in some meaningful and desirable way. Although at a given moment mortals might not be able to understand the design of providence, they could, nonetheless, find security in their awareness both of God's active presence and of the ultimate benefit arising from what might appear to be historical accident.

In Machiavelli's understanding, however, *Fortuna* does not necessarily display such beneficial intentions. Indeed citizens can not know the aims of *Fortuna*, be they good or evil. The lady *Fortuna* is variable, and where she rules there is great fluctuation and instability. Unlike Providence, which always intends the good for humanity, *Fortuna* may indeed seek its ruin. Yet the rule of *Fortuna* is only half the picture. As Machiavelli wrote in chapter 25:

> Nevertheless that our freedom will not be altogether extinguished, I think it may be true that *Fortuna* is the ruler of half our actions, but that she allows the other half or thereabouts to be governed by us.[12]

Machiavelli likens *Fortuna* to a woman. She is mastered by force and allows herself to be overcome by the impetuous and bold. Where she is not resisted, however, she shows her power. Yet when confronted by a leader of *virtu*, she may choose not to display her influence. This is not to suggest that one's way can always be had; for, indeed, *Fortuna* may choose to destroy the most virtuous of people. Yet inasmuch as *Fortuna* generally provides only the occasion for success, the truly great leaders " . . . owed nothing to fortune but the opportunity which gave them matter to be shaped into what form they thought fit; and without that opportunity their power would have been wasted, and without their power the opportunity would have come in vain."[13]

[12] Machiavelli, *The Prince*, p. 91.
[13] Machiavelli, *The Prince*, p. 20–21.

Leaders of *virtu*, therefore, appear as heroes who possess those qualities which enable them to aggressively seize an opportunity for the creation of order amidst disorder. Although by such an act a prince gains glory and honor, the order created is a public one, and public order is the *sine qua non* of the citizen's happiness. Disorder allows for rapine and bloodshed, and these as a rule injure the whole community. *Virtu* on the other hand allows a prince to establish an ordered regime, and such a foundation is neccessary if there is to be any form of civilizational accomplishment whatsoever. In his *Discourses*, Machiavelli wrote of the inevitable changes which every society must endure. There is, in effect, a cycle through which nations move: monarchy, tyranny, aristocracy, oligarchy, popular government, and anarchy. In those cases where the nation is fortunate, this latter condition is eventually overturned by the prince, and the cycle begins anew. Not only is such a pattern of continued change disorienting for the individuals whose private lives and cares are caught up in this larger movement, but it also serves to exhaust the very resources of the nation itself. Thus, rather than beginning the societal cycle again, most nations are so enfeebled by the process that they are easily conquered by a neighboring state. Consequently they cease to exist as a true civilizational order.

Based upon his understanding of reality Machiavelli never doubted that such fluctuations were inevitable. Change affected every form of government, and consequently all regimes were ultimately unstable and necessarily defective. Inasmuch as no society was totally immune from the effects of this historical cycle, the *virtu* of the prince consisted in his ability to create a temporary reprieve for his own people. By creating a relatively stable society the prince could delay the inevitable process of growth, decay, and extinction and establish, thereby, the necessary, although temporary, order which all civilizational accomplishments presupposed.

Inasmuch as the excellence of the virtuous prince was seen in terms of his historical efficacy, it is obvious that Machiavelli's understanding of *virtu* was quite different from that of traditional Christianity. Indeed for Machiavelli the prince was even justified in the judicious use of vice if such a practice would contribute to political ends. Consequently it would appear that for Machiavelli success, as measured in historical terms, had replaced eternal salvation as the operating standard for princely conduct. Whereas his contemporary, Erasmus, had advised princes that it was better to yield to defeat than to violate the principles of Christian justice, Machiavelli counseled precisely the opposite. Indeed in his *History of Florence* he admitted that he loved his country more than his own soul, and the teachings of *The Prince* are entirely consistent with such an admission.

By treating historical efficacy as the highest good Machiavelli broke with the classical-Greek and Christian traditions and returned, thereby, to the cosmological world-view of the ancient pagans. In particular he rejected the classical-Greek and Christian understanding of the bipolar nature of reality and replaced it with the ancient pagan view of reality as a strictly intramundane order.

The philosophical tradition of Plato and Aristotle and the theological perspective of Christianity understood both humanity and reality as participating in two levels of being. Accordingly there was first and most obviously the intramundane sphere of our physical-worldly existence. In addition there was the transcendental sphere of our psychic-spiritual existence. Given this background classical-Greek and Christian political theory attempted to understand the function of political society in terms of these two indices. As we have seen, these traditions tended to deemphasize the importance of politics as a worldly concern and thus subordinated it to the higher goals of spiritual development. It is here then that Machiavelli breaks with the traditional understanding.

This break can be illustrated by two examples. First, in his discussion of traditional political science, Machiavelli reinterpreted the classical understanding of the components of reality in a decidedly one-dimensional fashion. The transcendent pole of classical reality in which nature was revealed in its perfected form became for Machiavelli the realm of the "ought" about which humanity has "imaginings." The classical intramundane component, on the other hand, expanded to become the total content of that reality which was to be investigated by Machiavelli's new science.

A second example of Machiavelli's one-dimensional view can be found in his understanding of human nature. For the classical Greeks, humanity's uniqueness was found in its possession of a divinelike element. This element, reason, accounted for the human ability to participate in the transcendent while being bodily involved with the world. The classical view of humanity, therefore, saw it as existing in a state of tension created by the pull of the transcendent and the pull of the worldly. The transcendent pull was experienced in reason; the worldly, in the passions. Machiavelli's view of human beings, however, rejected this understanding. His psychology attempted to describe them entirely in terms of the pull of the passions. Thus for him, the human condition could be explained in essentially worldly terms. For example, he wrote in his *Discourses*:

> . . . nature has created men so that they desire everything but are unable to attain it; desire being thus always greater than the faculty of acquiring, discontent with what they have and dissatisfaction with themselves result from it.[14]

[14] Machiavelli, *Discourses*, p. 208.

By reducing the experience of human dissatisfaction to a question of mere physical desire, Machiavelli attempts to explain the quest for meaning and order in strictly mundane terms. Thus the purpose of life becomes simply the satisfaction of human passion. Yet at the same time Machiavelli's understanding of humanity does not imply that all passions are equal. Indeed his discussion of *virtu*, his attempt to construct human models for our imitation, and his distinction between power and glory attest to Machiavelli's desire to distinguish between the higher and the lower passions. Such a distinction, however, still operates strictly within a purely mundane understanding of reality. Although some passions may be higher than others, the passions function by their very nature as ties to the world. Thus it was that the Greeks understood the moderation of passion as the first step toward the life of reason. By disregarding humanity's search for the divine as the source for its dissatisfaction with the world and by reducing the experience of dissatisfaction to simply a clash among the passions, Machiavelli constructed a view of the human soul that was just as one-dimensional as was his view of nature.

Given this return to a cosmological understanding of reality, Machiavelli's emphasis upon politics is entirely understandable. Politics is that activity by which we order the affairs of the world. Since those affairs are everything in a one-dimensional universe, politics becomes the most important human activity. It provides the only true arena for human excellence. Consequently those who are successful in the creation of political order achieve thereby the highest reward obtainable in a one-dimensional reality, that is, to be known and remembered by others. Pagan glory has replaced Christian immortality; and to achieve such glory one must acquire princely *virtu*.

Machiavelli's *The Prince* ends with an appeal to Lorenzo di Medici to assume the task of unifying the Italian nation-state. Some scholars see this emotional plea as ill-fitted to the cool objectivity of the previous twenty-five chapters. Yet it is in many ways the capstone of the entire argument. Machiavelli has attempted to evoke a myth. He has created an image of the virtuous prince, described the necessity of a new state founding, and justified the deeds that must be done. In chapter 26, then, he presents the task at hand:

> This barbarous domination stinks in the nostrils of every one. May your illustrious house, therefore, assume this task with that courage and those hopes which are inspired by a just cause, so that under its banner our fatherland may be raised up. . . .[15]

---

[15] Machiavelli, *The Prince*, p. 98.

In times when traditions appear increasingly irrelevant vis-à-vis the events of the day and when the institutions of the old order have clearly failed, the attempt to evoke by myth those existential virtues required for a new founding is an obvious strategic alternative—an alternative employed as early as Plato's *Republic* when he created the myth of the philosopher-king.

ANALYSIS OF THE *DISCOURSES*

Generally Machiavelli's *Discourses on the First Ten Books of Titus Livius* has not received as much attention as has his *Prince*. It is much longer, more tedious, and repeats many of the themes of the earlier work. Yet it is important to examine the *Discourses* if only to dispel some popular notions about the character of Machiavelli's thought in general.

Some who have read only *The Prince* assume that Machiavelli is an advocate of tyranny for its own sake. Yet a reading of the *Discourses* makes it quite clear that Machiavelli actually favored a republican form of government. According to Machiavelli republics are preferable because they promote liberty and, as in the case of Rome, liberty is best secured in a mixed regime wherein the interests of both the nobles and the people are represented and can thereby act as checks against one another. Where free republics do exist, the primary task is to secure their continuation. This is best done by educating the citizen in those civic virtues which instill both an appreciation of and loyalty to the principles of the regime. Indeed this is the goal of Machiavelli's *Discourses*. Where such regimes do not exist, however, the primary task is to evoke a political founder who can create the necessary order upon which a republican civilization eventually can be built. This, in turn, was the task of Machiavelli's *The Prince*. Thus ideally the work of the prince should lead to the establishment of a republic. In such cases the prince actually succeeds by creating a form of rule that eventually requires his own removal from office. For Machiavelli, therefore, it is as if princely excellence can only become fully apparent when it is succeeded by the virtues of a republican government. Thus, as did Romulus, Machiavelli's prince is ultimately expected to sacrifice himself on behalf of the common good. The prince must first create a viable and stable society and then must step aside so as to allow the people to rule on their own behalf:

> But we must assume, as a general rule, that it never or rarely happens that a republic or monarchy is well constituted or its old institutions entirely reformed, unless it is done by only one individual. . . . A sagacious legislator of a republic, therefore, whose object is to promote the common good and not his private

interests . . . should concentrate all authority in himself. . . . Besides, although one man alone should organize a government, yet it will not endure long if the administration of it remains on the shoulders of a single individual; it is well then to confide this to the charge of many, for thus it will be sustained by the many.[16]

The method of the *Discourses* is similar to that of *The Prince*. Accordingly Machiavelli turned to an examination of history in an effort to call attention to those selected examples which he felt could serve as lessons for his own time. In particular he studied the practices and beliefs of the ancient Romans during the republican period. For Machiavelli Rome's stability and success were due primarily to that powerful love of liberty which was characteristic of its citizenry. The Roman's civic virtue, in turn, could best be explained in terms of the innate goodness of the regime's original principles. Thus, if Italy were to return to the principles of Rome's republican founding, it would be possible according to Machiavelli to share in its virtue:

> There is nothing more true than that all the things of this world have a limit to their existence; but those only can run the entire course ordained for them by Heaven that do not allow their body to become disorganized, but keep it unchanged in the manner ordained, or if they change it, so do it that it shall be for their advantage. . . . I say that those changes are beneficial that bring them back to their original principles.[17]

It should be remembered, of course, that these principles were those of a pre-Christian pagan Rome.

Many of the themes developed in the *Discourses* have already been introduced during our discussion of *The Prince*. Therefore it will be necessary to look only at the following. In a chapter entitled, "In Proportion as the Founders of a Republic or Monarchy Are Entitled to Praise, so Do the Founders of a Tyranny Deserve Execration," Machiavelli discussed his understanding of moral worth. The most general division that can be made among people is between those who deserve glory and those who deserve infamy. Examples of the former are founders of religion, founders of republics, commanders of armies, literary figures, and those who successfully practice the useful arts. The quality which they share in common and which qualifies them for praise is their ability to create order and stability according to the principles of a general design. Examples of those who deserve

---

[16] Machiavelli, *Discourses*, p. 138–139.
[17] Machiavelli, *Discourses*, p. 397.

infamy, on the other hand, are the destroyers of religion and republics and the enemies of virtue, letters, and the useful arts. These latter are to be condemned because they are destructive of human order and political stability. Granting that no order is permanent, stability, even if only temporary, is a fundamental human need. As we have seen Machiavelli believed that it is the personal *virtu* of a great founder which can serve as the source for a new beginning. Yet even if virtuous princes could be found, there must be some way of transferring their personal existential order to societies at large. At the same time there also must be some way of preserving that order once its living existential source is gone:

> But as the lives of princes are short, the kingdom will of necessity perish as the prince fails in virtue. Whence it comes that kingdoms which depend entirely upon the virtue of one man endure but for a brief time; for his virtue passes away with his life.[18]

According to Machiavelli the traditional means of embodying and transferring the personal virtue of individual princes to their people is through the creation and enforcement of good laws. Yet, "as good habits of the people require good laws to support them, so laws, to be observed, need good habits on the part of the people."[19] And, according to Machiavelli, the best means of developing the appropriate habits among the people can be found in religion. Indeed for Machiavelli the founders of religion deserve more glory than the founders of republics, because unless the people fear God they will not easily submit to those laws which they do not understand. Religion can enlist divine authority in the support of political goals and, in so doing, serve as a means for both uniting the people and inspiring in them a devotion to the regime. For Machiavelli, the Roman king Numa stands as an example for all:

> Numa finding a very savage people and wishing to reduce them to civil obedience by the arts of peace had recourse to religion as the most necessary and assured support of any civil society.[20]

Machiavelli's appreciation of the political benefits to be found in a civil religion was not an original discovery. Indeed Plato devoted a large portion of his *Laws* to an examination of the regime's official theology. Yet for Plato civil religion was important because it was the means by which a spiritual experience could be made available to all. That is to say, for Plato a

[18] Machiavelli, *Discourses*, p. 148.
[19] Machiavelli, *Discourses*, p. 168.
[20] Machiavelli, *Discourses*, p. 146.

true civil religion articulated a theological experience; as such its content must be nourished by the divine. Machiavelli's analysis, on the other hand, is concerned solely with the political benefits provided by a society's profession of a religious tradition. The positive meaning of a religious experience is replaced by the negative fear of God, and the theorist's concern about the theological adequacy of a particular tradition is replaced by Machiavelli's evaluation of its political efficacy. Religion is treated by Machiavelli as a purely secular force; it has become a form of ideology, simply a means of inculcating habitual obedience among the citizens. That religion can serve this purpose is obvious; that this, however, is the total significance of religion is, in fact, Machiavelli's "discovery."

This situation accounts, in part, for Machiavelli's critique of historical Christianity. Not only had the policies of the Papal States proved detrimental to the interests of Italy, but the very doctrines of Christianity itself—or at least their contemporary interpretation—made for an inefficient political religion. Machiavelli argued this point by comparing Christianity with the civil religion of pagan Rome. The Romans had a greater love of liberty because they were a stronger people. This strength, in turn, was established by their superior education and grounded in their superior religion. The pagans understood honor and possessions to be the highest goods; they deified those who distinguished themselves through honorable actions; and subordinated all concerns to the pursuit of grandeur and strength. As an immanent worldly religion, paganism concentrated all human energies on the achievement of worldly accomplishments—the highest being, of course, of a political nature.

Christianity, on the other hand, shared the classical-Greek orientation toward the transcendent "beyond." This had the effect of turning people away from the affairs of the world and discouraging, thereby, the development of worldly virtue. Christianity, accordingly, glorified the humble and contemplative rather than the heroic and bold. It taught patience, charity, and suffering and awaited the end of the world and history. Salvation, not remembrance, was the Christian goal.

For Machiavelli the historical failure of Christianity was evident in the failure of the Holy Roman Empire. To him, the Christian focusing upon the kingdom of God amounted to a turning away from his fellow citizens. Thus rather than seeing a concern for spiritual matters as a source of human strength, Machiavelli believed it to be a primary cause of political weakness. His response, therefore, was to advocate the creation of a civil religion which would successfully serve the promotion of secular ends. Thus for Machiavelli the church comes to serve the state, and it is this reversal of the traditional Christian arrangement which effectively marked the end of the feudal order.

BIBLIOGRAPHY

BUTTERFIELD, HERBERT. *The Statecraft of Machiavelli.* New York: Collier Books, 1962.

FLEISHER, MARTIN, ed. *Machiavelli and the Nature of Political Thought.* New York: Atheneum, 1972.

GILBERT, ALLAN H. *Machiavelli's Prince and Its Forerunners.* Durham: Duke University Press, 1938.

GILBERT, FELIX. *Machiavelli and Guicciardini: Politics and History in Sixteenth-Century Florence.* Princeton: Princeton University Press, 1965.

HALE, J. R. *Machiavelli and Renaissance Italy.* New York: Macmillan, 1961.

MEINECKE, FRIEDRICH. *Machiavellism.* Translated by Douglas Scott. London: Routledge and Kegan Paul, 1957.

PAREL, ANTHONY, ed. *The Political Calculus: Essays on Machiavelli's Philosophy.* Toronto: University of Toronto Press, 1972.

SKINNER, QUENTIN. *The Foundations of Modern Political Thought,* Vol. I: *The Renaissance.* Cambridge: Cambridge University Press, 1978.

STRAUSS, LEO. *Thoughts on Machiavelli.* Seattle: University of Washington Press, 1969.

7

THE PROTESTANT REFORMATION

THEOLOGICAL BACKGROUND: *DEVOTIO MODERNA* AND *VIA MODERNA*

Martin Luther's (1483–1546) nailing of his famous Ninety-Five Theses to the door of the Castle Church at Wittenberg in 1517 is typically portrayed as the beginning of the Protestant Reformation. Yet, at the same time, this event also marks the culmination of a series of earlier trends and important developments. At one level it represented the end of Luther's own personal spiritual struggle. As early as 1505 he appears to have entered into a deep spiritual crisis. Abandoning the idea of a legal career Luther entered the Augustinian monastery at Erfurt and there began a program of fasting, prayer, and study. During these studies he gave particular attention to the writings of Augustine and St. Paul and came under the influence of such late-medieval mystics as Suso, Ruysbroeck, Groote, and Tauler. Although the immediate issue which provoked Luther's act of defiance at Wittenberg was the Roman church's selling of indulgences to finance the construction of

St. Peter's in Rome, his overall position was based upon a series of fundamental disagreements with several of the church's teachings and practices. Having reached this impasse Luther felt compelled to speak out:

> Unless I am convinced by the testimony of the Scriptures or by clear reason (for I do not trust either in the pope or in his councils alone, since it is well known that they have often erred and contradict themselves), I am bound by the Scriptures I have quoted and my conscience is captive to the word of God. I cannot and will not retract anything, since it is neither safe nor right to go against conscience. I cannot do otherwise, here I stand, may God help me. Amen.[1]

The success of Luther's protest and the rapid spread of his ideas throughout Northern Europe suggest that the events of 1517 were not simply of a personal nature. Although Wittenberg may have represented the end of Luther's own personal struggle, it was at the same time the culmination of an entire series of larger cultural and political forces. In particular Luther's protest was an expression of Christianity's inability to continue as the source of political order for the modernizing West. Several expressions of this civilizational crisis had already developed by Luther's own time, and as a consequence his thought served as a symbol for the strength of these earlier movements.

In theology proper there were two developments which were particularly important: the *devotio moderna* and the *via moderna*. The *devotio moderna* was associated with the teachings of Gerard Groote and his followers in the Brethren of the Common Life. Groote (1340–1384), a Dutch mystic, spent his adult life preaching and organizing a series of free schools for the young throughout Europe. His teachings emphasized the need for a reformation of morals and extolled the virtues of a life devoted to poverty and sharing. Although he was ultimately silenced by the bishop of Utrecht, his influence was widely felt throughout Europe. His schools educated thousands, and the Carthusian monks in particular took a special interest in his teachings. Groote's most important work, *The Imitation of Christ*, was edited by one of his students, Thomas a Kempis, and enjoyed a wide-spread popularity. Central to Groote's teaching was his emphasis upon humanity's fallen nature. Accordingly human beings were understood to be creatures of sin. As such their nature was corrupted and consequently in need of the healing effects of God's grace. Yet inasmuch as all goodness rested in God, humans, themselves, were worthless. Thus although grace may be given, it was never merited. Christians can only turn themselves away from the

---

[1] George W. Forell, ed., *Luther's Works* (Philadelphia: Muhlenberg Press, 1958), XXXII, pp. 112–13.

world and submit in total resignation to God's will. In chapter 54 of his *Imitation of Christ* Groote has Christ say:

> But does it seem such a great thing that you, who are but dust and worth nothing, should submit yourself to another for God's sake when I, the Almighty and Supreme Who have created all things out of nothing, have humbly submitted Myself to men for your sake? . . . Learn to be submissive, you who are but dust; learn to be humble, you who are but clay and an outcast and bend yourself under the feet of all. . . . What reason have you, vain man, to complain? What can you, vile sinner, bring against your accusers, you who have offended God so often that you have deserved hell?[2]

Such an emphasis upon humanity's fallen nature, Augustinian in tone, was an expression of a theme that would become central to Luther's own theological speculations. Groote's importance, however, is not limited to his doctrinal influence upon latter-day Protestants. Just as significant is the fact that Groote was only one of the many mystics who appeared in the fourteenth century. Among other important mystics were Meister Eckhardt, Johannes Tauler, and William Langland, the author of *Piers the Plowman*. Again one could examine their works for evidence of certain themes that would later come to characterize reformist theology. For example, in *Piers the Plowman* it is possible to discover such "Protestant" elements as individualism, voluntarism, and nationalism. Yet on the other hand what is truly important is not any particular mystical teaching but the appearance of widespread mysticism itself. As a radically personal form of religious experience, mysticism represents a form of withdrawal from the external world.

A turning inward can, at the same time, represent a turning away. Consequently the rapid growth of mysticism in the fourteenth century may be interpreted as a serious expression of an increasing popular dissatisfaction with the traditional medieval order in general and the church's role in particular.

Medieval Christianity had long been confronted with the appearance of popular spiritual movements which operated outside of the traditional structures of the church. Yet in the past, the church had been able to successfully incorporate such movements and thereby absorb the spiritual energies which they contained. A good example of such a technique was the church's creation of the mendicant orders in the twelfth century as a means for tapping the popular religious movements of the time. For example, the

---

[2] Gerard Groote, *The Following of Christ*, trans. Joseph Malaise, S. J. (New York: America Press, 1937), pp. 200–01.

teachings of St. Francis of Assisi contained a fundamental critique of the feudal order—an order which included the privileged position of the institutional church. Yet rather than permitting this critical movement to be established as an independent force, the Roman hierarchy coopted Franciscan radicalism and channeled it within formal church structures by creating the Order of Friars Minor.

By the fourteenth century, however, the church's ability to accommodate such developments had diminished. Those who represented the mystical movement in the fourteenth century, as St. Francis had in the twelfth, were now treated as heretics and driven away from rather than incorporated into the organized structures. As the church hardened, the mystical movement spread, and with its spread the spiritual energy of the people assumed increasingly unorthodox forms. In his *The Two Sources of Morality and Religion* Henri Bergson has argued that the transformation of dynamic spiritual movements into static religious systems is due, in part, to the human need for assuring myths. The people require assurance against disorganization, depression, and the unforeseeable. Thus the institutions and dogmas of medieval Christianity served a real human need. The church's practices provided the mass of humanity with a needed structure, and its teachings supplied them with a sense of order. Yet if the leaders of such institutions are not sensitive to the continuing spiritual development of the people and to the never-ending task of reforming their institutions so as to accommodate popular energies, the spiritual process may in fact move outside of the established institutions. In some cases, such movements may even lead to the creation of counterinstitutions which are established in opposition to the former organization. Indeed the outburst of mysticism in the fourteenth century appears to indicate that some such process was in fact under way.

The second major theological event which preceded Luther's success was the *via moderna*. The *via moderna* was a development within medieval scholasticism which was designed as an alternative to the *via antica* of Thomas Aquinas. Its major spokesman was William of Ockham (1285–1347). And whereas the *devotio moderna* of Groote attested to the presence of a popular spiritual movement outside of the church, the *via moderna* of Ockham represented an intellectual tradition within scholasticism which provided Luther's theological speculation with a well-established foundation. Ockham's position, often referred to as *nominalism*, was in sharp contrast to that of Aquinas. Aquinas's blending of Christian theology and Aristotelian philosophy was based upon the belief that the teachings of faith and the dictates of reason formed a consistent and complimentary whole. The world was seen as a product of divine intellect, and inasmuch as human reason allowed its possessors to understand the substance of worldly reality, it also served, thereby, to introduce them to God's orderly plan. Accordingly God could be encountered both within His revelation to His faithful and through the order of reason. Faith for Thomas served to perfect reason—not to contradict it.

Ockham's theology, on the other hand, posited a fundamental division between the realms of faith and reason. Emphasizing God's absolute power, Ockham understood reality as the product of divine will. The world was simply the one possibility out of many alternatives which God chose to actualize. "Reality" was not an emanation of "eternal reason" but rather the product of divine choice; it did not have an essential structure. It could, therefore, be other than it was, and it was in God's power to change it as He wished. Reality might be structured by causes, but the causes, themselves, were not necessary ones. Hence, worldly existence was fundamentally hypothetical.

Ockham's emphasis upon divine will rather than reason implied a strict limit to the range of human reasoning. Since nature had no essential structure, it did not possess real universals. Inasmuch as reality had no real universals, human beings could not know its substance. Lacking a knowledge of substances humanity could only know reality in terms of its accidents. What reason showed humanity, therefore, was not reality in itself but only reality as it appeared to us or as it was thought by us. We could know our thoughts about reality but not reality itself. Thus within the realm of appearances human reason could aid in ordering its user's actions, but knowledge of the most fundamental things was not available to those who relied upon reason alone.

Ockham's purpose in developing his system was to restrict the claims of the rational sciences of his day. Science was valid for Ockham only when it remained within the limits of its own realm; it was only an aid for dealing with the hypothetical. The divine realm, on the other hand, was absolute and could be known only through revealed religion. According to Ockham, God's truths could not be reached by reason. Rather they are revealed to us through the miracle of faith—a miracle which was possible only because of God's absolute power. Given this situation, human salvation was to be found only by the faithful totally submitting themselves to the irrational will of God.

It would be an oversimplification, however, to suggest that Luther's teachings could be reduced to being simply an amalgamation of the *devotio moderna* and the *via moderna*. There is, however, little doubt that he was greatly influenced by both these traditions. Luther had studied the *devotio moderna* and was deeply impressed by some of its contemporary advocates, one being his mentor Johann von Staupitz. In addition Ockhamite teachings had been revived at the end of the fifteenth century by such influential theologians as John Mair and Gabriel Biel. And both men had an important impact upon Luther's studies.

POLITICAL BACKGROUND:
POWER AND STRUCTURE
OF THE CHURCH

The other major pre-Reformation controversy of a theological nature was one concerned primarily with the powers and structure of the church. The Conciliar Movement developed as an effort to resist Rome's continuing attempt to structure the Papacy in the form of an absolute monarchy. Although it is possible to trace the movement's beginnings back to the reaction of certain canon lawyers when confronted with Pope Gregory's reforms in the twelfth century, the most important event in the Conciliar Movement was the Great Schism of 1378–1414. Both William of Ockham and Marsilius of Padua had already developed theories which addressed the proper relationship between a general council of bishops and a heretical pope. But the question of papal legitimacy became an actual one when two popes (one Italian, the other French) were elected in 1378. The problem was further complicated by the emergence of a third pretender in 1409. It soon became apparent that the only way to resolve this schism was to evoke a supranational general council and then organize a new election. Consequently the Council of Constance met in 1414, deposed the claimants, and elected Martin V as the new pope. To accomplish this, of course, required that the council claim for itself an authority greater than that attributed to any of the individual pretenders. Accordingly the Council claimed that its authority came directly from Christ and that all Christians, including the pope, must obey it in matters of faith. Originally the idea of a general council was treated as an emergency measure brought about by the schism. Yet on October 9, 1417, the Council of Constance issued its decree, *Frequens*, which established the general council as a permanent institution of the church.

The most satisfactory theoretical elaboration of the conciliarist spirit is found in the work of Nicolaus of Cusa (1401–1464). Essentially a mystic, Cusa saw the conciliar arrangement as an institutional manifestation of the Christian mystical body. As such he viewed the council as a pragmatic expression of that harmony which should be characteristic of a spiritually united Christian people. Such a harmony according to Cusa would not tolerate any form of absolutism.

Unfortunately for both Cusa and the Conciliar Movement in general, however, the spirit which actually dominated the events of the day was decidedly more legalistic and nationalistic in character than Cusa had imagined. Once the schism had been settled, the usefulness of councils became less apparent. In addition, skillful maneuvering by the Papacy and the political support of the German princes in 1448 allowed the pope to dissolve the Council of Basel and, in effect, reestablish the monarchical form of church government.

Although conciliarism was defeated within the church, the widespread discontent with the Papacy continued. Indeed, just prior to Luther's protest, the conciliar spirit was revived in the context of a feud between Pope Julius II and King Louis XII of France. At this time, several conciliar arguments were resurrected in the work of such writers as Jacques Almain (1480–1515) and John Mair (1467–1550). It was quite natural, therefore, that the leaders of the Lutheran movement quickly associated themselves with this tradition of opposition to papal absolutism. Ironically the very concessions which the pope gave to the German princes in 1448 in order to win their support in dissolving the Council of Basel provided them with the essential territorial privileges and controls by which the princes were able to support Luther's campaign in the early stages of the Reformation.

It would be a mistake, however, to suggest that Luther's movement was entirely of a theological nature. Although his concern was primarily theological, Luther's protest managed to tap a number of other important themes, and these issues, in turn, played a major role in establishing the viability of his reform program. First, Luther's criticism of the practices of the clergy was, in part, a continuation of a tradition already successfully practiced by the humanists of his age. The clergy's abuse of its privileges had long ago given rise to a widespread feeling of anticlericalism among the laity. Thus Luther's attacks against the practices of the Papacy blended into a larger chorus of critical protests. Foremost among these protesters were the Renaissance humanists of Northern Europe. In their plays, satires, and essays they wrote against both the Church's shortcomings and the inordinate privileges granted the clergy by canon law. Some of the more famous examples of this form of humanistic literature are Sebastian Brant's *Ship of Fools* and Erasmus's *The Praise of Folly*.

In addition to the resentment provoked by the clergy's practices, the most important nontheological force supporting the spread of Lutheranism was the growing movement of political nationalism. Indeed as nationalism became a force in Europe local princes increasingly saw Protestantism as a vehicle for promoting their own special interests. Not surprisingly both the Holy Roman Empire and the church resisted the development of nationalistic identifications and the creation of the nation-state.

Although it is difficult to give precise dates for the beginnings of the nation-state movement, there is little doubt that by the thirteenth century the empire had ceased to be the political force it once was. At its periphery now, new national entities were developing wherein the loyalties of citizens were increasingly attaching to the national monarchs. For example, in France as early as 1202 the king had declared that he would not recognize the emperor as his superior when dealing with the temporal affairs of France. And by 1303 the theoretical claim of French independence had been established by John of Paris. Similarly, but by a different route,

England was moving towards a clearer understanding of its national character. Although the *Magna Carta* of 1215 was still essentially a feudalistic document, there was nonetheless a certain nationalistic tone to its rhetoric. And by the fifteenth century the English sense of nationalism was so developed that it enabled such theoreticians as Sir John Fortesque to suggest that English customs were actually superior to the traditional canon law. Indeed, in his *The Governance of England* Fortesque argued that it was the people of England who actually constituted the political society and that thus the nation should not be understood as being a mere possession of its sovereign. As these notions became more established it was clear that the imperial claim to legitimacy could no longer be seriously accepted. Even in Italy, which was somewhat slower in its development as a nation-state, one finds arguments against the imperial order as early as the fourteenth century. For example, Bartolus of Saxoferrato argued that the Italian city-states had a right to make and enforce their own laws independently of the emperor. And by 1513 Machiavelli was able to end his *The Prince* with an emotional appeal on behalf of Italian nationalism.

In addition to the Holy Roman Empire, the Roman Catholic church was the other major obstacle to the development of nationalism during this period. And here Luther's speculations proved to be most helpful. Within the balance of power achieved by the two-swords doctrine of Pope Gelasius I (492–496) the church had long maintained a traditional interest in temporal affairs. By the later Middle Ages, however, the Papacy had become increasingly interested in specifying a more exact interpretation as to the nature of its temporal claims. This initiative was resisted by the various secular authorities, and the resultant tensions between the spiritual and temporal realms became a major theme throughout the medieval period. At first the church attempted to exercise its political influence indirectly by instructing the clergy on its political duties and by governing them according to the special dictates of canon law. By the fourteenth century, however, tensions between the Papacy, France, and England produced a situation in which the church moved towards a more direct and immediate form of political interference. In 1302 Pope Boniface VIII published the papal bull *Unam Sanctum.* In it he declared that all humankind was under the direct authority of the pope of Rome and that thus both the temporal and spiritual powers (Gelasius's two swords) were in the hands of the pontiff. By arguing for virtually unlimited power over the temporal governments Boniface VIII had made a claim on behalf of the political supremacy of an absolute pope. Various theoretical attempts were made which sought to justify this action. Of these, the most influential was that made by the pope's counselor Aegidius Romanus (1246–1316).

Although *Unam Sanctum* did not specify a precise set of recommendations by which to institutionalize the pope's jurisdictional claims, a number of practices did develop over the years which limited the authority of the secular leaders. As a result by the sixteenth century there was a substantial hostility towards the powers of the church. Local political leaders found it extremely difficult to consolidate their rule in view of certain usages which had developed. For example, the clerical estate claimed an entire range of privileges not available to other citizens. Freedom from certain forms of taxation not only allowed clerics to accumulate large amounts of private wealth but also limited the ability of the political leaders to raise needed funds. Moreover, in many cases clerics were immune from prosecution in the ordinary courts and oftentimes were able to prosecute laypeople in their own specially constituted ecclesiastical courts.

In addition to such privileges and immunities, local political leaders resented the supranational presence of the Papacy within their societies. The pope claimed and exercised the right to both collect papal taxes and control the awarding of certain benefits within national churches. This arrangement led at times to a situation where secular authorities had to bargain for concessions within their own jurisdictions.

These claims and practices by the church served as a barrier to the formation of national secular regimes. And it is not surprising that in those areas where resentment against papal interference was most intense, the spread of Lutheranism was most rapid. Consequently it can be argued that Luther's theological movement both encouraged and was supported by the nationalistic aspirations that were emerging during this period. Indeed, Luther's "An Open Letter to the Christian Nobility of the German Nation Concerning the Reform of the Christian Estate" was as much an attempt to evoke German resentment towards a foreign pope as it was a theological treatise.

THE POLITICAL TEACHINGS
OF MARTIN LUTHER

As has been shown, Luther's theological position was in many ways a further development of themes which were already current at the time. For example, Luther shared with such mystics as Groote an Augustinian view of human nature: it was, they understood, fundamentally flawed by the presence of sin. Whereas the humanists of the period were celebrating the individual's capacities for action and excellence, Luther discounted such achievements as vain and carnal. Characterized by the deformity of sin, human reason was pictured as being fundamentally incapable of understanding God's plan for humanity. Thus, like Ockham, Luther emphasized the inscrutable quality of God's will. The faithful cannot know what it is that God wishes of them. Thus they are to obey God's commands not inasmuch as they appear to be reasonable, as the Thomists argued, but simply because they are God's wishes.

For Luther the relationship between God and His follower was an intensely personal and immediate one. God acted immediately upon the individual by the granting of grace, and the follower responded directly in an act of faithful submission to God's will. Given such an understanding, there was no place in this scheme for an institutional church which claimed to be God's authoritative representative on earth. Luther instead spoke of the priesthood of all believers. And if the church was nothing more than God's people, there could be no special estate among its members. All Christians were called to obey Christ's commandments, and each, in turn, was individually responsible for the continuation of his or her relationship with God. The church existed as a congregation of faithful who were gathered together in God's name. It could not, therefore, rightfully assume the characteristics of a political society.

Luther's analysis of the church as a congregation was an obvious rejection of the Roman Catholic argument that the church was a society which possessed jurisdictional powers and consequently had the authority to regulate the lives of its members. According to Catholic practice, the church's jurisdictional powers required the establishment of a priestly estate which enjoyed special jurisdiction, unique privileges, and its own canon law. In addition, the popes not only claimed jurisdictional powers over the spiritual lives of the faithful but also maintained an interest and influence in temporal affairs. Luther's understanding of the church as congregation, on the other hand, obviously served to reject all such claims. According to him, the true church was ruled solely by Christ and required no coercive power. As a spiritual affair, it was entirely removed from the temporal realm. God, as the *deus absconditus*, is unknown to human understanding. Our only contact with Him, therefore, is through His revelation in the Scriptures.

Luther's emphasis upon humanity's sinfulness carried with it several important implications. For example, inasmuch as people lacked all forms of true excellence, it was impossible for them to merit salvation. There simply was nothing they could do which would earn God's reward. As a consequence, salvation was a matter of faith alone. Only those who had received God's grace and thus lived in divine righteousness were saved. This decision to grant or withhold grace was God's alone, and His motives for deciding as He did were forever hidden from human reason. Luther found support for this position in his analysis of Scripture and in particular in his distinction between the Old and New Testaments. The Old Testament was a book of laws; it set forth commands which, given humankind's corrupted nature, were impossible to fulfill. Thus the message of the Old Testament was in the form of a lesson designed to teach the sinful about their inabilities and consequently prepare them for God's action. The New Testament, on the other hand, transcended the law. Having shown that humanity is incapable of accomplishing the works demanded by the law, the New Testament introduced God's redeeming grace. Through God's action human beings were saved and consequently were moved from a condition of despair to one of faith.

In examining the political consequence of Luther's arguments two items are particularly relevant. First, Luther's understanding of the relationship between God and humanity implied a view of the church which had important consequences for the social order of his time. Second, in searching Scripture for guidance concerning the faithful's political duties, Luther developed a theory of politics which was based upon his reading of the teachings of St. Paul. These factors, in turn, combined to provide a stimulus for the creation of secular political absolutism.

The effect of Luther's analysis was to argue for the removal of the institutional church from the temporal realm. However, inasmuch as the traditional social order had been one which was structured by the temporal presence of both church and state, the church's removal had the effect of creating a power vacuum which encouraged the expansion of secular authority. The church had traditionally been one of the major obstacles to the development of the European nation-state. With its removal, however, the secular authorities emerged as the only ones who could legitimately claim the right to the sovereign exercise of coercive power. Thus Luther's arguments concerning the nature of the church had the effect of sanctioning the wholesale extension of secular national power.

The second major element of Luther's political thinking was based upon his reading of the New Testament. Luther's attitude toward the church had provided certain negative guidelines vis-à-vis the social order. It remained, however, for Luther to consider such positive problems as the purpose of society, the duties of the secular authority, and the obligations of its subjects. In considering these issues, Luther was deeply influenced by the letters of St. Paul and, in particular, the Pauline notion that all authority ultimately comes from God.

Luther's advice to Kings and princes begins with an admonition to remember that inasmuch as they have received their powers from God, they must be certain to use them in a godly way. As such they are to care for the needs of their subjects and in general command for the sake of truth. Specifically they should strive to protect their people from external force, preserve internal peace, and do what they can to foster the true religion. Yet inasmuch as the true religion was held to be based on an inner experience, secular authority was warned to never use coercive force in its efforts to maintain that religion:

> Heresy can never be restrained by force. One will have to tackle the
> problem in some other way, for heresy must be opposed and dealt

with otherwise than with the sword. Here God's word must do the fighting. If it does not succeed, certainly the temporal power will not succeed either, even if it were to drench the world in blood.[3]

In general, Luther's analysis of secular authority encouraged an expanded role for the temporal ruler. From Luther's perspective original sin and the human inclination toward evil necessitated a government of force. And because the maintenance of order required the power of the sword, rulers could claim almost limitless control over the lives of their subjects. Yet there was one important qualification. Inasmuch as the rulers' authority was to be a direct expression of God's providence, their subjects were obliged in conscience to disobey them in those cases where they command them to undertake evil actions. Liberty of conscience, therefore, was established as a definte limit to the exercise of absolute political power.

Yet it is important to note that for Luther, at least up until 1530, the people's liberty of conscience did not imply the right of active resistance. Referring to Paul's warning, "Let every soul be subject to the governing authority, for there is not authority except from God," Luther insisted that subjects could not rightfully resist their leaders. Even the tyrant could not be resisted; for inasmuch as all authority came from God, the tyrant had to be respected as one sent by God to punish a people for its past sins. According to Luther, to resist a ruler was equivalent to resisting the will of God. This insistence, in turn, had the effect of removing a long-standing limitation upon the exercise of secular authority. Traditionally natural-law theorists had argued that humanity was capable of knowing nature's law and that such knowledge could provide an individual with a universal standard by which to judge the validity of particular political acts. As such, it enabled one to evaluate, criticize, and even condemn those rulers who repeatedly violated the law of nature. Luther, on the other hand, rejected this possibility. Not only was human reason too impaired by sin to be able to know the demands of natural justice, but Paul's admonition to the Romans was interpreted as commanding passive obedience to all rulers.

This argument changed dramatically in 1530, however, as the Lutherans found themselves in a critical situation. Emperor Charles V had convened the Diet of Speyer in 1529, and under his leadership the Catholic majority passed a resolution which called for the suppression of Luther's heresy, by force if necessary. Faced with this challenge Luther moved cautiously toward a doctrine of active resistance. Two arguments were introduced to justify this decision. The first was based upon an interpretation of the imperial constitution. It was argued that the constitution allowed

---

[3] J. M. Porter, ed., *Luther: Selected Political Writings* (Philadelphia: Fortress Press, 1974), p. 63.

local princes to resist the emperor if the emperor violated the terms of election by overextending the powers of imperial office. The second argument was based upon the private-law tradition. Here it was suggested that both the civil law and the canon law acknowledged instances where officials could be resisted when they acted outside of the duties of their office. By interfering in matters of faith, Emperor Charles V was acting within an area in which he had no legitimate role to play. Thus in these undertakings, he was not, strictly speaking, acting as emperor *per se* and could not, therefore, claim the protection of office.

Preoccupied with other concerns, Charles never fully followed through on his threats, and the crisis of 1530 soon passed. Thus Lutheranism continued to spread and was particularly successful in Germany, Scandinavia, England, Scotland, and France. Indeed by 1546 it was possible for the Protestant forces, united in the Schmalkaldic League, to declare war against the emperor. Although the Protestants were badly routed by Charles at Muehlberg, it was only the beginning of a series of battles which continued inconclusively until the compromise of the Peace of Augsburg in 1555. This peace was established upon the principle of *cuius regio, eius religio*, that is, the people shall adopt the religion of their ruler. With this compromise, the medieval vision of a politically and religiously united Europe finally disappeared. Whereas at one time the universal Roman church had claimed to pass judgment on the legitimacy of Europe's secular rulers, now individual national princes could, in effect, determine the religion of their subjects.

THE POLITICAL TEACHINGS OF JOHN CALVIN

The relationship between Luther and Calvin (1509–1564) was not a simple one. Although they shared in common many of the fundamental principles of the reformist theology, differences of emphasis, style, and character produced doctrinal distinctions. Thus, similar to Luther, Calvin emphasized humanity's total dependence upon God—even to the extent of acknowledging the doctrine of predestination. Yet, unlike Luther, Calvin accepted the possibility of a natural law and thus argued that the people "are not altogether lacking in knowledge of right and equity." Similarly, like Luther, Calvin considered the Scriptures to be God's direct revelation to his people. Its truth could be self-authenticated and thus did not require the exegesis of a clerical hierarchy. Yet—whereas Luther understood the New Testament as having superseded the Old Law—Calvin argued that the New Testament was essentially a reaffirmation of the principles of the Old Law and thereby a continuation of the holy covenant based upon humankind's promise to obey the Ten Commandments.

As far as the political theorist is concerned, however, the most important feature of Calvinist political thought is its development of the Lutheran theory of active political resistance. Calvin's original position was similar to that of Luther in the 1520s, that is, essentially a repetition of the Pauline doctrine of absolute nonresistance. Although the people did not have to obey those commands which would cause them to violate the wishes of God, resistance against rulers—even if they were tyrannical—was not permitted. As Calvin wrote in his "Commentaries on Romans":

> The reason why we ought to be subject to magistrates is because they are constituted by God's ordination. . . . For since a wicked prince is the Lord's scourge to punish the sins of the people, let us remember that it happens through our fault that this excellent blessing of God is turned into a curse.[4]

Like Luther, however, Calvin began to modify his position on resistance as the Holy Roman Empire intensified its persecution of the heretics. Indeed, by the 1560s he had adopted the Lutheran justification of active resistance, which was based upon the Protestant interpretation of the imperial constitution. As has been shown, this particular interpretation argued that lesser magistrates of the empire could legitimately resist the emperor when he acted beyond the scope of his original duties. In accepting this doctrine, however, Calvin introduced a fundamental modification. In its original version, the constitutionalist argument specified that the emperor could be resisted only by the lesser magistrates of the empire. Thus it was not a doctrine of popular resistance but rather one based upon a concept of federal powers. In his *Institutes*, however, Calvin referred to the tradition of the *ephorate*. Pointing to Sparta, Rome, and Athens he spoke of popular magistrates (*ephors*) elected by the people who were empowered to protect them from the cruelty of the king. Although the ephors were ordained by God, they were, nonetheless, empowered and elected by the people. Thus the suggestion of a popular right to resist seems clear.

Inasmuch as Calvin himself never really moved beyond certain modifications of the mature Lutheran position, the major development in resistance theory took place in the hands of his radical Continental followers. The immediate occasion for this development was the persecution of the Huguenots during the French religious wars. Under increasing pressure from certain Catholic nobility, Catherine de Medici of France had

---

[4] John T. McNeill, ed., *On God and Political Duty: John Calvin*, 2nd ed., rev., (Indianapolis: Bobbs-Merrill, 1956), pp. 84–86.

initiated a program of religious persecutions against the French Protestants which culminated in the massacre of the Huguenot leadership on St. Bartholomew's day in 1572. This act effectively destroyed any attempt to reach an accommodation between the monarchy and the Protestants and consequently was followed by a number of Huguenot cities withdrawing their allegiance to the crown. Within the context of these events radical Calvinist justifications for such actions soon began to appear.

At first these justifications tended simply to emphasize the defensive nature of the Huguenot action. Pointing to the tyrannical character of the regime and emphasizing the monarchy's violation of long-standing customs, the Calvinists sought to explain their actions in terms of justified self-defense. A more sophisticated analysis was required, however, and ironically it was achieved by turning to the scholastic arguments of the Counter-Reformation.

In an effort to combat the heretical arguments of the early Reformation, the church had encouraged the revival of Thomistic philosophy. Among those who led this movement were the Dominican Francisco de Vitoria (1485–1546) and the Jesuits Robert Bellarmine (1542–1611) and Francisco Suarez (1548–1617). This revival had a dual purpose. First, it attempted to correct the Lutheran view of the church, and secondly, it argued against certain features of the Lutheran attitude toward secular society. In particular, the Thomists were concerned with discounting the Protestant thesis that all political power was directly ordained by God.

In response, therefore, the Thomists emphasized both humanity's ability to comprehend the laws of nature and the purely secular character of political society. According to these arguments, humans were pictured as originally being in a state of nature in which a coercive society did not yet exist. In this condition humanity had enjoyed a natural community which was structured by a knowledge of the laws of nature and which was based upon a recognition of freedom, equality, and independence. Given this assumption, the central question, of course, was why did humanity leave this arrangement and create, thereby, a political society with its inevitable constraints upon freedom and consequent lack of equality. The general answer was that the decision was made because of the belief that if humankind remained in its natural condition, human weakness would bring about an increasing degree of injustice and insecurity. For the Thomists, the human being was a creature of sin and, therefore, ultimately required the guidance and discipline of the positive law.

The true importance of the Thomistic theory of the state of nature resided in its immediate political implications. First, according to this theory political society was not ordained by God but rather was simply a human creation established for purely mundane ends. Second, the idea that humans had agreed among themselves to establish a political society implied that consent was the true basis for all political authority. Accordingly, popular agreement, not divine grace, was the true foundation of political community, and thus the ruler's personal godliness was not an issue to be considered.

Although certain elements of the scholastic argument already appeared in three anonymous pamphlets published in 1574, the most famous Huguenot statement was Philippe Du Plessis Mornay's (1549–1623) *Defense of Liberty against Tyrants.* Mornay's argument drew heavily upon the Thomistic tradition. Accordingly, he emphasized that humanity had left its natural condition of liberty in order to secure the advantages of society. Consequently, the obvious purpose of society was to promote the subject's welfare, and, inasmuch as society was based upon consent, it was ordered by the terms of the contract to which the members, or their representatives, had agreed. This contract, in turn, implied on one hand a moral obligation on the part of the magistrates who had accepted it and, on the other, a moral right on the part of the people to see that through the offices of their representatives its terms were adhered to. The effect of this argument, then, was to provide a rational justification for resistance which was based upon a conception of representative popular sovereignty. Revolution now was no longer justified simply in terms of the need to secure a particular religious dogma; rather it was based upon an understanding of the moral rights of humans as natural beings.

The Huguenot theories of the 1570s enjoyed a wide influence throughout both France and the Netherlands. The final development of Calvinist thought, however, took place in Scotland and is most closely associated with the work of George Buchanan (1506–1582). Because of the influence of such reformers as John Knox (1505–1572), Scotland had become a Calvinist stronghold and in 1567 succeeded in deposing its Catholic queen, Mary Queen of Scots. Writing in defense of this action Buchanan began his argument with the typical Huguenot analysis of humanity's natural condition. Yet, unlike his French counterparts, Buchanan did not argue that the people had originally delegated their authority to their chosen representatives. His conception of popular sovereignty, on the contrary, was much more direct. The people had designated their own rulers directly and thus retained in themselves the right of resistance. In addition, Buchanan insisted upon the individualistic nature of the natural person. The people came together as individuals to form a society and, in so doing, retained their individuality. Thus society was formed not only for the sake of the common good but also on behalf of the individual interests of the consenting citizens. The implications of this particular approach were much more radical than the French or the Thomists would have allowed. For Buchanan, the right to resist a tyrant rested not only with the people as a whole but also with each individual citizen.

In developing an individualistic account of popular sovereignty, Buchanan had arrived at a position which appears remarkably similar to the modern constitutional theory which would be developed over a hundred years later by the Englishman John Locke. As such, Buchanan attests to a certain link between the modern age and its Calvinist, and therefore scholastic, predecessors.

BIBLIOGRAPHY

ALLEN, J. W. *A History of Political Thought in the Sixteenth Century.* New York: Barnes & Noble, 1960.

ANDERSON, PERRY. *Lineages of the Absolutist State.* London: Verso Editions, 1979.

COHN, NORMAN. *The Pursuit of the Millennium.* New York: Harper & Row, 1961.

CRANZ, F. EDWARD. *An Essay on the Development of Luther's Thoughts on Justice, Law and Society.* Cambridge: Harvard University Press, 1959.

ELTON, G. R. *Reformation Europe: 1517–1559.* Cleveland: Meridian Books, 1963.

FIGGIS, J. N. *Political Thought from Gerson to Grotius, 1414–1625.* New York: Harper & Row, 1960.

GIERKE, OTTO VON. *Natural Law and the Theory of Society, 1500–1800.* 2 vols. Translated by Ernest Barker. Cambridge: Cambridge University Press, 1950.

MURRAY, ROBERT H. *Political Consequences of the Reformation*, New York: Russell & Russell, 1960.

SKINNER, QUENTIN. *The Foundations of Modern Political Thought*, Vol. 2: *The Age of the Reformation.* Cambridge: Cambridge University Press, 1978.

TROELTSCH, E. *The Social Teaching of the Christian Churches.* Vol. 2. Translated by O. Wyon. Chicago: University of Chicago Press, 1976.

8

INTELLECTUAL REVOLUTION OF THE SEVENTEENTH CENTURY

Both the Renaissance and Reformation may be characterized as periods which attempted to strengthen Western society through a process of renewal and conservation. For example, Machiavelli looked back to the ancient Roman Republic as a model for contemporary political order, while both Luther and Calvin sought to purify Christianity by overcoming those compromises which the institutional church had made with humanity, society, and history. In each case the intention was to secure that element of the tradition which the theorist believed to be important for the preservation of a renewed order. In this sense, then, the political theory of the period exhibited an essentially conservative character. And as such it tended to emphasize the continuity of human political experience.

The seventeenth century marks a distinct departure from this attitude. In such writers as Hobbes, for example, an effort was made to begin anew. A new science of politics was to be created that would overcome the limitations of the past. Rather than being guided by the wisdom of the ancients, Hobbes sought to replace it. And the authority by which he would do so was that of unaided reason, that is, reason uninformed by and therefore unbound to any particular tradition or master. There shows in Hobbesian thinking the belief that a particular historical epoch was coming to a close. And as a new epoch begins, humanity is seen as capable of leaving behind the former and thereby starting anew. Beginning in the seventeenth century such an epochal consciousness gradually replaced the conservative character of the earlier period, and in the eighteenth, nineteenth, and twentieth centuries it became an ingredient in such diverse movements as positivism, progressivism, and Marxism.

An attempt to explain the emergence of this new form of consciousness serves as a reminder that political philosophy is conditioned by the events and developments of its day. Although it may claim a universal validity, it, nonetheless, emerges within a particular historical context. Political philosophers are responding to specific problems and challenges, and in doing so they address questions which are presented to them in a particular way. In a certain sense, then, the question forms the answer. As a response to a challenge political philosophy is, in part, engaged in a dialogue. And as participants within a dialogue, political philosophers are conditioned by those beliefs, assumptions, and expectations about what actually constitutes responsible and serious discussion. The ideas of political philosophers, therefore, are located within, although not necessarily limited to, the climate of opinion of their age. This situation becomes quite clear in an examination of the epochal consciousness that emerges in seventeenth-century political thought. For the climate of opinion at that time was profoundly affected by the development of modern science. Indeed for some, the new epoch actually began with the birth of modern science. Given this, it is impossible to understand the assumptions and ambitions of modern political philosophy without at the same time appreciating its basis within modern scientific civilization. The structure of this civilization, in turn, is most evident in the writings of Francis Bacon and Rene Descartes.

FRANCIS BACON

Born in 1561, Francis Bacon was a contemporary of Galileo and shared with him a profound enthusiasm for the promise of modern science. Although Bacon's scientific work was not particularly enduring, he, along with Rene Descartes, is often credited with providing the larger philosophical foundation for the scientific movement. Born to a politically involved family Bacon was to spend most of his life dealing in the affairs of the royal court. After several years at Cambridge he turned to the serious study of law. Soon Bacon established himself as an eminent legal authority and, in 1584, was given a seat in the House of Commons. During his thirty-six years in Parliament he championed such causes as the codification of English law, the modification of legal penalties, and the protection of parliamentary privileges vis-à-vis the monarchy. In 1603 he was knighted by King James and served in a number of capacities ranging from counsel to lord chancellor of the realm. Because of his political career Bacon was able to turn only periodically to his scientific and philosophic projects. In 1621, however, he left politics to devote himself full-time to the collecting and categorizing of natural history. While experimenting with the preservative powers of snow, he became ill and died in 1626.

Bacon's most important writings include his *Essays* (1597, 1625), *Advancement of Learning* (1605), *New Organon* (1620), and the posthumously published utopia *New Atlantis*.

The intention of Bacon's writing is revealed by the fact that both *Advancement of Learning* and *New Organon* (new rules of logic) were only parts of a larger and unfinished work entitled *The Great Instauration* (the great beginning). According to Bacon Western civilization was in need of a total renovation, and his call for a new science must be understood in terms of its contribution to that larger project. As he wrote in the poem to *The Great Instauration*:

> Now that the errors which have hitherto prevailed, and which will prevail for ever, should . . . either by the natural force of the understanding or by help of the aids and instruments of logic, one by one, correct themselves was a thing not to be hoped for, because the primary motions of things . . . are false, confused, and overhastily abstracted from facts; nor are the secondary and subsequent notions less arbitrary and inconstant; whence it follows that the entire fabric of human reason which we employ in the inquisition of nature is badly put together and built up, and like some magnificent structure without any foundation. . . . There was but one course left, therefore, to try the whole thing anew upon a better plan, and to commence a total reconstruction of sciences, arts, and all human knowledge raised upon the proper foundations.[1]

Bacon's Conception of Science

At the center of Bacon's analysis was his critique of traditional Western science. For him this traditional path had failed to penetrate to an adequate understanding of the deeper truths of nature. Rather than systematically investigating the fundamental coherencies of the natural order, traditional science had formed its arguments using only superficial

---

[1] Francis Bacon, *The New Organon and Related Writings*, ed. Fulton H. Anderson (Indianapolis: Bobbs-Merrill, 1960), p. 3.

evidence and operating according to the rules of an inadequate logic. Bacon's remedy was to propose the scientific method of induction and, his *New Organon* was a systematic attempt to present this understanding. Unfortunately this work was never completed. Of the eleven steps Bacon outlined, only three are developed in any detail. Yet, on the other hand, there is enough information to appreciate the general project which Bacon had in view. The scientific method was to serve as the means for disciplining and organizing the mind. In the past, according to Bacon, human beings had been plagued by certain innate and acquired mental habits ("the idols") which had both distorted their view of nature and, thereby, limited their ability to control it. Bacon believed that with the imposition of a uniform scientific method these distortions could be reduced.

His argument is fairly complex. After examining both the inadequacies inherent within the traditional interpretation of deductive logic and the weakness of Greek natural philosophy, Bacon developed his own program which would call for a new logic, a new natural history, and a new theory of causation. It is not necessary to describe all of those features in detail. Several themes, however, are important if we are to appreciate the climate of opinion which was forming during this period. In particular, one must examine Bacon's understanding of the role of the method, his view concerning the structure of nature, and his belief concerning humanity's proper place within it. Each of these arguments will have a decided influence upon the character of modernity.

Although he rejects many of the claims of traditional wisdom, Bacon was by no means a skeptic. On the contrary, he had an overwhelming faith in the power of reason. The past's failure to develop an adequate natural science was not due to an inevitable weakness within reason itself. Rather it was due to the simple fact that the proper scientific method had not yet been developed. According to Bacon humans can gain knowledge only with the assistance of the one, true, universal method, and—as the first element in his program to erect the new scientific civilization—it was his claim to have developed such a device. The purpose of the method was to discipline the mind, for without proper order humanity tended toward confusion. Indeed such confusion was the fatal flaw which characterized the scientists of the past:

> For they have been content to follow probable reason and are carried around in a whirl of arguments and, in the promiscuous liberty of search have relaxed the severity of inquiry. . . . Some there are indeed who have committed themselves to the waves of experience and almost turned mechanics yet these again have in their very experiments pursued a kind of wandering inquiry, without any regular system of operations.[2]

[2] Bacon, *New Organon*, p. 11.

A closer reading of Bacon's description of the method reveals that he hoped to achieve this state of mental order by reducing the role of the scientist's personality. The active personalities of scientists tended to interfere with and distort the flow of information which they were receiving from their environment. Accurate cognition, therefore, required that scientists assume a passive rather than an active role during investigations. If this could be accomplished, the uniform rules of an impersonal method would replace the vagaries of the individual personality:

> Wherein if I have made any progress, the way has been opened to me by no other means than the true and legitimate humiliation of the human spirit. For all those who before me have applied themselves to the invention of arts have but cast a glance or two upon facts and examples and experience, and straightway proceeded, as if invention were nothing more than an exercise of thought, to invoke their own spirits to give them oracles. I, on the contrary, dwelling purely and constantly among the facts of nature, withdraw my intellect from them no further than may suffice to let the images and rays of natural objects meet in a point, as they do in the sense of vision; whence it follows that the strength and excellence of the wit has but little to do in the matter.[3]

This particular understanding of the method's function in reducing the scientist to a passive spectator has several obvious implications. First, inasmuch as the personality of the knower is removed from the act of cognition, the particular qualities of individual scientists make no essential contribution to their inquiries. Thus, second, who you are does not determine what you can know. Rather each of us insofar as we submit to the discipline of the method has an equal access to the truth. Finally, as a consequence, there is no privileged status, no unique position which is available only to the few:

> But the course I propose for the discovery of sciences is such as leaves but little to the acuteness and strength of wits, but places all wits and understandings nearly on a level.[4]

By insisting upon the egalitarian quality of his method, Bacon undermined the arguments of those who would claim a privileged status because of unique insight. For example, Plato had argued that philosophers should rule because of their knowledge of the good; this knowledge, in turn, was something they possessed precisely because of who they were. As philoso-

3 Bacon, *New Organon*, pp. 13–14.
4 Bacon, *New Organon*, p. 58.

phers they were different than most citizens. This difference, based on the experience of conversion, gave them access to those levels of being of which most humans remain unaware. Thus the authority of philosophers was derived from their uniqueness—a uniqueness that could not be overcome by the simple application of a scientific method. If, as Plato argued, who you are does make a difference in what you can know, then a regime based upon such knowledge would necessarily be hierarchically structured.

Bacon's egalitarian epistemology, on the other hand, discounted the claim for a natural hierarchy and, as such, gave support to the democratic character of the modern age. In addition, it encouraged faith in the compelling power of reason. If all citizens can in principle come to know reality, then there is nothing in principle which denies the possibility of a future age marked by consensus and agreement. Disagreements and misunderstandings could no longer be attributed to the fundamental moral and personal differences among individuals. Rather the natural condition would be one of consensus. Truths firmly established through an exercise of the scientific method would easily replace the variety of opinions characteristic of traditional politics. Inasmuch as disagreement was not rooted in irreducible qualities of character and type, the viability of a universal method offered promise of an age of peace and accord. Modern science would serve, in effect, as the dogmatic core of a new society which would be free of strife and fundamental conflict.

Such a picture is the explicit theme of Bacon's *New Atlantis*. In this utopian novel, he develops a picture of life in the community of Bensalem. The central institution of this society is a community of scientists who undertake the fundamental scientific projects which Bacon had outlined in his *New Organon*. These scientists, members of the House of Solomon, are the intellectual and spiritual leaders of Bensalem; they bring to it the fruits of their research and serve as guardians of the popular culture. Bensalem in general represents a model society deliberately founded upon the central authority of modern science. What is most striking about Bacon's description is the relative absence of political conflict within such a society. The main political task is not the adjudication of conflict but the preservation of an existing harmony from possibly disruptive foreign elements. As the primary source of direction and counsel for Bensalem, the House of Solomon, composed of over fifty scientists and apprentices, speaks as if with one voice. Indeed there appears to be no mechanism for resolving conflict among the many offices of the house itself. Bacon's utopia appears to be suggesting that a society based upon modern science can successfully transcend the divisiveness and plurality so characteristic of traditional politics. This hope and its implied impatience with diversity was to become increasingly characteristic of the modern age in general and of the Enlightenment in particular.

The second element in Bacon's program for a new scientific civilization is concerned with the Western understanding of nature. Traditionally nature was understood to be a hierarchically ordered whole. Both the Aristotelian notion of final cause and the Christian concept of creation suggested that the natural world was part of a planned order which was both good and rational. Humanity did not picture itself as a master over nature; rather for the Greeks the human being was a participant, and for Christianity, a steward. As a meaningfully structured whole, nature appeared to have both a design and a purpose. Thus it possessed a dignity and stability which served as both a guide to and limitation upon human activity.

With the development of modern science in the seventeenth century, however, the traditional understanding of nature became increasingly questionable. This is reflected in Bacon's work in particular within his discussion of causation. For Bacon nature was essentially matter-in-motion. Natural phenomena could be understood solely in terms of efficient and material causes. "Efficient cause" is the motion which brings about a certain result; "material cause" is the matter out of which something is made. Accordingly nature appears to be nothing more than matter set into motion. If this is accepted, the traditional concepts of design (formal cause) and purpose (final cause) become superfluous to any description of nature. Bacon retained the term "formal cause" but redefined it to mean nothing more than a general law used to describe individual acts. The concept of final causation, on the other hand, was rejected completely. According to Bacon the notion of purpose was appropriate only in a description of human actions. To suggest that nature had a purpose would be to project the category into an area where it does not belong.

If nature is without design or purpose, then it is obvious that it cannot be the source for any legitimate standard by which to limit or guide human actions. Lacking formal cause, nature is unbounded. Lacking final cause, it has no goal. In short, nature is indifferent.

This view of nature's essential neutrality represented a radical challenge to traditional political philosophy. In the past political philosophers had attempted to base their speculations upon an understanding of the nature of things. For example, an understanding of human nature would allow one to comprehend the *human* good. Similarly an understanding of the nature of the political community would allow citizens to comprehend the *political* good. In both cases, then, the good was what particular natures intended it to be and thus what they existed for. If, however, nature is truly indifferent, it intends no particular good. The "good," consequently, becomes simply a value or preference which humans artificially create and bring to nature. In doing so, they impose a preferred "ought" upon a neutral "is."

This new understanding of nature posed a dilemma for the traditional ethical systems of the West. If humanity cannot point to nature as the source for its convictions, wherein lies their authority? Bacon himself was careful to avoid drawing such radical political and ethical conclusions from his arguments. On the contrary, he attempted to limit his discussion to the sphere of the natural sciences. Religious, ethical, and political beliefs were explicitly exempted from his discussion. In these matters Bacon accepted Christian revelation as the source of knowledge and professed thereby a loyalty to the tradition and practices of the past. Yet the logic of his arguments suggested otherwise, and that lesson was not lost on those who were to come.

Bacon's understanding of nature as mere matter-in-motion carried with it an explicit assumption concerning humanity's proper role in nature: lacking purpose and design, nature is simply material, and as material it is there to be used by and for humanity. Thus in the Baconian universe humans are primarily technicians. Their science provides the means by which they can extend their control over natural phenomena. This control, in turn, is to be exercised for the sake of human utility. As Bacon wrote in the *New Organon:*

> . . . I am laboring to lay the foundation, not of any sect or doctrine, but of human utility and power.[5]

According to Bacon, then, humans become the purpose-givers to a purposeless world. Nature is there to be used, and science becomes the pragmatic attempt to exploit such possibilities.

Several consequences follow from such a conception. First, the new science of the seventeenth century opened the door to modern industrial society. In a significant way the technological society of the twentieth century is simply a logical extension of the program first developed during the seventeenth century. Thus the plundering of nature today may be but an extreme form of Baconian exploitation and is possible only as long as Western people retain their belief that nature is essentially an object for their use.

Second, Bacon's suggestion that humans are essentially purpose-givers to a purposeless world challenges the classical commitment to the life of contemplation. Classical-Greek theory sought to understand the nature of the good society. Although the various theorists disagreed on many of the particulars, they shared in the common belief that the good society was intimately related to the life of contemplation (*bios theoretikos*). Accordingly

---

[5] Bacon, *New Organon*, p. 16.

the good society was to be ordered in such a way that the life of contemplation would be a dominant force in society's affairs. Its preeminent role was due to the classical belief that such a life represented the highest form of human excellence. Humans were seen as fulfilling their potential through the exercise of their rational faculties. Society, in turn, was to encourage and support such an achievement.

The classical understanding of the rational life assumed that other human activities were important precisely to the degree that they contributed to the development of rational excellence. The life of politics and the life of production were seen as subsidiary to the life of reason. They sustained life and thus made the good life possible.

With the development of Bacon's conception of nature and of science the life of production began to replace the life of reason as the highest form of human excellence. For Bacon, nature lacked design and purpose. Therefore it could not serve as an object for contemplation. Nature was to be used; and, as a used object, it stood over and against the human being, who now appeared as *homo faber*. The Baconian universe, therefore, posited a new philosophy of human nature and represented thereby a radical departure from the classical tradition. As the conception of human excellence changed, so too did the modern understanding of the good society. These changes became explicit in the writings of Thomas Hobbes and John Locke.

DESCARTES AND THE CARTESIAN METHOD

Another key representative of the modern spirit which was emerging in the seventeenth century was France's Rene Descartes (1596–1650). In addition to his scientific work in such fields as mathematics, geometry, meteorology, and optics, Descartes's philosophical writings have earned him the reputation as being a founder of modern philosophy. Among his most important philosophical publications are *Discourse on Method* (1637), *Meditations on First Philosophy* (1641), and *Rules for the Direction of the Mind* (published posthumously, 1701).

The *Discourse on Method* is particularly helpful in an effort to understand Descartes's experience of and reaction to the culture of his time. Although the title suggests that the treatise was primarily concerned with the rules of scientific inquiry, it does, in fact, contain only four sentences on the scientific method narrowly defined. This does not imply, however, that Descartes had not yet developed his method. Indeed from 1625 to 1628 he had been at work on his *Rules for the Direction of the Mind*, and it is evident that Descartes had already developed his understanding of this central feature for his philosophy by 1637. The *Discourse*, then, provides a simple introduction to Cartesianism in general and is particularly important for an understanding of those experiences which motivated Descartes's thinking.

The first part of the *Discourse* is entitled "Thoughts on Science." In this section Descartes related his fundamental dissatisfaction with the available intellectual traditions of the age. In particular Western culture, in both its formal and common forms, was characterized by a level of disagreement and variety which Descartes believed to be inappropriate. If, as Descartes assumed, reality was ultimately clear and simple, then our knowledge of it should be compelling and precise. Indeed Descartes understood precision and consensus to be characteristics of the most advanced mathematical sciences and proof, thereby, of their superiority. Thus it was the absence of such conditions in the nonmathematical sciences which led Descartes to reject their claims to legitimacy. Both his formal training and extensive traveling had failed to produce that body of certain knowledge which Descartes sought. Faced with this situation he resolved to disregard the available intellectual traditions and, in the spirit of Bacon, to begin anew:

> Nevertheless, as far as the opinions which I had been receiving since my birth were concerned, I could not do better than to reject them completely for once in my lifetime. . . . [6]

Descartes's analysis of the conditions accounting for the failures of Western science are particularly interesting. Assuming that diversity and disagreement are indeed indications of scientific failure, the question arises whether such conditions can be overcome and, if so, how? In the classical-Greek tradition, for example, there is a marked tolerance for such diversity because it was seen as unavoidable. Disagreement was accepted in part because of an appreciation of the tremendous richness and fecundity of reality itself. For example, Plato believed that reality was simply too rich and meaningful to be easily captured within the words and logic of a single dogmatic system. Second, the classical Greeks realized that the demands of philosophy were so great as to prevent all but a select few from achieving that rational insight which was characteristic of philosophical consciousness. Differences in insight were thus associated with irreducible differences in personal character. Indeed such thinkers as Plato and Aristotle understood the importance of rational persuasion; yet at the same time they appreciated its limits and restrictions. Accordingly neither philosopher pro-

[6] Rene Descartes, *Discourse on Method*, trans. Laurence J. Lafleur (Indianapolis: Bobbs-Merrill, 1956), p. 9.

jected the utopian vision of a political community free from internal discord and disagreement.

Descartes's analysis was decidedly different. In his view fundamental differences among the rational skills of human beings do not exist. Those obvious differences in degree which are evident to all do not in reality establish a qualitatively significant distinction among people. For Descartes, all individuals are essentially equal in their capacity for reasoned thought. Similar to Bacon, he therefore substituted an egalitarian view of human nature for the hierarchical model of the classical Greeks:

> Good sense is mankind's most equitably divided endowment, for everyone thinks that he is so abundantly provided with it that even those most difficult to please in other ways do not usually want more than they have of this. As it is not likely that everyone is mistaken, this evidence shows that the ability to judge correctly and to distinguish the true from the false—which is reality and what is meant by good sense or reason—is the same by nature in all men. . . .[7]

Given this fundamental equality among the rational capacities of people, how, then, can one explain the wide variety of opinion and disagreement which Descartes found so unsettling. Descartes's answer was essentially a methodological one. Humankind has heretofore failed in its effort to establish a uniform technique by which to govern human inquiry:

> . . . differences of opinion are not due to differences in intelligence, but merely to the fact that we use different approaches and consider different things. For it is not enough to have a good mind; one must use it well.[8]

With such an analysis Descartes had obviously indicated the form which his effort to establish a new scientific civilization would have to take. According to his understanding, disagreement and variety can be overcome precisely because there is a fundamental rational equality among people. The source of conflict, therefore, does not rest in human nature but rather in the variety of techniques and methods which humans have used throughout history. The solution is obvious: a single, universal method must be found and established as the dogmatic core for a new order. It is precisely this task which Descartes believed he had accomplished.

The Cartesian method is essentially a design for orderly thought. In

[7] Descartes, *Discourse on Method*, pp. 1–2.
[8] Descartes, *Discourse on Method*, p. 2.

its skeletal form, its components are the following. By a process of analysis complex ideas should be broken down into their simplest elements. These, in turn, should be examined in such a way that only those ideas which are so clear and distinct as to withstand all doubt are to be accepted as true. Complex structures can then be reassembled by progressing from the simplest and easiest concepts to the more complex. Finally this whole process should be carefully monitored and each step reviewed so as to insure that nothing is omitted.

Throughout the last 350 years, philosophers have commented upon and debated the numerous implications of Descartes's approach. For our purposes, it is necessary only to mention the following. Of the first implication (Cartesian Universality), it is important to note Descartes's own understanding of the character of his method. According to him, this method was *universal*. That is to say, it contained the single correct approach for all fields of study. As he wrote in his *Rules:*

> For this discipline ought to contain the first rudiments of human reason and be broad enough to bring out the truths of any subject whatsoever.[9]

It was precisely this belief in the universal applicability of his method which allowed Descartes to hope that he could overcome the cultural variety which was so characteristic of the past. Human reason, shared equally by all and aided by a single universal method, appeared to be capable of establishing a rational consensus among individuals. Although Descartes was careful to explicitly limit the scope of his method to the natural sciences, the logic of his argument transcended such a narrow limitation. Indeed Descartes was sensitive to the danger of appearing to be either a theological or political radical. Galileo's trial had made a deep impression upon Descartes, and he repeatedly affirmed his commitment to Roman Catholic doctrine. Yet such affirmations had little effect upon the logic and message implicit within his philosophy. In the third part of the *Discourse*, entitled "Some Moral Rules Derived from the Method," Descartes advocated a general rule of conformity and moderation:

> The first was to obey the laws and customs of my country, constantly retaining the religion in which, by God's grace, I had been brought up since childhood, and in all other matters to follow the most moderate and least excessive opinions to be found in the practice of the most judicious part of the community in which I would live.[10]

---

[9] Rene Descartes, *Rules for the Direction of the Mind*, trans. Laurence Lafleur (Indianapolis: Bobbs-Merrill, 1961), p. 14.

[10] Descartes, *Discourse on Method*, p. 15.

Such a rule has the obvious advantage of preserving the privacy and freedom of its practitioners. Those who follow it would be left alone thus enabling them to devote themselves more freely to their tasks. If we assume that Descartes followed his own advice, then we would expect him to deny that there were political or theological implications within his system. Yet the logic of his argument stood above such denials. If the method were truly universal, then it could, in fact, be applied to all of reality. If truth must be clear and distinct, then tradition cannot be a source of truths. And if all men have an equal access to reality, then revelation can claim no special authority.

Indeed Descartes, himself, labelled his morality as a "provisional" one. Thus the clear implication is that it would be replaced by a superior code at a later date. Although Descartes never published such a code, it was the logical culmination of his system. At one time he compared all of philosophy to a tree; its roots were metaphysics; its trunk, physics; and its ultimate branch, "the perfect moral science."

A second feature of the method, according to Descartes, was its sufficiency. The successful application of the method did not depend upon any additional set of skills or any particular excellence on the part of its user. Like Bacon, Descartes believed that he had succeeded in separating cognitive success from any particular set of personal or existential prerequisites. Who you are does not condition what you can know:

> And in the entire treatise we shall strive to follow so accurately and explain so simply all paths which lie open to men for the knowledge of truth that anyone who has learned this whole method perfectly, however humble his abilities may be, will nevertheless perceive that none of these ways is less open to him than to anyone else, and that there is nothing further of which he is ignorant because of any failure of ability or method.[11]

The several implications of the position are important. First, it sustains Descartes's prior belief that the civilization of modern science will be based upon a universally shared consensus. Not only is the method universally applicable, but it is also sufficient. That is to say, because there is nothing required beyond the method, its universal scope will necessarily be realized. Second, by denying that there is any essential contribution of the knower to the success of an act of cognition, Descartes is affirming an egalitarian view of human nature. All people share in the ability to know the truth as fully as is humanly possible. Thus in this essential feature of our nature, we are all equal. As in Bacon's system, it is apparent that Cartesian rationalism refutes the classical arguments on behalf of a natural hierarchy

---

[11] Descartes, *Rules for the Direction of the Mind*, p. 35.

among humanity. If a hierarchy does not in fact exist in nature, then it is difficult to justify its existence within society. Indeed it was precisely this problem which would occupy so much of the attention of the political theorists of the seventeenth century. Beginning with a fundamental assumption of human equality, such theorists as Thomas Hobbes and John Locke would proceed to analyze those conventions responsible for the introduction of a social hierarchy. Each in turn would then attempt to legitimate such a development.

There is a third and final feature of the Cartesian system which merits some notice. Given his particular analysis of the situation and assuming the adequacy of his solution, Descartes was led to expect that certain developments would naturally follow from the implementation of his system. That is, if the method is applied, the knowledge that will result will exhibit definite features. It will be certain, clear and distinct, and most importantly, universally persuasive.

> For if one person's argument were certain and evident, he could propose it in such a way to the other one that even the latter's mind eventually would be convinced.[12]

For Descartes, then, the truths of science were so compelling and persuasive that they could literally demand to be recognized. Such a belief in the persuasive power of truth, however, carries with it a certain threat of intolerance. If truth is understood as being clear, then it can be argued that those who do not see it our way are intentionally maintaining their disagreement for ulterior reasons. If, on the other hand, truth is not seen as self-evident or universally compelling to all, then there is an implied acceptance of diversity and a toleration for honest disagreement. Opinions may vary because honest people can disagree. From Descartes's perspective, however, such disagreement would be suspect. If facts can be secured from doubt once and for all, and if all individuals in principle understand this, then what is to be gained from continual challenge and discussion? This impatience with diversity and its accompanying intolerance is only implied in Descartes's writings. It becomes quite apparent, however, in such kindred spirits as Thomas Hobbes and latter-day positivists. Although modern science was born, in part, as a reaction against the dogmatic intolerance of a moribund medieval culture, it is apparent that it contained within itself a similar predisposition. This development will become apparent in later chapters.

[12] Descartes, *Rules for the Direction of the Mind*, p. 6.

BIBLIOGRAPHY

ANDERSON, FULTON H. *Francis Bacon: His Career and His Thought.* Los Angeles: University of Southern California Press, 1962.

BURTT, E. A. *The Metaphysical Foundations of Modern Science.* Garden City: Doubleday, 1954.

DONEY, WILLIS, ed. *Descartes: A Collection of Critical Essays.* Garden City: Doubleday, 1967.

FRIEDRICH, CARL J., and BLITZER, CHARLES. *The Age of Power.* Ithaca: Cornell University Press, 1957.

KOYRE, ALEXANDRE. *From the Closed World to the Infinite Universe.* Baltimore: Johns Hopkins University Press, 1957.

LEVINE, ISRAEL. *Francis Bacon.* Port Washington: Kennikat Press, 1970.

MARITAIN, JACQUES. *Three Reformers: Luther, Descartes, Rousseau.* New York: Sheed & Ward, 1936.

POPKIN, RICHARD. *The History of Scepticism from Erasmus to Descartes.* New York: Humanities Press, 1964.

WHITE, HOWARD B. *Peace Among the Willows: The Political Philosophy of Francis Bacon.* The Hague: Nighoff, 1968.

WHITE, LYNN JR. *Dynamo and Virgin Reconsidered.* Cambridge: M.I.T. Press, 1968.

WHITEHEAD, ALFRED NORTH. *Science and the Modern World.* New York: New American Library, 1948.

WILLEY, BASIL. *The Seventeenth-Century Background.* New York: Columbia University Press, 1934.

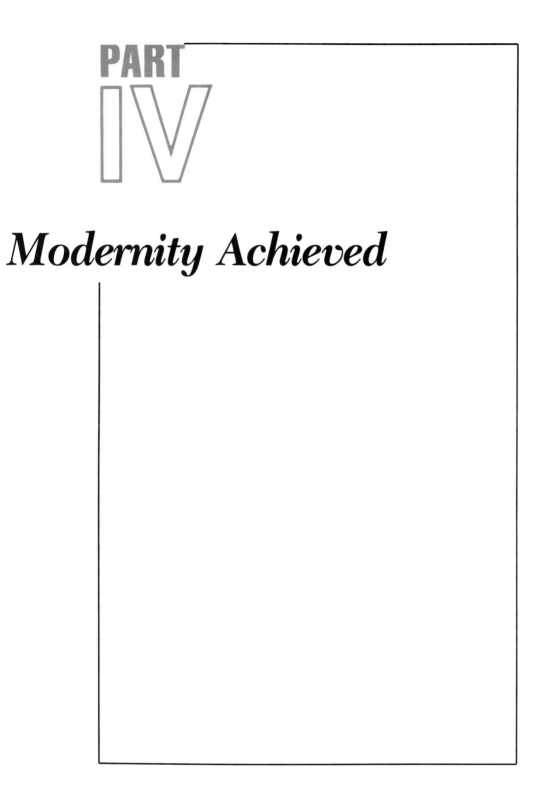

PART

IV

Modernity Achieved

9

THOMAS HOBBES

LIFE AND WRITINGS

The enthusiasm and certitude of the scientific spirit of the seventeenth century is no more clearly displayed than in the political writings of Thomas Hobbes. Born in 1588, Hobbes entered Oxford in 1602. He left the university five years later to become the tutor for the son of William Cavendish. As Cavendish would soon become the Earl of Devonshire, Hobbes became increasingly involved in political affairs. During one period, he became the tutor of the prince of Wales—eventually to become Charles II and by whose sponsorship Hobbes would escape being burned as a traitor. Having studied logic and having acquired a distaste for the official forms of Aristotelianism which dominated the English schools of his day, Hobbes soon developed a strong interest in modern science. For a period during the 1620s he served as a secretary to Francis Bacon, and during his travels to the Continent he met and corresponded with such notable scientists as Galileo and Descartes.

It was during a similar tour of the mainland in 1629 that Hobbes happened across a copy of Euclid's *Elementa*. He was so impressed by the rigor and clarity of Euclid's anlaysis that he resolved at that time to incorporate the methods of geometry into the domain of speculative philosophy proper. By 1634 Hobbes developed a scheme according to which he believed it would be possible to systematically treat all the problems of traditional philosophy within the structure of a trilogy. Beginning with an examination of matter (*De Corpore*), the argument was to proceed to the study of human nature (*De Homine*) and then end with a discussion of citizenship (*De Cive*). On the whole, the analysis was designed to move logically from the more elemental level toward the more complex. Each stage, in turn, was to begin from the foundations established by the conclusions of the previous study. The political events of the time, however, prevented Hobbes from realizing his initial plan. Indeed in 1642 he broke the sequence of his plan and published first what should have been the third and final volume of his study. He did so in the hope that its message would contribute to the reconstruction of the English political order during a period of decay and revolt. As he wrote in the preface:

> . . . it so happened in the interim, that my country, some few years before the civil wars did rage, was boiling hot with questions concerning the rights of dominion and the obedience due from subjects, the true forerunners of an approaching war; and was the cause which, all those other matters deferred, ripened, and plucked from me this third part. Therefore it happens, that what was last in order, is yet come forth first in time.[1]

Hobbes's intent was plain. He sought to restore the tradition of the English monarchy and prevent, thereby, the violence of war:

> . . . it [is] better to enjoy yourselves in the present state, though perhaps not the best, than by waging war endeavour to procure a reformation for other men in another age, yourselves in the meanwhile either killed or consumed with age.[2]

During Hobbes's lifetime England was involved in a series of serious political and religious disputes which eventually culminated in a civil war. Tensions between the monarchy and the parliament would come to entail the murder of a king, the rise and fall of Cromwell, and the restoration of Charles II. These disputes, in turn, were complicated by religious tensions and the activity of political factions associated with Roman Catholicism, Anglicanism, and Puritanism. In addition, the English were

---

[1] Thomas Hobbes, *Man and Citizen*, ed. Bernard Gert (Garden City: Doubleday, 1972), p. 103.
[2] Hobbes, *Man and Citizen*, p. 104.

preoccupied by efforts to extend and secure their rule in both Scotland and Ireland. The strain produced by such events exposed the extreme fragility of traditional English institutions. In 1640 Hobbes privately circulated a manuscript, *The Elements of Law: Natural and Political*, which forcefully argued on behalf of the monarchical position and, thereby, established him as an opponent of the parliamentary forces. As the monarchy weakened and the policies of the Long Parliament became more aggressive, Hobbes fled to France. With the restoration of the monarchy, however, Hobbes was able to return to England in 1660. Although he had supported the king throughout the civil war, the royalist forces were dissatisfied with certain arguments they found within his work. As a consequence, Hobbes gradually withdrew from political life and involved himself in strictly literary matters. In addition to writing his autobiography in Latin verse, he also produced an English translation of Homer's *Iliad* and *Odyssey*. His most important political work, however, is *Leviathan* (1651). Other important works not yet mentioned include *Dialogue between a Philosopher and a Student of the Common Laws of England* (1666) and *Behemoth* (1668).

INFLUENCE OF MODERN SCIENCE

The enthusiasm which the spirit of modern science engendered among some of its followers encouraged them to believe that it was possible to break from the traditions of the past. As we have seen, both Bacon and Descartes looked forward to a modern civilizational order which would be founded upon the dogma of a new scientific creed. In a similar spirit, Hobbes envisioned a grand trilogy which would systematically account for and settle all the traditional problems of speculative philosophy. Hobbes's belief in his own ability to accomplish such a task was sustained by his faith in the power of the mathematical sciences. These sciences, according to Hobbes, appeared to have achieved a degree of consensus and certitude which was obviously missing from the moral and political disputes of the day. Like Descartes, Hobbes assumed that true knowledge is characterized by its ability to compel agreement among people. The mere fact of disagreement, therefore, constituted an obvious proof that the traditional systems had not produced true knowledge and, therefore, that their claim to be respected was without authority. Writing in 1640, Hobbes announced his total rejection of traditional political philosophy:

> . . . as the writings of men from antiquity downward have still increased, so also have the doubts and controversies concerning the same. And seeing that true knowledge begetteth not doubt nor con-

troversy, but knowledge; it is manifest from the present contro-
versies, that they which have heretofore written thereof, have not
well understood their own subject.[3]

Hobbes's analysis of the reasons for the failure of traditional
political philosophy is important if we are to understand his own approach.
In *Elements of Law* he distinguished between two types of learning: the
mathematical and the dogmatical. The former are free from contradiction
and dispute and are primarily concerned with comparing figures and motions. Thus their discoveries do not affect human beings' passions and immediate interests. If they did, their condition would resemble that of the
dogmatical sciences. These sciences, examples being political science and
ethics, are concerned with humanity's rights and interests. As such, they inevitably compare people against one another and produce, thereby, conclusions which are bound to be offensive to some. In such cases, Hobbes argues:

> . . . as oft as reason is against a man, so oft will a man be against
> reason.[4]

Given this analysis, then, the task became one of reducing the dogmatical sciences into their appropriate mathematical form. For this to be
done, it was not necessary, according to Hobbes, to incorporate any new
discoveries concerning human nature: indeed, the relevant facts were
either well known or could be easily demonstrated. The problem as he saw it
was primarily one of developing an appropriate method—one based upon
the model of the mathematical sciences.

In his *De Cive*, Hobbes argued that the single cause for the failure of
traditional political philosophy was its inability to develop an appropriate
scientific method. Unlike the geometrician, moral philosophers had violated the simple procedures of critical reason:

> The only reason of which unluckiness should seem to be this; that
> amongst all the writers of that part of philosophy there is not one
> that hath used an idoneous [appropriate] principle of tractation.
> For we may not, as in a circle, begin the handling of a science from
> what point we please. There is a certain clue of reason, whose be-
> ginning is in the dark; but by the benefit of whose conduct, we are
> led as it were by the hand into the clearest light. So that the princi-
> ple of tractation is to be taken from that darkness; and then the light
> to be carried thither for irradiating its doubts.[5]

[3] Thomas Hobbes, *The Elements of Law—Natural and Politic*, ed. Ferdinand Tönnies (New
York: Barnes & Noble, 1969), p. 1.

[4] Hobbes, *The Elements of Law—Natural and Politic*, p. xv.

[5] Hobbes, *Man and Citizen*, p. 92.

Specifically, Hobbes argued that scientists should begin with an examination of particulars so as to discover the laws which are at work at that level and, having accomplished this, move systematically to an analysis of universal actions. As geometricians treat figures and physicists motions, so, too, should moral philosophers treat natural rights.

Hobbes's governing assumption was that it is possible to establish certain preliminary principles which are so obviously correct that there can be no possible grounds for mistrusting them. Then, by building the system carefully according to the laws of nature, it should be also possible to arrive at an argument whose conclusions exhibit the characteristics of a geometrical proof. By reducing both human nature and civil society to their simplest and most obvious elements, it would thus be possible according to Hobbes to construct a political science whose tenets are derived from true principles and established by self-evident argumentation. Such a political science, in turn, would have the effect of replacing disagreement with consensus and war with peace:

> For were the nature of human actions as distinctly known as the nature of *quantity* in geometrical figures, the strength of *avarice* and *ambition*, which is sustained by the erroneous opinions of the vulgar as touching the nature of *right* and *wrong*, would presently faint and languish; and mankind should enjoy such an immortal peace, that unless it were for habitation, on supposition that the earth should grow too narrow for her inhabitants, there would hardly be left any pretence for war.[6]

Hobbes's faith in the power of reason sustained his belief in the possibility of a peaceful political order. Indeed his desire for order and peace is understandable in view of the events of his day. Yet at the same time, Hobbes's rationalism implies a certain intolerance of diversity and carries with it a distinct threat of oppression. Assuming that reason can produce clear and compelling truth and assuming that a method has been found which can realize such a potential, how is one to explain the persistence of diverse opinions? Once scientific rationalism has established the expectation of consensus and order, how will it react to the frustration of such expectations? This, indeed, was the problem which confronted Hobbes.

In his *Leviathan*, Hobbes compared his work with that of Plato. According to Hobbes, both had developed elaborate theoretical systems which required that they be translated into practice if they were to be effective. The failure of Plato to achieve this, Hobbes maintained however, did not necessarily argue against the possibility of Hobbes's doing so. Indeed the Platonic experience should not be a precedent in the latter philosopher's

---

[6] Hobbes, *Man and Citizen*, p. 91.

case. According to Hobbes, Plato's inability to actualize his *Republic* was not an example of the inevitable gap between theory and practice. Rather Plato failed because he did not methodologically order and sufficiently prove the theorems of his system. His political failure, therefore, was based upon a prior scientific failure. Hobbes, on the other hand, was certain that he had transcended such limitations. His system was inevitable because it was rational. And its rationality was compellingly obvious because it

> . . . is so consonant to reason, that any unprejudicated man, needs no more to learn it, than to hear it.[7]

Hobbes's evocation of an "unprejudicated [unprejudiced] man" is reminiscent of both Descartes's "pure and attentive mind" and Bacon's "well-purged mind." Each in his own way was creating an image of a personality who, like himself, had succeeded in freeing his thoughts from the traditions of the past. Such individuals were to serve as models for the future order. More importantly, however, Hobbes's argument pointed to his final explanation of the only reason why diverse opinions could conceivably exist after the introduction of his perfect science: in the future, citizens might continue to hold their views only because it was in their selfish interest to do so. The truly honest and unprejudiced personalities, on the other hand, would willingly accept the arguments of his new science. Those who disagreed would do so because of personal avarice and social ambition.

An incident which occurred prior to the publication of his *De Cive* served to confirm Hobbes's analysis of this issue. Having privately circulated his manuscript to several readers, Hobbes was shocked to learn of their criticisms. Rather than analyzing their arguments, he explained them away as follows:

> These things I found more bitterly excepted against. That I made the civil powers too large; but this by ecclesiastical persons. That I had utterly taken away liberty of conscience; but this by sectaries. That I had set princes above the civil laws; but this by lawyers. Wherefore I was not much moved by these men's reprehensions, as who in doing this, did but do their own business; except it were to tie those knots somewhat faster.[8]

Given his assumption as to the perfectly rational character of his arguments, Hobbes expected agreement. The absence of actual agreement, however, did not cause him to question the adequacy of his own arguments. Rather he was forced to search for the irrational bias behind the ideas of

[7] Thomas Hobbes, *Leviathan*, ed. Michael Oakeshott (New York: Collier Books, 1962), p. 249.
[8] Hobbes, *Man and Citizen*, p. 105.

those who disagreed. He found such a bias in the economic and political ambitions of his critics. Here, then, is a clear case of the intolerance implicit in certain forms of modern rationalism: it argues that those who resist the self-evident truths of methodologically established arguments do so only because of base and selfish motives. This assumption would later become a key to Hobbes's interpretation of the events that led up to and culminated in the English Civil War.

ANALYSIS OF *BEHEMOTH*

Throughout this book the idea that creative political philosophy originates as a response to the experience of disorder has been underscored repeatedly. An attempt to fully comprehend a philosopher's meaning must, therefore, include an effort to reconstruct his or her particular experience of the historical situation. Unless the philosopher has written a history of that specific time, such a reconstruction depends upon an interpretive analysis of the reformer's suggested therapy. In the case of Thomas Hobbes, however, the task is simplified inasmuch as Hobbes did, in fact, prepare such a history. Written in 1668, Hobbes's *Behemoth: The Long Parliament* was his final attempt to summarize the lessons which were to be found in the English Civil War. By then the war was over and the king had been restored. At the same time, however, Hobbes was not yet convinced that all the proper lessons had been drawn. In studying the events between 1640 and 1660 Hobbes claimed to have discovered a certain pattern in the movement of political power. It was as if there were "a circular motion of the sovereign power through two usurpers."[9] In particular, sovereign power "moved from King Charles I to the Long Parliament; from thence to the Rump; from the Rump to Oliver Cromwell; and then back again from Richard Cromwell to the Rump; thence to the Long Parliament; and thence to King Charles II, where long may it remain."[10]

In part, Hobbes's *Behemoth* was an attempt to document this cyclical process. Yet, at the same time, this project was itself only part of a larger task which preoccupied Hobbes's attention throughout its writing. His first concern was to analyze the cause of the revolution itself. Why did it start and how did it develop? Assuming as Hobbes did that King Charles was "a man that wanted no virtue, either of body or mind, nor endeavoured anything more than to discharge his duty towards God, in the well governing of his subjects,"[11] how was it possible that such events developed? For

---

[9] Thomas Hobbes, *Behemoth or the Long Parliament*, ed. Ferdinand Tönnies (New York: Barnes & Noble, 1969), p. 204.

[10] Hobbes, *Behemoth or the Long Parliament*, p. 204.

[11] Hobbes, *Behemoth or the Long Parliament*, p. 2.

Hobbes the answer was to be found in the realm of ideas and opinions. The people had become corrupt; they had been misled by ambitious leaders and thus had become forgetful of both the rights of the sovereign and their corresponding duties as subjects. In short, the English revolution was due to a lack of true political knowledge. According to Hobbes the power of unfounded opinions had produced political chaos. The task of political science, consequently, was to once again demonstrate the rational foundation for the principles of the English regime. Indeed as early as 1640 and again in 1642 and 1651 Hobbes had published treatises which explained and proved the scientific foundation of order. According to his argument, *the* political science, based on *the* scientific method, had already been discovered. Why, then, did others continue to disagree? The problem apparently was one of civic education, and thus the majority of subjects were ignorant of their public duty. This condition, however, could be overcome if they could be taught the true science of politics.

According to Hobbes his own writings already contained such a teaching. Thus the problem was that Hobbes's science had not been given the opportunity to publicly demonstrate its merit. As long as the churches and the universities were in the hands of the enemy, opinion—not truth— would determine the beliefs of the masses:

> The rules of *just* and *unjust* sufficiently demonstrated, and from principles evident to the meanest capacity, have not been wanting; and notwithstanding the obscurity of their author, have shined, not only in this, but also in foreign countries, to men of good education. But they are few, in respect of the rest of men, whereof many cannot read; many, though they can, have no leisure; and of them that have no leisure, the greatest part have their minds wholly employed and taken up by their private businesses or pleasures. So that it is impossible that the multitude should ever learn their duty, but from the pulpit and upon holidays; but then and from thence, it is, that they learned their disobedience. . . . But out of the *Universities*, came all those preachers that taught the contrary. The *Universities* have been to this nation, as the wooden horse was to the Trojans.[12]

It is clear then that for Hobbes the disorder of the age was rooted in the inadequacies of orthodox opinion. Accordingly, his analysis of the churches and universities was designed in part as a criticism of that tradition. More importantly, however, it sought to expose the real motives of those who supported the orthodox view. For example, Hobbes accused the universities of resisting scientific reasoning and of resorting to rhetorical devices by which to establish specious distinctions and maintain theological

[12] Hobbes, *Behemoth or the Long Parliament*, pp. 39–40.

ambiguities. In particular, they had enshrined Aristotelianism as the ruling dogma. According to Hobbes, certain of Aristotle's metaphysical doctrines were patently false. The doctrine of separated essences and that of contingency were but two examples. Similarly in the realm of political theory, Hobbes accused Aristotle of having argued for democratic principles and consequently blamed the influence of such teachings for much of England's troubles. Likewise, Aristotle's ethical speculations were understood by Hobbes to have been a source of popular confusion, and they tended thereby to distract the subjects from an awareness of their obligation to obey sovereign law. According to Hobbes the motive behind the promulgation of such errors was quite clear. Indeed his study of history showed that philosophy had never contributed much to society; rather it had "much conduced to the advancement of the professors thereof to places of greatest authority."[13]

Similarly, the churches in England, who were resisting the claims of the monarch, did so by teaching doctrines which were theologically unfounded and politically dangerous. Although some may have actually believed in what they taught, Hobbes was convinced that the most important leaders were motivated solely by ambition and envy.

Given this analysis, then, Hobbes saw his task as one of frustrating the selfish ambitions of an envious few by exposing the inadequacies of their teachings. This, in turn, could best be done by promulgating the chief tenets of Hobbesian political science—a political science which was not concerned with the simple description and analysis of political events but rather was designed to instruct humanity in the principles of sovereignty.

ANALYSIS OF *LEVIATHAN*

Hobbes's most systematic effort to provide such an instruction is found in his *Leviathan*, which was published in 1651. The work is divided into four parts. The first is a discussion of human nature; the second examines the founding and preservation of the commonwealth; the third is an exploration of Christianity; and the fourth discusses the kingdom of darkness. Throughout the book Hobbes attempts to imitate the methods and principles of the mathematical sciences as he understands them. Accordingly, he builds his arguments logically from a set of initial presuppositions concerning life in general and human life in particular.

As the classical Greeks had done before him, Hobbes turns to nature as a model for his political order. Yet, unlike the Greeks, his view of nature is distinctly modern. For example, both Plato and Aristotle understood nature as a hierarchically ordered cosmic whole. For them, nature had design,

---

[13] Hobbes, *Behemoth or the Long Parliament*, p. 90.

form, and purpose. As such, it provided a model of order to which individuals were to conform and, in so doing, to discover thereby the purpose and dignity of their own particular existences. Such a view of nature was presupposed by Aristotle's discussion of final and formal causation. Yet it was precisely the attempt of the modern scientific revolution to formulate an understanding of nature which did not rely upon such notions as essence or purpose. Nature for the modern personality had become simply matter-in-motion. It exhibited no grand design and was indifferent concerning goals or objectives. As Hobbes wrote ". . . life is but a motion of limbs."[14] Given this approach, then, one understands both physical nature and human nature once one has specified their material and efficient causes. In a similar manner, one can understand the nature of a political society once one has specified both the material from which it is constructed and the activity of those who constructed it. In the case of politics, both these causes are the same—human beings. Humanity is, according to Hobbes, both the material and efficient cause of the commonwealth.

Before proceeding, it is necessary to specify some of the important consequences which are implied by Hobbes's approach. First, his scheme is ultimately reductionistic. As a consequence, for Hobbes an understanding of the whole can only be achieved in terms of an understanding of those particulars which constitute the whole. Society is but the sum of its parts. As such, it is an artificial creation composed of natural units. The natural unit is the human being, and thus society is nothing more than an artificial convenience created so as to serve humanity's natural needs. As such, the individual is the ultimate natural reality for Hobbes: society is constructed for the sake of the individual, and it seeks only to preserve singular interests and accommodate singular needs. Thus, on this particular issue, Hobbes adopts a fundamental assumption of liberalism.

To classify Hobbes as a liberal is at first a bit surprising. His *Leviathan* is an impassioned argument on behalf of an authoritarian and absolute form of government. The sovereign is above the law and the citizen has few rights vis-à-vis the sovereign's authority. Thus on one hand it is obvious that Hobbes does not share certain policies which are characteristically associated with the liberal perspective. Yet, on the other hand, he does agree with the fundamental liberal belief that society exists for the individual. Hobbes is not seeking to transform humanity, nor does he wish to model it after a preferred type. Rather he wishes to preserve human beings as individuals—free to do all that is not explicitly prohibited by the sovereign. It is only because of his pessimistic analysis of the human situation that Hobbes is forced to advocate absolute sovereignty. According to Hobbes, authoritarian regimes are required because of humanity's conten-

---

[14] Hobbes, *Leviathan*, p. 19.

tious nature; anything less would fail to preserve that minimal order which is necessary for the flourishing of our individuality. Thus Hobbes's authoritarianism is not derived from any organic theory of society which would threaten the very concept of individualism itself. Rather it is the result of his specific analysis of human passion and is motivated by his concern for the preservation of human individuality.

A second consequence of Hobbes's particular approach to the study of politics is his denial of a common good. Lacking design and purpose, that is, lacking formal and final causation, society cannot be understood in terms of a natural goal which it seeks to actualize. Such an approach would be too reminiscent of the teleological conception of reality which was discarded by the modern scientific revolution. In effect, then, there is no final achievement or state of completion that directs society's actions. On the contrary, according to Hobbes society was formed in order to avoid certain consequences. In particular, human beings joined in society to avoid a premature and painful death. As a consequence Hobbes's society is informed by the threat of a *summum malum* (greatest evil) rather than by the promise of a *summum bonum* (greatest good).

Being both the matter and the maker of society, humanity is the central object of Hobbes's concern. He begins his analysis, then, with an examination of human nature—that is, with an examination of natural humans before they entered the artificial environment of society and culture. Just as modern science reduced nature to its simplest elements in order to understand its more complex expressions, so, too, does Hobbes attempt to simplify his understanding of humanity by focusing upon its most elemental features. Accordingly, for Hobbes human nature is seen most clearly in its most primitive form. Unlike the classical Greeks who developed their understanding of human nature by examining that nature in its most perfected or mature form, Hobbes looks to the common, the primitive, and the elemental. Thus, whereas the Greeks focused upon the psyche of the philosopher as their guide for a discussion of human nature, Hobbes begins his analysis with an examination of the passions of the solitary individual. As modern science had discarded the classical teleological conception of physical nature, so, too, has Hobbes replaced the teleological conception of human nature. For him, humanity is best understood in terms of the appetites and aversions which move it.

In developing Hobbes's conception of human nature it is helpful to list several characteristics of humans as they appear in their natural state.

Pursuit of Pleasure in the State of Nature

Humans as matter-in-motion are set into motion by their appetites. They move toward those things which appear pleasant and away from that which appears painful. As such human life is spent in the pursuit of pleasure and the happy individual is the one who enjoys continual success in obtaining those things which are desired.

Two aids are particularly helpful for assuring the success of such a quest. The first is power; for power is but the present means for obtaining some future good. Given this life becomes, in fact, the pursuit of power. Happiness is the result of a continual success in gaining pleasure, and power is the indispensable and always necessary means for that task. As Hobbes writes in chapter 11:

> Felicity is a continual progress of the desire, from one object to another; the attaining of the former, being still but the way to the latter. The cause whereof is, that the object of man's desire, is not to enjoy once only, and for one instant of time; but to assure for ever the way of his future desire. . . . So that in the first place, I put for a general inclination of all mankind, a perpetual and restless desire of power after power, that ceaseth only in death. And the cause of this . . . [is that a man] cannot assure the power and means to live well, which he hath present, without the acquisition of more.[15]

A second major aid in the service of the passions is knowledge in general and scientific reason in particular. In seeking the objects of their passions, humans are necessarily involved in a calculation concerning means and ends. Assuming that the end is pleasure or the avoidance of pain, people seek to choose those means which will produce the desired effects. Their thoughts, therefore, are concerned with understanding the relationships between cause and effect. Like the animals, they wish to be able to know which events will follow which actions. Unlike the animals, however, humans are aided in this task by the invention of speech. Speech, then, is the means by which humanity can " . . . register, what by cogitation, we find to be the cause of any thing, present or past; and what we find things present or past may produce, or effect."[16] Simply put, speech is the process by which we name things; but, if used carefully and consistently, it aids us in remembering those relationships between cause and effect which were first discovered through immediate experience. The careful use of speech requires that names be used consistently and that the subject and predicate of a statement affirm the same thing. According to this perspective, then, to reason is

> . . . nothing else but [to] conceive a sum total, from *addition* of parcels; or conceive a remainder, from *subtraction* of one sum from another; which, if it be done by words, is conceiving of the con-

---

[15] Hobbes, *Leviathan*, p. 80.
[16] Hobbes, *Leviathan*, p. 34.

sequences of the names of all the parts, to the name of the whole; or from the names of the whole and one part, to the name of the other part.[17]

And if this is reason, scientific knowledge is nothing but the knowledge of the consequences of using names in one way or another. For Hobbes, then, the philosopher is simply one who can demonstrate the logical consequences of maintaining specific affirmations.

Without going into the detailed epistemological debate which Hobbes's conception of speech has provoked, it is possible to point to several consequences of his position. First and most obviously is its nominalism. For Hobbes, we cannot, in fact, know what is really good, evil, beautiful, or ugly in itself but can only know what people call as such. The good is simply a name given to whatever is the object of an individual's appetite. Inasmuch as people have different pleasures, the good means different things to different people. The obvious fact that humans disagree as to what is good was handled by the classical theorists in their distinction between that which *is* good and that which *appears* good. What *appears* good varies from person to person; what, in fact, *is* good is known to "right reason." Hobbes, however, denies that "right reason" exists in nature. There is no naturally correct way of naming things because there is no true knowledge of their nature. Human knowledge is limited to the realm of appearances because thought is simply a matter of sense perception. Thus Hobbes's nominalism implies a natural ethical relativism.

A second consequence of Hobbes's theory of reason is to subordinate reason to the passions. According to Hobbes, reason does not guide the passions so much as it serves them. It is humanity's appetites which specify the objects of human desire, and reason simply advises on how to best acquire that which is being sought. For Hobbes, it is apparent, then, that reason is not a separate faculty of the soul, that is, one with its own proper ends and appropriate virtues. Rather than being an independent faculty seeking its own appropriate good, reason is simply a subsidiary of the passions. As such, it finds its purpose and establishes its claims only within the tasks assigned to it by the passions. Hobbes's human being is harmonious not because of any proper ordering among the soul's diverse faculties but because of the single reality of his or her quest for pleasure. Every psychic state can be explained in terms of this quest—even the spiritual. In a remark clearly directed at the Puritans of his day, Hobbes explains the mystic's experience of spiritual possession as a form of madness engendered by the extreme passion of pride and vainglory. In effect, then, Hobbes has achieved a reversal of the traditional Christian interpretation of psychic order. For him, pas-

---

17 Hobbes, *Leviathan*, p. 41.

sion is the spirit's foundation rather than the source of its ultimate corruption. Thus, as in the example of reason, Hobbes has succeeded in reducing the spiritual faculty of human beings to nothing more than a by-product of their natural passions.

Total Equality and Perpetual Conflict

A second major characteristic of humans in the state of nature is their equality. For Hobbes, all humans are equal by nature, and their equality is established in the very nature of things. Although some may be physically stronger than others, none is so strong as to be free from the risk of being killed. Even the strongest must sleep and are thus vulnerable to the weapons of the weakest. Similarly, according to Hobbes, wisdom is essentially a matter of experience and all people gain in experience by the mere passing of time. Time is essentially equal on all accounts for the fundamental equality of human wit—an equality attested to by the fact that every individual seems contented with his or her own share.

The argument that all men are naturally equal implies that there are no true distinctions by which any one person can establish the priority of his or her claim over the claims of any other. No one is naturally superior to another and thus no one is entitled to any particular benefits or advantages vis-à-vis another. In the case where two people desire the same object but only one can have it, each has a naturally equal right to claim it. Inasmuch as nature provides no way of distinguishing between the two, contention and struggle is the inevitable result. According to Hobbes, this state of conflict tends to escalate to a state of war. Not only do people compete for limited goods, but they lack any sense of pity or social concern which would serve to moderate their struggle. Indeed, for Hobbes, human beings do not enjoy one another's company. In addition to seeking pleasure, people are driven by a desire for glory. They want to be esteemed by others and in the pursuit of such acknowledgement are concerned with establishing their superiority over others. Thus even in a situation where there is a sufficiency of material goods contention among human beings is the natural condition. People struggle, therefore, for the sake of gain, safety, and glory. The effect of this is to produce the condition of war. Summarizing his analysis of the state of nature, Hobbes wrote:

> Hereby it is manifest, that during the time men live without a common power to keep them all in awe, they are in that condition which is called war; and such a war, as is of every man, against every man.[18]

---

[18] Hobbes, *Leviathan*, p. 100.

A war of every one against every other denies the possibility of a civilized life. Lacking security, people have no opportunity to devote themselves to the creation of culture or the development of industry. Inasmuch as there is no order in savage nature, there can be no principles of right and wrong or justice and injustice which can mediate the struggle of each against each. The reigning virtues, therefore, are simply force and fraud. Personal possessions are determined only by what one can get and how long one can keep it. The entire atmosphere, in effect, is poisoned by the continual fear and danger of violent death. In Hobbes's words, the life of the individual in such a state is "solitary, poor, nasty, brutish, and short."[19] Given this, human beings seek to flee from nature. Their only remedy is to construct an artificial convention which will form the basis for a political society.

Moved by passion and instructed by reason individual humans quit the state of nature through the creation of a social contract. The purpose of society, therefore, is given in those passions which originally motivated humanity to form its laws:

> The passions that incline men to peace, are fear of death; desire of such things as are necessary to commodious living; and a hope by their industry to obtain them. And reason suggesteth convenient articles of peace, upon which men may be drawn to agreement.[20]

In the state of nature all people enjoyed the fundamental right to do anything for the preservation of their lives. Inasmuch as this right was exercised within a situation characterized by the total absence of external restraints, a contradiction quickly became apparent. The very preconditions of peace and security which were necessary for the successful pursuit of pleasure were, in fact, destroyed by the radically egalitarian nature of the human being's quest for power. The result was the absence of a natural pattern or hierarchy which could serve as a model for the ordering of human social and historical existence. Responding to this situation, humanity turned to reason—or to what Hobbes terms "the laws of nature." These laws were not as the name might suggest, principles operating within reality; for reality, being but matter-in-motion, contained no such formal ordering. Rather they were precepts of human reasoning, that is, practical advice designed to relieve humans of the burden of their natural condition. Specifically, they forbade that which was destructive to human life or which attempted to take away those means necessary for its preservation.

Focusing upon humanity's common fear (fear of painful death) rea-

---

[19] Hobbes, *Leviathan*, p. 100.
[20] Hobbes, *Leviathan*, p. 102.

son sought to establish peace by denying those conditions which accounted for the war of each against each. In particular, reason advised each human to lay down his or her rights to everything. If this were done by all, then all individually, in effect, would have voluntarily surrendered the original liberty to resist another in the other's pursuit of one's own claims. This promise, in turn, served to establish the legitimacy of the sovereign's rule.

The Social Contract

In the state of nature, each individual had a right to everything. Since all claims were in principle equal, each individual had, in effect, the right to resist the attempts of any other individual to benefit from the exercise of his or her own rightful claim. Thus, the exercising of one's rights was in every case equivalent to resisting the exercise of the rights of others. By contracting to drop all claims, the individual promises at the same time not to resist the claims of others. In Hobbes's understanding, then, this is precisely what the members of a civil society do. They promise not to resist the rightful claims of others. Yet, if each has already waived his or her natural claim to everything, a citizen's rightful claim can only arise if it is granted by one who has such a power. Such a person is the sovereign. Thus sovereigns now become the source of all rights. Their will establishes the claims that their subjects may make and no citizen has the right to resist. Thus, for Hobbes, the sovereign became the source of all rights—including the right to name things. Consequently good is what sovereigns call good; just is what they call just. In effect, then, the power of sovereigns extends to the right of defining reality. Their law has become the final word.

The totality of a sovereign's power, however, should not distract one from appreciating the nature of its source. Inasmuch as all people are equal by nature, no one has a natural right to rule another. Consequently legitimate authority arises only when people consent to be governed. Thus for Hobbes the freely willed consent of equal and autonomous individuals was the sole basis for political obligation. Subjects are obligated to obey only because they have agreed to do so. Consequently the duty to fulfill one's obligations is not a natural duty but simply the result of a prior promise. In short, for Hobbes obligation was based on the will, and it acquired its "moral" force through an act of voluntary consent.

Hobbes's emphasis upon the role of consent as the basis of obligation is typical of liberal political theory in general. According to liberalism citizens are obligated to obey only those authorities to whom they have given their consent. Thus the giving of consent, which is an act of free will, is both the basis for all authority and at the same time the means by which the exercise of authority can be controlled. Even in Hobbes the sovereign cannot legitimately demand that a citizen voluntarily accept to be killed. Inasmuch as humans consented to join society in order to live, the taking of a life breaks that fundamental agreement which is the source of the sovereign's legitimacy. Thus just as Hobbes considered the will to be the only fundamental reality within human nature, so, too, did he believe that human consent was the sole justification for political rule. Having replaced classical reason as the source of personal order, he must at the same time replace it as the source of political and historical order.

Given the extent to which all individuals must subordinate themselves to the will of a sovereign, the question arises as to why anyone would keep the original promise to obey. The answer for Hobbes is quite simple: the alternative to such a society is the state of nature, and the disadvantages of the state of nature are so immense as to make such an alternative unacceptable. Rational individuals can be made to see that it is in their own ultimate self-interests to submit to the will of a sovereign. Indeed, there are only two exceptions to this rule. If the sovereign attempts to kill one of the citizens or subjects the person to punishment or imprisonment, then the citizen has a practically compelling reason to resist the sovereign's will. In all other cases, however, the disadvantages of our political existence are minor in comparison with those of our natural state.

The above analysis, based as it is on a theory of enlightened self-interest, is theoretically plausible only if an individual's waiving of rights is, in fact, reciprocated by all others. If one were to waive the right to resist while others, in turn, retained theirs, that would be exposing oneself to increased danger and pain rather than its opposite. In addition, if all appeared to waive their rights but only a few kept their word, then those few would, in turn, suffer disproportionately. It is apparent, therefore, that the legitimacy of the social contract depends upon its being rigorously upheld. For Hobbes, inasmuch as human society does not have a basis in nature, it can exist only as long as it is held together. Although cool and dispassionate argument can demonstrate the logically compelling reasons for obeying the contract, such reasons, in themselves, are not sufficient to insure that it will in fact be obeyed. The reciprocity of the contractual pledge can be secured only by coercion. Sovereigns, therefore, become necessary if societies are to exist.

Society's continuing need for a sovereign to enforce its contractual base is explained by the fact that individuals do not change their human nature simply by leaving their natural condition. They continue to be concerned with the pursuit of pleasure and the avoidance of pain. Unlike some animals, therefore, humans cannot be trusted to maintain their society without the coercive restraints of a sovereign government. The reasons for this situation are found in certain unique features of human nature. First, unlike the animals, humans enjoy a certain pleasure from gaining honor and fame. Thus they are driven to excel. However, this striving for eminence not only sets one against another but also serves to distinguish an individual's private good from society's common good. Rather than seeking the common good, individuals each seek their own preeminence and, as such, are each interested in rising above and withdrawing from the common.

In addition, humanity has both reason and speech. Whereas such thinkers as Heraclitus and Aristotle understood these faculties to be indications of humankind's appropriateness for political life, Hobbes sees them as sources of social disruption. For example, reason produces innovation and innovation threatens the social order. Speech, in turn, is the means by which individuals can propagate false opinions, and false opinions are, according to Hobbes, one of the causes of warfare. Finally, human beings' extreme vainglory encourages them to take offense even in those situations where no damage was intended. Thus human conflict is a continual possibility even among well-intentioned citizens. According to Hobbes, therefore, it is these and similar considerations which lead people

> . . . to confer all their power and strength upon one man, or upon one assembly of men, that may reduce all their wills, by plurality of voices, unto one will . . . and therein to submit their wills, every one to his will, and their judgments, to his judgment.[21]

In the dedication of his *Leviathan* to Francis Godolphin, Hobbes characterized his argument as follows:

> . . . I speak not of the men, but, in the abstract, of the seat of power, (like to those simple and unpartial creatures in the Roman Capitol, that with their noise defended those within it, not because they were they, but there).[22]

This characterization successfully underscores an important feature of Hobbes's political analysis. The sovereign is necessary simply because the system requires that someone maintain those artificial conditions which make the political order possible. Someone has to be in a position to enforce the governing conventions which determine the claims and privileges of the citizens. Inasmuch as nature does not favor the claims of any particular individual, the sovereign must. Indeed the need for someone to settle disputes by establishing an order of preferences and obligations was the very need that compelled human beings to leave the state of nature in the first place. Put simply, someone must rule.

Typically, in the long history of Western political philosophy, this

[21] Hobbes, *Leviathan*, p. 132.
[22] Hobbes, *Leviathan*, p. 5.

sort of assertion—that someone must rule—immediately provoked the question as to who that someone should be. The need for leadership thus acknowledged, logic led naturally to an examination of those qualities which leaders should have if they are to rule well. For example, Plato argued that only philosophers could master the true art of political rule, for only they possessed the necessary personal virtues. Similarly, Aristotle's plea on behalf of the rule of the morally mature was based upon his analysis of the virtues and his particular understanding of the rational soul. Both men agreed that only a certain type of person should rule because the art of ruling well presupposed a definite type of human excellence. This presupposition was shared throughout the Middle Ages and even by such modern thinkers as Machiavelli.

Hobbes, however, breaks radically from such a tradition. As he argues in *Leviathan*, the important issue is not who occupies the seat of power but simply that there be a seat of power. Whereas Plato and Aristotle felt that a political leader should have a certain knowledge of such realities as justice, goodness, and fairness, Hobbes argued that such terms did not designate realities at all but were simply names. For example, nobody can know what is good because there is no such reality as goodness. Goodness is simply a name used by people to designate that which they like. So far as one person's taste and likes are as valid as another's, one person's usage of the term "good" is as valid as another's. No one, in fact, can claim to know more concerning such things because human knowledge, limited to sense experience, does not extend to such affairs.

If Hobbes's analysis is correct, then the issues which preoccupied such thinkers as Plato and Aristotle are, in fact, unimportant. If justice and goodness do not exist, then human beings cannot be better or worse. If all people are, in fact, equal, then indeed it makes no difference who rules—just as long as someone does. A sovereign is necessary, therefore, not because society needs to be guided by reason but because it must be empowered by will. The will of the sovereign, not the character of a person, is Hobbes's foundation for political order.

The sovereign for Hobbes is that person or group of persons who occupy the seat of power. However, depending upon the conditions and customs of a particular society, that seat may, in turn, be occupied by one person, several, or many. Although for reasons of convenience and efficiency Hobbes prefers a monarchical government, he emphasizes that his arguments apply with equal force to both an aristocracy and a democracy. The important concern is with sovereignty as such. Regardless of how it is organized, sovereignty, as the ability to act for society as a whole, must be preserved and therefore must remain unlimited. It cannot be divided, delegated, restricted, or withdrawn. As an absolute, it rightly determines both the standards of conduct and the content of what can be taught. As the source of law, it is above the law. As the interpreter of the law, its decisions are the sole means by which subjects may distinguish right from wrong. As the executor of the law, it demands total and complete obedience.

Although Hobbes attempted to base his argument strictly upon a natural philosophy, at the same time he had to acknowledge, and thereby accommodate, the perspectives of Christian theology. This was so for several reasons. First, Christianity had deeply influenced the assumptions and beliefs of Western peoples. European civilization was as much, if not more, a product of the Judaic-Christian traditions as it was a result of Greek culture. Thus political speculation, like all forms of discourse, was partially rooted in a perspective formed by Christian revelation. Second, the political implications of Christianity had assumed a particular importance in contemporary English political affairs. Inasmuch as certain leaders of the Anglican church, the Puritans, and the Roman Catholic church had sided with various elements in the civil war, the struggle among the forces of the monarchy, Parliament, and Cromwell had assumed certain theological overtones, Indeed, it was this situation which encouraged Hobbes to expand his naturalistic arguments. As he wrote in his dedication:

> That which perhaps may most offend, are certain texts of Holy Scripture, alleged by me to other purpose than ordinarily they use to be by others. But I have done it with due submission, and also, in order to my subject, necessarily; for they are the outworks of the enemy, from whence they impugn the civil power.[23]

Thus it is that half of *Leviathan* was devoted to an interpretation of the Holy Scriptures, which according to Hobbes supported the conclusions of his own theory.

Before examining Hobbes's reading of the Scriptures, however, it may be useful to recall his earlier and more generalized treatment of religion as such. In chapter 12 of the *Leviathan*, Hobbes explained what he considered to be the "seeds" of religion. In effect, it was Hobbes's attempt to account for religion in terms of those experiences which support it. Specifically, he based the religious tradition in humanity's desire to know the cause of things, to consider their beginnings, and to understand the relationships among events. These qualities, which are peculiar to humanity, produce anxiety, and this, coupled with human ignorance, accounts for humanity's characteristic fear of invisible powers. Inasmuch as people tend to worship what they fear, Hobbes believed that the entire panoply of pagan gods can be explained away in terms of natural psychological events.

---

[23] Hobbes, *Leviathan*, p. 5.

In addition, throughout history some have taken advantage of these human traits in order to develop specific religious doctrines whose sole utility was to secure people's obedience to particular political regimes.

Throughout his analysis, Hobbes was careful to exempt the Judeo-Christian tradition from such a charge. First, he allowed that a monotheistic understanding of god may be due more to humanity's desire to know the causes of natural bodies than to human fear. Yet even granting this, it is evident that for Hobbes there was no need for a particularly religious explanation for the phenomenon of monotheism. God was experienced as a logical postulate, not as the ground of humanity's being. Thus there is no sense of the sacred or the divine in Hobbe's account. Second, Hobbes suggested that the Judeo-Christian tradition was exempt from the reductionism implicit in his general account because the particular peoples of this tradition who developed the natural seeds of religion did so, not according to their own imaginations, but according to divine commandments. Thus one can distinguish Abraham, Moses, and Christ from other religious leaders because they were acting as agents of God. Yet at the same time, they, too, had as their purpose, " . . . to make those men that relied on them, the more apt to obedience, laws, peace, charity, and civil society."[24] It is in an attempt to demonstrate this thesis that Hobbes devoted the second half of his *Leviathan* to an interpretation of the Bible.

Earlier Hobbes had argued that proper scientific reasoning presupposed the careful and consistent use of terms as developed through their usage. Accordingly a true understanding of the Bible presupposes that the terms of discussion will be used in a manner consistent with their meaning in the Scriptures. The primary task of a biblical commentator, therefore, is to rediscover the original sense which the words carried when they were written down. According to Hobbes one of the major failings of historical Christianity has been its tendency to misuse biblical terms either by introducing certain foreign philosophical connotations or by relying upon far-fetched allegorical interpretations in order to arrive at a predetermined conclusion. If one were to follow Hobbes, on the other hand, a careful scrutiny of the biblical texts would reveal the following:

1. Man does not possess an immortal soul. Thus a particular church's claim of being able to grant either eternal damnation or reward is, in fact, without force.

2. God's kingdom is an earthly one and will be established during a future age. There is neither heaven nor hell after history, for there is no life after death. Thus those institutions which claim to be an earthly representation of an already existing heavenly kingdom are, in fact, violating the message of Scripture.

---

[24] Hobbes, *Leviathan*, p. 90.

3. Until Christ's second coming the church is but a civil government of Christian people. Inasmuch as all government is temporal government, the political sovereign is, in effect, also the chief pastor of the church. The church, in turn, is simply concerned with the teaching of Christian doctrine. Its ministers possess only the power to teach and are subordinate to the ecclesiastical power which all Christian sovereigns exercise within their own realms.

These and similar arguments lead Hobbes to conclude that the true Christian message is essentially an attempt to reaffirm our loyalty and obedience to the temporal sovereign whosoever that individual may be:

> For our Saviour Christ hath not given us new laws, but counsel to observe those we are subject to; that is to say, the laws of nature, and the laws of our several sovereigns: nor did he make any new law to the Jews in his sermon on the Mount, but only expounded the law of Moses, to which they were subject before. The laws of God therefore are none but the laws of nature, whereof the principal is, that we should not violate our faith, that is, a commandment to obey our civil sovereigns, which we constituted over us by mutual pact one with another.[25]

Thus Hobbes's task is completed, and by implication, so too is the task of political philosophy. The civil rights and ecclesiastical powers of the sovereign have been demonstrated by references to the natural inclinations of human beings, the laws of nature, and the texts of Scripture. Insofar as these references agree totally with one another, the resultant teaching is simple and direct. Thus it is that Hobbes's original infatuation with the mathematical sciences appears once again in the conclusions of his arguments. This is evident in that political problems are treated as if they were similar to mathematical problems, that is, as if they lend themselves to a final solution. Once that solution has been achieved, the problem no longer exists as a problem and citizens can turn their attention to other things—for example, to the private and the commercial.

In an important sense, then, Hobbes has assumed for himself the ultimate political task—that of founding a political order. And in this respect he is similar to Machiavelli. Yet there is an important and enlightening difference between the two. Machiavelli sought to establish a regime that would encourage and enable other citizens to confront the challenges and thus enjoy the glory of political life. Hobbes, on the contrary, attempted to establish a regime which, having solved the issue of political order, would allow its citizenry to turn away from politics and toward the

---

[25] Hobbes, *Leviathan*, p. 426.

private. In this sense, then, his political excellence sought to deprive others of the opportunity for similar accomplishments.

In classical Greek thought it was common to distinguish among three forms of human life—the life of philosophy, the life of politics, and the life of pleasure. The weight of classical thought argued for a hierarchical arrangement which placed the life of philosophy first and the life of pleasure last. In Hobbes, however, the life of pleasure is all that remains. Having transformed philosophy into a science of systems and dogma and having formally solved the problems of political life by acknowledging the totally artificial character of human society, Hobbes has removed the existential substance which grounded both the life of philosophy and the life of politics. What remains real for humanity therefore, is quite simply the life of pleasure—or in modern terms, economics.

By subordinating the political realm to the service of economic interests, Hobbes once again demonstrated his distance from the classical tradition. For example, in his *Politics* Aristotle devoted most of Book I to an examination of the household. For him the household, which included husband and wife, parent and child, and master and slave, was an association concerned primarily with satisfying the recurring needs of life. As such the art of household management was an art concerned with both the acquisition and use of wealth. For Aristotle the economic art, like all the arts, was ultimately concerned with securing the best possible results. This concern for the best, in turn, necessarily implied an understanding of humanity's economic good. Yet central to Aristotle's argument was his insistence that the good of the members of the household could only be determined in view of that which was good for the social whole, of which the household was but a part. In simpler terms Aristotle believed that economic activity must be subordinated to and thus disciplined by political considerations. The household existed for the sake of life, whereas politics was concerned with the pursuit of the good life. Thus as important as economic success was, its ultimate worth could only be measured in terms of its contribution to the political goals of society. As a subsidiary art economics acquired its final legitimacy only in the service of larger ends.

This relationship between politics and economics, which was typical of both Greek and Christian political theory, was reversed in the writings of Hobbes. For Hobbes human beings created the political realm in an effort to support commodious living. Thus for him political considerations were clearly subordinate to economic concerns. Humanity tolerates the inconveniences of political life for the sake of pursuing its economic, and thus essentially private, interests. Inasmuch as economic activity is primarily concerned with the production and use of value, it is governed by the laws of efficiency and technique. Thus in reversing the classical relationship between politics and economics, Hobbes was, at the same time, subordinating the principles of political and moral order to the dictates of efficiency and production. Consequently, just as he reversed the classical understanding of the proper relationship between reason and the passions, so, too, did Hobbes deny the classical belief that the good was always superior to the useful.

BIBLIOGRAHY

BOWLE, J. *Hobbes and His Critics*. Oxford: Oxford University Press, 1951.

GOLDSMITH, M. M. *Hobbes' Science of Politics*. New York: Columbia University Press, 1966.

HOOD, F. C. *The Divine Politics of Thomas Hobbes*. Oxford: Oxford University Press, 1964.

MACPHERSON, C. B. *The Political Theory of Possessive Individualism: Hobbes to Locke*. Oxford: Oxford University Press, 1962.

MINTZ, SAMUEL. *The Hunting of Leviathan*. Cambridge: Cambridge University Press, 1962.

PETERS, RICHARD. *Hobbes*. London: Penguin Books, 1956.

STRAUSS, LEO. *Natural Right and History*. Chicago: University of Chicago, 1953.

STRAUSS, LEO. *The Political Philosophy of Hobbes: Its Basis and Its Genesis*. Chicago: University of Chicago Press, 1952.

WARRENDER, HOWARD. *The Political Philosophy of Hobbes: His Theory of Obligation*. Oxford: Oxford University Press, 1957.

WATKINS, J.W.N. *Hobbes's System of Ideas*. London: Hutchinson, 1965.

10
JOHN LOCKE

LIFE AND WRITINGS

John Locke's (1632–1704) political theory was deeply rooted in the tensions and troubles of his day. During the preceding one hundred years, the English middle class had gradually succeeded in acquiring an increasingly larger share of Britain's economic and political power. In doing so, they attempted to delineate and thereby restrict the traditional jurisdictional claims of the English monarchy, which had based its rule on the support of the landed nobility. In 1628 Parliament's *Petition of Rights* denied such customary royal prerogatives as the levying of direct taxation, the waiving of *habeas corpus*, and the denial of a trial by jury. Again, several years later in 1641, Parliament went further and attempted to assert its own institutional autonomy. Thus in the *Triannual Act* of that year Parliament was empowered to meet in session every three years even without being summoned by royal initiative. And, at the same time, the dissolution and re-election of its members was to take place regularly regardless of the crown's own wishes. In effect, then, the middle class was attempting to develop a constitutional form of government for England which would limit the powers of the monarchy and establish, thereby, the centrality of parliamentary rule.

The growing tensions between the royalists and the parliamentarians came to a head between 1648 and 1688. In 1648 the forces of Parliament, led by Oliver Cromwell, tried and executed King Charles I. After several years of ineffective parliamentary rule Cromwell established himself as the protector of England and ruled in an absolute fashion for almost five years. However, with his death in 1658 Parliament again proved incapable of governing, and it eventually moved to restore the monarchy by inviting the return of the Stuart king Charles II in 1660. The restoration of the monarchy, however, did not resolve the tensions that had produced the original crisis. The immediate issue that sparked renewed conflict concerned Charles's intention to pass the crown onto his brother, James, who was a Roman Catholic. Parliament, representing the largely Protestant middle class, attempted to pass an Exclusion Bill which was designed to prohibit such a transfer. With the bill's failure, however, selected Whig leaders began to prepare for armed rebellion. James assumed the throne in 1685 but was deposed three years later. Finally in 1688, in what is referred to as the "Glorious Revolution," the House of Orange replaced the Stuarts as the English ruling family. By accepting Parliament's invitation to assume the English crown, William and Mary did, in effect, acknowledge parliamentary sovereignty. Thus the constitutional issue was resolved in practice.

Born into a moderately wealthy bourgeois family, Locke originally intended to pursue an academic career. Having completed the prestigious Westminster school he entered Christ Church, Oxford, at the age of 20. There, as an instructor in Greek and rhetoric, Locke became increasingly involved with current developments in the natural sciences and eventually became an acquaintance of the master chemist Robert Boyle. Partially because of the influence of Boyle and partially because he was denied a professorial appointment in light of his refusal to be ordained, Locke turned to the study of medicine. Having completed his studies he began a private practice. One of the first patients was Anthony Ashley Cooper.

At the time of their meeting Ashley was one of the most powerful political leaders in England. Soon he would become Lord Ashley, then the earl of Shaftesbury, and eventually lord chancellor of the Realm. Impressed with Locke's overall abilities Ashley became his patron and secured several appointments for him. In return he relied heavily upon Locke for advice and guidance. When Ashley became finance minister in 1668, Locke turned to the study of economics and soon became involved with the major political issues of the day. As a parliamentary leader Ashley was one of the major forces behind the drafting of the Exclusion Bill. With its failure he became involved in a plot to overthrow the king on behalf of his illegitimate son

Monmouth. With the plot's discovery, however, Ashley was forced to flee England and died an exile in Amsterdam in 1683. Given this turn of events, Locke's previous association with Ashley necessarily complicated his own situation. Fearing for his safety, he fled to Holland in 1683 and did not return to England until the "Glorious Revolution" five years later. Upon his return, however, he enjoyed such a reputation as a philosopher that he was able to exercise a considerable influence on the political affairs of the time. Serving as an advisor and mentor to such politicians as John Somers, the lord chancellor, Locke was able to effect in an immediate way the formation of practical governmental policies. Withdrawing from politics at the turn of the century in order to translate and comment on the Epistles of St. Paul, Locke died on October 29, 1704.

Among his most important books are *A Letter Concerning Toleration* (1689), *An Essay Concerning Human Understanding* (1690), *Two Treatises of Government* (1690), and *The Reasonableness of Christianity* (1695). It is interesting to note that Locke published his *Two Treatises of Government* anonymously and strongly denied persistent rumors that he was their author for as long as he lived. One of the reasons he may have had for doing so is that certain arguments within the *Treatises* are difficult to reconcile with some of the conclusions found within his philosophical masterpiece *An Essay Concerning Human Understanding*.

ANALYSIS OF *AN ESSAY CONCERNING HUMAN UNDERSTANDING*

Locke's philosophical reputation was primarily dependent upon the authority of his *Essay*. Begun nearly twenty years before its eventual publication, the *Essay* was Locke's attempt to "examine our own powers, and see to what things they were adapted."[1] Locke's answer to his own question was essentially that of an empiricist, and the quality of his arguments supporting this position placed him at the forefront of the Enlightenment tradition.

At the center of Locke's effort was his concern to confront the challenge of the skeptics. Earlier, philosophical rationalists had succeeded in undermining Europe's confidence in its traditional religious and cultural beliefs. Expanded travel, contact with non-Western civilizations, and the Protestant challenges to Catholic orthodoxy had had the effect of encouraging a spirit of critical doubt. In response, Locke's empiricism promised to

[1] John Locke, *An Essay Concerning Human Understanding*, ed. Alexander Fraser (New York: Dover Publications, 1959), I, p. vi.

provide a certitude of sorts. According to Locke reason was, indeed, capable of producing certain knowledge, but only if it recognized its own proper and relatively narrow scope.

Specifically Locke argued that one must begin by accepting the fact that human knowledge consists in the perception of ideas:

> Since the mind, in all its thoughts and reasonings, hath no other immediate object but its own ideas, which it alone does or can contemplate, it is evident that our knowledge is only conversant about them. Knowledge then seems to me to be nothing but the perception of the connexion of and agreement, or disagreement and repugnancy of any of our ideas. In this alone it consists.[2]

According to this view, knowledge is reduced to a concern for the relationships between ideas within the individual's mind. It becomes, in effect, an interior operation and, as such, does not involve a confrontation between a subject and an object. Rather it becomes the subject's concern with the thinking self.

Locke was an empiricist inasmuch as he argued that all of our ideas ultimately were derived from physical sensations. Our bodies receive sensual experience from the environment, and these sensations, in turn, impress themselves upon the mind. It is as if the mind were a sheet of white paper (*tabula rasa*) upon which sensations record their perceptions. The mind, in response, operates upon these perceptions by reflecting upon their relationship with one another. The result is human knowledge.

Locke's philosophical speculation is at times ambiguous and becomes somewhat complex. For example, in addition to discussing experience, he also undertook an examination of how it is that human beings come to intuit their own existence and how one can actually demonstrate the existence of God. Without developing the details of these and related arguments, it is possible nonetheless to mention several consequences which followed from Locke's overall position. First, by insisting that all ideas begin with physical sensation, Locke rejected the traditional belief in innate truth. For him, God had not impressed any set truths on the minds of individuals. Thus what at first may appear to be innate truths were, in fact, only the prejudices, opinions, and beliefs of a particular group of people. Inasmuch as true knowledge could not be gained by an examination of other's thoughts, each individual simply had to turn to a consideration of his or her own experience. Thus, for Locke, the rational person was the autonomous individual. Equipped with the power of sensation and reflection, each individual was capable of that experience which is the source of all knowledge. To turn away from direct experience in order to rely upon

[2] Locke, *An Essay Concerning Human Understanding*, II, p. 167.

the thoughts of others was to remove oneself from that condition which makes all knowledge possible. Thus the individual, liberated from the bonds of social belief, is Locke's epistemological model. This same individual will become his political model in the *Second Treatise.*

Second, Locke's strict empiricism had the effect of denying the possibility of a metaphysics. According to Locke, humans experience the effect of physical stimuli upon their five senses. Thus they can know such primary qualities as motion, solidity, figure, and extension. But, inasmuch as humans cannot directly experience any substantive reality behind these qualities, it is impossible for them individually to ultimately know the essence or nature of anything. A true metaphysics, therefore, is an impossibility. Inasmuch as a knowledge of essences or causes is denied humanity, those who claim to have it are claiming an achievement which is beyond the capabilities of the human mind. According to Locke, therefore, by honestly accepting the limitations of reason people can acquire true wisdom. It is not, however, a wisdom about ultimate things. It is rather a knowledge of useful things:

> It is of great use to the sailor to know the the length of his line, though he cannot with it fathom all the depths of the ocean. It is well he knows that it is long enough to reach the bottom at such places as are necessary to direct his voyage, and caution against shoals that may ruin him. Our business here is not to know all things, but those which concern our conduct. If we can find out those measures whereby a rational creature, put in that state which man is in this world, may and ought to govern his opinions and actions depending thereon, we need not be troubled that some things escape our knowledge.[3]

Restricted and properly disciplined, human reason is capable of discovering a form of knowledge whose truthfulness can be secured against further doubt. Thus, although a scientific comprehension of nature was beyond anyone's grasp, the tenets of a rational morality could actually be demonstrated mathematically. This was possible because for Locke moral action did not presuppose a comprehensive understanding of the principles of reality. Unlike traditional moralities which argued for the necessity of attuning oneself to the order of creation, Locke's moral system was based totally upon the priority of sensation. In such a system humans were understood as directing their actions entirely in terms of their own immediate experience of pleasure and pain. Accordingly actions were desirable inasmuch as they promoted the experience of pleasure. Pain, on the other hand,

---

[3] As quoted in Paul Hazard, *The European Mind 1680–1715*, trans. J. Lewis May (New York: New American Library, 1963), pp. 244–245.

was an evil which was to be avoided. In either case, however, it was possible to derive the concept of harm and benefit from a mere physical sensation. As a result, Locke's moral code was based entirely upon psychological realities. As a system, it did not require the knowledge of a law external to itself, and thus its tenets were both certain and demonstrable.

In describing the human mind as a "white paper" or "an empty closet," Locke emphasized thereby the passive nature of human cognition. Inasmuch as knowledge was the result of external sensations impressing themselves upon the material of the mind, cognition did not depend upon any specific personal powers. As such, Locke's epistemology did not require a theory of the human personality. For Locke, who one was did not determine what one could know, and thus epistemologically all people were potentially equal. On this point, Locke's rational egalitarianism differed sharply with certain traditional theories. For example, Plato had argued that only certain individuals were capable of encountering the highest truths. This was so because for Plato philosophical awareness presupposed specific personal and psychological powers. Only those whose souls were ordered by the love of wisdom were in a position to experience the ground of being. Thus, according to Plato, it was possible to establish a hierarchy among citizens which was determined by their differing capacities for knowledge. Ideally such an epistemological hierarchy would be reflected politically. Thus, in Plato's *Republic*, the social classes were differentiated primarily by their ability to respond to and benefit from philosophical education. Locke, on the other hand, denied such implications. All people were fundamentally equal in their ability to learn, because learning was simply a matter of experience. In this sense then, Locke's epistemology was entirely consistent with his political theory. In both instances, the natural human condition was one of fundamental equality.

REASON VERSUS REVELATION

One of the consequences of Locke's empiricism is expressed in the following passage:

> *Reason*, therefore, here, as contradistinguished to *faith*, I take to be the discovery of the certainty or probability of such propositions or truths, which the mind arrives at by deduction from such ideas, which it has got by the use of its natural faculties; viz. by sensation or reflection. *Faith*, on the other hand, is the assent to any proposition, not thus made out by the deductions of reason, but upon the credit of the proposer, as coming from God, in some extraordinary

way of communication. This way of discovering truths to men, we call *revelation*.[4]

In establishing this dichotomy between faith and reason Locke broke with a tradition which included both the pagan Plato and the Christian Aquinas. For them faith and reason were but aspects of a single process characterized by the interpenetration of human and divine consciousness. Locke, on the other hand, argued that reason and faith should be sharply differentiated. For him each had its own particular sphere of inquiry, and thus, in turn, each was characterized by its own specific mode of operation. Given this separation, one of Locke's primary objectives was to establish the boundaries between these two spheres and subsequently to determine their proper relationship to one another. Specifically he attempted to establish the place of Christianity within a rationalistic civilization. Typically his solution presaged that of the Enlightenment.

Although Locke had argued that the existence of God could be demonstrated by reason alone, he, nonetheless, accepted the fact of revelation. Indeed, according to Locke, the New Testament actually revealed the entire law of nature and thus its teachings did not, in fact, contradict the teachings of natural reason. In those cases where revelation appeared to go beyond the teachings of reason, however, statements of faith were still acceptable if it could be shown that God was their author. On the other hand, this claim of authorship was something that only reason itself could judge. Thus, Locke wrote:

> *Reason is natural revelation*, whereby the eternal Father of light and fountain of all knowledge, communicates to mankind that portion of truth which he has laid within the reach of their natural faculties: *revelation* is *natural reason enlarged* by a new set of discoveries communicated by God immediately; which reason vouches the truth of, by the testimony and proofs it gives that they come from God.[5]

In short, "*Reason must be our last judge and guide in everything.*"[6]

The real significance of Locke's argument is not to be found in his emphasis upon the priority of reason. Rather what is more important is his diminution of what is meant by both revelation and reason. For Locke, revelation was no longer the experience of a mysterious inrush of the sacred into the profane. Rather, it was simply a body of dogma—the propositions

---

[4] Locke, *An Essay Concerning Human Understanding*, II, p. 416.

[5] Locke, *An Essay Concerning Human Understanding*, II, p. 431.

[6] Locke, *An Essay Concerning Human Understanding*, II, p. 438.

of which could be tested and approved. Similarly, reason for Locke was no longer humanity's questioning response to the promise of a hidden meaning. Rather, it was simply an autonomous faculty standing outside of the faith experience and critically testing the acceptability of dogmatic formulas. In both cases, the mysterious experience of a guided quest had disappeared. In effect, truth had become a matter of correct doctrine.

This change in meaning is quite clear in Locke's *The Reasonableness of Christianity*. For Locke, Christian revelation is true because reason had demonstrated that God was its author. The question remained, however, as to the meaning of its revealed truth. Whereas traditional Christianity would emphasize the fundamentally mysterious experience of a god-human, Locke attempted to answer this question by isolating a few key propositions which he believed formed the core of Christian teaching. Rejecting the church's continuing historical attempt to express its own experience of the Christian message, Locke settled on three dogmatic propositions: God exists; Christ was the Messiah; and mortals should repent in order to live a righteous life. According to Locke, each of these propositions could be tested and affirmed by natural reason. Whereas the "thinking part of mankind" had already discovered the one god, natural philosophers independent of revelation had already set forth the moral rules for a righteous life—albeit in a nonsystematic form. Thus according to Locke there was, in effect, nothing in Christianity that reason could not accept. Yet, if this were so, what, then, was the purpose of Christ's coming as the Messiah? For Locke the answer to this question could be found by examining Christ's teaching authority. Inasmuch as Christianity was essentially a set of moral precepts, Locke's Christ essentially became the means for their authoritative promulgation. Natural reason had discovered moral truth slowly and had had little success in persuading "laboring and illiterate men" of its veracity. However, with Christ lending the authority of his divine command to such teachings they could now be accepted easily and quickly by the simplest of people. Thus for Locke Christianity was essentially a device for moral instruction. Through its appeal "the illiterate bulk of mankind" could be taught the moral rules which are necessary for its salvation.

The intellectual tension between revelation and reason was mirrored at the political level by the institutional tension between church and state. In both cases, Locke attempted to solve the tension by separating the two components and isolating each within its own appropriate sphere. In both cases, however, the unintended consequence was to produce the diminution of both components and the eventual domination of one by the other. Thus just as Locke's autonomous reason would eventually come to dominate Christianity's revealed dogma, so, too, would Locke's secular state expand so as to monopolize the public order.

During Locke's time the major church-state issue was that of toleration. Should the state permit a variety of religious practices, and, if not, how could it promote religious uniformity? Locke's answer to these questions was to argue on behalf of a conditional religious liberty. Generally, he favored a mutual toleration among Christians. Thus atheists were excluded in principle, and—although they were Christians—Catholics were not to be tolerated because of their allegiance to Rome. Locke's tolerant society, therefore, presupposed the existence of a functioning Protestant civilization. Given this condition, he sought to secure both religious liberty and political freedom.

Locke's method of achieving religious toleration presupposed a distinction between two spheres of concern. On one hand, there was the temporal order. It was to be organized as a political society and was to be concerned only with the procuring, preserving, and advancement of its citizens' civil interests. These interests, in turn, were defined as life, liberty, and the pursuit of property. On the other hand, there was the spiritual realm. Here the primary concern was with the salvation of souls, and the proper organizational form was that of the voluntary church. According to Locke, the temporal and spiritual orders could operate independently of one another, and thus their respective institutions should not need to interfere in one another's work. If this were accepted, the political society would have no legitimate interest in the religious beliefs of its various churches. Concerned only with the outward prosperity of society, the state would thus respect the priority of personal conscience in those matters concerning eternal salvation.

By distinguishing between the spiritual and temporal order, Locke hoped to minimize the number of issues over which the two realms would come into conflict. To further support this effort, he also distinguished between the public and private order. Inasmuch as political society was concerned with material prosperity, it operated within the public order. It was concerned not only with the individual but with society as a whole. The spiritual realm was different, however. Inasmuch as "the life and power of true religion consist in the inward and full persuasion of the mind . . . ,"[7] spiritual concerns were essentially a personal and, therefore, private affair. Thus in separating the spiritual from the temporal order Locke also privatized the former. As a consequence, religion became a purely private matter.

At first glance, Locke's attempt to achieve religious toleration appears to have been a pragmatic success. There are, however, certain theoretical issues which merit further investigation. First, by separating the spiritual from the temporal and by defining the care of the latter as the sole

---

[7] John Locke, *A Letter Concerning Toleration*, ed. Patrick Romanell (Indianapolis: Bobbs-Merrill, 1950), p. 18.

concern of politics, Locke achieved a radical break from the classical tradition. For the classical theorist, the purpose of politics was not simply life but the good life. Accordingly, society was to help citizens live well and, thus, by necessity was concerned with the question of virtue and human fulfillment. According to Locke's scheme, however, society is concerned simply with living. Thus it is life and the prerequisites of life which become the purpose of political existence. Questions concerning the good or the virtuous, on the other hand, now become the private concern of individual citizens. Society, as such, takes no position on such matters. With Locke, therefore, the problem of preserving mere biological and social existence has expanded to fill the entire public arena. As a result, the public order becomes totally dedicated to the pacification of material existence, while the issues of spiritual fulfillment are relegated to the private choices of autonomous individuals.

Second, Locke's effort to develop a tolerant society raises the question as to whether it is based upon realistic assumptions. In reducing the political to the mere pursuit of material ends, Locke had the effect of trivializing the public order. Such trivialization, in turn, succeeded in limiting the range of interests and passions that could become involved in an eventual conflict. Yet, at the same time, it is questionable whether citizens will long accept a trivial politics. Indeed, there seems to be a human need to relate the political order to a set of higher values. By removing the spiritual meaning of a Christian political order, Locke hoped to achieve religious liberty. Yet at the same time he may have created instead a spiritual vacuum. It may be that the modern creation of political ideologies and the popularity of such political religions as fascism and national socialism are, in part, responses to the void created by a radically privatized spiritual world. In short, by removing Christianity from the public order, Locke may have inadvertently encouraged the development of its perverted forms.

ANALYSIS OF *TWO TREATISES* OF *GOVERNMENT*

Locke's most important political writings are contained in his *Two Treatises of Government*, which was published anonymously in 1690. Generally the *Treatises* represent Locke's response to the doctrine of political absolutism. Specifically, the *First Treatise* is a critique of the absolutist position as represented in the writings of Robert Filmer, while the *Second Treatise* presents Locke's own preferred theoretical alternative, that is, a limited government based upon popular consent.

During the struggles between the king and Parliament at the close of the sixteenth century, the monarchy had attempted to justify its position by appealing to a doctrine of political absolutism. Indeed by Locke's time the absolutist tradition had developed several distinct schools. One was the rationalistic school as represented in the work of Thomas Hobbes. As we have seen, however, Hobbes's absolutism was based upon an individualistic perspective which presupposed a belief in natural human equality. As such, it was rejected by the royalist forces and remained politically ineffective. The more popular form of political absolutism, on the other hand, was that developed by Robert Filmer in *Patriarcha*, written around 1637 but published in 1680. As an absolutist Filmer shared many of Hobbes's assumptions. For example, he believed that the human will was the source of all law and authority, that the population's total submission to the dictates of a sovereign was a necessity, and that no form of mixed government could be tolerated. Yet, unlike Hobbes, Filmer denied natural equality, stressed the social nature of humanity, and rejected any theory which presupposed the existence of a state of nature.

Filmer based his understanding of absolutism on a reading of the biblical account of creation. Accordingly, he first interpreted the Old Testament in such a way as to justify patriarchal kingships and then subsequently applied such arguments to the monarchies of his own day. According to Filmer the Old Testament established the fact that Adam was granted original political authority over other humans. Over time this original sovereignty was transferred to other earthly princes, and, thus, the monarchs of Filmer's day were, in effect, Adam's heirs and, as such, enjoyed the full exercise of biblical sovereignty.

Locke's response to Filmer was cast in the form of scriptual exegesis. Examining the Bible, Locke attempted to document the many cases wherein Filmer had obviously misinterpreted the meaning of selected passages. The result, according to Locke, was a series of logical contradictions and historical misstatements. Thus even if one were inclined to accept such a form of argumentation, Locke denied that Filmer had made his case. And by showing how Filmer's case had failed, Locke believed that the correct alternative could be easily established:

> But if this foundation fails, all his [Filmer] Fabric falls with it, and Governments must be left again to the old way of being made by contrivance, and the consent of Men making use of their Reason to unite together into Society.[8]

It is in his *Second Treatise* that Locke attempts to make the case for returning to the "old way." The *Second Treatise* begins with an examina-

---

[8] John Locke, *Two Treatises of Government*, ed. Peter Laslett (New York: New American Library, 1965), p. 178.

tion of political power. As a form of power, political power must be distinguished from all other types. Specifically, political power, unlike the power of father over children or masters over servants, implies the right of making and enforcing laws. These laws, in turn, are concerned first with the regulation and preservation of property and secondly with providing for the common defense of the nation. Like Hobbes, Locke believed that one could best comprehend the nature of political power by first examining how it came about. Thus it was necessary to recreate the original logic which compelled subjects to form society in the first place. As a state-of-nature theorist Locke believed that this logic was most apparent during the drafting of the social contract.

Like Hobbes, Locke believed that human nature was revealed most fully in its primitive rather than perfected forms. Thus, in an effort to know humanity it was necessary to recreate that state of nature which existed before the development of civil society. According to Locke, the following conditions existed in such a state. First, all people were free to dispose of themselves and their property as they saw fit. This freedom, however, did not imply a state of total license, for, according to Locke, God had promulgated certain natural laws which functioned to structure and order humanity's original condition. Specifically, inasmuch as each person was the property of God, no one possessed the right of destroying either oneself or another. Locke's reference to God as providing the basis for human relationships appealed to a long-standing theme in Christian social theory. Yet Locke's particular version differed in a significant way. Traditionally Christian theory had argued that a proper human relationship was based upon that love which one experienced while seeing the image of God in another. For Locke, however, it was God's property relationship with each individual which provided the basis for human interaction. In effect, then, proprietary interests appear to have replaced Christian love as the model for human and social order.

A second characteristic of the state of nature, according to Locke, was its fundamentally equalitarian condition. No one was subordinated to the will of another. Locke based this theory of equality on the fact that all human beings were equally members of a common biological species. Whereas Christianity had traditionally argued that all people were equal because they were all equally loved by God, Locke grounded human equality on a mere biological fact. According to Locke, therefore, political equality was derived from biological equality. Differences in spiritual development, on the other hand, were relegated to the private sphere of religious concern.

Locke's description of life within the state of nature is at times ambiguous. On one hand, he insisted upon the fact that the state of nature was not characterized by warlike conditions. Whereas Hobbes had seen violent war as natural, Locke understood peace to be the more typical situation. This difference was due, in part, to the fact that Locke did not conceive of natural humanity in the same radically individualistic manner as had Hobbes. For Locke, the natural ancestors were indeed motivated by the requirements of self-preservation. Yet, at the same time, they exhibited a certain degree of sociality. The very same natural law which dictated self-preservation also demanded that each individual attempt to preserve the rest of humankind in those cases where his or her own preservation was not directly threatened. Consequently, Locke's natural individual was involved in both self-regarding and other-regarding actions. As a result, war was possible but not inevitable. Yet, having deemphasized the warlike conditions of the state of nature on one hand, Locke nevertheless wrote later:

> . . . that though in the state of Nature he hath such a right, yet the Enjoyment of it is very uncertain, and constantly exposed to the Invasion of others . . . the enjoyment of the property he has in this state is very unsafe, very unsecure. This makes him willing to quit a condition, which however free, is full of fears and continual dangers . . . [9]

Despite such ambiguities concerning the precise character of life in the state of nature, Locke, nevertheless, was clear as to its central feature. Referring to the conditions which existed between rulers of independent countries as an example, Locke argued that the state of nature existed wherever the executive power of the law of nature remained exclusively in the hands of individuals. For Locke, the natural law was intelligible and clear to all rational creatures, and in the state of nature each individual was charged with executing and enforcing its requirements. In short, every person had the right to punish those who invaded the rights of others:

> Men living together according to reason, without a common Superior on Earth, with Authority to judge between them, is *properly the State of Nature.* [10]

In entering society, natural individuals forfeited definite, concrete advantages. First, they moved from a condition of equality to one of inequality. Second, they exchanged natural liberty for the more limited benefits of civil liberty. And, finally, they ultimately had to relinquish the right to enforce that law of nature which had previously guaranteed their own self-preservation. The question arose, therefore, why humans would consent to such developments. For Locke, the answer was to be found in the ex-

---

[9] Locke, *Two Treatises of Government*, p. 395.
[10] Locke, *Two Treatises of Government*, p. 321.

istence of certain inconveniences which were endemic to the natural condition. Specifically, inasmuch as each person was charged with interpreting and executing the law of nature, certain consequences could not be avoided. First, biased by their own interests and hampered by a lack of study the natural ancestors disagreed as to the exact dictates of the natural law. As a result, there was no established, known, and settled law. The inevitable variety of interpretations, therefore, could only encourage a multiplicity of conflicts. Second, inasmuch as each individual was empowered to serve as a judge, there was no way of guaranteeing an impartial judge for any particular case. Consequently, a situation arose wherein any individual could demand to be the judge in one's own case, which was a development that created an obvious dilemma. Finally, although each individual was charged with punishing crimes against the natural law, each individual necessarily lacked sufficient power with which to enforce those judgments. As a consequence, crimes would often go unpunished. According to Locke, these inconveniences had the combined effect of producing a single result. Together they made the pursuit and preservation of property extremely difficult. Thus it was that in order to ease these difficulties natural humanity consented to form civil society. In short, society was created for the sake of preserving property. On one hand, it was to preserve humanity, understood as God's property, while, on the other hand, it was to protect life, liberty, and estates, referred to by Locke as "man's property." To achieve this goal, the natural ancestors simply had to agree to waive their right to enforce the law of nature:

> . . . there only is *Political Society*, where every one of the Members hath quitted this natural Power, resigned it up into the hands of the Community in all cases that exclude him not from appealing for Protection to the Law established by it. . . . And thus the Commonwealth comes by a Power to set down, what punishment shall belong to the several transgressions which they think worthy of it, committed amongst the Members of that Society, (which is the *power of making Laws*) as well as it has the power to punish any Injury done unto any of its Members, by any one that is not of it, (which is the *power of War and Peace*) and all this for the preservation of the property of all the Members of that Society, as far as is possible.[11]

According to Locke, therefore, the natural human consented to society because of a carefully calculated judgment. The benefits of securing one's property apparently outweighed the benefits of living in a condition of pure equality and perfect freedom. It is obvious, however, that such a cal-

---

[11] Locke, *Two Treatises of Government*, p. 367–8.

culation makes sense only if property exists. If human beings cannot claim a natural right to property, then all calculations designed to protect such a right would be without force. Given this, it was absolutely essential that Locke develop a compelling theory of property rights.

Locke's justification of property faced an immediate difficulty: he himself accepted the argument that both reason and Scripture proved that God had given the Earth to humankind in common. If this were the case, how was it then possible to justify an individual's claim to possess a particular item? By what right could a person appropriate alone something that was originally intended for humankind in general? For Locke, the answer to this question was to be found through an analysis of labor. Yet to do so he had to amend somewhat his earlier work. Previously Locke had argued that each individual was essentially the property of God. Now, however, he insisted that each individual's person was in fact his or her own property. In addition to admitting a certain ambiguity into his work, Locke's suggestion that all individuals were the sole proprietors of their own person and capacities also forced him to break with the traditional understanding of labor. Traditionally, it had been argued that property and labor were social functions and thus that the ownership of property implied certain social obligations. According to Locke, on the other hand, individuals as the absolute proprietors of their capacity to work owed nothing to society on this account. Possessing their own persons as property, the natural forebears labored in order to appropriate the goods of nature for their own personal use. By laboring, the natural workers acted in such a way as to mix a part of themselves, that is, their labor, with nature in general, and thus by doing so they each established a property claim on the eventual products of their individual labors.

> The Labour of his Body, and the Work of his Hands, we may say, are properly his. Whatsoever then he removes out of the State that Nature hath provided, and left it in, he hath mixed his Labour with, and joyned to it something that is his own, and thereby makes it his *Property*. It being by him removed from the common state Nature placed it in, hath by his *labour* something annexed to it, that excludes the common right of other Men.[12]

For Locke, therefore, labor was not merely a necessary device for producing economic values. Rather, in Locke's system it served at the same time as the theoretical justification for human acquisition.

In the early state of nature, there were two fundamental limits which controlled human acquisitive actions. First, inasmuch as people

---

[12] Locke, *Two Treatises of Government*, p. 329.

labored so as to enjoy the fruits of their individual work, any labor that produced a surplus which could not be consumed before it spoiled lacked a basic logical justification. To acquire products simply to allow them to be destroyed was senseless. Second, individuals could acquire as much as they could consume alone if they left enough, and of equal quality, in common for others. This was an obvious restriction, since each individual had a right to self-preservation and thus no one could deprive others of the necessities they required. The effect of these qualifications was to limit human acquisitiveness and thereby create a bounded property system. According to Locke, therefore, the natural forebear had a right to property; but, as in the case of freedom, it operated within the limits of the natural law.

The original balance of the bounded property system existed during the early stages of human history when the population was small and land plentiful. Before long, however, human beings introduced a factor which both disrupted this original balance and destroyed the limitations on human acquisitiveness. That factor was the invention of money. By agreeing to give value to gold and silver, humanity created a means by which the original limits to the appropriation of property could be transcended forever. This occurred in two distinct ways. First, money allowed individuals to exchange their surplus products for a commodity which could not spoil. The acquisition of land for the production of a surplus which eventually could be converted to gold or silver was no longer a meaningless activity. Thus, the limitation due to spoilage was no longer operative. In a similar manner, the introduction of money transcended the demand that the individual leave behind land which was enough and of equal quality for others. After all, it was not the land but the product of the land which people required. And if, by accumulating a large amount of land and investing in its productivity, an individual was able to increase its yield, what was created, in effect, was more for others. By cultivating the land and creating wealth, the individual actually increased the product of the whole. Thus private appropriation increased the amount of product available for others and became, thereby, a positive accomplishment. Unlimited appropriation, in turn, promised unlimited productivity. As such, it transcended the earlier limitation originally established by the demand for sufficiency. For Locke, unlimited acquisition by an individual was justified because it contributed to social wealth. And the purpose of society thereby became the growth of property rather than its mere preservation. Whereas originally humanity labored in order to consume, with the invention of money they now labored in order to acquire. As a consequence laboring was no longer simply a means of preserving life. It had become instead preoccupied with the demand for unlimited acquisition.

Locke's effort to justify unlimited acquisition has led some scholars to suggest that he was a spokesman for the merging capitalist order. And it is true that his doctrine of property does reflect the interests and needs of the capitalist class. Limits to the accumulation of capital were not only removed, but this removal was seen as both just and proper. Such an argument was truly revolutionary during Locke's own time. Even his contemporary, Hobbes, shied away from those conclusions which Locke calmly accepted. Whereas Hobbes feared that the spiritual madness which produced the unrestricted passion for possession would eventually destroy society, Locke, on the contrary, saw it as a primary source for social improvement. Thus it is that in Locke's work the entrepreneur's passion for property actually replaced the philosopher's love of wisdom as the existential source for social order.

Locke's doctrine of property served several functions within his argument. First, in specifying the rationale for the formation of political society, it established, thereby, the purpose of the political community. Accordingly, society, for Locke, existed solely for the sake of preserving life, liberty, and property. Second, by specifying the purpose of the political community, Locke's doctrine of property also served to set definite limits to the exercise of political power. Political power was legitimate only when it was used to pursue those goals for which it was created. Any attempt to use such a power for different ends, therefore, was arbitrary and, as a consequence, lacked binding authority. In particular, political power was limited to serving the public good and preserving the social order. In doing so, it was to be exercised according to promulgated, standing laws and administered by known, authorized judges. Most importantly, it could not deprive a person of property without that individual's consent. In essence, therefore, Locke was arguing on the behalf of a limited, constitutional government. Its fundamental concerns, powers, and privileges were established and defined by the terms of that social contract to which the citizens had originally consented. Thus, as Locke had argued in his *First Treatise*, consent was the only basis for legitimate government.

According to Locke's reconstruction, the original social contract actually contained several elements. First, humans each agreed to forfeit their own original right to enforce the laws of nature. Second, in forfeiting such a right, those individuals effectively transferred it into the hands of the community. Third, in allowing the community to exercise this entrusted right, each agreed that it should act according to the determinations of the majority. In short, political society was founded when each of its members agreed to be ruled according to the decisions of the majority. Thus a commitment to majority rule was the actual device by which individuals consented to take themselves out of the state of nature.

According to Locke, the giving of consent can take one of two forms. First, one may explicitly consent to majority rule. In such cases, there is no ambiguity, and thus one's membership in the commonwealth is for all intents and purposes perpetual. The second form involves an expression of tacit consent whereby a person's acceptance of the government is assumed because of his situation:

> And to this I say, that every Man, that hath any Possession, or Enjoyment, of any part of the Dominions of any Government, doth thereby give his *tacit Consent* and is so far forth obliged to Obedience to the laws of that Government, during such Enjoyment, as any one under it; whether this his Possession be of land, to him and his Heirs for ever, or a Lodging only for a Week; or whether it be barely travelling freely on the Highway; and in Effect, it reaches as far as the very being of any one within the Territories of that Government.[13]

Although Locke's notion of tacit consent may appear somewhat strained, it was, nonetheless, absolutely necessary for his argument. Essential to Locke's view was his belief in the original freedom of each human being. Given this, there appeared to be no consistent scheme by which the subordination of one to another could be justified except by the granting of consent. Thus to expand the notion of consent so as to include its tacit expression was a necessary development in view of Locke's underlying moral commitment to equality and freedom.

Once the political community has been formed and empowered to enforce the laws of nature and pursue the goals for which it was established, it must be organized for action in history. Accordingly, Locke suggested that there be a certain division of labor. First, the ability to do whatever is necessary for the preservation of society within the bounds established by the laws of nature should be placed in the hands of the legislative power. The legislative power, in turn, exists to express the consent of society. As such, it formulates the positive law and sees to the public good by deciding how the forces of society shall be utilized. Second, the task of administering the law and overseeing the punishment of those who disobey should be delegated to the executive power. Unlike the legislative, which meets only periodically, the executive should always be in session. Its task, however, is clearly subordinate to that of the legislative. As the supreme power, the legislative necessarily establishes those general rules which set the agenda for the executive branch. Even allowing for that degree of discretion which is necessary for any fair administration of the law, the executive is always bound in principle by the intention of the legislative power. Finally, although the federative powers of declaring war and determining foreign relations are distinct from those of punishing domestic criminals, they should, nonetheless, be placed in the hands of the executive. As distinct as

[13] Locke, *Two Treatises of Government*, p. 392.

the federative powers may be, they do, nonetheless, require that discretion and efficiency which is typical of an executive power in continuous session. At the same time, however, inasmuch as the federative power is placed within the executive, it is, thereby, clearly subordinated to the will of the legislative.

In his discussion of the creation and organization of the government, Locke carefully distinguished between the means by which society was created and those by which the government was formed. Having created their communal existence by contract, the members of society then proceeded to entrust political power to their particular government. Thus, although society itself is understood to have been created by a contract, no such contract exists between the society and its government. On the contrary, the relationship between a society and its government is fiducial rather than contractual. As a consequence, if the legislative power betrays its trust, it may be removed:

> . . . yet the Legislative being only a Fiduciary Power to act for certain ends, there remains still *in the People a Supream power* to remove or alter the Legislative, when they find the *Legislative* act contrary to the trust reposed in them. For all *Power given with trust* for the attaining an *end*, being limited by that end, whenever that *end* is manifestly neglected, or opposed, the *trust* must necessarily be *forfeited*, and the Power devolve into the hands of those that gave it, who may place it anew where they shall think best for their safety and security.[14]

In short, Locke had presented a justification for revolution.

Locke's justification depended upon a fundamental distinction between society and government. Society arose from the human decision to leave the state of nature and incorporate with others so as to act as one body. As a result, a society can only be dissolved by foreign conquest. A government, on the other hand, exists only as a recipient of society's trust. It, therefore, can be dissolved whenever that trust is withdrawn. If, for example, the legislative were to act in such a way as to appropriate rather than preserve the life, liberty, and property of the people, they, in turn, would be justified in rebelling. Yet, in doing so, they would not be returning to the state of nature, for in withdrawing their trust from an arbitrary government, they would, in effect, simply be reaffirming the intention of their original contract with one another.

At one time, it was argued that Locke's *Second Treatise* was written as a defense of the Glorious Revolution. More recently, however, others, namely Peter Laslett, have argued that the *Treatise* was composed prior to

---

[14] Locke, *Two Treatises of Government*, p. 413.

the revolution and thus was intended to promote it rather than simply to defend it. Similarly, scholars have consistently emphasized Locke's influence upon the American Revolution in general and Thomas Jefferson in particular. Indeed, even those who question whether Locke was the single-most important theoretician for the American Revolution do not deny that Lockeanism at least played a major role. Yet, as significant as Locke's justification of rebellion was, it would be a mistake to limit his importance to this theme. On the contrary, it can be argued that Locke's acceptance of the passionate human as the sole criterion for political order was his most important theoretical accomplishment. Whereas classical theory had insisted that only humans at their best could serve as the standard for personal and social order, Locke, to the contrary, was willing to accept them at their most elemental. Thus not only were the passions to be accepted, but, if properly organized, they actually served as the motor for social progress. For Locke, then, inasmuch as the acquisitive life had replaced the good life as the standard of personal excellence, freedom necessarily replaced virtue as the purpose of political existence.

BIBLIOGRAPHY

AARON, R. I. *John Locke.* Second edition. Oxford: Oxford University Press, 1955.

Cox, RICHARD. *Locke on War and Peace.* Oxford: Oxford University Press, 1960.

CRANSTON, MAURICE. *John Locke: A Biography.* London: Longmans, Greene & Co., 1957.

GOUGH, J. W. *John Locke's Politial Philosophy.* Oxford: Oxford University Press, 1950.

KENDALL, WILMORE. *John Locke and the Doctrine of Majority Rule.* Urbana: University of Illinois Press, 1941.

LAMPRECHT, S. P. *The Moral and Political Philosophy of John Locke.* New York: Columbia University Press, 1918.

MACPHERSON, C. B. *The Political Theory of Possessive Individualism: Hobbes to Locke.* Oxford: Oxford University Press, 1962.

STRAUSS, LEO. *Natural Right and History.* Chicago: University of Chicago Press, 1953.

YOLTON, J. W. *John Locke and the Way of Ideas.* Oxford: Oxford University Press, 1956.

11

THE ENLIGHTENMENT

The success of modern science accounted for the spirit of optimism that was so characteristic of eighteenth-century European political thought. For many the discoveries of Copernicus, Kepler, Galileo, and Newton appeared to inaugurate a new age of scientific promise. These successes, in turn, were understood by such philosophers as Descartes and Bacon to be the inevitable results of the modern scientific method. In either its rationalist or empiricist form this method appeared to accurately describe the principles of reason itself. Thus if humanity could learn to follow the laws of critical inquiry rather than the dictates of prejudice, custom, or authority, there appeared to be every reason to believe that the moral and political sciences would soon imitate the progressive development of the natural sciences. Similarly, unlike its medieval predecessor, modern science taught that nature was continuous, uniform, and simple. Thus assuming that the natural order was, indeed, the basis for the political order, it seemed apparent that a rationally justified pattern of uniform political order could be discovered and implemented. Indeed the faith that such an achievement was in fact possible extended throughout much of Western Europe during the eighteenth century. Ultimately it was a faith in the power of autonomous reason, and, as such, it eventually included the following tenets:

> The essential articles of the religion of the Enlightenment may be stated thus: (1) man is not natively depraved; (2) the end of life is life itself, the good life on earth instead of the beatific life after death; (3) man is capable, guided solely by the light of reason and experience, of perfecting the good life on earth; and (4) the first and essential condition of the good life on earth is the freeing of men's minds from the bonds of ignorance and superstition, and of their bodies from the arbitrary oppression of the constituted social authorities.[1]

Although the Enlightenment spirit found important advocates in England, Scotland, and Germany, its true home was in eighteenth-century France. At the same time, however, it is obvious that its French representatives consciously took their lessons from the masters of seventeenth-century English thought.

VOLTAIRE AND THE FRENCH ENLIGHTENMENT

One thinker who typified this pattern was the French writer Voltaire. Voltaire, the author of such works as *Candide* (1759), *The Philosophical Dictionary* (1764), and *The Philosophy of History* (1766), was born in Paris in 1694. Educated by the Jesuits and originally intending a career in law, Voltaire quickly became acquainted with several of the current intellectual trends of his day.

Accordingly as a youth he began to develop doubts about Christianity and, at the same time, became increasingly interested in both the natural sciences and the empirical philosophy upon which they were based. In 1726 Voltaire left for a two-year visit to England. There he became acquainted with the teachings of such English writers as Hume, Berkeley, and Thomas Woolston. More importantly, however, he learned of the work of John Locke and Isaac Newton. Eventually it would be English philosophy and science as represented by Locke and Newton which would serve as the inspiration not only for Voltaire in particular but for the French Enlightenment in general.

---

[1] Carl Becker, *The Heavenly City of the Eighteenth-Century Philosophers* (New Haven: Yale University Press, 1973), pp. 102–03.

Newton's influence can be traced to two particular achievements. First, his substantive work in science seemed to succeed in establishing a rigorous and empirically demonstrable world-view. Newton's theory of gravity brought together into one picture the astronomical discoveries of Copernicus, Brahe, and Kepler on one hand with the physical conceptions of Galileo on the other. Accordingly all change in motion could be explained in terms of force, and all objects, whether terrestrial or heavenly, could be treated as units of mass. The result was a conception of the universe as a machine. Whereas medieval science had pictured nature as striving towards an hierarchical ideal, Newton's model suggested that nature was simply a mechanical succession of events. Physics, accordingly, was the study of motion, and, as such, it could be practiced with the precision of the mathematical sciences. In summarizing the world-view of Newtonian science, the philosopher E. A. Burtt wrote:

> First, the real world in which man lives is no longer regarded as a world of substances possessed of as many ultimate qualities as can be experienced in them, but has become a world of atoms [now electrons], equipped with none but mathematical characteristics and moving according to laws fully statable in mathematical form. Second, explanations in terms of forms and final causes of events, both in this world and in the less independent realm of the mind, have been definitely set aside in favour of explanations in terms of their simplest elements, the latter related temporally as efficient causes, and being mechanically treatable motions of bodies wherever it is possible so to regard them.[2]

The Newtonian view of nature as a machine, or as a watch, created certain problems for both theologians and philosophers. In particular it was not clear where God and humanity fit within the mechanized universe. Attempts to deal with these issues formed a major element within Enlightenment thought. Yet at the same time, the Newtonian model of nature was widely accepted because it seemed to work. Nature appeared to be ordered and regular. Those occasional irregularities which Newton, himself, could not explain disappeared as other mathematicians, such as Maupertius, Clairaut, and D'Alembert, extended Newton's findings and confirmed his theories with more sophisticated measurements and experiments. Not surprisingly, therefore, the cosmology of Descartes and Leibnitz, the other modern alternative to medieval science, eventually lost its supporters.

[2] E. A. Burtt. *The Metaphysical Foundations of Modern Science* (Garden City: Doubleday, 1932), p. 303

Newton's second major contribution to Enlightenment theory was his method—a blend of both mathematical and experimental reasoning. Assuming that nature was, in fact, nothing but matter-in-motion, Newton believed that the science of mechanics (a fundamentally mathematical discipline) provided the model for all scientific reasoning. Consequently, the task of the natural scientist was to reduce all physical phenomena to their engendering mathematical laws. Yet Newton was not interested in mathematically pure speculation for its own sake. Unlike Galileo, Kepler, or Descartes, Newton did not believe in *a priori* certain truth. Thus all mathematical explanations of nature had to be verified and guided by experiment. For Newton, it was experience which posed the problem that mathematics sought to solve, and ultimately it would have to be experience which would test the solution. Newton's method, therefore, has three distinct phases: First, experiments are used to simplify the phenomena; second, the governing principles are expressed mathematically; and finally, the resulting laws are tested experimentally by extending them to new fields.

Newton's emphasis upon experimental testing accounts for his critique of hypothetical reasoning. For Newton ideas could claim scientific legitimacy only if they were deductions from sensible phenomena and thus capable of being verified within experience. As a result he refused to use rationalistic hypotheses in his scientific work, and this refusal, in turn, placed a strict limit upon the range of phenomena which could be investigated legitimately. For example, although Newton could specify the mathematical characteristics of gravitational forces, he refused to speculate about gravity's ultimate nature or the reason for its existence. For Newton scientific reason was a powerful but limited tool. For Voltaire and other Enlightenment thinkers, Newton's sober assessment of reason represented a nondogmatic and open attitude which they found refreshing. By admitting the limits of what reason could know, Newtonian science seemed to advocate toleration and acceptance. Thus rather than building an absolute system, modern science encouraged the process of questioning and criticism. Such an attitude in turn could be applied not only to science but also to religious and social practice. Indeed such an extended application soon became a major concern for Englightenment theorists.

Influence of John Locke

Whereas Newton appeared to have provided the world with the means to understand and control physical nature, it was another Englishman John Locke, who seemed to have discovered the secrets of human nature itself. Referring to him as a "physicist of the soul," Voltaire wrote:

Such a multitude of reasoners have written the romance of the soul, a sage at last arose, who gave very modestly its history. Mr. Locke has displayed the human soul in the same manner as an excellent anatomist explains the springs of the human body. He everywhere takes the light of physics for his guide.[3]

For Voltaire and others, John Locke was the preeminent philosopher. His empiricism not only confirmed the methodology of modern science but at the same time suggested a view of human nature that was entirely consistent with the Newtonian universe. In addition Locke's religious, political, and educational writings seemed to provide those practical conclusions which were necessary in order to reform society according to the new teachings of English physics and psychology. For example, during the autocratic reign of Louis XIV in France, religious and political persecution were common. With the repeal of the Edict of Nantes the monarchy set its full weight behind the persecution of Protestantism. Voltaire and other intellectuals were horrified by the dogmatic intolerance which was implicit in such events and found in Locke's *A Letter Concerning Toleration* powerful arguments with which to oppose such a practice. Similarly Locke's political philosophy as expressed in his *Treatise of Government* articulated a liberal program with which to combat the absolutism of the French monarchy. In teaching that a spontaneous harmony in nature produced a situation wherein the individual's pursuit of enlightened self-interest eventually led to the good of all, Locke not only emphasized the importance of the individual but at the same time suggested that the proper role of government was limited to that of aiding the individual in the pursuit of life, liberty, and property. Such a program not only supported the intellectuals' interest in freedom and toleration, but it also promoted the social and economic interests of the emerging French middle class. Finally, Locke's argument that the human mind began as a white sheet upon which experience could imprint its teachings engendered a great faith in the possibilities of education. Discounting innate ideas, Lockean psychology suggested that, inasmuch as education was simply a matter of experience, the people could improve themselves by expanding their horizons and opening themselves to the new truths of science. As such, humankind was not determined or stagnant, rather it could progress and improve itself by the simple act of turning from the ignorance of its past. Accordingly a faith in the power of education, obviously bolstered by the progress of science, became a fundamental tenet of Enlightenment thought. Indeed such a faith was the animating spirit of the *philosophes*.

[3] Voltaire, "On Mr. Locke," in Norman Torrey, ed., *Les Philosophes* (New York: Capricorn Books, 1960), p. 75.

THE *PHILOSOPHES* AND THE *ENCYCLOPEDIA:* DIDEROT AND D'ALEMBERT

The *philosophes* were a group of French intellectuals who were dedicated to the popularization of the teachings of such scientific geniuses as Newton, Locke, Descartes, and Bacon. Although their particular viewpoints were often quite diverse, they did share a common commitment to the teachings of English science. Accordingly they argued on behalf of the experimental method and advocated the use of free reason as the final guide in all human affairs. And because these ideas were foreign to the French culture of their day, the *philosophes* often exhibited a certain contempt for the traditions of their own society. They consequently saw their role as one of both criticism and instruction. Prejudice, superstition, and traditional practices were denounced as remnants of an irrational age. In their place, the *philosophes* advocated the principles of a rational order.

The Enlightenment criticism of tradition and superstition drew support from the work of the English philosopher, scientist, and statesman Francis Bacon. In his *New Organon* Bacon had called attention to the distorting effects of certain "idols" that occupied the mind. According to Bacon, the unpurged mind tended to distort the information which it received from the senses. Thus true knowledge required that the mind somehow be cleansed of its idols, and such was the task of the scientific method. Inasmuch as Bacon's main concern had been to promote the study of nature, he carefully demarcated the realm of nature from both the political sphere and the religious domain. Specifically he applied his theory of the idols only to the study of nature. Thus for him both tradition and authority, which had no place in the practice of science, could play a legitimate role in the ordering of religious and political affairs.

The Enlightenment theorists, however, went beyond Bacon's original intention. In their work, the theory of idols became a general theory of prejudice, and it was thereby extended to include a critique of both religious and political practices. As a consequence, the practical wisdom gained through political practice was now expected to meet the same criteria governing the theoretical wisdom sought in scientific inquiry. Describing this development, the philosopher Hans Barth has written:

> At this point the critique of the Enlightenment departed from Bacon's position. It asserted the existence of a natural, lawful order of state and society that could be disclosed; if it did not exist in actuality, the reason simply was that prejudices concealed it from common view. The theory of idols, broadened into a theory of prejudice, now acquired a pronounced political character: it claimed to replace a social order founded on divine authority and sover-

eignty with a secular order justified by reason. The irrational basis of the state and religion, already admitted by Bacon, was now perceived as one more idol to be brought before the court of reason. If it did not pass the test, it would be exposed as the machination of class interest and group will![4]

Thus the combination of Newton's mechanized universe, Locke's rationalistic political theory, and Bacon's theory of idols equipped the *philosophes* to undertake a total critique of existing society. Among those who joined Voltaire in this project were Bernard Le Bovier de Fontenelle (1657–1757), Pierre Bayle, (1647–1706), Julien Offray de La Mettrie (1709–1751), and Baron d'Holbach (1723–1789).

The clearest expression of the Enlightenment spirit of the *philosophes* was found in a project directed by two of their most important members. In 1747 a group of Parisian publishers commissioned Denis Diderot (1713–1784) and Jean Le Rond D'Alembert (1717–1783) to prepare a French translation of Englishman Ephraim Chambers' *Cyclopedia or an Universal Dictionary of Arts and Sciences.* Originally the project was a relatively simple one and entailed the production of only two volumes. However, in 1750 Diderot published a *Prospectus* which outlined his plan for a new and greatly expanded undertaking. Instead of translating a mere reference work, Diderot announced plans for a much more ambitious project. As he later explained in an article describing the *Encyclopedia*, the new work sought to demonstrate the "interrelation of all knowledge":

> In truth, the aim of an encyclopedia is to collect all the knowledge scattered over the face of the earth, to present its general outlines and structure to the men with whom we live, and to transmit this to those who will come after us, so that the work of past centuries may be useful to the following centuries, that our children, by becoming educated, may at the same time become more virtuous and happier, and that we may not die without having deserved well of the human race.[5]

Diderot's *Encyclopedia* was to become a project which would cover the globe and cross the ages. More importantly it was a project which would provide for a certain type of knowledge. Bacon had taught that knowledge was power. Accordingly the *Encyclopedia* was to devote a great deal of time to the study of technology and the manual arts. Science in the form of technology was to provide humanity with the tools it needed in order to gain

[4] Hans Barth, *Truth and Ideology*, trans. Frederick Lilge (Berkeley: University of California Press, 1976), p. 27.
[5] Denis Diderot, "Encyclopedia," in Stepen Gendzier, ed., *Denis Diderot's The Encyclopedia* (New York: Harper & Row, 1967), p. 92.

the power necessary for human freedom. In addition, the aim of knowledge was the promotion of human virtue and happiness, and thus the purpose of Enlightenment education was moral knowledge in the service of humanity and its needs and not knowledge for its own sake. So defined, Diderot's *Encyclopedia* would grow to a project involving over 150 contributors, requiring twenty years to complete, and filling seventeen volumes with an additional eleven folios of prints.

The *Encyclopedia* was designed, in part, to function as a dictionary. Consequently its chapters were arranged alphabetically, and its articles served as up-to-date summaries of the various disciplines which were being examined. Yet, at the same time, the encyclopedists sought to demonstrate the interrelationship among all ideas. Thus this larger task necessarily imposed its own structure upon the work. This structure was explained in a preface prepared for the book by Jean Le Rond D'Alembert. In his *Preliminary Discourse to the Encyclopedia*, D'Alembert claimed that the work was intended as an illustration of Francis Bacon's conception of the tree of knowledge. The various branches of knowledge were categorized according to Bacon's understanding of the three faculties of the mind: memory, reason, and imagination. For example, under memory were grouped the various branches of history; under reason, the various forms of philosophy; and under imagination were included both moral and profane poetry. All were related to one another inasmuch as each of the mind's faculties was defined by its own particular way of processing sense perception. Consequently, as a whole, the *Encyclopedia* was based upon a version of English empiricism. At the same time its ethics was a form of utilitarian sensationalism. Thus for the encyclopedists, just as humanity's ideas can be traced back to their origin in physical sensation, so too, then, can its understanding of good and evil. For example, according to D'Alembert, justice was simply a feeling which was evoked by humankind's prior experience of oppression. Although Bacon's tree of knowledge provided a certain formal structure to the work, other philosophical assumptions were also quite apparent. For example, in addition to its empiricism and thus its subsequent rejection of teleology, the *Encyclopedia* also embodied a distinct spirit of rationalism. Like Descartes, D'Alembert was a skeptic. As such he distrusted any arguments that appealed to authority and expected, instead, that all propositions demonstrate their basis in clear and distinct sensations.

The range and scope of the articles included within the project suggests that the *Encyclopedia* was intended to be more than a simple reference work. In fact, it was to serve as the intellectual foundation for a secular and naturalistic civilization. In this capacity it functioned as a modern day equivalent to the traditional Christian *Summa Theologica*. Whereas Thomas's *Summa* was written from the perspective of Christian revelation, the *Encyclopedia* of Diderot and D'Alembert presupposed the fundamental assumptions of modern science. In effect, then, it represented a new understanding of what was important to know from the perspective of a post-Christian world-view. As the philosopher Eric Voegelin has noted:

> The *Summa* of the type that was fixed by St. Thomas embraced systematically what appeared as relevant knowledge within the categories of the Christian view of man in the universe; the *Encyclopédie*, at least in the original conception of d'Alembert and Diderot, attempted the equivalent organization of relevant knowledge within the categories of the new anthropology that had become fixed by the middle of the eighteenth century.[6]

This tension between the secularism of the *Encyclopedia* and traditional Christian religion accounts, in part, for the difficulties encountered by the project during its production. It was banned twice; once in 1752 and again in 1759. On both occasions the censors reacted to the implicit and explicit critique of morals and religion which could be found in the articles. The central issue concerned the status of traditional Christianity. Many of the *philosophes* such as Voltaire, D'Alembert, and Diderot followed John Locke in advocating the principle of deism. *Deism* was a religion of reason. It argued that God existed; that He desired that humans be virtuous; and that the virtuous will be rewarded and the wicked will be punished in a future life. These principles, in turn, were understood to be truths which were established by reason and thus were available independently of any particular tradition of revelation. Inasmuch as a revealed religion taught such principles or enforced their implications, it was accepted as confirming what reason taught. Thus John Locke's *The Reasonableness of Christianity* (1695) could argue that Christian revelation performed an important service by dramatically bringing supernatural sanctions to the support of rational moral teachings. For Locke, inasmuch as Christianity supplemented the moral code of scientific rationalism, it was acceptable. Yet a Christianity reduced to this subsidiary role would be a religion which was necessarily devoid of its spiritual center. And to the extent historical Christianity refused to accept this reduction, it became the object of powerful Enlightenment criticism. Thus Voltaire's advice to "crush the infamy" typified the militant hostility which the *philosophes* felt toward orthodox Christianity.

Among such deists as Voltaire the critique of Christianity was, in part, an attempt to articulate a form of religion that would be fitting in a world as conceived by modern science. Christian miracles did not have a place within a mechanized world-view. God was necessary to make

---

[6] Eric Voegelin, *From Enlightenment to Revolution* (Durham: Duke University Press, 1975), p. 76.

nature's machine, but His constant intervention could only destroy those uniform and consistent laws which science had so carefully described. In addition much of Christianity's traditions, offices, and rituals were based upon a mythical view of humanity and nature which could no longer be readily believed. Consequently by stripping Christianity of its "superfluous elements"—such as the divinity of Christ—Enlightenment rationalism attempted to preserve a core of intellectually acceptable religious truths. Thus Voltaire defended Locke from those who accused him of being anti-Christian, and insisted that he, himself, was not an atheist. On the contrary, according to Voltaire, modern science had actually succeeded in establishing the tenets of a deistic theology:

> What conclusion shall we draw from all this? That atheism is a most monstrous evil in those who govern; that it is the same in councilors, . . . that even though it is less disastrous than fanaticism, it is almost always fatal to virtue. Above all, let us add that there are fewer atheists today than ever . . . and as a well-known author has said, a cathechist announces God to children, and Newton demonstrates Him to the wise.[7]

MATERIALISM: d'HOLBACH AND HELVETIUS

The early *philosophes*, therefore, positioned themselves between the "fanaticism" of Christianity and the "evil" of atheism. It was a position which they believed was justified by the teachings of English empiricism and Newtonian science. Yet to their critics, such a justification was not so obvious. Indeed the assumptions of the *philosophes* seemed to imply a much more radical conclusion than they, themselves, were at first willing to draw. In a review of D'Alembert's *Discourse*, a contributor to the *Journal des Scavans* acknowledged that D'Alembert himself espoused the deist belief in God's existence but went on to warn: "The system of Locke is dangerous for religion, . . . although one has no objections to make when those who adopt it do not draw noxious conclusions from it."[8] From the religious point of view the danger in the Lockean-Newtonian perspective was materialism, and, although Voltaire, D'Alembert, and Diderot denied such an implication, their arguments were based upon a refusal to draw those conclusions which were implicit in the principles they had already accepted. It was therefore only a matter of time before such contradictions

---

[7] Voltaire, *Philosophical Dictionary*, trans. Peter Gay (New York: Harcourt, Brace & World, 1962), p. 104.

[8] As quoted in R. J. White, *The Anti-Philosophers* (New York: St. Martin's Press, 1970), p. 104.

became apparent. And, indeed, materialism soon became a public teaching in the works of such Enlightenment thinkers as Julien Offray de La Mettrie (1709–1751), Paul Henri d'Holbach (1723–1789), and Claude Adrien Helvetius (1715–1771). Common to these various forms of materialism was the belief that all of reality was ultimately of a material nature and consequently could be explained in strictly material terms. Assuming that Newtonian science had established the mechanical nature of material reality, the materialist extended the argument to insist that the principles of mechanics could, in fact, explain all of human behavior. It then followed that once the principles of human behavior were known, they could subsequently be manipulated in such a way as to improve the lot of humankind and, thereby, promote human happiness. Central to the materialist perspective, therefore, was a reconsideration of human nature itself. Whereas the Christian tradition had understood that what made humanity "human" was its unique relationship with the divine, the materialist denied the existence of a spiritual reality and, thereby, brought mortals back entirely into the natural realm. Similarly, whereas the classical tradition had understood human reason as the means by which humanity participated in a spiritual realm which was beyond the purely immanent, the materialist simply redefined the concept in such a way that reason now appeared to be based upon an organization of the material realm itself. Humankind, accordingly, was understood to be grounded in the material rather than in the spiritual, and such a grounding, in turn, established the coordinates for human existence. Expressing this new orientation, Baron d'Holbach wrote:

> To discover the true principles of morality, men have no need of theology, of revelation, or of gods; they need only common sense. They have only to commune with themselves, to reflect upon their own nature, to consult their visible interests, to consider the objects of society and the individuals who compose it, and they will easily perceive that virtue is advantageous, and vice disadvantageous, to such beings as themselves. Let us persuade men to be just, beneficent, moderate, sociable, not because such conduct is demanded by the gods, but because it is a pleasure to men. Let us advise them to abstain from vice and crime, not because they will be punished in the other world, but because they will suffer for it in this . . . [9]

The immanentist, utilitarian, and progressive features of French materialism are expressed clearly in d'Holbach's statement. Yet for the fullest development of the materialist program, one must consult the work of Helvetius.

Strictly speaking Helvetius was not associated with the *En-*

---

[9] Baron d'Holbach, "Common Sense," in Torrey, *Philsophes*, p. 197.

cyclopedia. He was, however, an acquaintance of both Diderot and Voltaire, and his ideas were popularly identified with those contemporaries. Indeed the scandal created by the publication of his *On the Mind* in 1758 encouraged the censors to ban the first seven volumes of the *Encyclopedia* a year later. His system was completed with the posthumous publication of his *On Man* in 1772. Helvetius's major achievement was to apply the principles of Locke's *An Essay Concerning Human Understanding* to the problems of politics. Radicalizing Locke's critique of innate ideas, Helvetius began by defining the human being strictly in terms of physical sensibilities. Given this, all people were understood to be simply the results of the impressions and experiences to which they had been exposed. Human differences could, therefore, be reduced to differences in experience, and by modifying those experiences it would be possible to recondition people so as to produce those qualities which were thought to be desirable. For Helvetius, human beings were both plastic and passive. Thus radicalizing Locke's concept of the mind as a *tabula rasa*, he wrote: "Born without ideas, without voice, and without virtue, everything in man, even his humanity, is an acquisition. . . ."[10] Given this view that *Homo Sapiens* is pure potential, human nature for Helvetius had become a strictly historical concept. Men and women are formed solely by their experience, and, inasmuch as all experience is ultimately a matter of physical sensation, human nature is actually created through the administration of pleasure and pain. As a consequence, then, Helvetius's materialism led logically to an ethical utilitarianism. For Helvetius, as for all utilitarians, pleasure is the only good. By arguing that humanity seeks only pleasure Helvetius broke from the more complicated psychology of the classical Greeks. Whereas both Plato and Aristotle acknowledged the human love of pleasure, they also insisted that the love of honor and the love of wisdom were distinct and separate drives. Thus for the Classics, one of the tasks of ethics was to achieve a certain balance or harmony among these distinct psychological forces. For Helvetius, on the other hand, humanity was a somewhat more simplified being. It has only one love—the love of pleasure. Knowledge, power, and honor are not sought for themselves but only for the pleasures which they represent. Thus for Helvetius the ethical life was not primarily concerned with harmony—and the consequent subordination that such a concept implied—but rather with acquisition and the need to satisfy human self-love:

> It is to clothe himself and adorn his mistress, or his wife, to procure them amusements, to support himself and his family, in a word to enjoy the pleasures attached to the gratification of bodily desires

[10] Helvetius, *On Man*, in Nicolas Capaldi, ed. *The Enlightenment: The Proper Study of Mankind* (New York: Capricorn Books, 1968), p. 112.

that the artisan and the peasant thinks, contrives and labors. Corporeal sensibility is therefore the sole mover of man. . . [11]

Having found the single force that determines human behavior, Helvetius believed he was in a position to effectively engineer human action. Inasmuch as human nature was malleable and sensual pleasure was the sole focus of human interest, it was theoretically possible to make citizens act morally by rewarding them for socially beneficial actions and punishing them for those which were harmful. In short, ethical action could be induced by education and legislation. Consequently by making individual's personal interests coincide with the general interest of society, the law could use their self-love in such a way as to promote the greatest happiness for the greatest number. This, in turn, was for Helvetius the purpose for which all government was constituted, and it presupposed the talents and abilities of an enlightened legislator.

For Helvetius humans were simply mechanisms in pursuit of pleasure. Thus in order for them to live together, they must first become virtuous, and this, in turn, could be accomplished only when the wise legislator created an educational and legal system which effectively wove together their otherwise purely selfish individual interests. The legislator, in effect, manipulated citizens for the good of society. Originally the human race was neither good nor bad; its members were simply self-interested. Human beings become good, however, when in the pursuit of their enlightened self-interest they actually contribute to the public utility. Thus the greatest happiness of the greatest number became the standard for social justice, and it could be achieved only by creating a stable balance among private interests. Once this balance was achieved, however, Helvetius believed that humankind would move necessarily towards its own immanent perfection and self-fulfillment. In short, for Helvetius, Enlightenment materialism necessarily implied a doctrine of historical progress. The materialist understanding of human nature had emphasized humanity's plastic quality. At the same time utilitarian psychology had discovered the principal forces that propelled the human machine, and finally the standard of social utility had provided the immanent goal for all political action. Together these doctrines suggested the possibility of a progression towards a superior yet realizable state of human existence. For Helvetius education and wise legislation would both increase human happiness and improve the species at the same time. Thus it was that the belief in historical progress became one of the dominant themes of Enlightenment political theory. It was also one of the major contributions of the eighteenth century to the nineteenth; for the

---

[11] Capaldi, *The Enlightenment*, p. 112.

idea of progress would reappear as a central tenet in the two major political traditions which developed during the nineteenth century—the socialism of Karl Marx and the liberalism of John Stuart Mill.

THE BELIEF IN PROGRESS:
TURGOT AND CONDORCET

History had become a major theme in post-Hellenic political speculation because of Christianity's unique position within Western civilization. Indeed the Christian tradition had always maintained a particular interpretation of historical meaning. As first articulated by Augustine in the fifth century, Christianity distinguished between sacred and profane history. Sacred history was concerned with those events related in the Old and New Testaments. Thus it was primarily a history concerned with the relationship between God and humanity. As recorded in the Bible this relationship could be divided into six ages; the last beginning with the birth of Christ and extending until the end of the world. The significance of these ages, however, was always the same; they represented moments within the divine drama of humankind's movement from alienation to reconciliation. In short, Christian history was a history of salvation, a time between original sin and redemption. Its meaning, therefore, was apparent only in view of the Christian understanding of humanity's relationship to God. It was, in fact, constituted by an experience of faith. Describing Augustine's understanding of history, the political scientist Gerhart Niemeyer remarks:

> [Augustine] could formulate a concept of order in time because certain events dispersed over many centuries appeared related by a common inner meaning and a continuous human experience of a dimension transcending time. In the chaotic multitude of fleeting moments, some were lifted above oblivion and statistical insignificance through an experience of holiness . . . . Augustine's perception of the inner meaning that links these moments to each other added up to a concept of time-directed-to-a-goal which in turn enables men to conceive of history as a whole.[12]

The inner meaning of Augustine's related events was salvation, and the events, themselves, were the components of his sacred history. All other events, such as military conquests, political change, or scientific and intellectual advances, belonged to profane history and consequently were relatively unimportant. From the perspective of Christian faith, *real* history

[12] Gerhart Niemeyer, *Between Nothingness and Paradise* (Baton Rouge: Louisiana State University Press, 1971), p. 55.

existed only at the sacred level, and its meaning had already been fully revealed in the writings of Scripture. Worldly events, on the other hand, were relatively meaningless and acquired significance only if they in some way entered into the sacred dimension.

This Christian view of history continued throughout the Middle Ages and was represented even as late as the seventeenth century by such writers as the French bishop Jacques Bossuet (1627–1704). Yet by this time Christian orthodoxy was facing significant challenges. The Renaissance had encouraged interest in historical scholarship, and in the sixteenth-century humanist scholars had undertaken a large number of studies which were concerned exclusively with profane history. The real break, however, occurred during the French Enlightenment with the publication of Voltaire's *Essay on the Manners and Mind of Nations* in 1756. With this publication Voltaire abandoned the traditional Christian understanding of history and thereby initiated the process of secularization. From the secularist perspective history is conceived of as a strictly worldly phenomenon. Its events are purely human events, and its significance, if any, is to be described in properly mundane terms. Whereas God was the primary subject of history according to Christianity, the object of Voltaire's essay was the human spirit. In particular Voltaire wished to study the advance of the human spirit from its original barbarism to its present "politeness." To do so, he reviewed the civilizations of China, India, Persia, Arabia, Rome, and Christianity. Generally he found a pattern of moderate progress. Setbacks, however, did occur, and it was shown that the two most important obstacles to progress were those erected by war and dogmatic religion. Whereas Christianity understood the meaning of history to be the awarding of salvation, Voltaire saw it as that process by which humankind became "better and happier" through the use of human reason. Accordingly it was people and not divine providence who determined the course of empirical history, and it was a secular and not a religious accomplishment which marked its culmination.

Although the idea of human progress was implicit in the materialism of Helvetius and Holbach, and although empiricism's emphasis upon the accumulation of experience lent itself to a progressivist interpretation, it was primarily Jacques Turgot and the Marquis de Condorcet who first established a systematic philosophy of historical progress. Jacques Turgot (1727–1781) enjoyed a successful career as an administrator for the French state. During the period from 1774–1776 he served as Louis XVI's economic minister and used this opportunity to introduce several major reforms which supported the interests of the rising commercial classes. Although his policies were later repealed, his economic theory exerted a significant influence upon the thought of Adam Smith. In 1750 when he was just twenty-three, Turgot delivered two lectures at the Sorbonne entitled "Discourse on the Advantages which the Establishment of Christianity Has Procured for Mankind" and "Philosophical Tableau on the Successive Advancements of the Human Mind." Within the context of these two lectures Turgot developed the first systematic theory of history which accounted for human progress in terms of natural causation. For Turgot history was the story of the mind's development through three distinct phases.

First, there was the age of barbarism. It was a period of equality and was typified by the fact that early peoples explained the causes of natural events in terms of the actions of intelligent, invisible beings. The second age was a period dominated by the influence of Greek philosophy and Christian theology. Within it, natural forces were explained in terms of abstract forces or essences and society was characterized by a marked inequality among nations. The third and present stage of history was dominated by the influence of modern science. Accordingly the teachings of Bacon and Descartes were to teach people to explain the causes of events in terms of mechanical interactions which were to be expressed in mathematical formulas and could be verified by experience. Socially the third age would witness the reestablishment of equality, while the French civilization would expand to unite the world as in a single republic. The establishment of such a commercial civilization, however, was not the actual goal of history. Such a social and political accomplishment would be but a manifestation of that real underlying progress which, for Turgot, could only be understood in terms of the evolution of the human mind. Accordingly, for Turgot, history appeared as a process of purification in which the mind was cleansed of its earlier barbaric and theological-philosophical forms. In short, history was the story of the mind's growing capacity for the practice of the mathematized sciences.

The influence of modern science upon the thought of Turgot is obvious. First, Turgot's total acceptance of the procedures of modern science explains his general assumption that the movement from a theological-philosophical civilization into a scientific one is equivalent to a movement from a lower order to a higher. Indeed the notion that such a change is progressive at all presupposes that science is good. And, while many of Turgot's contemporaries shared this assumption, it was by no means a self-evident truth. Second, Turgot's commitment to science had the effect of predetermining his attitude towards history. For him, history was like any other reality, an external object that could be studied according to the methods of the natural sciences. Unlike Augustine for whom history was the creative expression of an underlying faith experience, Turgot understood history as if it were a worldly thing—an external reality that could be studied objectively and then empirically analyzed in terms of cause and effect. In short, Turgot wished to study history in the same manner that Newton studied physics. Accordingly the study of history was, for him, the study of causation. In particular it was a study of that pattern of causes which had had the cumulative effect of moving humankind into the scientific age. For Turgot it was as if humankind had been pushed ahead from behind as the result of an interplay among blind forces. Progress, consequently, was not the result of a divine intervention but was rather the by-product of an interaction among mechanical and impersonal forces. Specifically Turgot argued that humanity's passions and appetites inevitably lead to wars and revolutions. These, in time, bring hitherto distinct civilizations into contact with one another and eventually result in the mixing of cultures and beliefs. Such cultural mixtures, in turn, provide the rich and flexible environment which stimulates the work of people of genius, and it is their work, ultimately, which brings about those intellectual advances which mark humankind's progress toward perfectability. Thus it is that progress is the eventual result of humankind's lowest self-centered motives. Yet, inasmuch as these motives, appetites, and passions are natural to humanity, progress itself is a natural and hence analyzable achievement:

> We see the establishment of societies and the formation of nations which one after the other dominate other nations or obey them. Empires rise and fall; the laws and forms of government succeed one another; the arts and sciences are discovered and made more perfect. Sometimes arrested, sometimes accelerated in their progress, they pass through different climates. Interest, ambition and vain glory perpetually change the scene of the world inundating the earth with blood. But in the midst of these ravages man's mores become sweeter, the human mind becomes enlightened, and the isolated nations come closer to each other. Commerce and politics reunite finally all the parts of the globe and the whole mass of humankind, alternating between calm and agitation, good and bad, marches constantly, though slowly, toward greater perfection.[13]

Turgot's vision of history was at once both optimistic and pessimistic. Its optimism was due to its progressivism. Humankind was naturally assured of improving. Yet, at the same time, there was an unavoidable sadness expressed by this vision. This sadness was based in the fact that it was the abstraction, "the mass of humankind," and not the concrete individual which was progressing. Inasmuch as progress is marked by the growth of culture and science, history's real meaning is determined at the civilizational level. As a consequence, history does not seem as meaningful to the individual in daily life. For Turgot it was only the person of genius who directly contributed to the growth of civilization. Thus the rest of

[13] As quoted in Karl Loewith, *Meaning in History* (Chicago: University of Chicago Press, 1949), p. 100.

humankind was apparently excluded from the drama. Whereas the Christian view of history was a view which incorporated each individual inasmuch as its meaning was that of each sinner's personal salvation, Turgot's progressivism spoke to "humankind" in general or "civilization" at large and not to the concrete individual personality. For Augustine everyone could belong simultaneously to the city of God and to his own particular social community. Because membership in the city of God depended upon one's immediate relationship with the sacred, people could find ultimate meaning in their life regardless of their contribution in the demands of their profane existence. As such, each individual was secure in a context of religious meaning and could subsequently face the ambivalence of profane history with a relative calm. In Turgot's progressivism, however, no such security existed. Rather than possessing dual citizenship, each individual belonged only to the abstraction "humankind," and any meaning which existed, existed only for the abstraction in general. Referring to the personal problem posed by such a scheme, Eric Voegelin writes:

> Of what concern can it be to a man, who lives and dies in his finite present, whether mankind has progressed in the past or will progress in the future, if he himself leads a miserable life in an unenlightened, isolated community where the mores are restrictive? Turgot's answer is the *masse totale*. The triumphant brutality of the answer is unsurpassable. History has no meaning for man. What does it matter? It has meaning for the *masse total*.[14]

The Enlightenment blend of scientism and progressivism that was typical of Turgot was also clearly expressed by his contemporary, the Marquis de Condorcet. An associate of such *philosophes* as D'Alembert, Voltaire, and Turgot, Condorcet was a mathematician who soon became involved in political affairs. At one time he was a member of the Directory of the Paris Commune, and in 1791 he was elected a representative to the French legislature and eventually became its president. As a republican, Condorcet opposed the Jacobin radicalization of the French Revolution, and in 1793 he was ordered arrested for his criticism of the newly written constitution. After hiding for several months Condorcet was finally arrested and died in March 1794 while in prison. A year later the Directory vindicated his good name and allowed for the posthumous publication of his *Sketch of a Historical Portrait of the Progress of the Human Mind*. The purpose of the essay was explained in the author's introduction:

> Such is the object of the work I have undertaken; the result of which will be to show, from reasoning and from facts, that no bounds

---

[14] Voegelin, *From Enlightenment to Revolution*, p. 93.

have been fixed to the improvement of the human faculties; that the perfectibility of man is absolutely indefinite; that the progress of this perfectibility, henceforth above the control of every power that would impede it, has no other limit than the duration of the globe upon which nature has placed us. The course of this progress may doubtless be more or less rapid, but it can never be retrograde. . . .[15]

Condorcet's faith in human progress was supported, in part, by his understanding of the potential of natural science. In its systematic pursuit of truth and in its reliance upon mathematics and experimentation, science had developed powerful analytical techniques which could be applied to the study of moral and political phenomena. Applying these techniques to the study of history itself Condorcet believed that he had discovered a table of progress which specified the ten stages in the history of humanity's accumulation of knowledge. The stages, however, had no obvious structural principle. Some referred to social and economic movements—for example, stage 2: the transition from the pastoral to the agricultural state. Others referred to intellectual and technological developments—for example, stage 7: from the revival of the sciences in the West to the invention of printing. And still others appear to be simply convenient chronological distinctions—for example, stage 9: from the time of Descartes to the French Revolution. In spite of such conceptual diversity, however, Condorcet was convinced that his tables exhibited the precision of the most vigorous of the empirical sciences. Inasmuch as the stages were subject to a general law of development, each was both a necessary complement to the one which preceded it and the inevitable preparation for the one that followed.

Condorcet's review of intellectual history had not only provided him with information about past events, it had also taught him the general laws whose principles had determined the phenomena which he observed. Thus inasmuch as natural science had taught that the general laws which regulate the universe are both regular and constant, it was reasonable to assume that one could just as well predict the future development of the moral and intellectual faculties. Specifically Condorcet wrote: "Our hopes, as to the future condition of the human species, may be reduced to three points: the destruction of inequality between different nations; the progress of equality in one and the same nation; and lastly the real improvement of man."[16] For Condorcet, the "real improvement of man" implied several concrete achievements. First, the growth of science and technology would make possible a higher level of general prosperity. As reason advanced to replace the practices of religious superstition and the limitations of political tyranny, individuals would be able to reform their agricultural and in-

---

[15] Capaldi, *The Enlightenment*, p. 160.
[16] Capaldi, *The Enlightenment*, p. 291.

dustrial techniques so as to insure greater productivity. As wealth increased and the amount of necessary labor declined people could look forward to longer, healthier, and happier lives. Better food and housing and the improvement of medical science could actually postpone, if not eliminate, death. In addition to such physical and economic improvements, Condorcet foresaw the possibility of improving humanity's intellectual and moral character. Through a process of cumulative inheritance parents could pass along to their children those principles of social organization which their experience had shown to make moral improvement possible. Thus each generation would be starting from where the previous one had left off, and the species as a whole would move forward without interruption or limitations. Such an argument suggests that Condorcet's vision of historical progress went far beyond that of Turgot. Whereas Turgot equated historical progress with a development of the culture and content of various civilizations, Condorcet seemed to envision history as the progressive change in the very structure of human nature itself. Yet in spite of an apparent openness to alternatives, such a change was to take place within an increasingly standardized environment. Condorcet's future was to be an age characterized by the destruction of inequalities among nations. Accordingly all societies would come, sooner or later, to resemble those of the French or the Anglo-Americans. Thus for Condorcet, international equality meant, in fact, cultural uniformity. And although he insisted that such changes could not be forced upon unprepared cultures, Condorcet was fully confident that the natural course of history would eventually bring about his foreseen transformations. In the past, the power of enlightenment had effected only a small intellectual elite. In the future, however, it was to become the condition for humankind in general. The task that remained, therefore, was essentially one of propagation. Those truths which had been discovered and certified by science were now to be carried to the people. Thus philosophy would no longer remain the search for truth; on the contrary, it would now become the intellectual means for the popular transmission of accepted dogma:

> Philosophy has no longer anything to guess, has no more hypothetical combinations to form; all it has to do is to collect and arrange facts, and exhibit the useful truths which arise from them as a whole, and from the different bearings of their several parts.[17]

For Condorcet, therefore, philosophers were no longer those who were characterized by their sense of wonderment before the richness and mystery of reality. On the contrary, as intellectuals, they were simply manipulators of public opinion. Thus unlike Plato's philosopher-kings who taught the love of wisdom and its concomitant radical openness to all levels of reality,

[17] Capaldi, *The Enlightenment*, p. 164.

Condorcet's intellectuals taught the authoritative propositions of the empirical sciences. As such, they became the essential instrument for the inauguration of the future age of perfection.

The elitism implicit in Condorcet's thought was typical of the *philosophes* in general. As cultural liberals they were not necessarily political democrats. As intellectuals the *philosophes* wished to be free from the rigidified traditions and intolerant authority which they associated with both secular and church officials. Thus their programs were often only differing versions of a basic political liberalism. Here again, John Locke was the model. However, political liberalism does not necessarily imply a commitment to democratic political institutions. Although all enlightened people should be free to innovate, experiment, and pursue knowledge, the *philosophes* did not believe that all people, therefore, should necessarily share the right to exercise political authority. The important issue was the promulgation of the Enlightenment, and in those cases where a prince, such as Frederick the Great of Prussia, appeared to be capable of such a program, the *philosophes* were generally supportive of such arrangements. Indeed democracy's only strong advocate during this period was that of the Enlightenment's greatest critic, Jean Jacques Rousseau.

BIBLIOGRAPHY

BECKER, CARL.   *The Heavenly City of the Eighteenth-Century Philosophers*. New Haven: Yale University Press, 1932.

CASSIRER, ERNST.   *The Philosophy of the Enlightenment*. Translated by Fritz Koelln and James Pettegrove. Boston: Beacon Press, 1955.

CROCKER, LESTER.   *Nature and Culture: Ethical Thought in the French Enlightenment*. Baltimore: Johns Hopkins University Press, 1963.

FRANKEL, CHARLES.   *The Faith of Reason: The Idea of Progress in the French Enlightenment*. Oxford: Oxford University Press, 1948.

GAY, PETER.   *The Enlightenment: The Rise of Modern Paganism*. New York: Random House, 1966.

GAY, PETER.   *The Enlightenment: The Science of Freedom*. New York: W. W. Norton & Co., 1977.

HAZARD, PAUL.   *European Thought in the Eighteenth Century*. Translated by J. Lewis May. Harmondsworth: Penguin, 1954.

HAZARD, PAUL.   *The European Mind: 1680–1715*. Translated by J. Lewis May. New York: New American Library, 1963.

MANUEL, FRANK.   *The Age of Reason*. Ithaca: Cornell University Press, 1951.

POLLARD, SIDNEY.   *The Idea of Progress: History and Society*. Baltimore: Penguin, 1971.

WHITE, R. J.   *The Anti-Philosophers*. New York: St. Martin's, 1970.

WILLEY, BASIL.   *The Eighteenth-Century Background*. New York: Columbia University Press, 1940.

12

ROUSSEAU

Although the Enlightenment intellectuals may have rejected the political and intellectual traditions of their own immediate environment, they, nonetheless, enjoyed the security of belonging to a larger history-in-the-making. Confident that the scientific and philosophical discoveries of the seventeenth century had effectively marked the end of an epoch, the Enlightenment intellectuals looked forward to the beginning of a new age.

Perhaps the sharpest contrast to this sense of identification and its attendant feeling of security can be found in the work of Jean Jacques Rousseau. Unlike his contemporaries Rousseau was deeply affected by his own personal experience of alienation. As a consequence he attempted to discover a form of community which would allow him to overcome his sense of isolation while at the same time preserving the independence of his ego. In an effort to achieve this balance Rousseau managed to both criticize and, at the same time, embody some of the central features of his day. His writings, therefore, exhibit a truly paradoxical quality.

LIFE AND WRITINGS

Jean Jacques Rousseau was born on June 28, 1712, to a watchmaker in the city-republic of Geneva, Switzerland. Because his mother had died soon after his birth, Rousseau was left alone much of the time and, as a result, devoted himself to the reading of novels and histories. In particular, he was attracted to the characters portrayed in Plutarch's *Lives* and, as a consequence, developed both an appreciation for Western antiquity and a certain romantic fascination with the heroic personality. When his father was exiled from Geneva for dueling, Rousseau was abandoned and thus was forced to care for himself. For the next fourteen years he moved about from job to job and city to city. Finally, at the age of 29, he succeeded in inventing a new system of musical notation and moved to Paris in the hope of making his fortune. Although this financial scheme failed, Rousseau, nonetheless, managed to meet a number of influential intellectual and social leaders. Through his friendship with Denis Diderot he became acquainted with those *philosophes* who had come together in Paris to publish the *Encyclopedia*, and this association eventually led to Rousseau, himself, being asked to contribute several pieces on music and political economy. While in Paris Rousseau undertook a number of projects in order to support himself; however, he always remained dependent upon the favors of rich patrons and during this period failed to produce much of lasting merit. This changed dramatically, however, one day in 1749.

Walking to Vincennes to visit the imprisoned Diderot, Rousseau read that the Academy of Dijon was offering a prize for the best essay examining the effect of the arts and sciences upon the development of morals. At that moment, Rousseau experienced an insight which he later recalled in a letter written to Malesherbes:

> Suddenly I felt mind dazzled with a thousand illuminations; crowds of striking ideas came to me at once with such force and so jumbled together that I was thrown into an inexpressible agitation . . . . Oh, if I could ever have written a quarter of what I saw and felt under that tree, how clearly I should have brought to view all the contradictions of the social system, how powerfully I should have laid bare all the abuses of our institutions, how simply I should have demonstrated that man is naturally good, and that it is only through these institutions that men become evil![1]

[1] As quoted in John C. Hall, *Rousseau: An Introduction to His Political Philosophy* (London: MacMillan Press, 1973), pp. 12–13.

The immediate product resulting from this insight was Rousseau's *Discourse on the Science and Arts* which won the competition at Dijon in 1750. Although the arguments of the *Discourse* were neither original nor entirely satisfactory to Rousseau himself, it is, nonetheless, necessary to appreciate the importance of this original vision for all of Rousseau's subsequent work. Referring to this event in his *Confessions*, Rousseau wrote that during it he "beheld another world" and "became another man." Indeed it was this insight into "another world" which actually provided Rousseau with the necessary theoretical categories by which he could express and analyze his own fundamental sense of alienation. Rousseau's vision had shown him that humanity was naturally good. Consequently the appearance of evil could only be explained in terms of a series of accidental or conventional abuses which had the effect of alienating humankind from its original condition. Given this, Rousseau was faced with two distinct but related projects. First, it was necessary for him to analyze the history of the human race's fall from this visionary state of original innocence. And, second, it was necessary to provide an appropriate therapy which would allow humankind to recover both its original integrity and its lost communal wholeness. In short, Rousseau's political theory was intended as the means by which humankind was to transcend its historical alienation by recreating as far as possible the conditions of its own primal godlike form.

The fame which Rousseau enjoyed after winning the Dijon prize and the financial rewards which followed from the successful production of his opera *Le Devin du Village* allowed Rousseau to devote an increasing amount of his time to writing. In 1755 he published his *Discourse on the Origin of Inequality*, and for the next six years he worked under the patronage of Madame di Epinay while finishing his *Émile*, *The Social Contract*, and the novel, *Julie, ou la Nouvelle Heloise*.

However with the publication of his *Émile* in 1762 Rousseau's fortunes took a sudden turn for the worse. Certain theologically sensitive passages in the book caused it to be banned in Paris, Geneva, and Bern. Thus fleeing arrest Rousseau was forced to seek the protection of a number of sponsors throughout Europe. By 1765 Rousseau had become convinced that there was a worldwide effort to persecute him. This fear soon assumed manic proportions, and by the end of his life Rousseau was obsessed with escaping from those whom he imagined were plotting against him. Ill and disturbed Rousseau returned to Paris in 1767. There, living in a poor house, he was forced to earn his keep by copying music. However, before he died in 1778, Rousseau managed, nonetheless, to finish a series of candid and deeply personal autobiographical writings. The most important of these were *The Confessions, The Reveries of a Solitary Walker,* and *Dialogues de Rousseau juge de Jean Jacques.*

ANALYSIS
OF THE *FIRST DISCOURSE*

Written as an entry for an essay contest sponsored by the Academy at Dijon, Rousseau's *Discourse on the Sciences and Arts* constituted a direct attack upon one of the central tenets of the Enlightenment tradition. The *philosophes'* enthusiasm for science was, in part, based upon their belief that advances in the sciences would necessarily eventuate in a form of political progress. As philosophy succeeded in destroying irrational superstition and as the fine arts contributed to the development of higher and more civilized pleasures, it was assumed that the unfettered pursuit of truth would necessarily lead to an improvement in the political condition. Rousseau, however, argued to the contrary. For him a fundamental and ultimately unavoidable tension existed between the needs of the city on one hand and those of science on the other. This tension was unavoidable, according to Rousseau, because it was based upon a likewise fundamental division within human nature itself, that is, the separation between the mind and the body. For Rousseau society was primarily concerned with satisfying the needs of the body. Specifically, it sought to provide for human beings' safety and well-being. The mind, however, had its own needs, and they accordingly were best served through the pursuit of science and art. Given the fact that society and science are by nature serving two different sets of needs, Rousseau believed that the Enlightenment assumption concerning their harmonious and mutual improvement was naive. Indeed, Rousseau argued that in some cases the pursuit of Enlightenment science could actually harm the city by corrupting the character of its citizens.

Throughout his *First Discourse* Rousseau wrote from the perspective of the citizen. Within that perspective the needs of the political society were assumed to be paramount. Specifically all political societies require that their citizens be virtuous, and virtue, according to Rousseau, implied political and military excellence. If a city were to prosper, it required that its citizens be willing to devote themselves to the serving of its needs. Indeed, in the extreme case of war it even required the sacrificing of their lives. As examples of such prosperous communities Rousseau cited ancient Persia, Scythia, Germany, primitive Rome, and above all Sparta. In each case the society succeeded in evoking a sense of patriotism and courage within the hearts of its citizens. Having done this, therefore, it could, as a consequence, presuppose that its citizens would willingly obey its laws. Indeed, without such automatic obedience, no city could prosper. Yet, at the same time according to Rousseau, true political virtue actually required more than simply passive obedience. Virtuous citizens must not only obey their regime but actually serve it. Thus true political virtue implied the notion of duty, and this, in turn, required that citizens be willing to actively participate in the political life of their own society. Or, as Rousseau put it: "In politics as in ethics, it is a great evil to fail to do good, and every useless citizen may be considered a pernicious man."[2]

Having assumed the priority of political virtue, Rousseau argued that the desirability of any particular enterprise could best be measured in terms of its contribution to the formation of a virtuous citizenry. Given this standard, Rousseau believed that modern science and philosophy had failed the test. Indeed he argued that unlike such ancient philosophers as Socrates and Cato, the modern philosophers were, in fact, harming their fellow citizens. Whereas the early philosophers attempted to teach people their duties and civic virtues, the moderns by preaching a morality of self-interest had, thereby, loosened citizen's ties to their society. In doing so, such modern thinkers as Hobbes and Mandeville had, in fact, endangered what they sought to protect.

In general, Rousseau's indictment of modern science rested on four main ideas: (1) The technological application of science makes possible both increased luxury and greater convenience. (2) Because scientists and artists achieve notoriety through their discoveries and innovations, they are motivated by self-interest to attack the common opinion and accepted principles of society. Thus not only do they place their own fame above the interests of society as a whole, but in attacking the beliefs, traditions, and commitments of their fellow citizens they undermine the very possibility of a civic education. As a consequence, the scientist's skepticism, which is a means to fame and serves truth only indirectly if at all, actually destroys the patriot's fervor. (3) The pursuit of knowledge presupposed the existence of leisure, and a society which desires a flourishing scientific and artistic culture must necessarily generate a great deal of leisure time. Yet the existence of leisure necessarily represents a withdrawal from political activity, and thus it would appear that intellectual excellence requires a diminution of political virtue. (4) The practice of silence unavoidably introduces an antiegalitarian theme into civic culture. By rewarding intellectual and artistic talent society necessarily calls attention to the differences among its citizens. According to Rousseau "this . . . is the most evident effect of all our studies and the most dangerous of all their consequences."[3]

To this point, Rousseau's critique of modernity had been made by a

---

[2] Roger Masters, ed., *Jean Jacques Rousseau: The First and Second Discourses*, trans. Roger D. and Judith R. Masters (New York: St. Martin's Press, 1964), p. 49.

[3] Masters, *Jean Jacques Rousseau*, p. 58.

comparison with the practices of antiquity. Thus reversing the progressivism of the Enlightenment tradition Rousseau treated the teachings and practices of the ancients as possible correctives for the failings of the modern age. Thus although he admitted that human failings have existed since the beginning of time and although he treated Athens and imperial Rome as early examples of decayed societies, Rousseau, nonetheless, argued that as far as corruption was concerned " our century and our nation will no doubt surpass all times and all peoples."[4] This dichotomy between the ancients and moderns is nowhere more dramatically expressed than in Rousseau's discussion of civilized humanity. Ultimately, according to Rousseau, modernity can best be judged by its product, that is, the modern bourgeois. Referring to "civilized" humanity, Rousseau wrote:

> Today when subtler research and a more refined taste have reduced the art of pleasing to set rules, a base and deceptive uniformity prevails in our customs, and all minds seem to have been cast in the same mold. Incessantly politeness requires, propriety demands; incessantly usage is followed, never one's own inclination. One no longer dares to appear as he is; and in this perpetual constraint, the men who form this herd called society, placed in the same circumstances, will all do the same things, unless stronger motives deter them. Therefore, one will never know well those with whom he deals . . . . No more sincere friendship; no more real esteem; no more well-based confidence.[5]

Rousseau had, in short, accused the modern civilized citizen of being inauthentic. Adopting the artificial customs of the day, the bourgeoisie attempted to please others by playing those roles which society created for them. They were, in effect, people of semblances who sought to appear virtuous without actually possessing the virtues. In appearing to live for others rather than for themselves, the civilized citizens were, in fact, people without qualities. Being such, they necessarily remained unknown to their acquaintances. Thus in spite of appearances to the contrary, the civilized person was lonely. And it was this experience of loneliness or alienation which motivated Rousseau's original critique of the modern order. The modern person cannot be known, cannot be trusted, and consequently, cannot be loved. Rather than being a wholesome personality who is known and accepted by others, the bourgeois man or woman is, in fact, a radically private individual who is estranged from fellow humans by the very roles he or she is forced to play. On one hand, such alienation is the cause of a tremendous amount of personal unhappiness. At the same time, however, it

[4] Masters, *Jean Jacques Rousseau*, p. 37.
[5] Masters, *Jean Jacques Rousseau*, p. 37–38.

makes society all but impossible. For Rousseau, a true society presupposes the active love of one citizen for another. Without such beneficence, therefore, society would soon break apart.

In part, Rousseau's critique of bourgeois civilization was based upon his rejection of the Enlightenment solution to the problem of social alienation. Following Locke, Enlightenment theorists had argued that individual selfishness and avarice actually produced specific political benefits. Indeed, accepting selfishness as a fundamental human drive, Enlightenment theorists suggested that a form of social harmony would result if each individual were allowed to pursue his or her own enlightened self-interest. For example, Locke had argued that a social good such as lawful peace would result from the pursuit of such individual goods as property and wealth. To assure this, all that was required was a constitutional mechanism by which individuals could be persuaded that their submission to the social contract would eventually result in the improvement of their private situation. Thus employing an analogy with the commercial marketplace both Hobbes and Locke had assumed that the public order could be based upon a rational appeal to private interest. Consequently although the citizens would be motivated solely by their private interests, they would, nonetheless, appear to be public spirited and act accordingly as long as it was to their own advantage to do so. In short, Enlightenment theory had produced the very model of bourgeois citizen against which Rousseau argued:

> But there is more. Indeed, of all the truths I offer here to the consideration of wise men, this one is the most astonishing and the most cruel. Our writers like to regard absolutely everything as "the political masterpiece of the century": the sciences, the arts, luxury, commerce, laws—and all other bonds which, in tightening the social knot with the force of personal interest, make men mutually dependent, give them reciprocal needs and common interests, and require that all pursue the happiness of others in order to be able to pursue their own. These ideas are to be sure, quite attractive, and can be presented in a most favorable light. But upon attentive and impartial examination, many of the advantages they first seem to offer must be discounted. Is it really such a wonderful thing to have made it impossible for men to live together without mutual bigotry, mutual competition, mutual deceit, mutual treason and mutual destruction? How careful we must be, henceforward, never to see ourselves as we are! After all, for every two men whose interests converge, there are perhaps one hundred thousand who are adversaries; and there is but one way to succeed in deceiving or ruining all these thousands. Here is the deadly source of violence, of the betrayals and perfidies, of all the other horrors necessary in a condition where each—in pretending to work for the fortune and reputa-

tion of others—seeks in truth, at the expense of others, only to enhance and enlarge his own.[6]

According to Rousseau, the Enlightenment failed when it accepted the alienated individual as the fundamental unit of society. Whereas Rousseau acknowledged the fact that the primacy of self-love required that morality begin with the concept of self-interest, he, nonetheless, believed that it was possible to go beyond such a point. By extending the individual's love to include other people, Rousseau sought to create a political unit which would allow the person to transcend his or her estranged condition. Accordingly humanity would have to discover itself to be both the subject and object of history. Such was the purpose of Rousseau's *Second Discourse*.

ANALYSIS OF THE *SECOND DISCOURSE*

Rousseau's *Discourse on the Origin and Foundation of Inequality Among Men* was, like the *First Discourse*, written as an entry for the Academy of Dijon essay contest. Unlike the *First*, however, Rousseau's *Second Discourse* did not win the competition. The argument of the *First Discourse* was based upon a comparison between antiquity and modernity. Rousseau's analysis of the alienated bourgeois was developed in contrast to the classical view of the person as a fully integrated social being. At first glance, therefore, Rousseau appeared to be reintroducing the classical emphasis upon both the city and political virtue as a corrective to the modern preoccupation with the individual and alienated private interests. Yet, Rousseau's appeal to the classical model was a complex one for, unlike the classical theorists, Rousseau did not believe that the human being was by nature a political animal. The modern scientific revolution had taught him that nature, being simply matter-in-motion, intended nothing. Thus one could not argue, as the Greeks had done, that the individual was naturally intended for membership in a political community. Given this, to speak of political society as the means for perfecting human nature would be to employ a language which no longer seemed appropriate. Thus, although Rousseau rejected the bourgeois morality of the enlightened age, his critique of modern humanity required further elaboration. It was no longer sufficient simply to point to the needs of the city. Given Rousseau's modernistic assumptions, the city itself had to be justified, and following the example of

[6] Jean Jacques Rousseau, "A Preface to *Narcisse*," trans. Benjamin Barber & James Forman, *Political Theory*, 6, no. 4 (November 1978), 549. By permission of Sage Publications, Inc.

Locke and Hobbes, such a justification had to be made in terms of the state of nature.

The original question posed by the Academy at Dijon was, "What is the origin of inequality among men; and is it authorized by natural law?" According to Rousseau, however, an answer to this question presupposed a knowledge of human nature and such a knowledge, in turn, meant that the human being must "see himself as nature formed him."[7] Thus, like the Classics, Rousseau began his political inquiry with an effort to comprehend the meaning of human nature. Yet his effort was distinctively modern in its approach. Whereas the classical thinkers believed that human nature was most clearly revealed in its perfected form, Rousseau, following the teachings of modern science reduced humanity to its simplest elements. Thus whereas Plato and Aristotle looked to the philosopher as the most accurate expression of human nature, Rousseau, like Hobbes and Locke, looked to the primitive. In line with this, then, Rousseau hypothetically recreated a state of nature so as to examine the original condition of its natural members.

In physical terms, the natural humans were gifted specimens. Although they were subject to such natural infirmities as sickness and old age, they nevertheless possessed sharp instincts by which they could defend themselves and, as a consequence, they were well adapted to their environment. Being strong, quick, and essentially fearless, the natural humans were capable of satisfying their minimal desires with relative ease. Thus Rousseau wrote of this primitive "man": "His desires do not exceed his physical needs; the only goods he knows in the universe are nourishment, a female, and repose; the only evils he fears are pain and hunger."[8]

In describing the primitive humans' psychological condition, Rousseau exphasized three traits. First, like all animals, they faced the task of procuring the means for their own continued existence, and, as with the other species, they were guided in this effort by their instincts. Yet, unlike the animals, natural humans possessed the additional power of free choice. Thus according to Rousseau the natural humans were free agents and thereby distinguished themselves from the other animal species precisely to the extent that they exercised this distinctive faculty. Unlike Hobbes, who tried to reduce all of reality to a single level and thus analyzed both humans and animals as simple machines within a mechanical universe, Rousseau attempted to differentiate between humans and animals, and in so doing he distinguished between the realm of the mechanical and that of the spiritual. Animals possessing only instincts were indeed "ingenious machines."

[7] Masters, *Jean Jacques Rousseau*, p. 91.

[8] Masters, *Jean Jacques Rousseau*, p. 116.

Humans, however, transcended the mechanical domain by virtue of their power to choose. Thus, like Descartes, Rousseau attempted to construct a human realm beyond the mechanics of nature. Yet, unlike Descartes, he did so by pointing to the power of choice rather than to that of reason.

According to Rousseau, the second feature of humanity in its natural state was its faculty of self-perfection. This, unlike the animals, the humans were capable of responding to their own historical experience and changing themselves accordingly. In short, humankind is truly an historical species. The animals, according to Rousseau, are constant throughout time. As such, they do not evolve in light of their species experience. Humankind, on the other hand, does. The faculty of self-perfection allows humans to adapt and change throughout time. Thus modern humankind has become quite a different creature than was natural humankind. And in Rousseau's eyes, the changes have not been for the better:

> Men are wicked; sad and continual experience spares the need for proof. However, man is naturally good; I believe I have demonstrated it. What then can have depraved him to this extent, if not the changes that have befallen his constitution, the progress he has made, and the knowledge he has acquired?[9]

For Rousseau, the faculty of self-perfection has been the source of all of humanity's misfortunes. As it has moved away from its original condition of natural goodness, humanity has become so different that it would be impossible for it to go back. Having developed new needs, the modern bourgeois is incapable of returning to the state of nature. Indeed, if one were to try, such a person would be both unhappy and incapable of existing in such a state. The irony of this situation was that this original development was neither necessary nor inevitable. By emphasizing both the priority of human choice and the faculty of self-perfection, Rousseau, in effect, presented a view of natural humanity which implied that it actually lacked a given nature. Malleable and open to choice, the natural ancestor had been pure potentiality, who thus could have become either good or evil. That the human race developed as it did was simply due to the accidents of history, and history could not be undone. Thus rather than returning to the state of nature, the best that modern humanity could do would be to create a society which approximated the state of nature as closely as possible. In particular, it would have to create a society characterized by the absence of both political and moral inequality. Such, in turn, was the task which Rousseau undertook in his *Social Contract.*

The classical definition of human being had emphasized the qualitative differences which were introduced into human nature by the ac-

---

[9] Masters, *Jean Jacques Rousseau*, p. 193.

tive presence of reason. For the Greeks, reason was that divine quality which raised humanity to the level of its humanness. For Rousseau, however, rationality was not a distinguishing characteristic of humanity's primitive nature. Indeed, in discussing the third feature of this hypothetical state of nature, Rousseau argued that human reasoning was, in fact, essentially equivalent to the animal's processing of sensations: "Every animal has ideas, since it has senses; it even combines its ideas up to a certain point, and in this regard man differs from the beast only in degree."[10] By refusing to set the order of reason apart from the realm of the senses, Rousseau broke with long-standing Western tradition. The human being was no longer distinguished as the rational animal. Rather, reason was now reduced to the simple combination of sensual information and, as such, was phototypically present in all sensate creatures. Rousseau had arrived at this conclusion in turn by radicalizing the logic of Hobbes and Locke. Both men had argued that natural humanity must be investigated in that condition which existed before the formation of society. Yet, according to Rousseau, neither Locke nor Hobbes rigorously followed his own logic. Indeed, if humans actually existed before society, they could not possess those things which only society makes possible. For example, inasmuch as language was a social creation, humanity in the state of nature could not possess language, and without language there could be no thought or reflection. Any knowledge that required

> . . . the linking of ideas and perfected only successively seems to be altogether beyond the reach of savage men for the want of communication with his fellow men—that is to say for want of the instrument which is used for that communication and for want of the needs which make it necessary.[11]

For Rousseau, therefore, primitive people were effectively enclosed within that environment which was formed by their own immediate experience. Although each could experience images, the individual was neither self-conscious nor capable of generating ideas.

Through a similar process of radicalization, Rousseau discounted Hobbes's suggestion that the natural primitive was warlike and mean-spirited. Hobbes had argued that such primitives had been vain and therefore sought to appease their vanity by defeating others. Rousseau, on the other hand, distinguished between vanity and the love of self. The latter, being the concern for self-preservation, was a natural sentiment and, if properly guided, was capable of producing virtue. Vanity, on the other hand, could not arise in the state of nature because it presupposed the very

[10] Masters, *Jean Jacques Rousseau*, p. 114.

[11] Masters, *Jean Jacques Rousseau*, p. 188.

existence of society. Vanity, or a human's desire to be esteemed, requires comparison, and comparison, in turn, requires the presence of others. If "naturals" existed without society, such comparisons would be impossible, and thus the existence of vanity must be understood as a result of and not the cause of social evolution.

In addition to requiring a reconsideration of Hobbes's view of the natural human, Rousseau's radicalizaton of that logic which was implicit within traditional state-of-nature theories forced him to reconsider the principle of natural right. If primitives were rational, they would not be motivated by the fear of death because the concept or idea of death did not yet exist. Similarly, inasmuch as they were deficient in reason, primitives could not perform those utilitarian calculations which both Locke and Hobbes had presupposed as being necessary for the transition from the natural to the civil state. According to Rousseau, therefore, the natural law had to be able to "speak directly by nature's voice."[12] As such, its principles were anterior to reason. Consequently Rousseau reduced the natural law to two basic principles. First, the natural human was primarily concerned with personal self-preservation; and second, when this self-preservation did not demand otherwise, the primitive was moved by feelings of compassion and pity. Thus, unlike Hobbes's brutal warrior, Rousseau's noble savage found the suffering and death of another to be repugnant.

By assuming that self-preservation was the fundamental law of nature Rousseau's theory was typical of the modern natural-right tradition. Unlike the Classics, whose teleological view of nature supported the belief that human perfection was the primary natural task, Rousseau shared the reductionistic view of his contemporaries. At the same time, he also accepted the modern belief that the human being was not naturally social. Thus, for Rousseau, the dynamics of the natural soul could be fully explained in terms of the two passions of self-preservation and pity. Accordingly, no principle of sociability was required in order to account for natural humanity's behavior and needs. If humanity was not social by nature, then society was obviously the result of a convention or agreement. Accordingly, Rousseau's next task was to explain those circumstances which led to the creation of a society based upon consent. This, in turn, could only be done by reviewing the history of human evolution.

For Rousseau, natural humanity had existed in a state of moral and political equality. This meant that humanity had not yet consented to the creation of privileges for some at the expense of others. Accordingly, no individual was obligated to serve the will of another, and each free to follow his or her desires as best one could. Independent and capable of satisfying their own primitive desires, such natural humans enjoyed an almost

[12] Masters, *Jean Jacques Rousseau*, p. 95.

godlike state of self-sufficiency. Unfortunately, however, such a condition did not last long. Equipped with the faculty of self-perfectability, the natural human soon found himself in a variety of historical and geographical situations which eventually transformed its very nature. Thus Rousseau wrote:

> After having shown that perfectability, social virtues, and the other faculties that natural man had received in potentiality could never develop by themselves, that in order to develop they needed the chance combination of several foreign causes which might never have arisen and without which he would have remained eternally in his primitive condition, it remains for me to consider and bring together the different accidents that were able to perfect human reason while deteriorating the species, make a being evil while making him sociable, and from such a distant origin finally bring man and the world to the point where we see them.[13]

In his *Second Discourse*, therefore, Rousseau attempted to reconstruct the history of humanity's accidental fall. Within this story two moments are of particular importance: the founding of civil society, and the founding of political society. After a series of developments, including the introduction of the division of labor and the establishment of the household, humankind created the arts of metallurgy and agriculture. These, in turn, had the effect of heightening people's dependency upon others. Metalsmiths, for example, could provide tools for farmers only if they themselves were freed from the demands of farming. Farmers, in turn, realized that in order to receive the tools they needed they had to acquire surplus provisions so as to provide for the smiths who worked on the farmers' tools. Moreover, this exchange of provisions for tools presupposed the existence of property; for people had to possess something before they could exchange for it. The eventual result of this development was the creation of the "private property" system. Given both their expanding needs and their developing technologies, people agreed among themselves to respect one another's claims to ownership. Property, therefore, did not exist in nature. As such, it was essentially a convenient device created by humanity in response to its changing historical condition. And according to Rousseau, with the creation of private property civil society was, in effect, established: "The first person who, having fenced off a plot of ground, took it into his head to say *this is mine* and found people simple enough to believe him; was the true founder of civil society."[14]

Although there was a certain compelling logic for the creation of

---

[13] Masters, *Jean Jacques Rousseau*, p. 140.

[14] Masters, *Jean Jacques Rousseau*, p. 141.

the property system, it did, nonetheless, produce specific negative consequences. Given the fact that talent is unevenly distributed among people, some were necessarily more successful than others in the acquisition and management of property and its products. As a result, therefore, a new form of inequality became inevitable. With the development of civil society the distinction between the rich and the poor soon became apparent, and radical economic inequality soon became a fact of social life.

The irony of the property system was found in the fact that it was based upon an agreement. In effect, the poor had agreed to the creation of the rich. Therefore as economic tensions worsened the legitimacy of the original contract became increasingly questionable. It appeared to be only a matter of time before the impoverished masses would act to negate the cause of their condition by withdrawing their original consent. To prevent this, therefore, the rich created the political society. With the formation of the state, magistrates were appointed to enforce the social contract, and with their appointment another form of inequality emerged, that is the difference between the powerful and the weak. Thus, for Rousseau, the state was essentially an enforcement mechanism operating on behalf of the interests of the wealthy while appearing to serve the common good. As political power became hereditary, the people came to accept their servitude and eventually became like slaves to their master. Yet, in spite of such developments, the poor and weak continued to consent to political society because without it their position would become even worse. As humankind moved away from its original condition, the principles of the natural law became increasingly ineffective. For example, the first principle, self-preservation, could no longer be met by the efforts of a single individual. As people became more and more interdependent and the division of labor became more pronounced, none could satisfy their needs without the cooperation of others. Thus individual self-preservation presupposed the existence of social cooperation, and this cooperation, in turn, required the exercise of state authority. Similarly, the second law of nature, compassion, also became ineffective as humanity became increasingly civilized. With the growth of society, vanity and pride emerged to challenge the sentiment of pity. Thus one's regard for fellow citizens had to become a duty if it were to be effective at all. The law, therefore, emerged as a replacement for compassion. Without a political society to enforce the law and to impose a morality, individuals risked their very existences. Thus, having become evil, human beings actually required the state. Yet, according to Rousseau, the fact that civilized humanity required the state did not at the same time imply that every form of political association was equally desirable. Indeed for him—although a return to the state of nature was out of the question—it was still possible to devise a political mechanism by which humans could approximate the most desirable features of the natural condition, that is, liberty and equality. Such was the program of his work, *Social Contract.*

ANALYSIS
OF THE *SOCIAL CONTRACT*

Published in 1762, Rousseau's *Social Contract* served as the inspiration for an entire age. Written during a time when political absolutism was a dominant force, the *Social Contract*, more than any other single work, succeeded in popularizing the idea of democratic self-government. Prior to Rousseau, the concept of democracy had carried with it the dual implication of political instability and moral chaos. As such, it was often argued that a regime's democratic tendencies had to be carefully checked by the judicious use of selected institutional arrangements and constitutional balances. The age which followed Rousseau, however, quickly came to be characterized by the more or less whole-hearted acceptance of traditionally democratic aspirations. Thus, already beginning with Robespierre in the French Revolution, democracy soon appeared to many to be the only morally acceptable form of government. Indeed, by believing this, the modern citizen was, in fact, accepting Rousseau's central argument.

The *First* and *Second Discourses* had had the cumulative effect of questioning the moral legitimacy of all existing regimes. As portrayed by Rousseau, political societies were achieved at the price of sacrificing natural human equality. Yet, at the same time, the physical and psychological transformations of civilized humankind meant that political life had become a necessary evolutionary accomplishment. The task, therefore, was not to destroy society. Rather what was required was an effort to find an arrangement by which the necessary existence of society could at the same time be made morally acceptable. Or, as Rousseau wrote:

> Man is born free, and everywhere he is in chains. One believes himself the master of others and yet he is a greater slave than they. How has this change come about? I do not know. What can render it legitimate? I believe that I can settle this question.[15]

In his effort to legitimate society, Rousseau had to justify the fact that the people are bound by the law. This, however, was difficult inasmuch as

---

[15] Charles M. Sherover, *The Social Contract or Principles of Political Right by Jean Jacques Rousseau*, trans. Charles M. Sherover (New York: New American Library, 1974), p. 5.

Rousseau had argued that humanity was distinct from the animal precisely because it possessed the freedom to choose. Thus any attempt to justify obedience had to do so without at the same time violating this distinctively human quality.

Before offering his own arguments, Rousseau began by discounting two alternative solutions. First, others such as Aristotle had argued that the existence of natural inequalities could be used to justify the existence of political and social inequalities. Thus, just as nature had made some humans the slaves of others, so, too, could society demand the subordination of the lower to the higher. For Rousseau, however, such arguments were without merit. First, according to him, all people are by nature free, and thus there was, in fact, no such thing as a natural slave. Second, those men who appear to be among the naturally lower elements appear so only because they were born into a social environment which condemned them to such appearances. Thus Aristotle had, in effect, confused cause and effect. For Rousseau, some people appeared to be born *for* slavery only because they were in fact born *in* slavery.

A second traditional defense of political inequality was represented by the arguments of such thinkers as Hugo Grotius. According to Rousseau, Grotius and others had attempted to justify political rule as a direct consequence of success in combat. Accordingly their version of natural law would support the right of the victorious to rule the vanquished. Rousseau, on the other hand, denied such an interpretation. Power was simply a political fact; and, as such, its exercise could make no moral claim. Indeed, even if the strong did compel the weak to obey them, such success would not be the same as establishing a moral right to such obedience. In short, the concepts of force and duty referred to different types of relationships and, as a consequence, were not logically interchangeable.

Given the fact that, for Rousseau, there was no such thing as natural authority and that force could not be understood as a source of right, the only possible source of legitimate authority which remained was that which was based in consent. Yet, if the consent were to be morally acceptable, it had to be of a certain kind; for according to Rousseau, any convention which denied the essential characteristic of our human nature would by this very denial be devoid of moral force:

> To renounce one's liberty is to renounce one's quality as a man, the rights and also the duties of humanity. For him who renounces everything there is no possible compensation. One such renunciation is incompatible with man's nature; for to take away all freedom from his will is to take away all morality from his actions.[16]

[16] Sherover, *The Social Contract*, p. 15.

The task, therefore, was to construct a political mechanism which would preserve human liberty while at the same time acknowledging human moral obligations. Rousseau's solution to this dilemma was contained in his notion of the general will. For Rousseau the formation of the general will began with an act of individual alienation. Through an act of total alienation each individual transferred all of his or her rights to the whole community. By totally alienating all such rights, each individual became, in effect, a member of the newly formed political association. Inasmuch as one's rights were given to the associated whole rather than to another individual, no single person was thereby subordinated to the will of another. Similarly, inasmuch as each individual transferred all of personal rights without reserve, each individual was placed in an equal condition with every other associate. The social contract, in effect, had created a public person, and each individual became, as a result, an indivisible part of this newly created moral and collective body. Moreover, as a public person, the political association is moved by the exercise of its general will. This general will, in turn, seeks the public advantage, that is, the defense of the person and property of each associate. Since such a defense is precisely what each individual willed for himself/herself while in the state of nature, in following the general will each associate was, in effect, obeying only himself/herself. As a member of the political association all individuals speak for and to themselves through the general will. Thus by fulfilling the obligation imposed upon them by the general will, each associate was, in fact, listening to himself/herself. As a consequence, individual freedom was preserved inasmuch as, by submitting to the general will, each associate obeyed only that law which he or she, in fact, had prescribed. Thus whereas in the state of nature individuals enjoyed the natural liberty of doing only that which each desired, all people enjoy in the political association the civil liberty of obeying only self-set obligations. We are free because we obey ourselves; yet we are moral because we act from a sense of duty. Through the device of the general will, therefore, Rousseau attempted to reconcile the apparent tension between morality and freedom. The success of this reconciliation, however, has been an issue of some debate.

On one hand, Rousseau's concept of the general will functioned as a justification for popular rule. The people, as the political association, are sovereign. They come together to decide as a unit what is to the advantage of the community. Having done this they then empower the government to administer their decision. From this perspective, then, the government is clearly subordinated to the will of the people. Whether it is organized as a monarchy, aristocracy, or democracy, the government is of necessity bound by those pronouncements which serve as an expression of the general will. Strictly speaking, therefore, only the assembled people possess the power to legislate. The government, in turn, is simply charged with executing their laws and maintaining, thereby, those conditions which are necessary for civil and political liberty. Rousseau's insistence upon both popular sovereignty and the superiority of the political association vis-à-vis the government accounts for his criticism of all forms of representative democracy. According to Rousseau only a direct democracy was actually democratic. Consequently popular sovereignty required that the members of a political association actually participate in the making of the laws. To delegate this task to a set of representatives, even if they were popularly elected, is to sacrifice self-rule for the sake of convenience and efficiency. Democracy for Rousseau meant direct or participatory democracy and, as such, required the active exercise of political virtue by citizens who were simultaneously both the subjects and objects of the political association.

Whereas on one hand the concept of the general will functioned to justify popular rule, at the same time it has been interpreted as allowing for political authoritarianism. This was due, in part, to certain characteristics which Rousseau attributed to the general will's functioning. For example, according to Rousseau, the general will was indivisible, unerring, absolute, and sovereign. It could not be limited by any fundamental or superior law, and it alone could judge as to what was in the best interest of the community. Similarly, individual citizens possessed no rights vis-à-vis the sovereign, and, in those cases where one refused to obey, the sovereign was fully justified in compelling obedience. As Rousseau wrote:

> In order, then, that the social pact may not be a vain formula, it tacitly includes this engagement, which can alone give force to the others—that whoever refuses to obey the general will shall be constrained to do so by the whole body; which means nothing else than that he shall be forced to be free. . . .[17]

Given the power and capabilities assigned to the general will, it is absolutely essential that its intention be easily discerned. One way of doing this would be simply to count the votes of the individual citizens and equate the general will with the preferences of the majority. Yet, according to Rousseau, this technique was inappropriate inasmuch as each citizen, insofar as action as an individual, is concerned primarily with personal self-interest. The majority will, therefore, would be simply the aggregate of such private interests, while the general will, on the other hand, would be concerned with the good of the whole. As an expression of everyone's concern for the good of each, the general will was both impersonal and universal. Inasmuch as its pronouncements were intended to apply to all and thus did not designate certain classes within the association for special consideration, the general will was oblivious to both the peculiarities of individual persons and the specifics of particular cases.

[17] Sherover, *The Social Contract*, p. 31.

As a consequence Rousseau distinguished between the general will and the will of all. The latter, being merely the sum of private wills, was not necessarily representative of the former. Accordingly the people are not an infallible guide as to the intention of the general will. For Rousseau, the general will was infallible but the people were not. It would appear, then, that at the very heart of Rousseau's formula there exists a certain ambiguity.

The proper functioning of the general will presupposed the existence of a virtuous citizenry which was capable of choosing the association's common interest over its own numerous private interests. Yet, such a display of public virtue was by no means natural, for nature itself taught only the principle of self-preservation. As a consequence the public morality had to be created, and that, in turn, presupposed the existence of certain conditions.

First, Rousseau believed that true public-spiritedness would be endangered by severe economic inequalities. Thus the sovereign must watch over the economic system in order to insure that the two extremes of poverty and wealth were avoided. Inasmuch as the individual had no right to property, the sovereign was empowered to regulate the economic system in such a way that all citizens would have something while none would have too much. Second, inasmuch as public virtue becomes more difficult to maintain as the size of the state increases, the sovereign should be concerned not only with the extent of the state's territory but also with the ratio of the land to the population. Ironically, it is worth noting that the tendency of the modern nation-state is to deny the possibility of ever achieving such a set of conditions. Even in Rousseau's time it was apparent that the "logic" of the nation-state called for both large territorial acquisitions and the destruction of limited and balanced agrarian economies.

Finally, according to Rousseau, the most important condition for establishing a successful regime was to be found in the character of the people themselves. The people had to be educated so as to learn to care for the association. As long as rationalistic self-interest prevailed, a true general will could never develop. Thus, according to Rousseau, the sovereign was necessarily concerned with watching over and influencing the manners, customs, and opinions of the populace. In this effort, religion necessarily played a major role.

In his discussion of civil religion, Rousseau distinguished among three types. First, the "religion of man" was that form of religion which was limited to the purely internal worship of god and the external performance of moral duties. For Rousseau, this religion was the appropriate form for a pure and holy Christianity. Yet, although it recognized the universal family of humankind, the "religion of man," nonetheless, had several unfortunate political consequences. Being fundamentally other-worldly, the spiritualism of the "religion of man" tended to detach the believer from affairs of the state. In so doing, it made the state vulnerable to both the attacks of foreign armies and the ambitions of private individuals. Thus rather than promoting the republican spirit, it actually allowed for the weakening of the state and thus the possible imposition of slavery. Rousseau called the second form of religion the "religion of the priest." Religions of this type tend to develop elaborate institutional structures. Thus churches eventually emerge as counterinstitutions to the state and thereby divide the loyalties of the citizen. Politically this form of religion introduces a contradiction within humanity itself and, in so doing, destroys the necessary conditions for social unity. The last form of religion, according to Rousseau, was the "religion of the citizen." Here the spheres of the sacred and the secular are identified with one another. The country is treated as an equivalent to the church, and a whole series of public cults and dogmas are created so as to distinguish the citizen from the infidel. Politically the religion of the citizen is most useful because it equates one's service to the state with one's service to god. Unfortunately, however, the religion of the citizen also encourages a degree of fanaticism. Thus, if it becomes tyrannical, it threatens to make its citizens intolerant and warlike.

According to Rousseau's analysis, every form of religion has certain negative political consequences. Yet, at the same time, a relationship between religion and the state was unavoidable. Historically, religions of the citizen were typical of humanity's early development. Thus all wars tended to be religious wars, and conversions were achieved through conquest. With the emergence of Christianity, however, an effort was made to separate the religious sphere from its political equivalent. Yet, in both its forms, either as a "religion of the priest" (Roman Catholicism) or as a "religion of man" (Calvinism), Christianity, according to Rousseau, had proven to be injurious to social and political unity.

Rousseau's *Social Contract* was essentially an effort to describe those conditions within which such dichotomies as morality and freedom or authenticity and alienation could be resolved. As such, it was not meant to be a description of an historically existing regime. On the contrary it was, instead, a call to creative action. There was in Rousseau's program, however, an unavoidable difficulty. The society described in the *Social Contract* presupposed the existence of a type of citizen who was actually the product of that very society. The problem, therefore, was one of foundations. Once the society had been founded and once it could produce the public morality it required, its existence or continuation was only a matter of preservation. The question remained, however, as to how the society could be established in the first place? How could the general will be affected as long as bourgeois humanity still existed? The problem was a serious one for Rousseau, and he was not optimistic that it could be solved. If it could, however, it would only be because of the efforts of the legislator.

Modeled after Moses, Rousseau's legislator would be the founding genius who, standing outside of society, would draft its constitution and mold its citizens in such a way as to make the social contract concretely effective. Legislators, being neither members of sovereign associations nor of governments, would be the ones to establish the appropriate laws for a given people. Thus would people undergo that process of educational formation which would make them into viable citizens. Once that had been accomplished, however, the people themselves could assume the tasks of the sovereign, and legislators would no longer be necessary. They would have transformed their charges into moral citizens, and the now-created moral citizens could then live according to the dictates of the general will. To accomplish such a transformation, however, legislators would have to claim the authority of a god, for they could not presuppose the willing consent of those who had not yet developed their social consciousness. Consequently, the laws and customs of society would have to acquire a certain weight so that they could evoke that sense of moral obligation which would eventually provide their force. In effect, then, Rousseau's regime of liberty and equality was based upon an act of duplicity. The legislators *appear* to blend nature and art in such a way as to promote the well-being of their citizens. That such a blending is in itself artificial and neither divine nor natural is the secret upon which these regimes are necessarily founded.

Throughout Rousseau's work, there exists a variety of tensions. Thus the tensions between nature and civilization, compassion and self-interest, integrity and alienation, privacy and fame, and the particular and the general actually serve to create a field within which Rousseau's thinking develops. His uneven handling of these polarities necessarily introduces a certain ambiguity into his work; yet his unwillingness to suppress one or the other is indicative of a basic existential honesty. At one point in his *Confessions* Rousseau attempted to reduce the many tensions to one essential dichotomy: the dichotomy between his heart and his understanding. Although this split is never totally resolved, it may be argued that the final logic operating within Rousseau's work is a logic which is dictated by the heart. Alienated from both his fellow people and from his own natural goodness, Rousseau sought a logical way of extending humanity's compassion outward so as to include society as a whole.

BIBLIOGRAPHY

CASSIRER ERNST.   *The Question of Jean Jacques Rousseau.* Translated by Peter Gay. Bloomington: Indiana University Press, 1963.

COBBAN, ALFRED.   *Rousseau and the Modern State.* London: George Allen & Unwin, 1934.

COLLETTI, LUCIO.   *From Rousseau to Lenin*. Translated by J. Merrington & Judith White. New York: Monthly Review Press, 1972.

CRANSTON, MAURICE, and RICHARD PETERS, eds.   *Hobbes and Rousseau: A Collection of Critical Essays*. Garden City: Doubleday, 1972.

CROCKER, LESTER.   *Rousseau's Social Contract: An Interpretive Essay*. Cleveland: Case Western Reserve University Press, 1968.

EINAUDI, MARIO.   *The Early Rousseau*. Ithaca: Cornell University Press, 1967.

GRIMSLEY, RONALD.   *The Philosophy of Rousseau*. Oxford: Oxford University Press, 1973.

HENDEL, CHARLES W.   *Jean Jacques Rousseau*. 2 vols. Oxford: Oxford University Press, 1934.

MASTERS, ROGER.   *The Political Philosophy of Rousseau*. Princeton: Princeton University Press, 1968.

SHKLAR, JUDITH.   *Men and Citizens: A Study of Rousseau's Social Theory*. Cambridge: Cambridge University Press, 1969.

TALMON, J. L.   *The Origins of Totalitarian Democracy*. New York: Praeger, 1960.

VAUGHAN, C. E.   *Studies in the History of Political Philosophy Before and After Rousseau*. Manchester: Manchester University, 1925.

13

EDMUND BURKE

LIFE AND WRITINGS

Edmund Burke was born in Dublin, Ireland, in 1729. Due to poor health he was sent away for elementary schooling and consequently did not return to Dublin until the age of fifteen, when he did so to enter Trinity College. After graduation and under pressure from his father, who was a relatively successful attorney, Burke traveled to London so as to prepare for the bar. In time, however, he became increasingly unhappy with his legal studies, and eventually abandoned them in order to pursue a literary career. At the age of twenty-seven he published his first work, *A Vindication of Natural Society: A View of the Miseries and Evils Arising to Mankind from Every Species of Artificial Society*. Published anonymously in 1756, Burke's *Vindication* was intended as a parody of the work of the recently deceased Lord Viscount Bolingbroke. Bolingbroke's collected works had just been published in 1754, and among them was an analysis of certain undesirable influences which he saw developing within English political life. As a corrective Bolingbroke suggested the desirability of returning to the traditional principles of aristocratic rule. In making his case, however, he argued on behalf of the superiority of natural as opposed to revealed religion. Burke—an Anglican who had been educated in both Catholic and Quaker schools—responded by extending the logic of Bolingbroke's original argument in such a way as to effectively undermine the legitimacy of Bolingbroke's own preferred aristocratic order. In a manner reminiscent of Rousseau, whose *Second Discourse* had first appeared a year earlier, Burke criticized all forms of "artificial society" in the name of "natural society." Yet in doing so, he so effectively mimicked Bolingbroke's style that many commentators took the *Vindications* to be a posthumous publication of Bolingbroke himself.

Rumors that Burke was, indeed, the author of *Vindications* earned him a small literary reputation. With the publication of two additional works in 1757, however, he soon acquired a well-established name. The first publication was a two-volume study entitled *An Account of the European Settlements in America.* Although the manuscript was originally the work of Burke's cousin, William, Burke aided him by editing it and in doing so revised it extensively. Inasmuch as Britain was engaged in the Seven Years' War at that time, there was considerable public interest in the American colonial situation. The book, as a consequence, was extremely popular and went through a number of editions. Its primary historical importance is due to its containing the first examples of Burke's thinking regarding America and its proper role within the British Empire.

AESTHETICS AND EMPIRICISM

Burke's second publication in 1757 was entitled *A Philosophical Inquiry into the Origin of Our Ideas of the Sublime and the Beautiful.* It, too, reached a large audience—especially in Germany where it is said to have influenced the thinking of both Lessing and Kant. The exact relationship of this work to Burke's political thinking, however, is somewhat complex. Breaking with the teachings of classical aesthetics Burke rejected the notion that there was a necessary connection between beauty on one hand and order, appropriateness, or proportion on the other. As a consequence art could no longer be considered as an attempt to imitate the beautiful as such: the ugly as well as the beautiful was to be regarded as a legitimate aesthetic phenomenon. This celebration of ugliness as an appropriate concern of the artist had already begun with the Italian mannerists of the sixteenth century and would continue to develop up to the eighteenth. Thus Burke's work contributed to the philosophical legitimation of an ongoing artistic movement. A second consequence of his aesthetic position was to effect a separation between physical-sensual beauty on one hand and intellectual beauty on the other./ For the classical theorists a true appreciation of physical beauty presupposed a sense of order, proportion, and appropriateness. These, in turn, were obviously intellectual categories. Thus the classical tradition logically implied a necessary relationship between the realm of the visible and that of the intellectual. By denying this relationship Burke, in effect, emancipated both artistic sentiment and creative instinct from the governance of reason.

/To a certain extent Burke's aesthetic theory can be deduced from his prior allegiance to philosophical empiricism./ Such empiricists as John Locke had traditionally argued that all knowledge was simply a matter of sensual experience. Thus an empiricistic account of our ideas of the beautiful and the sublime could only trace such concepts back to their origin in specific sensual perceptions. As a result empiricism could explain how ideas arose, but it could not know their why or wherefore. In accepting the empiricist program Burke wrote the following:

> When I say, I intend to inquire into the efficient cause of sublimity and beauty, I would not be understood to say, that I can come to the ultimate cause. I do not pretend that I shall ever be able to explain why certain affections of the body produce such a distinct emotion of mind, and no other; or why the body is at all affected by the mind, or the mind by the body. A little thought will show this to be impossible. But I conceive, if we can discover what affections of the mind produce certain emotions of the body; and what distinct feelings and qualities of body shall produce certain determinate passions in the mind, and no others, I fancy a great deal will be done.[1]

Burke's extension of empiricism into the realm of aesthetic experience was perfectly consistent with the general sensualist perspective. Beginning in the seventeenth century with such thinkers as Hobbes, Bacon, and Locke and continuing throughout the eighteenth in the work of such writers as Hume, Berkeley, and Hartley, British empiricism had succeeded in becoming a dominant form of philosophical speculation./As it evolved empiricism sought to explain the whole range of human experience in terms of relatively simple physical sensations./In doing so, therefore, it necessarily implied a specific conception of human nature./Accordingly, for the empiricist, the human being could be reduced to the level of its physical existence and bodily sensations./ Within the scope of this reduction the empiricists believed that they could account for such human experiences as the will to live, human passion, the power of memory, the functioning of in-

[1] Edmund Burke, *A Philosophical Inquiry into the Origin of an Idea of the Sublime and Beautiful*, ed. James Boulton (London: Routledge and Kegan Paul, 1950) and (Atlantic Highlands, N.J.: Humanities Press), p. 129.

strumental reasoning and foresight, and the fear of death. They could not, however, sufficiently comprehend such phenomena as human spirituality, the exercise of moral consciousness, and humanity's relationship with God. As a consequence, these latter experiences tended to be ignored, and thus the understanding of human nature which resulted was decidedly limited. By ignoring precisely those experiences in which the human being perceived itself to be a participant within a larger spiritual order, empiricism created an image of the human being as a strictly immanent being.

Burke's analysis of aesthetic theory shows that he was deeply influenced by the empiricist tradition. Yet typically he avoided committing himself to the radical philosophical implications of the entire program. Whereas he could accept a sensualist approach to aesthetic phenomena, Burke resisted the empiricist vision of the person as a purely immanent or autonomous being. Thus he retained an appreciation for the traditional belief that humanity is a participant within a structured common order. This is evident in the opening lines of his essay, in which he refers to the concept of human nature:

> On a superficial view we may seem to differ very widely from each other in our reasonings, and no less in our pleasures: but, notwithstanding this difference, which I think to be rather apparent than real, it is probable that the standard both of reason and taste is the same in all human creatures. For if there were not some principles of judgment as well as of sentiment common to all mankind, no hold could possibly be taken either on their reason or their passions, sufficient to maintain the ordinary correspondence of life. It appears, indeed, to be generally acknowledged, that with regard to truth and falsehood there is something fixed. We find people in their disputes continually appealing to certain tests and standards, which are allowed on all sides, and are supposed to be established in our common nature.[2]

Indeed although unable to articulate the precise order of that structure which binds it to all of creation and God, the human being, nonetheless, is capable of experiencing that reality. As Burke wrote:

> That great chain of causes which, linking one to another, even to the throne of God himself, can never be unravelled by any industry of ours.[3]

Or again as he would write thirty-three years later:

---

[2] Burke, *A Philosophical Inquiry into the Origin of an Idea of the Sublime and Beautiful*, p. 11.
[3] Burke, *A Philosophical Inquiry into the Origin of an Idea of the Sublime and Beautiful*, p. 129.

Each contract of each particular state is but a clause in the great primeval contract of eternal society, linking the lower with the higher natures, connecting the visible and invisible world, according to a fixed compact santioned by the inviolable oath which holds all physical and moral natures, each in their appointed place.[4]

This early essay on aesthetics illustrates an important feature of Burke's thinking. Although he could accept certain philosophical assumptions that informed the social and political thinking of the Enlightenment philosophers, Burke would not allow such dogma to interfere with his commonsense experience. Whereas Enlightenment theory attempted to adjust reality so as to conform with preconceived rational postulates, Burke, to the contrary, insisted upon acknowledging the structure of experienced reality itself. As a consequence, although he could use the arguments of empiricism, Burke never could become simply an empiricist himself.

With the publication of these two works in 1757, Burke enjoyed a growing reputation with the English literary classes. In 1758 he was appointed the anonymous editor of a yearly review of world affairs entitled the *Annual Register*. While working as editor Burke became increasingly interested in English political affairs and, in 1759, became the secretary of William Hamilton, who was soon sent to Ireland to help administer the restless English colony. Returning to London in 1764 Burke joined a group within the Whig party which was united in its common opposition to the crown's policy toward the American colonies. The leader of this faction was the Marquis of Rockingham. When Rockingham became prime minister on July 13, 1765, he arranged for Burke, who had been his private secretary, to be elected to Parliament as a representative of the pocket borough of Wendover. Thus in 1766 Burke began a career as a British politician that would continue for almost thirty years until his death in 1797.

During his years as a member of Parliament Burke was associated with many attempts to reform English political life. For example, he championed such causes as religious toleration and economic reform, and he was a strong opponent of the African slave trade. Although he opposed extending the franchise, Burke did resist efforts by both the monarchy and the landed aristocracy to interfere with the representative functions of the parliamentary system. Finally he was a tireless critic of the corruption and mismanagement which were typical of British imperial rule in both Ireland and India. Yet, granting the importance of these problems, perhaps the most pressing issue of Burke's day was the question concerning the status of the American colonies. Eventually Burke became one of the most outspoken supporters of the American cause within Parliament and, for a time, was

---

[4] Edmund Burke, *Reflections on the Revolution in France*, ed. Thomas H. D. Mahoney (Indianapolis: Bobbs-Merrill, 1955), p. 110.

even commissioned by the state of New York to represent its interest in London.

BURKE ON THE AMERICAN REVOLUTION

The original controversy between England and its American colonies was over taxation. After defeating the French in the Seven Years' War, England attempted to meet the financial burdens produced during the war by levying a series of taxes upon its American colonies. The Sugar Act (1764), the Quartering Act (1765), and the Stamp Act (1765) were designed to lessen the burden on the British taxpayer by extending it to America. Quite to London's surprise, however, the colonists resisted this effort and claimed that they had been taxed without their consent. In addition they argued that, inasmuch as they were not represented in Parliament, only their own colonial assemblies could legitimately impose a tax burden upon them. With this, then, there began a series of moves and countermoves which would eventually lead to outright rebellion.

Burke's position throughout this struggle was ultimately based upon considerations of expediency. Although he argued that, in principle, Britain retained the right to tax its imperial subjects, he nonetheless believed that the Stamp Act was impractical and thus should be repealed. Indeed, according to Burke, the Americans were correct in arguing that they had not been adequately represented in Parliament. He maintained that those who spoke of "virtual [or indirect] representation" were naively unaware of the nature of the situation. Thus imposing a tax upon America was not only at variance with the American temperament (and thus an impracticable policy) but also represented a threat to English liberty in America and thus, by extension, a challenge to English freedom at home. For Burke the best policy would be to return to the situation prior to 1764. In short, Britain would claim its right to tax, but at the same time it would refrain from exercising it. America, in turn, would refrain from disobeying.

Central to Burke's analysis was his belief that the British parliamentary and imperial systems were fundamentally sound. The problem was not one of institutions or law. Rather it was matter of leadership. Burke, like the other Rockingham Whigs, was convinced that the tensions between England and its colonies were rooted in the diplomatic failures of the British leadership. Rather than responding with tact, grace, and care, the British leadership clumsily moved from confrontation to confrontation. Indeed even after the war had begun Burke continued to insist that the colonists were, in fact, only fighting for the cause of English liberty. Burke's perception, however, was fundamentally mistaken. As the situation worsened Burke failed to appreciate the truly radical nature of the American Revolution. At first he treated the tension as an essentially commercial affair. Thus, although Parliament retained the right to tax, Burke saw no financial benefits to be gained by insisting to do so. Given this perspective, then, the colonial rebellion appeared to be nothing more than a legitimate resistance to an invasion of ancient privileges (taxation). Yet the American Revolution was more than that. Under the influence of Enlightenment thought the revolution's leaders saw the issue as being one of rights rather than of privileges. Indeed, to a certain extent the American Revolution was being fought on behalf of the abstract natural rights of all peoples. Thus Burke's solution that England should retain but not exercise the sovereign right of taxation did not, in fact, satisfy the radical demands of the American leadership. For the Americans the problem was not simply one of the ill-will or abusive policies of the British gentry. Rather the issue involved the legal structure of the British imperial order itself. In short, the colonies did not want the *privilege* of taxation. Instead they claimed it as a *right*. As the nature of the conflict became clearer, Burke was one of the first to insist that Britain should be willing to revise its imperial constitution. In his famous speech of conciliation in November 1775, he encouraged the British to recognize the *de facto* right of America to tax itself. The government, however, refused to listen, and war became inevitable. Finally on April 10, 1778, Burke announced his unreserved support of total American independence.

ANALYSIS OF *REFLECTIONS* ON THE *REVOLUTION* IN FRANCE

Of all of Burke's writings, the one which has proven to be most influential is his *Reflections on the Revolution in France* which was first published in 1790. Ostensibly Burke's *Reflections* was a letter addressed to a French correspondent, M. Victor Dupont. In reality, however, it was a response to Dr. Richard Price's public sermon which praised the principles espoused by the French revolutionaries. As an example of political rhetoric Burke's argument proved to be extremely effective. Originally the French Revolution of 1789 enjoyed the enthusiastic support of a great many English. With the publication of Burke's *Reflections*, however, a much more cautious attitude soon began to prevail. This success eventually provoked a series of counter-arguments which attempted once again to rally the English behind the French cause. Among the most important of these responses were William Godwin's *Enquiry Concerning Political Justice*, Mary Wollstonecraft's *A Vindication of the Rights of Woman*, and Thomas Paine's *Rights of Man*.

Throughout the *Reflections*, Burke presented himself as a person who is primarily concerned with the preservation of English peace and liberty. His fear was that the English supporters of the French Revolution would, in their enthusiasm, actually destroy what they claimed to love most. Specifically Dr. Price and others were accused of misunderstanding the principles upon which the British political order was based. According to Burke, Price supported the French Revolution out of his mistaken belief that it was similar to the English revolution of 1688, which, according to Price, was the source of current English liberties. For Burke, therefore, the problem was twofold. First, one had to correctly understand the sources and principles of British order so as to preserve and extend them. And second, one had to correctly perceive the exact nature of the French Revolution so as to comprehend its relationship with the British experience. From Burke's standpoint Price and his followers had failed on both counts.

Burke believed that the Glorious Revolution of 1688 had essentially been a reaffirmation of the principles of British politics. Unlike Price who interpreted that event as a new beginning, Burke argued that the Glorious Revolution was defensive in character. Through it the English sought to defend their traditional liberties and practices rather than allow them to be modified according to the interests of the overly ambitious. In short, the 1688 revolution was fought in order to preserve the English inheritance:

> The Revolution was made to preserve our *ancient*, indisputable laws and liberties and that *ancient* constitution of government which is our only security for law and liberty . . . . We wished at the period of the Revolution, and do now wish, to derive all we possess as *an inheritance from our forefathers*. . . .[5]

Specifically Burke argued that the principle of a hereditary monarchy was well established in both English common law and in recent statutes. Consequently although the English did not accept the divine-right theory of monarchy, neither did they hold that a monarch was a servant of the people, and thus no king or queen could be removed at the people's pleasure. According to Burke, English tradition had established this understanding, and it continued to function as the source of the current regime's legitimacy. At the same time, however, tradition was not an absolute for Burke. Political power existed for a rational purpose. Specifically, political society was required as the necessary means for humanity's intellectual and moral development. Inasmuch as the fulfillment of human nature required society and inasmuch as the existence of society presupposed the exercise of governmental authority, political power existed for a specific end—the

---

[5] Burke, *Reflections on the Revolution in France*, p. 35.

general advantage of the people. Government, in effect, was entrusted to act with this purpose in mind. In those extreme cases when the government seriously violated the people's trust and the future appeared to offer no remedy, the people, in turn, were justified in exercising their right to revolt. According to Burke, however, this was not the situation in 1688. Thus Price's attempt to suggest an analogy between the British Revolution of 1688 and the French Revolution of 1789 was based upon a fundamental misunderstanding of the British political experience.

Although Burke was concerned with the accuracy of Price's analogy, his deepest fears concerned the nature of the French Revolution itself. To him it was "the most astonishing [revolution] that has hitherto happened in the world" because it was more than just a radical rearrangement of governmental institutions.[6] It was, rather, "a revolution in sentiments, manners, and moral opinions."[7] For Burke the events of the revolution indicated that France was suffering from a pathological condition. Yet in order to examine this situation it first was necessary for Burke to develop his own understanding of those standards of normalcy which correctly defined the good political order. Therefore Burke undertook an examination of what he considered to be both the true rights of citizens and the true principles of government. In both instances he wished to distinguish between the valid concepts and those posited by the theorists of the French Revolution.

Enlightenment theory had typically begun by reconstructing a view of natural primitives as they had existed before the formation of society. Given this view the theorist would then abstract certain rights which were said to adhere to the very nature of the human being as such. These rights were then used, in turn, as the standards against which to judge the conventions of any given historical society. Burke, on the other hand, considered such a "metaphysical" approach to be entirely inadequate, that is, mistakenly based upon the assumption that humanity's nature could be clearly and meaningfully distinguished from its historical and social forms. Returning to the classical natural-law tradition instead, Burke acknowledged that society was, indeed, artificial; but, given humanity's natural need for social conventions to develop the full potential of its rational capacities, the artificial structures of society actually formed humanity's natural milieu.

> The state of civil society . . . is a state of nature; and much more truly so than a savage and incoherent mode of life. For man is by na-

---

[6] Burke, *Reflections on the Revolution in France*, p. 11.

[7] Burke, *Reflections on the Revolution in France*, p. 91.

ture reasonable; and he is never perfectly in his natural state, but when he is placed where reason may be best cultivated, and most predominates. Art is man's nature.[8]

Given Burke's approach, the "metaphysical" distinction between nature and history had little merit. Rights were established by the requirements of humanity's nature, but that nature, in turn, achieved its proper fulfillment only in the context of the human historical and social situation. Thus there are no politically meaningful abstract rights which exist independently of humanity's actual historical being. Metaphysically the human being may have rights, but historically they are real only in the form of specific liberties and privileges provided by a particular society at a particular time. Even the fundamental human right of self-defense is surrendered when, as they are directed by their very nature, humans enter society. It is replaced in turn by the particular concrete rights of that society to which they have adjoined themselves:

> One of the first motives to civil society, and which becomes one of its fundamental rules, is *that no man should be judge in his own cause.* By this each person has at once divested himself of the first fundamental right of unconvenanted [natural] man, that is, to judge for himself and to assert his own cause. He abdicates all right to be his own governor. He inclusively, in a great measure, abandons the right of self-defense, the first law of nature. Men cannot enjoy the rights of an uncivil and of a civil state together. That he may obtain justice, he gives up his right of determining what is in points the most essential to him. That he may secure some liberty, he makes a surrender in trust of the whole of it.[9]

Burke's argument allowed him to deny that one could legitimately criticize the civil practices of a particular society by contrasting them with the universal standards of an abstract metaphysical condition. Rather, according to Burke, government's practices must be evaluated in strictly political terms. In this perspective, therefore, the true rights of humankind would consist solely of those concrete advantages for which civil society was originally formed. A listing of such advantages would include:

> Men have a right to live by that rule; they have a right to do justice, as between their fellows, whether their fellows are in public function or in ordinary occupation. They have a right to the fruits of their industry and to the means of making their industry fruitful.

[8] As quoted in Francis Canavan, S.J., "Edmund Burke," in *History of Political Philosophy*, eds. Leo Strauss and Joseph Cropsey (Chicago: Rand McNally, 1963), p. 604

[9] Burke, *Reflections on the Revolution in France*, p. 68.

They have a right to the acquisitions of their parents, to the nourishment and improvement of their offspring, to instruction in life, and to consolation in death. Whatever each man can separately do, without trespassing upon others, he has a right to do for himself; and he has a right to a fair portion of all which society, with all its combinations of skill and force, can do in his favor. In this partnership all men have equal rights, but not to equal things. He that has but five shillings in the partnership has as good a right to it as he that has five hundred pounds has to his larger proportion. But he has not a right to an equal dividend in the product of the joint stock; and as to the share of power, authority, and direction which each individual ought to have in the management of the state, that I must deny to be amongst the direct original rights of man in civil society, for I have in my contemplation the civil social man, and no other. It is a thing to be settled by convention.[10]

Having discussed the notion of rights Burke then turned to an examination of the positive principles of political order. In doing so he paid particular attention to the issue of political leadership. For Burke this issue was important because of the essential and unavoidable role assigned to the exercise of personal judgment in political life. Given the intricacies of human nature and the complicated workings of any society, there could never be a single political or constitutional arrangement which would be suitable for all conditions. Consequently good government always depended upon the good judgment of its leaders. The art of judging well, however, was a skill that had to be acquired through practice and developed by effort. Thus those who were particularly successful in developing their powers of judgment constituted, thereby, a natural political aristocracy, and the best society was one which allowed its natural aristocracy to rule.

According to Burke the rise of the natural aristocracy tended to be resisted by other classes competing for political power. Traditionally such resistance was practiced by the social gentry which based its claim to rule on the principle of inheritance. More recently, however, the natural aristocracy was being challenged by those who argued that all people, being equal, have an equal right to rule. Such, according to Burke, was the claim of the intellectuals who had inspired the French Revolution. In both their elitist and democratic form, however, Burke believed that such arguments denied the natural fact that political skills were distributed unevenly among citizens and throughout the classes:

You do not imagine that I wish to confine power, authority, and distinction to blood and names and titles. No, Sir. There is no qualification for government but virtue and wisdom, actual or presump-

---

[10] Burke, *Reflections on the Revolution in France*, p. 67.

tive . . . . Woe to the country which would madly and impiously reject the service of the talents and virtues . . . that are given to grace and serve it . . . . Woe to that country, too, that passing into the opposite extreme, considers a low education, a mean contracted view of things, a sordid, mercenary occupation as a preferable title to command! Everything ought to be open, but not indifferently, to every man.[11]

In speaking of virtue and wisdom Burke was referring specifically to that form of practical wisdom which he called "prudence." Prudence to Burke was the ability to "compute morally" rather than "mathematically" or "metaphysically." By that he meant that prudence was primarily concerned with the good rather than with the true. The good is the object sought by action, and action occurs in the realm of the particular and the contingent. Theory, on the other hand, seeks truth, and truth, by definition, is universal and unchanging. Thus the theoretical attitude is incapable of guiding action because it is insensitive to the very mode within which actions necessarily take place. According to Burke whenever theory is forced upon politics, as in the case of France, it tends toward extremism. This is the case inasmuch as the theoretical mind seeks to create a true form which is unchanging and perfect. The prudent mind, to the contrary, acknowledges humanity's historical character and thus is capable of dealing more realistically with the situations it encounters. The prudent mind seeks to make better that good which it already finds and, as a consequence, seeks to preserve rather than to create.

It is important to understand that in emphasizing the historical and particular nature of prudential wisdom Burke was not at the same time advocating moral relativism. In speaking of the *true* rights of citizens, Burke wrote:

> The pretended rights of these theorists are all extremes; and in proportion as they are metaphysically true, they are morally and politically false. The rights of men are in a sort of *middle*, incapable of definition, but not impossible to be discerned. The rights of men in government are their advantages. . . .[12]

This analysis places Burke firmly within the traditional natural-law perspective. The person seeks what is to personal advantage, and that, in turn, is determined by what is appropriate for or required by human nature. For Burke God had created human beings intending their intellectual and moral perfection. This purpose, therefore, established that end toward which humanity and society must work. Reason, in turn, is capable of

---

[11] Burke, *Reflections on the Revolution in France*, p. 57.
[12] Burke, *Reflections on the Revolution in France*, p. 70–71.

recognizing this project and thus commanding those actions which are necessary for its attainment. Since the natural law commands action, it cannot generate those precise and uniform definitions which are characteristic of the theoretical sciences. It can, however, be discerned, and discerning judgment is the trademark of the prudent mind. The natural law, therefore, according to Burke, was not that dogmatic code of rights as envisioned by the rationalistic philosophers of the Enlightenment. Rather it was for him, as for Aristotle, that principle of action which became apparent in the informed judgments of the prudent person.

In part Burke's prudent person was characterized by the appreciation of the limits of intellectual individualism. The Enlightenment faith in autonomous reason supported the attempts of certain theorists to create elaborate systems of ideas which would then stand as total critiques of existing societies. Burke, on the other hand, was extremely skeptical of such intellectual endeavors. According to him, the type of wisdom necessary to govern well was not the creation of a single person's imagination. Rather it was the product of a long social experience. As a consequence, Burke believed that practical wisdom was to be found in the traditions and customs of a society, and that they, in turn, were to be revered and respected. Whereas the Enlightenment understood prejudices as irrational social barriers to the discovery of truth, they were, for Burke, the necessary means by which an individual was introduced to an ongoing body of knowledge. Rather than opposing the growth of knowledge they were, in fact, the essential means for its preservation. In praising the British attitude toward prejudices, Burke wrote:

> We are afraid to put men to live and trade each on his own private stock of reason, because we suspect that this stock in each man is small, and that the individuals would do better to avail themselves of the general bank and capital of nations and of ages. Many of our men of speculation, instead of exploding general prejudices, employ their sagacity to discover the latent wisdom which prevails in them. If they find what they seek, and they seldom fail, they think it more wise to continue the prejudice, with the reason involved, than to cast away the coat of prejudice and to leave nothing but the naked reason; because prejudice, with its reason, has a motive to give action to that reason, and an affection which will give it permanence. Prejudice is of ready application in the emergency; it previously engages the mind in a steady course of wisdom and virtue and does not leave the man hesitating in the moment of decision skeptical, puzzled, and unresolved. Prejudice renders a man's virtue his habit, and not a series of unconnected acts. Through just prejudice, his duty becomes a part of his nature.[13]

[13] Burke, *Reflections on the Revolution in France*, p. 99.

Burke's argument on behalf of prejudices was not intended to be a critique of reason as such. Rather it was a defense of a particular understanding of reason which was, itself, based upon two prior principles. First, Burke's understanding of the way in which reason operated included an appreciation of the intellectual contributions which are found in tradition. For Burke reason operated through traditions not in spite of them. Thus belief and inquiry were mutually supportive rather than contradictory. Second, Burke's rejection of intellectual individualism was, in part, motivated by his moral disapproval of those who would set themselves above and apart from their past/ In rejecting their past and subordinating its truth to their own, such intellectuals were in fact displaying an inordinate amount of pride. In claiming to speak for humankind they were actually acting "like the flies of summer" and thereby denying the true social contract which linked past, present, and future generations:

> Society is indeed a contract . . . . It is to be looked on with other reverence, because it is not a partnership in things subservient only to the gross animal existence of a temporary and perishable nature. It is a partnership in all science; a partnership in all art; a partnership in every virtue and in all perfection. As the ends of such a partnership cannot be obtained in many generations, it becomes a partnership not only between those who are living, but between those who are living, those who are dead, and those who are to be born.[14]

After having developed his understanding of the principles of political order Burke completed his *Reflections* by comparing the prerevolutionary and postrevolutionary conditions within France. According to his analysis contemporary France had entered into a period of dramatic decline. On one hand, its leaders were vulgar and materialistic individuals who possessed little virtue and no political experience. On the other, its cultural and religious traditions were being destroyed by the teachings of the Enlightenment philosophers. Moreover, the government's policies in general and its monetary policy in particular were ill-conceived and promised disastrous results. Finally, according to Burke, France's extreme democratic passions threatened to overturn the rule of law and implied, thereby, the rule of a tyrannical majority.

In comparing this situation to prerevolutionary France Burke attempted to defend the ancien régime. It is generally agreed that in this defense he exhibited a marked blindness towards the inadequacies of the French monarchy. In particular in reviewing the political and religious features of the old regime, Burke quickly passed over the obvious economic and social inadequacies which were characteristic of the traditional system.

---

[14] Burke, *Reflections on the Revolution in France*, p. 110.

In addition in his enthusiasm to protect the English system from any French influence, Burke failed to notice the actual continuities which did, in fact, exist between the old and the new.

Unlike other opponents of the French Revolution Burke never attempted to create a theoretical order which could serve as an alternative to the apocalyptic and secular model of the French Revolution. To have done so would have been to engage in the very style of theorizing which he criticized. Thus Burke's accomplishment was essentially that of a commonsense critic of the French experiment. As such he could provide a telling analysis of the events of his day. Yet at the same time, inasmuch as the fundamental assumptions of his commonsense perspective remained unquestioned, Burke's analysis could never serve as a total substitute for serious political theory. For one who accepted the perspective of an English society which was informed by elements of the Greek, Christian, Jewish, and Germanic traditions, the French Revolution appeared to be an obvious mistake. Yet in order to demonstrate the adequacy of that perception itself, it would have been necessary to examine theoretically those principles which were presupposed by that society which Burke accepted. This Burke declined to do. Thus as an example of political rhetoric, Burke's *Reflections* are quite important. They justified and thereby protected his community in the judgment of those who already shared in its commitments. Such a task is, in part, the duty of the statesman. However, such justification does not describe the activity of the theorist. Eventually political theorists must proceed to question the adequacy of their society's commitments. Thus although political theorists may begin their inquiry from the perspective of the concerned citizen, they must, sooner or later, abandon it for that of the concerned philosopher.

BIBLIOGRAPHY

CANAVAN, FRANCIS. *The Political Reason of Edmund Burke*. Durham: Duke University Press, 1960.

CHAPMAN, GERALD W. *Edmund Burke: The Practical Imagination*. Cambridge: Harvard University Press, 1967.

COBBAN, ALFRED. *Edmund Burke and the Revolt Against the Eighteenth Century*. London: George Allen and Unwin, 1929.

CONE, CARL. *Burke and the Nature of Politics*. 2 vols. Lexington: University of Kentucky Press, 1957, 1964.

KIRK, RUSSELL. *Edmund Burke: A Genius Reconsidered*. New York: Arlington House, 1967.

MacCUNN, JOHN. *The Political Philosophy of Burke*. London: E. Arnold, 1913.

MANSFIELD, H. C.   *Statesmanship and Party Government: A Study of Burke and Bolingbroke.* Chicago: University of Chicago Press, 1965.

NAMIER, LEWIS.   *England in the Age of the American Revolution.* London: Macmillan, 1966.

PARKIN, CHARLES.   *The Moral Basis of Burke's Political Thought.* Cambridge: Cambridge University Press, 1956.

STANLIS, PETER.   *Edmund Burke and the Natural Law:* Ann Arbor: University of Michigan Press, 1958.

14
MODERN LIBERALISM AND THE UTILITARIAN ETHIC

The early English liberal program sought to develop a political environment which would stimulate and sustain the growth of individuality. Based upon a tradition of natural-rights speculation, early liberalism attempted to protect individuals by creating for them a private space within the public realm. For example, the individual's right to property, the freedom of religious belief, and a citizen's right to resist governmental oppression functioned in such a way as to create for people a private sphere within which they could partially determine their own destiny while being shielded from social control. As England moved into the nineteenth century, however, certain changes occurred which disrupted the original equilibrium of the former age. One was at the theoretical level, where the natural-rights tradition, which had originally supplied the ethical basis for political liberalism, came under increasing criticism. Inasmuch as natural-rights theory presupposed that human beings could know their original rights, it was based upon the rationalistic assumption that humans were capable of discovering specific universal principles which existed independently of particular historical and social conditions. John Locke, for example, had believed that the principles of justice were, in fact, eternal laws of nature which could be discovered by unaided reason and thus used as guides for human conduct. Yet in time, this faith in the mind's ability to know such things began to appear less and less plausible as philosophical empiricism became more and more radical.

DAVID HUME AND THE CRITIQUE OF NATURAL-RIGHTS THEORY

The thinking of David Hume (1711–1776) was typical of this development. Hume radicalized the teachings of English empiricism by pushing them to their logical limits until he arrived at a thorough-going skepticism. If, as empiricism taught, all perceptions are, in fact, unique existences, then according to Hume it becomes impossible to know the necessary connections between such perceptions. In short, according to Hume, the human mind can know neither cause nor effect, and without this knowledge it can never achieve an understanding of the nature of reality itself. While Hume's skepticism obviously challenged the rationalistic assumptions of modern science, it also served to undermine the very foundations of natural-rights philosophy. According to Hume, inasmuch as the mind cannot know nature, it is at the same time incapable of knowing what is naturally right or what is naturally just. Thus those moral doctrines which claimed a knowledge of the natural law were in fact mere fictions. Indeed, according to Hume, reason is incapable of judging the truth or falsity of any moral proposition. Reason cannot teach humanity how to act because it cannot know which desires are naturally good and which are by their nature evil. Thus rather than guiding the passions, reason is ultimately their slave.

Hume's analysis led to the obvious conclusion that natural rights do not exist. From his perspective all morality was simply a matter of convention, and convention, in turn, was simply a matter of convenience. With this criticism, then, political liberalism faced a fundamental crisis. As the natural-rights tradition became increasingly questionable, liberalism was threatened with the eventual loss of its own ethical foundation. Thus if liberalism were to remain an ethically defensible political doctrine, it would have to develop a moral theory which could confront the challenge of a radically skeptical empiricism.

The second challenge to early liberalism stemmed from changes in the English economic and social order. By the nineteenth century England was beginning to experience the first effects of the industrial revolution. The large-scale introduction of machinery into the production process had a number of important, if unintended, consequences. For example, mechanized technology increased the division of labor and, thereby, routinized the tasks of production. The increased division of labor, however, required more planning and consequently encouraged the centralization of administrative authority. Similarly the use of coal power markedly increased the economy's productive capacities. This, in turn, created the need for more workers and eventually led to the rapid expansion of the urban areas. Rapidly growing cities, however, demanded new techniques of municipal governance and soon challenged the adequacy of the traditional English system of political representation. Most importantly, however, the sudden development of industrial wealth led to the emergence of new classes whose appearance constituted a challenge to the older social order. The bourgoisie not only threatened the prerogatives of the landed aristocracy, but at the same time it was separated from the working classes because of a growing disparity in wealth and social power. As this disparity increased, class antagonism intensified.

Each of these developments eventually created its own specific problem for the liberalism associated with such natural-rights theorists as John Locke. For Locke and others, government was to act both as an impartial judge and as a protector of individual rights. Therefore it was to refrain as much as possible from intervening in the economic and social processes of its day. As the social and economic environment changed in response to industrialization, however, liberalism's formal commitment to the safeguarding of rights had the substantive effect of protecting and preserving distinct social and economic privileges. As a consequence, its theoretical impartiality actually appeared to favor the partisan interests of the commercial classes. As the demands upon government increased, it became more and more apparent that liberalism would have to assume an activist attitude towards social issues. Whereas the extremely individualistic perspective of the natural-rights tradition had only allowed for a minimal level of governmental involvement in economic affairs, the political realities of the day seemed to dictate a more positive approach.

Given this situation, then, utilitarianism may be understood as liberalism's response to the intellectual and social crises which were characteristic of nineteenth-century English society. Among the utilitarian reformers, the two most important were Jeremy Bentham and John Stuart Mill.

JEREMY BENTHAM

Jeremy Bentham was born in London on February 15, 1748. His father, intending that his son should become a lawyer, planned Bentham's education accordingly. Bentham, who was reading and writing at the age of three and studying Latin at four, was sent to Queens College, Oxford, at twelve years of age.

During his four years at Oxford Bentham developed an interest in both the natural sciences and in the study of modern logical theory. Upon graduation he began preparing for a career in law, and in 1769, at twenty-one, he was admitted to the bar. After having successfully completed his legal studies, however, Bentham decided against being either a lawyer or a judge. He resolved instead to devote himself to the task of creating a scientific basis for the practice of jurisprudence and the art of legislation. Thus, supported by a small private income, he began to study and write with this singular goal in mind. The range of his interest was truly remarkable, and his writings were both numerous and influential. A partial listing of his almost sixty publications would include: *Defense of Usury* (1787), *The Panopticon* (1787), *Essay on Political Tactics* (1791), *Manual of Political Economy* (1793), *Chrestomathia* (1816), and *Handbook of Political Fallacies* (1825). It is generally agreed, however, that his most important works in the field of political theory were *Fragment on Government* (1776) and *An Introduction to the Principles of Morals and Legislation* (1789).

British Politics and the Reforms
of the Philosophical Radicals

In addition to his many writings, Bentham was, on occasion, involved with political projects. Throughout his career he was a strong advocate of legal codification. Bentham believed that as the law grew slowly by judicial interpretation and tradition it became increasingly complex and unwieldy. As such it also became increasingly inaccessible to the average citizen who, as a consequence, became almost totally dependent upon the service of lawyers. By codifying the law Bentham hoped to rationalize the legal system and thereby promote citizen involvement in politics. Thus, on several occasions, he offered his services as a codifier to various regimes. After having approached both Catherine II of Russia in 1786 and the American president, James Madison, in 1811, he was finally commissioned by the Portuguese Cortez (parliament) in 1821 to undertake a codification project.

Of all of Bentham's practical schemes, however, the most famous was his plan for a model prison first developed in his *Panopticon* of 1787. For over twenty-three years Bentham worked unsuccessfully to gain the economic and political support necessary to build his model project. Returning from a visit to Russia in 1788 Bentham developed his plans for the construction of a modern penitentiary which would be designed so as to allow for the maximum supervision of prison life. At first, in 1794, the English Parliament accepted Bentham's scheme, but in 1811 it rejected the concept and voted to pay him 23,000 English pounds in compensation for his time and expenses.

Bentham's disappointment in the political process that had resulted in the rejection of his scheme paralleled his increasingly radical analysis of the limitations of entrenched political power. Earlier in his career, Bentham had believed that the English governing classes were essentially well meaning but misinformed. Subsequently he argued that political reform was primarily a matter of enlightenment. Thus according to Bentham once the leadership had seen the error of its ways it would enthusiastically adopt those reforms which were obviously necessary for good government. As Bentham's efforts to reform British politics met with increasing resistance, however, he gradually began to reject his earlier optimism. Indeed it soon became apparent to him that poor political judgment was not simply the result of bad logic. Rather it was due in part to the influence of "sinister interests."

> . . . it is apparent that the mind of every public man is subject at all times to the operation of two distinct interests: a public and a private one . . . . In the greater number of instances, these two interests, the public and the private, are not only distinct but opposite, and that to such a degree that if either is exclusively pursued, the other must be sacrificed to it.[1]

Given this unavoidable conflict of interests, political reform could no longer be considered simply a matter of public education. On the contrary, true reform could be accomplished only if certain mechanisms were created whereby the particular interests of the political leadership could be made to coincide with the general interests of the public. Specifically Bentham believed that this could be accomplished through the practice of frequent elections based upon an extended franchise. If the political leaders were held accountable by means of periodic elections, their own interests as politicians would depend upon their serving the general interest of the public at large. Therefore Bentham recommended the establishment of annual elections which would be based upon a universal franchise and carried out with the fullest publicity possible. To insure such publicity he supported the existence of a free press, advocated unlimited access to government offices, and fought for the right to visit the legislature in session.

As he pursued these reforms Bentham gathered around him a group of like-minded liberals. Referred to as the "philosophical radicals," this group finally succeeded in becoming a political force within Parliament it-

---

[1] Harold Larrabee, ed., *Bentham's Handbook of Political Fallacies* (New York: Thomas Y. Crowell Co., 1971), p. 229.

self. Whereas the English Parliament had traditionally been content merely to supervise the administration of existing law, under the influence of the "Benthamites," it began to use its legislative powers to reform the legal and political practice of the day. Indeed, through their initiative, the Benthamites gradually succeeded in transferring the weight of English social power away from the traditional land-owning classes and towards the emerging commercial bourgeoisie.

Although Bentham never produced one particular work which systematically set forth his complete political theory, it is nonetheless possible to specify certain features of that vision which inspired his overall reform efforts. First, according to Bentham, the basic task of government was to create and maintain an ordered and rational legal system. Inasmuch as a society's laws determined the duties and rights of its citizens, it was absolutely essential that they be as clear and consistent as possible.

Second, government should be concerned with securing the wealth and prosperity of its citizens. Bentham held that generally this can best be done by guaranteeing that each individual receive those rewards for which he or she has worked and, therefore, by insuring that all are secure in the enjoyment of their possessions. Beyond this, the government should interfere with the efficient working of the economic system as little as possible.

Third, although economic, political, intellectual, and moral inequalities are both unavoidable and necessary, government should attempt to moderate their extreme forms whenever possible. Such efforts, however, must always be guided by the principle of utility and based upon a respect for secured property. Finally, government should make an effort to cultivate a spirit of benevolence among its citizens. The happiness of society increases precisely to the degree that its citizens are willing to render services to one another. Such a spirit may be encouraged in turn by combating religious and sectarian prejudices, establishing charitable organizations, and teaching a morality of public spiritedness in all the schools and churches. In each case, however, the goal was always to increase the greatest happiness of the greatest number.

Bentham's preoccupation with legal reform accounts, in part, for the particular style of his theoretical work. As a legal reformer, he was primarily concerned with the relationship of the individual citizen to government. Whereas political theorists had traditionally investigated such larger issues as regime theory, authority, and the nature of political legitimacy, Bentham focused upon ways of improving the day-to-day operation of the English government. As a consequence, his theory reflected a certain individualistic bias. Rather than analyzing the spiritual principles which necessarily inform a given social order, Bentham sought only to comprehend the nature of those specific exchanges which formed the concrete relationships between the individual governor and particular subjects. As a consequence, Bentham was primarily concerned with the impact of governmental sanctions upon the individual. In particular, he was interested in discovering those mechanisms by which such sanctions could be regulated according to the utilitarian principle of the greatest happiness for the greatest number.

Utilitarianism

Although Bentham's individualism was appropriate in view of his reformist intentions, it also appears to have been required by his understanding of the scientific method. Indeed Bentham was convinced that the methods of modern natural science could at the same time be employed by the social scientist. In particular, he admired the conceptual clarity and precision which he assumed to be characteristic of scientific analysis.

According to Bentham, the physical and mathematical sciences had finally succeeded in decoding the "logic of understanding" and thus were capable of reaching a state of near perfection. This same progress, however, could not be found among the moral sciences. Given this, the moral sciences appeared to have failed in their efforts to achieve precision and certainty. Yet, if the scientific method had worked in the realm of nature, why would it now work in the realm of action? Bentham, for one, believed it could.

> There is, or rather there ought to be, a *logic* of the *will* as well as of the *understanding*: the operations of the former faculty, are neither less susceptible nor less worthy, than those of the latter, of being delineated by rules.[2]

Thus morality was to imitate physics. In doing so, measurement would replace imitation, and calculation would take the place of judgment. According to Bentham, science proceeded analytically. Specifically, by breaking down complex wholes into their simple component parts, scientific reason appeared capable of understanding nature's fundamental principles. Thus by a similar move from the general to the specific and from the abstract to the concrete, it would be possible for the moral and legal tradition to achieve its own scientific basis. In particular, scientific analysis promised to solve the difficult problem of conceptual "fictions." These fictions arise when people mistakenly assume that there is a corresponding reality for each and every concept contained in their language. Rigorous analysis, however, demonstrates that in many cases words, themselves, are simply the product of our own creative imagination. Therefore by getting

---

[2] Jeremy Bentham, *Fragment on Government and An Introduction to the Principles of Morals and Legislation*, ed. Wilfred Harrison (Oxford: Basil Blackwell, 1967), p. 123.

behind the language to the thing itself, scientific analysis could provide that clarity and precision necessary for a true understanding of political reality. According to Bentham, a science of morality would require that abstract terms be reduced to either their empirical objects or their engendering emotions. This was especially important in the area of political theory; for there, according to Bentham, the use of "fictions" was an all too common practice. As an example of such fictions, Bentham cites "justice," "power," "rights," and "community." In each case, a term is created for which there is no corresponding object in reality. For example, those who use the term "community" speak as if it were a separate entity with its own structure, purpose, and interests. Typically, in such cases, the common good of the community is juxtaposed to the particular interests of the individual citizen. Yet according to Bentham:

> The Community is a fictitious *body*, composed of the individual persons who are considered as constituting as it were its *members*. The interest of the community then is what?—The sum of the interests of the several members who compose it.[3]

It is apparent, then, that for Bentham the political community is essentially the sum of its parts. As such, its good is simply the aggregate of the individual goods of its members, and its principle of order, as a consequence, must be the same as that principle which orders the life of its members. In short, for Bentham, both political and personal order can be explained strictly in utilitarian terms. In appropriating the analytical method, Bentham was forced to reject any attempt to explain complex realities in terms of those higher principles which emerge from the integration of contributing particulars. On the contrary, analysis demands both that the higher principles be reduced to the lower and that the complex be explained in terms of the simple. Accordingly, from this perspective the political community must be explained in terms of its simplest unit, its individual citizens; and similarly, the individual citizens must be explained in terms of their most primitive qualities, the passions:

> Nature has placed mankind under the governance of two sovereign masters, *pain* and *pleasure*. It is for them alone to point out what we ought to do, as well as to determine what we shall do. On one hand the standard of right and wrong, on the other the chain of causes and effects, are fastened to their throne. They govern us in all we do, in all we say, in all we think: every effort we can make to throw off our subjection, will serve but to demonstrate and confirm it.[4]

[3] Bentham, *An Introduction to the Principles of Morals and Legislation*, p. 126.
[4] Bentham, *An Introduction to the Principles of Morals and Legislation*, p. 125.

Bentham's summary of the utilitarian position expressed clearly the two claims of this tradition. First, as a psychological theory, utilitarianism claimed to be able to correctly explain human action. Thus, its major teaching contended that the human being is motivated solely by the desire for pleasure and the corresponding dislike of pain. According to this approach then, human beings are described solely in terms of their instrumental functions. Secondly, as a moral theory, utilitarianism claimed to be able "to rear the fabric of felicity by the hands of reason and of law." Here its primary teaching was that of hedonism. Pleasure is the good; and thus it is both rational and admirable to pursue it. Inasmuch as pleasure is *the* good, there is no other quality which can possibly enhance its moral value. Thus an ethical decision necessarily takes the form of a quantitative calculation which is concerned with acquiring the greater rather than the lesser. As a moral system, then, utilitarianism may be summarized as follows:

> By the principle of utility is meant that principle which approves or disapproves of every action whatsoever, according to the tendency which it appears to have to augment or diminish the happiness [pleasure] of the party whose interest is in question. . . . [5]

Bentham's Fragment on Government

Bentham attempted to illustrate the explanatory power of psychological utilitarianism in his *Fragment on Government*, published in 1776. This work was originally written as a response to a section in William Blackstone's *Commentaries on the Laws of England*. Bentham had attended Blackstone's lectures at Oxford in 1763 and considered his work to be typical of the confused thinking which supported the prejudices of the day. According to Bentham, if serious politico-legal reforms were to be accomplished, it was necessary to explore the theoretical weaknesses within Blackstone's work, because he, in particular, had become one of the most influential legal scholars of the time. Accordingly, Bentham's *Fragment* is devoted to examining Blackstone's understanding of sovereignty, which was originally introduced as a digression during his discussion of municipal law.

In form *Fragment on Government* simply parallels Blackstone's original discussion. As Bentham reconstructs Blackstone's argument, he pauses to call attention to certain ambiguities, fictions, and logical inconsistencies—the combined weight of which is intended to demonstrate Blackstone's general confusion and theoretical inadequacy. In particular, Bentham focuses upon two themes. First, he accuses Blackstone of ignoring the logical distinction between the realm of the *de facto* and that of the *de jure*. The realm of the *de facto* is concerned with the law as it is; as such, it is the task of "expositors" to relate the facts as they see them. The realm of the

---

[5] Bentham, *An Introduction to the Principles of Morals and Legislation*, p. 126.

de jure, on the other hand, is concerned with the law as it ought to be. Here it is the task of "censors" to give reasons justifying their preferences. For Bentham, these two tasks are logically distinct inasmuch as each operates according to its own rules of correct procedure. In Blackstone's *Commentaries*, however, these distinctions are not recognized. Accordingly Bentham accuses Blackstone of arguing in such a way as to present the existing laws as always being justified, that is, the *de facto* is presented as the *de jure*. Consequently from Blackstone's perspective existing English law is necessarily correct and as a result does not require reform.

Bentham's second and major effort was concerned with demonstrating the explanatory power of utilitarianism itself. Like many of his contemporaries Blackstone employed a state-of-nature model in his analysis of political society: here, the sovereign was supposed to have acquired certain "powers" and "rights" in light of the citizens' "promise" to obey as they moved from a "state of nature" to civil society by the means of an "original contract." For Bentham, however, such an explanation appeared to be both unnecessarily clumsy and dependent upon a series of meaningless fictions. For him it was much more accurate to explain the existence of political society strictly in terms of the principle of utility. First, political society, as Bentham had learned from Hume, is characterized by the simple sociological fact that its members are obedient:

> When a number of persons (whom we may style *subjects*) are supposed to be in the *habit* of paying *obedience* to a person, or an assemblage of persons, of a known and certain description (whom we may call *governor* or *governors*) such persons altogether (*subjects* and *governors*) are said to be in a state of *political* SOCIETY.[6]

Second, having established the habit of obedience as the defining characteristic of political existence, Bentham, then, explains the fact of that habit in purely utilitarian terms. Accordingly, citizens obey only because the pain of disobedience is greater than the pain of obeying. Or in other words, citizens keep their promises only because it is in their own self-interest to do so:

> . . . they should obey in short *so long as the probable mischiefs of obedience are less than the probable mischiefs of resistance:* why, in a word, taking the whole body together, it is their *duty* to obey just so long as it is their *interest*, and no longer.[7]

According to Bentham, then, political life can be fully explained in strictly nonpolitical terms. That is to say that through the process of analysis

---

[6] Bentham, *Fragment on Government*, p. 38.
[7] Bentham, *Fragment on Government*, p. 55.

the principles of social order can eventually be reduced to an individual's desire for selfish pleasure. In short, for Bentham, "fictions" have given way to "facts." Yet it is important to note that the "facts" in this case are defined very narrowly so as to include only the data of sensual experience. The higher "facts" of spiritual or moral experience are not recognized. Consequently the analytical adequacy of Bentham's strictly utilitarian explanation presupposed a prior restriction of the range of human phenomena which are to be explained. Specifically the reality of the human spirit is made to disappear inasmuch as it is classified as a mere "fiction." In a certain sense, then, Bentham used the power of an arbitrary definition as a necessary means for securing his scientific logic.

Analysis of An Introduction to the Principles of Morals and Legislation

Bentham's arguments for considering utilitarianism as a moral theory were given their fullest expression in his *An Introduction to the Principles of Morals and Legislation* (1789). Bentham began his *Introduction* by showing how utilitarianism has, in fact, served either explicitly or tacitly as the basis for all principled moral thought. Even philosophical and religious asceticism, which at first glance may appear to be the opposite of the utilitarian view, were in Bentham's mind only misconstrued versions of an ultimately hedonistic ethic.

Although Bentham admitted that the principle of utilitarianism could not be directly proven, he was, nonetheless, convinced of its ultimate truth. Consequently he argued that all principles which differed from utilitarianism were proven by that very difference to be wrong. Secure in this faith, Bentham attempted to apply utilitarian teachings to some of the central issues of political life. In particular, he was interested in the problem of despotism.

According to Bentham despotism existed when governments acted in an arbitrary manner. They acted arbitrarily, in turn, when their decisions were based upon emotions and preferences rather than upon principles and reason. Although few regimes would openly admit to the charge, most according to Bentham were in fact truly despotic. Indeed even those regimes which claimed to represent a moral truth, such as the "natural law" or "natural right," "the will of God," or the "requirements of good order," were in fact despotic because the ambiguities and contradictions of such moral systems simply served to cloak the arbitrary and capricious nature of the government's rule.

As a moral system, utilitarianism argued that the government's sole aim is to foster the pleasure and security of those individuals who constitute the political community. In particular two issues received special consideration. First, how can the government determine the amount of pleasure its various policies will produce? And second, what means are available to the government as it attempts to actualize its plans? The former concern is essentially a matter of calculation; the latter is one of sanction.

In deciding which policies it is to pursue, the government must calculate each action's tendency to augment or diminish the happiness of the party whose interest is in question. Ideally, therefore, the government would be able to quantify and thereby measure the amount of pleasure which any particular action promises. The appeal here is obviously to the precision and objectivity of a purely arithmetical operation. The operation itself, however, is nonetheless somewhat complex. This complexity arises from two sources. First, the quantitative value of a particular pleasure will, to a certain extent, depend upon specific external circumstances. Bentham mentioned seven in particular. Each represents a dimension of value which must be considered in determining the weight of any particular pleasure. These seven elements of pleasure include its intensity, its duration, its certainty or uncertainty, its propinquity or remoteness, the fecundity of the act which produces it, and finally the number of persons who will be affected by it. The second complication arises from the fact that a given act in a given set of circumstances will produce different amounts of pleasure in different individuals because of differing degrees of sensibility. Some people are more susceptible to or more disposed toward certain pleasures than others. Indeed in his survey Bentham mentioned thirty-two different factors which may influence a person's sensibility. Among these were health, strength, sex, age, rank, education, climate, and religious faith. As is evident from this listing, the utilitarian calculation could become a rather prolonged and difficult operation. In acknowledging this, Bentham wrote:

> It is not to be expected that this process should be strictly pursued previously to every moral judgment, or to every legislative or judicial operation. It may, however, be always kept in view: and as near as the process actually pursued on these occasions approaches to it, so near will such process approach to the character of an exact one.[8]

Once having determined its preferred policy, the government is still faced with the task of enforcing its decisions. Specifically, what means are available to the government as it attempts to bring about the greatest happiness of its citizens? For Bentham, the answer is obvious. Just as pleasure is the goal which the government seeks, so, too, is it the means or instrument which the regime can use in approaching its goal. In short, pleasure is both the final and efficient cause in determining human behavior. By granting pleasures or threatening pain the government can in-

---

[8] Bentham, *An Introduction to the Principles of Morals and Legislation*, p. 153.

duce its citizens to act in conformity with its preferred policies. Bentham referred to the sources of pain and pleasure as "sanctions" and distinguished among four types: physical, political, moral, and religious. Specifically, political sanctions are those sources of pleasure and pain which are available to and used by the officials of the regime. Like their moral and religious counterparts, however, they operate through the medium of the physical. That is, all sanctions regardless of their source are based upon the threatened or actual imposition of physical pleasure and pain. According to Bentham, however, the threat of pain is a much more efficient cause than is the promise of pleasure. Thus, as a consequence, the primary means by which a government can promote the general happiness of its citizenry is through the imposition of physical punishment. Given this understanding, a government's general concern to augment society's total happiness is manifested most concretely in its effort to prevent those mischievous acts which would tend to subtract from that sum. Inasmuch as the best means for doing so is the threat of punishment, the basic task of government, according to Bentham, becomes that of creating and maintaining a system of civil and penal laws.

The importance of Bentham's theory of punishment, however, is not restricted to its place within his discussion of political sanctions. On the contrary, for Bentham the theory of punishment actually served as the theoretical foundation for his understanding of legal rights and duties. As a scientific analyst, Bentham had already dismissed the entire natural-rights tradition as a mere verbal fiction. Similarly, as an empirical psychologist, his understanding of people was based upon an examination of human actuality rather than of human potential. Yet, inasmuch as the natural-law tradition based its understanding of human obligation on humanity's natural duty to fulfill its potential, Bentham was forced to reject its teachings. As a consequence, for Bentham there were neither rights nor duties in nature. How, then, do they come to exist in society? To answer this question, Bentham had to reintroduce the concept of punishment. By deciding to punish certain offenses the government creates an obligation that requires that its citizens refrain from certain acts. Inasmuch as citizen A is obligated not to act in a certain way, citizen B has the right to expect that A will fulfill his or her obligation. If A does not, he or she will be punished, and the threat of such punishment acts to secure A's habitual obedience to the law. Such habitual obedience, in turn, has the effect of securing B's rights inasmuch as A has refrained from acting against him or her according to the intention of the original law.

Given this perspective, it is clear that, for Bentham, rights do not exist in nature but rather are derived from obligations. Obligations, in turn, are not found in nature but rather are created by the threat of punishment. Where there is no threat of punishment, there are no obligations. And where there are no obligations, there are no rights. Thus it is clear that Bentham regarded human rights as purely a matter of convention. They are created by the positive law and exist only as long as that law is held in force. The law itself, however, is justified only if it promotes the principle of utility. Thus once again utilitarianism was presented as the necessary and sufficient means for political order.

Earlier it was shown that Bentham's commitment to the method of scientific analysis required that he reduce the realm of the "factual" to include only that aspect of reality which is available to humanity through sensual experience. Similarly, his understanding of the political good seemed to require that the government's role be reduced to simply eliminating mischievous acts. These reductions, however, are related and thus have a common source. Ultimately they can be traced to Bentham's impoverished understanding of human nature. For Bentham the human being is simply the processor of perceptions and the possessor of passions. Lacking a spiritual center Bentham's individual appears be be without spiritual needs. Devoid of spiritual needs, this person thus appears oblivious to the requirements for a spiritual order. As a consequence, Bentham apparently believed that humanity's life could be properly fulfilled at the level of mere biological existence. For Bentham, therefore, sheer life, rather than the good life was the principle of the political order; given this, power replaced virtue as the essential means for accomplishing political ends. It is power which assures us that the utility of obedience will ultimately outweigh the utility of disobedience. If it does not, the habit of obedience will soon weaken, and with its disappearance the political society, by definition, would dissolve. Given such possibilities it is not surprising that utilitarianism tended to be preoccupied with the issue of power. For according to its own tenets, it is power and power alone which establishes the necessary link between the individual governor and the individual citizen.

JOHN STUART MILL

James Mill and the Benthamites

The success of Bentham's work was due in large measure to the efforts of a group of liberal reformers who dedicated themselves to promulgating the teachings of their master. This group included among others the political activist Francis Place, the economist David Ricardo, and the legal theorist John Austin. United by their efforts to support the interests of the emerging middle class, the Benthamites, or Philosophical Radicals, worked for the repeal of those laws which sanctioned and, thereby, secured the traditional privileges of the English landed aristocracy. In their effort to spread Benthamite ideals, they founded the *Westminster Review* in 1824 and established London's University College in 1828. Politically they supported reform in such diverse areas as education, public health, civil law, foreign trade, imperial governance, and public administration. Their greatest success, however, was achieved in 1832 when the right to vote was finally extended to include the more prosperous male members of the commercial and trading classes.

Perhaps the most important of the Philosophical Radicals was the Scott James Mill. Born in 1773 Mill originally prepared himself for a career as a preacher within the Scottish church. However, in 1802, he left the ministry to devote his full energies to the practice of journalism. In 1817 Mill published his three-volume *The History of British India.* The book was an immediate success. It not only brought Mill a certain literary fame but, at the same time, led to his appointment with the East India Company. This appointment, in turn, provided Mill with a steady income and thus allowed him to raise his family of nine while pursuing his literary and political interests.

Mill had met Jeremy Bentham in 1808 and was, as a result, quickly converted to the main principles of utilitarianism. Soon he and Bentham not only became good friends but also formed a close working relationship which was based upon complementary needs. On one hand, Bentham's withdrawn personality and cumbersome writing style had hindered the spread of his doctrines. Mill, on the other hand, possessed a real ability to both systematize and explain utilitarianism's general teachings. Thus the Benthamite circle actually formed around Mill. As a widely read publicist he quickly became the chief representative of the utilitarian school. Both his *Elements of Political Economy* (1821) and his *Analysis of the Phenomena of the Human Mind* (1829) were faithful renderings of utilitarian doctrine. Yet, perhaps the most successful expression of the Benthamite creed can be found in a series of essays which Mill wrote for the *Encyclopedia Britannica* between 1816 and 1823. One of these, his *Essay on Government* (1820), is generally regarded as the definitive statement of traditional utilitarian political theory.

Although Bentham's *Fragment on Government* contained a few hints for a larger, more inclusive, political theory, it was Mill's *Essay* that provided utilitarianism's final political statement. In it, James Mill accepted the fundamental utilitarian assumptions concerning human nature and ethical values. Accordingly, he set himself the task of explaining the proper relationship between the individual and the government in terms of the individual's rational self-interest in happiness. In the utilitarian spirit, Mill assumed that all human behavior could be explained in terms of individual self-interest and that, subsequently, the common good was nothing more than the aggregate sum of all the particular goods of the individual citizens. Given this, it appeared that the purpose of government was to pursue the greatest happiness of the greatest number. This, in turn, could best be done by allowing individuals to secure those objects whose possession gave them pleasure. In other words, government existed to support individuals' attempts to satisfy their desires. Inasmuch as this attempt generally requires labor, a government which is concerned with promoting the greatest happiness of the greatest number is, in effect, practically concerned with securing for each individual as much of the product of his or her labor as possible. In short, happiness increases to the degree that each individual is free to acquire as much wealth and pleasure as personal talents allow. To do so, of course, it is necessary that the individual's private property be protected from the designs of other people. Thus government arises primarily as a means for protecting the property of its citizens and thereby insuring that all individuals can pursue their own self-interests without undue interference from others.

> That one human being will desire to render the person and property of another subservient to his pleasures, notwithstanding the pain or loss of pleasure which it may occasion to that individual, is the foundation of government.[9]

Given this understanding as to the true character of the political relationship, the obvious concern is that of power. Individuals will exploit one another if they have the power to do so. To prevent such a development, the government must be in a position to exert as much opposing power as is necessary to deny the utility of such an attempt. For James Mill, therefore, government was essentially a reservoir of power which is necessary to maintain an arena for competition among individuals who are pursuing their own selfish interests. Yet placing sufficient power in the hands of public officials creates an unavoidable dilemma. Public officials, like all other citizens, are motivated by their own selfish interest in happiness. Thus, given the opportunity, they, too, will attempt to render all others subservient to their own will.

In short, Mill had reintroduced the ancient problem of who will guard the guardians. Whereas classical theorists attempted to solve this dilemma through a program of moral education which would produce virtuous and moderate leaders who were capable of controlling their selfish interests, Mill accepted such interests as the very foundation for his preferred regime. According to Mill's argument, if the interests of the political authorities can be made to coincide with those of the citizens, then in pursuing

---

[9] James Mill, *Essay on Government*, ed. Currin V. Shields (Indianapolis: Bobbs-Merrill, 1955), p. 56.

one the officials are necessarily pursuing the other. In Mills's view, such a coincidence of interest occurs only in a representative government where there are frequent elections based upon adult male suffrage. In such a situation, either elected representatives promote the interests of their constituents by checking the abuses of the governors or they suffer the consequence of being turned out of office. Thus governmental responsibility is assured not by an appeal to honor or virtue but by representatives' own calculations as to how they can best obtain the offices they desire. For the Benthamites, the utility of such calculations presupposed that logic which was built into the operation of representative institutions. It was, however, a logic ultimately based upon the realities of self-interest and power. Yet power and self-interest are essentially abstractions. Within the Benthamite calculus they do not refer to the concrete experience of particular human beings. Rather they are the units within an abstract mathematical operation which is oblivious to the particulars of time and place. As a consequence, the Benthamite solution to the problems of political order exhibited a certain rationalistic and ultimately mechanical quality. Given this quality, Benthamite political theory was entirely consistent with the utilitarian view of human nature. Humanity was understood to be uniform, predictable, and consistent. This, in turn, allowed the Benthamites to believe that they had discovered the general laws of human behavior and thereby could eventually establish a rigorous science of human governance. Yet, ironically, it was precisely this description of humanity as a rational machine which provoked the reformist efforts of that person who was originally intended to be the greatest of all the utilitarians, John Stuart Mill—the son of James Mill.

Life and Writings of John Stuart Mill

In his *Autobiography*, (published in the year of his death, 1873) which he wrote with his stepdaughter, Helen Taylor, John Stuart Mill gave an account of his intellectual training and of his career as a writer and scholar. His father had decided that John Stuart should be thoroughly educated according to Benthamite principles, and consequently, in cooperation with Bentham, devised "an unusual and remarkable" curriculum for his eldest son. Kept from other children and with his father as his tutor, Mill learned Greek by the age of three. Subsequently he studied arithmetic, history, and Latin, and at twelve he began the study of logic, political economy, and analytical psychology. In 1820, he went to France to stay with the brother of Jeremy Bentham. Upon his return later that year, he studied law under the guidance of John Austin who would eventually become the first professor of jurisprudence at the newly founded Benthamite University College, London. At sixteen, Mill's period of planned instruction ended as he joined his father as a junior clerk in the India Office. The effect of this rigorous training was precisely what James Mill intended. His son had become a dedicated disciple of Jeremy Bentham:

> The "principle of utility" understood as Bentham understood it, and applied in the manner in which he applied it . . . fell exactly into its place as the keystone which held together the detached and fragmentary component parts of my knowledge and beliefs. It gave unity to my conceptions of things. I now had opinions; a creed, a doctrine, a philosophy; in one among the best senses of the word, a religion; the inculcation and diffusion of which could be made the principal outward purpose of a life.[10]

While John Stuart Mill's education had exposed him to the fundamental dogma of a particular creed, it also had the inevitable effect of shaping his personality according to the standards implicit in such dogma. Consequently, according to his own description, Mill had become a "reasoning machine." Beginning in 1826 and lasting about five years, Mill suffered through a period of depression and mental torment. During that time, he came to realize that Bentham's mechanistic and universalistic conception of human nature had failed to appreciate the individual's need to develop his emotional and personal faculties. In short, Bentham failed to realize the importance of those individual and unique qualities that combine to form the human personality. An educational program that ignored such features eventually permits them to atrophy. And a political system which ignores them is essentially incapable of producing that happiness which all utilitarians considered to be fundamental.

The Revision of Utilitarian Ethics

John Stuart Mill continued to proclaim his allegiance to utilitarian principles. But at the same time Mill sought to introduce a series of necessary reforms. First, the Benthamite view of humanity had to be enlarged to include an appreciation of such things as the human spirit, the human conscience, and human idealism. Similarly, the utilitarian view of society would have to be expanded so that it could address itself to such issues as society's interest in humanity's self-education and the nation's concern for its own spiritual character. In any case, however, such reforms necessarily presupposed a reconsideration of utilitarianism's most fundamental concept: pleasure.

In an essay entitled *Utilitarianism*, published in 1863, Mill attempted both to defend utilitarianism from its critics and to expand the notion of pleasure to support what he felt were necessary reforms. In his at-

---

[10] John Stuart Mill, *Autobiography* (Indianapolis: Bobbs-Merrill, 1957), p. 44.

tempt to establish a mathematical calculus, Bentham had implied that pleasure was simply a quantitative concept. As *the* good, the value of pleasure could not be increased by bringing any other quality to it. More pleasure was better than less simply because of the amount involved. A distinction among types of pleasure, however, presupposed qualitative differences and, therefore, was unacceptable. For Mill, on the other hand, utilitarianism did not require such a limitation. As a utilitarian, he believed that it was possible to make qualitative distinctions and indeed argued for the recognition of a fundamental qualitative difference between intellectual and sensual pleasure:

> It is quite compatible with the principle of utility to recognise the fact, that some *kinds* of pleasure are more desirable and more valuable than others. It would be absurd that while, in estimating all other things, quality is considered as well as quantity, the estimation of pleasures should be supposed to depend on quantity alone . . . . It is better to be a human being dissatisfied than a pig satisfied; better to be Socrates dissatisfied than a fool satisfied.[11]

In creating a scale from the animal to the human and from the foolish to the wise, it is obvious that Mill is suggesting that the value of pleasure is increased by the presence of intellectual activity. It is not simply that intellectual activity increases the amount, permanency, or fecundity of pleasure; for such changes are purely of a quantitative nature. Rather, according to Mill, intellectual pleasure is superior because of the kind of pleasure which it is.

Although Mill, himself, was convinced that the recognition of qualitative distinctions among pleasures was consistent with utilitarianism, his arguments are not necessarily persuasive. By admitting that some pleasures are superior in kind to others, Mill is claiming that there is a source of value other than pleasure itself. Inasmuch as the absence or presence of the active intellect adds to or detracts from the value of pleasure, it is obvious that pleasure alone is not the sole source of value. Something other than mere pleasure is good, and pleasure alone, consequently, cannot be *the* good simply. Whereas Mill's distinction between Socrates and the fool may appeal to common sense, it is difficult to justify such a distinction on strictly utilitarian grounds.

In differentiating between the sphere of the intellectual and the realm of the physical, Mill reintroduced a fundamental theme of classical political philosophy. Indeed for the ancient Greeks the central problem of political order was based upon the fact that, as complex beings, humans

---

[11] Mary Warnock, ed., *John Stuart Mill: Utilitarianism, On Liberty, Essay on Bentham* (New York: New American Library, n.d.), pp. 258–60.

have both spiritual and physical needs. Participating in both the transcendent and mundane poles of reality, humanity requires various goods which are different in kind. Thus it is faced with the constant challenge of creating a harmonious personal and social order. Typically for the Greeks such a harmony was achieved by recognizing a certain rank among humankind's interests and needs and, consequently, subordinating the lower to the higher. Thus, in the classical spirit, Mill proposed a similar solution. The intellectual pleasures are not only different from their physical counterparts but are, at the same time, superior in kind to them. The good life, therefore, is the rational life, and the good society is the one which elicits and supports the life of reason among its citizens.

Mill's emphasis upon the relationship of reason to politics has led some commentators to suggest that there is a certain similarity between his thinking and that of Aristotle. Indeed such comparisons find further evidence in the fact that Mill, like Aristotle, argued that existing societies should be directed towards a realization of the "best polity." Thus, unlike many of his contemporaries, Mill drew his model of political order from an understanding of what was required for the "ideal" society. In doing so, he broke from a tradition that can be traced back through such thinkers as Bentham, Hobbes, and Machiavelli. As we have seen these men had argued that political order must be created according to an understanding of the human being as it appears in actuality rather than as it is potentially. Mill, on the other hand, like the Greeks, sought to govern the lower in light of the higher. Accordingly, from this perspective, an ethical education should be modeled after Socrates rather than after the fool, and a political society should be constructed in view of the rational polity rather than according to the "merely *business* part of the social arrangements." [12]

Both Mill's concern for the relationship between reason and politics and the "idealism" of his political writings do, indeed, suggest a certain similarity with the Greeks. Yet the basic character of his work becomes clear only if one is aware of what actually distinguishes Mill from the classical tradition. This becomes apparent if one looks at those arguments which Mill introduced to support his position that the intellectual pleasures are superior in kind. Essentially, he based his arguments for reason upon an appeal to opinion:

> Of two pleasures, if there be one to which all or almost all who have experience of both give a decided preference . . . that is the more desirable pleasure . . . . Now it is an unquestionable fact that those who are equally acquainted with, and equally capable of appreciating and enjoying, both, do give a most marked preference to the manner of existence which employs their higher faculties. [13]

[12] Warnock, *John Stuart Mill*, p. 105.
[13] Warnock, *John Stuart Mill*, p. 259.

In short, Mill is appealing to the *fact* that people prefer the intellectual life in order to argue for the claim that they *ought* to do so. Yet, this form of argumentation necessarily overlooks the differences that exist between the realm of the empirical and the realm of the moral. Logically, it is difficult to establish that what people, in fact, do can at the same time legitimately proscribe what, in theory, they ought to do. By emphasizing that the great majority of intellectuals are happy with their lot, Mill is, in effect, simply giving a statistical argument.

The classical tradition, on the other hand, based its justification of the rational life on metaphysical grounds. Accordingly people ought to pursue the life of reason because such a pursuit was intended by the very structure of human nature itself. For the Greeks the soul was intended for reason. Thus humanity's obligation to live the rational life was given by nature and, as a consequence, existed regardless of whether individuals factually fulfilled their obligations or not. Mill, on the contrary, does not rely upon such an argument because, unlike the Greeks, he does not believe in the possibility of metaphysical truth. For Mill, reason is empirical not transcendental. And thus when he called for the life of reason or evoked the ideal of the rational polity, he had a radically different intention than did either Plato or Aristotle.

Analysis of A System of Logic

Mill's understanding of reason was clearly expressed in his *A System of Logic*, published in 1843. The purpose of the book was to show that all knowledge must be based upon empirical experience. In particular, it attempted to argue against those who claimed that intuition could serve as a possible source of knowledge. The intuitionists, according to Mill, had maintained that certain mathematical, metaphysical, and moral principles were necessarily innate. Mill, on the other hand, was an empiricist. Accordingly, for him all knowledge rested ultimately upon experience, and the purpose of all science was to establish the antecedent causes for each empirical event. Although the various methods scientists chose ultimately depended upon the particular objects each was studying, the primary and common technique was that of inductive reasoning. Where appropriate, deduction was acceptable, but it always had to be informed by that data which induction alone made available. In the social sciences, in particular, two methods were considered to be both appropriate and necessary. First, in such disciplines as political economy, where one is seeking to determine the effect of a particular change within the given conditions of a particular society, Mill recommended the concrete deductive method, which he modeled after the practices of the astronomer. Second, in those disciplines where one is seeking to discover how entire states of society develop and evolve, Mill recommended the inverse deductive or historical method, which he borrowed from Auguste Comte. Together these two methods formed the basis for all of social science. In other words, for Mill, the highest form of social knowledge was contained in the philosophy of history. Reason, empirically understood, could comprehend the laws of succession which condition historical evolution, but it could not in principle transcend the historical realm itself. Accordingly human reason can know material and efficient causation but cannot know formal and final causes. It can determine the means which are appropriate for achieving a given end but cannot decide among the ends in themselves. In short, for Mill, reason was defined in strictly instrumental terms:

> A scientific observer or reasoner, merely as such, is not an adviser for practice. His part is only to show that certain consequences follow from certain causes, and that to obtain certain ends, certain means are the most effectual. Whether the ends themselves are such as ought to be pursued and if so, in what cases and to how great a length, it is not part of his business as a cultivator of science to decide, and science alone will never qualify him for the decision.[14]

It should be clear, then, that what Mill meant by reason was fundamentally different than which was understood by the classical tradition. For the Greeks, reason was that source of spiritual order which allowed the human being to participate in and be transformed by an experience of transcendence. The best polity, consequently, was that which encouraged such spiritual achievements and structured itself accordingly. For Mill, on the other hand, reason had simply become the ability to calculate. As an instrumental power, it allowed humans to efficiently manipulate the immanent order. Thus the rational polity was, in fact, one which was dedicated to the practice of modern science. By so defining reason, Mill, in effect, transformed Plato's original philosopher into his own image, that is, that of the modern intellectual. In view of this, it is not surprising that Mill's political theory was primarily concerned with creating a social environment that would encourage such a transformed human to prosper. Human prosperity, in turn, was defined primarily in terms of historical progress and intellectual improvement. For Mill humankind was a progressive species. As such, it was capable of entering into a higher form of civilization which would be characterized both by individual liberty and intellectual consensus. In a vision which was obviously inspired by progressivist beliefs, Mill foresaw:

> . . . a future which shall unite the best qualities of the critical with the best qualities of the organic periods; unchecked liberty of

14 Henry M. Magid, ed., *On the Logic of the Moral Sciences: A System of Logic*, Book VI (Indianapolis: Bobbs-Merrill, 1965), pp. 145–46.

thought, unbounded freedom of individual action in all modes not hurtful to others; but also convictions as to what is right and wrong, useful and pernicious, deeply engraven on the feelings by early education and general unanimity of sentiment, and so firmly grounded in reason and in the true exigencies of life, that they shall not, like all former and present creeds, religious, ethical, and political, require to be periodically thrown off and replaced by others.[15]

However, inasmuch as Mill saw his own age as one of "loud disputes but generally weak convictions," it was obvious to him that any significant human improvement would ultimately depend upon the possibility of an historical emancipation.[16] This emancipation was, in turn, the central theme of two of Mill's most important books, *On Liberty* and *Considerations on Representative Government.*

Analysis of On Liberty

Published in 1859, Mill's *On Liberty* was intended to be both a utilitarian and a progressivist tract. In the spirit of utilitarianism, it attempted to examine the necessary conditions of human happiness. Yet, in the spirit of progressivism, its understanding of human happiness was one which presupposed "utility in its largest sense, grounded on the permanent interests of a man as a progressive being."[17] Thus inasmuch as humankind was an evolving rather than a fixed species, all calculations concerning happiness had to take into account the prospect for human improvement. Programs which promoted the advance of civilization were legitimate because they contributed to social excellence. Similarly, once a specific program had achieved its purpose and raised the civilizational level of a particular society, that program, thereby, lost its original justifying rationale. Mill, for example, believed that political despotism was a legitimate form of government for those societies which had not yet evolved beyond the level of cultural barbarism. However, once its citizens had become capable of being improved by free and equal discussion, the despotic regime no longer served a progressive function and, according to Mill, should be replaced by a more liberal form of rule. Similarly, such liberal institutions and practices as constitutionalism and the recognition of political rights were appropriate techniques for securing intellectual progress in the more modern societies of Europe. Yet, as means to an end, their real value depended upon the efficiency with which they performed their function. Thus in those cases where progress demanded additional safeguards, new techniques would have to

[15] Mill, *Autobiography*, p. 107.
[16] Mill, *Autobiography*, p. 107.
[17] Warnock, *John Stuart Mill*, p. 136.

be developed. This, according to Mill, was the situation in England during his own time.

In Mill's analysis, the traditional concern of liberal political theory had been to restrict the range of state power. Thus Anglo-American liberal theory had succeeded in subordinating the state to society by promoting the doctrine of political rights and encouraging the recognition of constitutionalism. In time, however, the liberal promotion of society over the state evolved in such a way as to create its own particular challenge to progress. Specifically, now that society had succeeded in capturing the government, the numerical majority was placed in the position of exercising a tyrannical power over any given minority. This power was most apparent in the realm of ideas. For Mill, social progress was essentially the result of intellectual development. Such development, in turn, presupposed that individuals would be allowed to question and challenge the most respected elements of public opinion. Thus, for Mill, real cultural progress required that the state not only tolerate but actually foster and protect the practice of individual criticism and dissent.

In the realm of ideas such dissent should be unlimited because, by its very nature, dissent served utility. If an orthodox belief were false, dissent promoted utility by serving truth. If an orthodox opinion were correct, dissent served truth by fostering debate and thereby reaffirming one's commitment to the orthodoxy on intellectual grounds. Finally, if both the orthodox belief and the dissenting opinion reflected partial aspects of the whole truth, utility was ultimately served by their mutually corrective effect upon one another. In each case, then, according to Mill, intellectual dissent promoted social progress.

Mill's concern to protect dissent went beyond the realm of pure thought. Indeed, he extended his principle of liberty so as to include the public expression of private ideas. It is obvious that such public expression moves one toward the realm of action and thereby raises a series of questions. Yet, because Mill believed that the liberty of thought was so closely related to the liberty of speaking and writing, it was inconceivable to him that it was possible to limit one without at the same time limiting the other.

Eventually, the realm of action is fully and finally entered when one attempts to carry out dissident ideas and beliefs. Here, then, Mill admitted that the principle of absolute liberty must be abandoned. Because of their effects, actions cannot be as free as thoughts. Yet here, too, progress demands that society permit as much freedom in action as is possible. Thus Mill wrote:

> That principle is, that the sole end for which mankind are warranted, individually or collectively, in interfering with the liberty of action of any of their number, is self-protection. That the only purpose for which power can be rightfully exercised over any mem-

ber of a civilised community, against his will, is to prevent harm to others. His own good, either physical or moral, is not a sufficient warrant.[18]

This argument presupposed a distinction between self-regarding and other-regarding actions. Self-regarding actions were those which directly and in the first instance affected only the individual actors themselves. According to Mill, society has no legitimate interest in monitoring such acts. Other-regarding actions, on the other hand, were those which directly and immediately affected someone other than the actors themselves. In those cases, Mill acknowledged that society was permitted to act in order to protect its members from harm and, thereby, promote the greatest happiness of the greatest number. In both instances, however, the role of government was strictly limited. For Mill, the classical belief that the state was concerned with the creation of human and social order in both its temporal and spiritual aspects was simply untenable. This was so primarily because of his concern for the preservation of individuality.

Mill's commitment to individualism introduced a certain ambiguity into his work. On one hand, he defended individualism in strictly instrumental terms. Accordingly, individuality was to be valued inasmuch as it served utility. Yet, at other times, Mill appeared to treat individualism as if it were a value in and of itself. Thus on one occasion he spoke of it as having "an intrinsic worth," and on another he praised nonconformity because it was different even if not better. Now, if "better" is defined in utilitarian terms as Mill insisted, then "being different" must be praiseworthy and, hence, valuable in its own right. In either case, however, there is no doubt as to the importance which individualism had for Mill.

Mill's appreciation of individuality obviously implied a specific view of human nature. Seen as individuals, human beings are characterized more by what sets each apart from others than by what each shares with all in common. Given such diversity, there can be no single model for humanity's spiritual development. Thus, for Mill, the human being is essentially self-defined, and, as a consequence, authenticity rather than virtue becomes the preeminent mode of human excellence. This emphasis upon authenticity becomes especially clear if one compares Mill's understanding of reason with that of the classical Greeks. Whereas the classical tradition understood reason as the means by which the person participated in the community of being, Mill, on the contrary, sees it primarily as a means of self-expression:

> There is no reason that all human existence should be constructed on some one or some small number of patterns. If a person possesses

---

[18] Warnock, *John Stuart Mill*, p. 135.

any tolerable amount of common sense and experience, his own mode of laying out his existence is the best, not because it is the best in itself, but because it is his own mode.[19]

Indeed, the traditional argument that there was one pattern for human existence was ultimately based upon the idea of a set human nature. Similarly the traditional attempt to find the best mode for laying out one's existence presupposed that the needs of that nature determined what was desirable and appropriate for it. However, in his advocacy of eccentricity, Mill effectively questioned the validity of both presuppositions. This challenge, in turn, created certain problems for his own thinking. If humanity has neither a set nature nor a specifically appropriate way of life, the question arises as to what ultimately is the end or goal of that pattern of progress which appears to underlie all of Mill's thought? Humanity cannot be progressing towards a more humane era if humanity, itself, has no standards or limits. Thus the ambiguity implicit within Mill's individualistic conception of personality is repeated on a larger scale as the ambiguity of history itself.

Analysis of Considerations on Representative Government

The importance that history be understood as a process of emancipation and progress is shown once again in John Stuart Mill's *Considerations on Representative Government*, written for the most part in 1860. According to Mill, the quality of a government ultimately depends upon its ability to improve its people. That is to say, the purpose of government is to promote progress on the basis of order. This is best achieved, however, when the people are allowed to actively exercise their talents and thereby develop new skills and abilities. Logically then, Mill's emphasis on an active citizenry implied a governmental system which would encourage a large degree of political participation. Whereas despotism with its emphasis upon such passive qualities as obedience may be appropriate for backward nations, Mill believed that civilized societies require that their citizens actively participate in governing so that they may progress even further. Thus once a society has reached that stage of civilization wherein the desire not to have power exercised over oneself is greater than the desire to exercise power over others, it has achieved that particular moral condition which suits it for popular government. Ideally such a government would allow for all people to share in the exercise of sovereign power. Practically, however, Mill believed that such a situation could exist only among the smallest political units—such as a small town. Thus given the fact that modern

---

[19] Warnock, *John Stuart Mill*, p. 197.

civilization seems to require the large nation-state, a representative form of government appears to be the best that is possible.

Having argued on behalf of both political participation and representative government, Mill was anxious, nonetheless, to distinguish his ideal regime from the American model of representative democracy. According to Mill, the American model was, in fact, an example of a false democracy which merely represented the interests of the majority rather than the will of all. Influenced by his reading of Alexis de Tocqueville's *Democracy in America*, Mill feared that the form of popular democracy practiced in America would eventually undermine the very conditions of progress which make self-government possible in the first place. Progress, according to Mill, depended upon the intellectual and moral excellence of a few select geniuses. Accordingly, the unique individual who was capable of leading the masses was the key to social emancipation. Yet, in America, popular sovereignty was practiced in such a way as to threaten true individuality. According to Mill, the radically democratic insistence upon political equality and majority rule eventually would result in a fundamentally egalitarian society. Such a society, in turn, would negate the very conditions of future progress. In short, Mill sought to strike a compromise. On one hand, he continued to share in the Benthamite commitment to popular self-rule. On the other hand, he was convinced by the Saint-Simonist argument that the true interest of all the people was best served in a society which was governed by those experts who knew the "true principles" of political science. Inasmuch as a methodologically rigorous political science could achieve valid insights into the requirements for political order, it seemed only sensible that those who possessed such knowledge should be in the position of serving the community as a whole.

Mill's compromise between democracy and elitism was based upon his prior distinction between the act of governing and the act of controlling. Actual governing should be left to the experts. Inasmuch as the executive, administrative, and legislative functions of government presuppose highly trained and skilled practitioners, they are best left to those experts who are protected from the uninformed demands of the general populace. Thus, according to Mill, a true democracy does not require that the power of governing rest with the people. At most, democratic theory demands that the people ultimately retain the sovereign power of controlling those who govern. Accordingly, Mill suggested that a popularly elected representative assembly should be established in order to oversee and control the performance of the governing elite. Such an assembly would not only serve as a forum for ideas and opinion but, at the same time, would watch over and control the professional elite by approving or rejecting their legislative proposals. In effect, then, Mill sought to establish a "skilled democracy" wherein governing power was at least two steps removed from the people at large.

According to Mill's analysis, representative self-government faced two essential challenges. First, there was the problem of sheer governmental incompetence. And, second, there was the possibility that popular legislation which was theoretically intended for the benefit of all would, in fact, become mere class legislation which favored either the capitalist or working class exclusively. In the hopes of minimizing such possibilities, Mill suggested a number of reforms. First, in order to insure that minorities would be adequately represented in the popular assembly, Mill advocated the practice of proportional representation. By rejecting the arrangement by which the majority alone determined the representatives from a geographical district, Mill's scheme assured that each minority could be represented according to its proportion of the total vote. Second, in order to insure that everyone's interests were represented, Mill favored extending the franchise far beyond the current British practice. He did, however, allow for certain qualifications. Thus a voter had to be able to read and write and should, at the same time, be a taxpayer. Consequently those on relief or aid would not be permitted to vote. Third, inasmuch as class legislation was due, in part, to short-sighted ignorance, Mill advocated a scheme for weighted voting. Although all qualified voters should be heard, Mill did not believe that all should be heard equally. Thus those who were mentally superior should be allowed to cast more than one ballot. Such a program, according to Mill, would give preponderance to reason and intelligence rather than to mere numbers. Finally, in order to promote responsibility among both the representatives and the voters, Mill favored direct rather than indirect elections and open rather than secret balloting. In both cases, the intent was to increase public spirit and, thereby, strengthen the role of political intelligence.

BIBLIOGRAPHY

ANSCHUTZ, R. P. *The Philosophy of J. S. Mill*. Oxford: Oxford University Press, 1953.

BAUMGARDT, DAVID. *Bentham and the Ethics of Today*. Princeton: Princeton University Press, 1952.

HALEVY, ELIE. *The Growth of Philosophical Radicalism*. Translated by Mary Morris. London: Faber & Faber, 1949.

HAMBURGER, JOSEPH. *Intellectuals in Politics: John Stuart Mill and the Philosophical Radicals*. New Haven: Yale University Press, 1965.

HIMMELFARB, GERTRUDE. *On Liberty and Liberalism: The Case of John Stuart Mill*. New York: Alfred Knopf, 1974.

MACCOBY, SIMON. *English Radicalism: 1832–1852*. Chicago: University of Chicago Press, 1935.

MACK, MARY. *Jeremy Bentham: An Odyssey of Ideas*. London: Heinemann, 1962.

MACPHERSON, C. B. *The Life and Times of Liberal Democracy*. Oxford: Oxford University Press, 1977.

McCLOSKEY, HENRY J. *John Stuart Mill: A Critical Study*. London: MacMillan, 1971.

PACKE, MICHAEL ST. JOHN. *The Life of John Stuart Mill*. New York: Macmillan, 1954.

PAREKH, BHIKHU, ed. *Jeremy Bentham: Ten Critical Essays*. London: Frank Cass, 1974.

PLAMENATZ, JOHN. *The English Utilitarians*. Oxford: Blackwell, 1949.

RYAN, ALAN. *John Stuart Mill*. New York: Pantheon Books, 1970.

STEPHEN, LESLIE. *The English Utilitarians*. 3 vols. London: Duckworth & Co., 1900.

WILLEY, BASIL. *Nineteenth Century Studies*. London: Chatto & Windus, 1949.

15

SOURCES OF MARXISM

With the development of socialism as a major political movement during the nineteenth and twentieth centuries, it has become increasingly important for both its critics and supporters to comprehend its claims as clearly as possible. Scholars accordingly have turned to the task of analyzing the central tenets of the socialist tradition. Often in doing so, they have searched for various historical precedents in the hope of clarifying the specific meaning of what may be at times a vague and abstract doctrine. For example, some historians have argued that one could find instances of socialism in the traditions of ancient Greece. As examples, they could point to selected arguments in Plato's *Republic* and to certain practices in the traditions of Sparta and Crete. Similarly others have suggested that the Mosaic law of the Old Testament and certain Christian doctrines, especially those found in the writings of St. Luke and Thomas Aquinas, could be interpreted as part of a continuing socialist development.

In general, however, such efforts have not proven particularly helpful. In many cases the interpretations of Plato or Thomas as protosocialists have been somewhat strained and therefore less than convincing.

More importantly, however, by positing the existence of a continuous tradition of Western socialism such arguments tend to distract one from those concrete events and specific circumstances which surrounded its emergence in the eighteenth and nineteenth centuries. This is important because to a significant degree socialism is a particularly modern phenomenon. Historically it arose under the combined influence of the Industrial and French Revolutions, and theoretically it accepted the essentially modern commitment to fundamental human equality.

UTOPIAN SOCIALISM

In 1880 Karl Marx's collaborator, Friedrich Engels, published a pamphlet entitled, *Socialism: Scientific and Utopian.* The booklet was originally intended as an aid for distinguishing between Marx's version of socialism and the alternate varieties against which it was competing at the time. Central to Engels's argument was the claim that Marxist socialism was based upon an understanding of the real "material economic facts." Thus unlike its "utopian" competitors Marxism's doctrines were the result of an historical discovery and not simply the end-product of an evolution of ideas. Its validity, therefore, was derived from the scientific insight upon which it was based, and it was, as a consequence, essentially independent of its own historical evolution. Nonetheless after having argued this case Engels wrote:

> But, in its theoretical form, modern socialism [Marxism] originally appears ostensibly as a more logical extension of the principles laid down by the great French philosophers of the eighteenth century. Like every new theory, modern socialism had, at first, to connect itself with the intellectual stock-in-trade ready to its hand, however deeply its roots lay in material economic facts.[1]

Thus having recognized this situation, Engels devoted the rest of his essay to an analysis of Marxism's theoretical precedents. As such *Socialism: Scientific and Utopian* serves as the central document for any discussion of the sources of Marxism.

Before examining the writings of the utopian socialists Engels called attention to certain historical events which were important for the development of socialist thinking and the creation of the proletarian class. According to Marx the proletariat emerged fully only within capitalism. Thus its development as a class depended upon the development and growth of the capitalist economic and social system. In order for capitalism

[1] Robert C. Tucker, ed., *The Marx-Engels Reader* (New York: W. W. Norton & Co., 1972), p. 605.

to grow, however, it had first to overthrow and destroy the remnants of feudalism. This, in turn, required that the bourgeoisie successfully replace the nobility as the dominant class within society. The history of this struggle between these two classes included such events as the Peasant Wars in Germany (1524–1526), the English Revolution of 1688, and the French Revolution of 1789. Although each of these events was essentially a part of the bourgeoisie's campaign against feudalism, Engels discovered within each a prototypical example of a developing workers movement. Specifically he mentioned the Anabaptist movement which was organized during the German Peasant Wars by Thomas Muentzer (1488–1525), the Leveller Movement (1647–1650) within the English Civil War which attempted to steer the liberal revolution in a more radically democratic direction, and the Conspiracy of Equals led by Gracchus Babeuf (1760–1797) which plotted against the French Directory on behalf of the abolition of private property. In each case, however, the fledgling worker's movements failed; and they did so, according to Engels, for essentially the same reason. As forerunners of the modern proletariat none of the movements had, in fact, the necessary support of the appropriate economic class. Inasmuch as the proletariat had not yet fully evolved, it was not yet capable of acting in an historically decisive manner. Thus rather than being examples of a truly revolutionary working-class movement, these instances were actually premature outbursts which gave early expression to forces still in need of further development.

Likewise, just as the proletariat was not yet in a position to act decisively, so, too, was the proletarian theory of that time limited by its immature form. As examples of prototypical, yet immature, socialist theory Engels referred to the literary utopias of Thomas More (1478–1535) and Tommaso Campanella (1568–1639). In addition he mentioned the communist schemes of such French theorists as the Abbe de Mably (1709–1785) and Morelly, who published his *Code de la Nature* in 1755. Although both men wrote total critiques of society and appear, in fact, to have influenced the conspiratorial politics of Babeuf, neither developed any specific relationship with the industrial working class.

Of all the individuals whom Engels included under the category "founders of socialism," special treatment was reserved for those he called "the three great utopians." By this he meant Henri de Saint-Simon, Charles Fourier, and Robert Owen. Each in his own way introduced a theme of analysis which would later be appropriated and developed by Marx. Thus, although Marxism cannot be reduced to a mere compilation or synthesis of their ideas, there is little doubt that the "utopians" played an important role in the formation of Marx's system. However, in spite of this debt Engels was, nonetheless, anxious to demonstrate the important differences between Marx's scientific socialism and that of his utopian predecessors. According to Engels they, unlike Marx, were the victims of a naive faith which relied more upon the inventions of reason than upon a careful analysis of economic and historical forces:

> One thing is common to all three. Not one of them appears as a representative of the interests of that proletariat which historical development had, in the meantime, produced. Like the French philosophers, they do not claim to emancipate a particular class to begin with, but all humanity at once . . . . For, to our three social reformers, the bourgeois world, based upon the principles of these philosophers, is quite as irrational and unjust, and, therefore, finds its way to the dust-hole quite as readily as feudalism and all the earlier stages of society. If pure reason and justice have not, hitherto, ruled the world, this has been the case only because men have not rightly understood them. What was wanted was the individual man of genius, who has now arisen and who understands the truth. That he has now arisen, that the truth has now been clearly understood, is not an inevitable event, following of necessity in the chain of historical development, but a mere happy accident.[2]

Henri de Saint-Simon

Saint-Simon (1760–1825) was the eldest of nine children born to an aristocratic French family. In spite of his background, however, he soon developed a sympathy for the revolutionary causes of his day. In 1777 he entered the French army and two years later sailed to America to fight in the Revolutionary War. At home he did not fight in the French Revolution, but he did follow it with enthusiasm and voluntarily exchanged his aristocratic title for the egalitarian one of "citizen." After an initially successful career as a land speculator, Saint-Simon turned to a life of philosophy and supported himself by selling subscriptions to a series of journals which he founded with the assistance of such secretaries as August Comte and Augustin Thierry. Toward the end of his life Saint-Simon suffered through a bitter feud with his protege August Comte and attempted suicide in 1823. He died two years later.

Saint-Simon's writings are both fragmentary and incomplete. This was due, in part, to the fact that he wrote primarily as a publicist and, therefore, was faced with the responsibility of responding to a variety of rapidly changing issues. For example, his writings covered such topics as suggesting the digging of the Panama Canal, planning the construction of roads and waterways in Spain and Holland, and weighing the merits of a national bank for France. Among his philosophical and political works, however, it is generally agreed that his most important are *Letters from an*

---

[2] Tucker, *The Marx-Engels Reader*, p. 607.

Inhabitant of Geneva, The Reorganization of the European Community, and *New Christianity.* For the purposes of an overview, it is possible to group Saint-Simon's writings into four general periods. From 1800 to 1813 he was primarily concerned with the attempt to construct a unified system of a priori, deductive knowledge built upon Newton's law of gravity. Between 1814 and 1816 he turned his energies towards advocating the development of a European political community. From 1816 to 1825 Saint-Simon was chiefly concerned with analyzing and defending the political and cultural principles of the emerging industrial order. Not surprisingly, it is the work of this particular period which latter-day socialists found to be of interest. Finally in the year of his death, 1825, Saint-Simon began to outline what he considered to be the model for a new and reformed Christianity.

According to Saint-Simon Christianity was in need of a thorough reform because both Roman Catholicism and contemporary Protestantism had evolved into heretical versions of the original Christian truth. For Saint-Simon, primitive Christianity was essentially a moral system. Consequently both the practice of worship and the various theological doctrines were originally intended only to remind the faithful of their binding moral obligations. As such, the essence of true Christianity could be summarized in the moral demand to "Treat each other as brothers." According to Saint-Simon, however, this original command could be formulated in an even more precise manner. Accordingly he wrote:

> Now according to this principle which God gave to men to guide their conduct, they should organize their society in the way which can be most advantageous to the greatest number; they should have as their goal in all their work, in all their actions the speediest and most complete improvement possible of the moral and physical existence of the most numerous class.[3]

The most numerous class, of course, was the poor. Thus the effect of Saint-Simon's interpretation was to argue that society, as a whole, should be organized in such a way as to systematically serve the needs of the poor. Eventually this concern for the poor became a major theme for those who continued to identify with Saint-Simon's organization after his death in 1825. Indeed under the leadership of Enfantin and Bazard, the Saint-Simonists began to radicalize the teachings of their founder. Although Saint-Simon had preached against exploitation and had warned of the anarchy which resulted from the operation of the free-market competitive system, he never directly attacked the institution of private property. Yet, by the 1830s, his followers had come to the conclusion that the poor could

---

[3] Ghita Ionescu, ed., *The Political Thought of Saint-Simon* (Oxford: Oxford University Press, 1976), p. 206.

never be served as long as the private ownership of property, as secured by an inheritance system, was allowed to continue. Indeed the actual term "socialism" was coined by Pierre Leroux in 1832 to refer to the doctrines of these radicalized followers of Saint-Simon. The appropriateness of applying this term to Saint-Simon himself, however, is less clear. In many ways, his understanding of the emerging technological society was a rather faithful reflection of the highest aspirations of the developing industrial bourgeoisie.

Saint-Simon's political and social thought were essentially dependent upon his general theory of historical progress. For him historical change could only be understood in terms of the growth and development of the human mind. Accordingly history could best be seen as that process through which the mind matured over time. Beginning at the most primitive level, people once believed in the existence of a great number of independent causes and thus expressed their experience of nature polytheistically. In time, this perspective gave way to monotheism, wherein what had formerly appeared to be a variety of independent causes now came to be understood as simply various aspects of a single cause. In short, as the human mind progressed it replaced the multitude of gods with a single deity and used its existence as the means by which to explain the obscure happenings within nature. More recently and most importantly for Saint-Simon, however, the modern mind had finally reached the realization that the relationship between God and the universe was essentially an incomprehensible one. Given this, traditional metaphysical and religious speculation appeared to be pointless. The truly mature and scientific mind, as a consequence, would devote itself entirely to an examination of the factual world and simply seek, thereby, to discover the antecedent causes of empirical events. According to Saint-Simon, this most recent development in human consciousness had occurred in his own time. Such scientific thinkers as Bacon, Descartes, and Newton had succeeded in bringing the natural sciences into their mature form. Thus it remained only for a person of equivalent genius to transform the social and human sciences in a similar manner.

According to Saint-Simon's analysis, this development of the mind throughout history had not occurred in a simple linear fashion. Rather history appeared to move through a sequence of organic and critical periods. During the organic periods order prevailed. Inasmuch as the mind had achieved a specific stage in its development stability, synthesis, and consensus characterized the period. In the critical ages, however, chaos emerged. As the mind began to evolve out of its earlier form instability, conflict, and confusion appeared. These characteristics, in turn, were indicative of the fact that a transition towards a new organic period had begun.

In developing this scheme Saint-Simon argued that the first organic period had lasted up until the third and fourth centuries A.D. During this time polytheism prevailed and the social system was based upon slavery. After an intervening critical transition the second organic period lasted up to the eleventh and twelfth centuries. During that period monotheism provided the official ideology, and the social system was arranged according to the principles of feudalism. Finally, Saint-Simon argued that the third and ultimate organic period had been in the process of formation since the late Middle Ages. With the French Revolution representing the last element of the critical interregnum, he predicted that the final age would be fully established during the nineteenth century. Inasmuch as the mind would have achieved its mature and positive form, this final organic period would be characterized by the cultural dominance of the scientific attitude and, at the same time, would be based upon a sophisticated industrial system. Saint-Simon's predictions as to the particular features of this new society are to be found in his *Letters from an Inhabitant of Geneva*.

In general, Saint-Simon predicted that his future society would be organized in such a way as to overcome most of the unwelcome features associated with the nascent industrial order. In particular, he argued that poverty and the recurring crises of industrialization could be removed if the state were to assume an active role in the planning and administration of the economy. Therefore, although private property would be preserved, production itself would be planned according to the needs of society, and the abolition of inheritance would insure that only those who contributed to the production of wealth would, as a consequence, enjoy the privileges of ownership.

All of Saint-Simon's efforts to reform the industrial order were based upon his fundamental acceptance of both its goals and culture. For him, the entire purpose of the political community was to engage in the production of useful things. As a consequence this mission provided the model according to which the perfect society could be organized, that is, the workshop.

Saint-Simon's understanding of the industrial society acknowledged the existence of three distinct classes. Unlike Marx, however, Saint-Simon believed that the various classes could work in harmony with one another. Assuming that society could be structured according to the efficient principles of the workshop, Saint-Simon argued that social harmony was possible because each class would share in contributing towards the common goal of material production. As such, each would be aware of the necessary contribution of the other and accept them accordingly. The workers would provide the labor; the industrialists would contribute the necessary managerial skills; and the scientists, organized within the Council of Newton, would establish overall policy and set, thereby, the general direction of society.

Saint-Simon's belief in the possibility of cooperation and consensus was rooted in his understanding of the powers of the scientific mind. Having matured beyond the polytheism and monotheism of an earlier age, humanity was now capable of scientifically grasping the laws of social existence. By expelling the moralists and the metaphysicians the scientists of social behavior could achieve a system based upon facts rather than upon particular interests. In such a case, political power would no longer be a matter of governing people but rather one of administering things. As a consequence the new industrial order would be immune to political instability and social unrest. In this sense, then, the third organic age would be the final one, and history, in effect, would be at the end.

The impact of Saint-Simon's ideas on Western thinking has been immense. Some have argued that the Saint-Simonists have had more influence on the contemporary world than any other socialist school except that of the Marxists. Rather than tracing the full range of Saint-Simon's influence, however, our concern is with its effect upon Marxism. On this point, the philosopher Leszek Kolakowski remarks:

> As far as Marxian socialism is concerned, the most important features of [Saint-Simon's] doctrine may be listed as follows: the firm belief in the regularity of history and its inexorable march towards socialism; the ruinous consequences of anarchic competition and the necessity of state economic planning; the replacement of political government by economic administration; science as the instrument of social progress; and the internationalist approach to politico-economic problems. What is contrary to Marxism, on the other hand, is the idea that the state as it now exists can be used to bring about a socialist transformation; likewise Saint-Simon's appeal for cooperation between classes, and the religious overtones of his "industrial order."[4]

However, it would be misleading if one simply limited Saint-Simon's influence to such a selection of particular themes and issues. Indeed, of equal importance is the fact that Saint-Simon succeeded in transmitting a certain spirit to the general tradition of nineteenth-century socialism, that is, the spirit of Enlightenment rationalism. Throughout his writings Saint-Simon exhibited the rationalist's faith in scientific reason. His reading of history suggested that it is essentially the story of the origin and growth of modern science. Similarly even his religious theory reflects this assumption. Saint-Simon's "New Christianity" was not, in fact, an attempt to express his own personal religious experience. It was, rather, only a cult form for scientific

[4] Leszek Kolakowski, *Main Currents of Marxism*, trans. P. S. Falla (Oxford: Oxford University Press, 1978), I, p. 191.

ideas. Similarly in his political theory, Saint-Simon's hope for order and stability was based upon his prior belief in the efficacy of that consensus made possible by the dominance of instrumental reason and scientific logic. Indeed, as has been shown, such a belief was characteristic of Enlightenment theory, and it will appear again forcefully in the thought of Karl Marx.

Charles Fourier

The second great utopian socialist mentioned by Engels was Charles Fourier (1772–1837). His work, however, represents a sharp contrast with that of Saint-Simon. Whereas the latter embodied the faith of the rationalist, Fourier rejected that tradition in the spirit of the romantic. His theory of history, his understanding of human nature, and his vision of the future society manifest a common rejection of the achievements of the commercial and scientific age. Indeed Fourier sought a closer association with nature. Accordingly he rejected the artificiality and coldness of bourgeois society and spoke of a potential universal harmony wherein individuals would be integrated with themselves, with their neighbors, and with nature as a whole. These themes, which are typical of romanticism, will later reappear in the so-called scientific socialism of Karl Marx.

Charles Fourier was born to a wealthy cloth merchant in Besancon, France, in 1772 and, after a minimal education, was rushed by his parents into a business career against his will. His firm prospered for a while, but the counter-revolution of 1793 destroyed all his assets and drove him into poverty. After several years in the army he moved back and forth between Lyons and Paris while pursuing minor jobs. His major effort, however, was directed towards formulating and promulgating his idea of the perfect social order. For forty years he spent his spare time writing about and seeking a sponsor for his experiment in harmonious living. Although he never found a patron to support his project, he did manage to acquire a sizeable following. Briefly, under the leadership of Victor Considerant (1808–1893), the Fourierists were involved in the political developments which followed the collapse of the Orleans monarchy in 1848.

Fourier's ideas were known throughout much of Europe, and several attempts to found Fourierist communes were undertaken in such diverse places as Romania and the United States. Among the thirty or so Fourierist communes in America the most famous was at Brook Farm in West Roxbury, Massachusetts. Both Nathaniel Hawthorne and Ralph Waldo Emerson were associated with it at one time or another during the community's five-year existence.

Among Fourier's most important works are *Théorie des quatre mouvements et des destinées genérales* (1808), *Traité de l'association domestique et agricole* (1822), and *Le Nouveau Monde industriel et sociétaire* (1829). Fourier's attempt to analyze the relationship between sex and socialism, a theme rediscovered by some socialists in the twentieth century, was published for the first time in 1967 as *Le Nouveau monde amoureux*.

Unlike Saint-Simon who appropriated the intellectual history of the West as a progressive development upon which modernity could be built, Fourier began with an almost total rejection of humanity's past:

> Whoever seeks for real discoveries should know that he who proposes anything new is obliged to disregard the opinions of his age and give a denial to its dominant prejudices . . . . I am in the same position—I bring a theory whence will spring riches, truth, and social unity. . . . But let no one be deceived in this—where there is incense for the age, there are no new ideas. If we sincerely desire new truths and real discoveries, we must not demand flattery from him who brings them.[5]

Perhaps the only exception to Fourier's wholesale condemnation of the past was the work of Isaac Newton. According to Fourier, Newton had succeeded in understanding the mechanics of nature when he formulated his law of gravity. What remained, therefore, was to formulate an equivalent description of the mechanics of society. This Fourier did with his law of passionate attraction.

Fourier's law of passionate attraction was based upon his understanding of human nature. His ability to discover this law, in turn, was due to what he considered to be his unique appreciation of the human personality. According to Fourier, he alone understood human nature to be fundamentally good. Consequently those emotions and desires which are natural to humanity must be both acknowledged for what they are and accepted as desirable. Indeed the passions are God's work, and thus rather than repressing them the true moralist must seek the appropriate means for their satisfaction. It was precisely this failure of traditional morality to appreciate its true task that allowed Fourier to disregard the totality of its teachings.

According to Fourier traditional moral theory failed in several ways. First, it recognized only nine out of the twelve passions which actually motivate human beings, and of these it understood only four with any degree of precision. Second, traditional morality sought to correct and repress the passions rather than to support them. In doing so, it created a series of duties which actually violated natural justice and produced, thereby,

---

[5] Mark Poster, ed., *Harmonian Man: Selected Writings of Charles Fourier*, trans. Susan Hanson (Garden City: Doubleday, 1971), pp. 158–59.

conflict, antagonism, and social discord. For Fourier a true morality would allow the passions their natural play and, consequently, it would be capable of organizing a social order which would support their combined development:

> Passionate attraction alone, without constraint and without aid other than the charm of voluptuousness, is going to establish universal unity upon the globe, and will cause war, revolution, indigence, and injustice to disappear during the seventy thousand year period of social harmony which we will enter.[6]

At the core of Fourier's political theory was his belief that it would be possible to achieve a harmonious social order by balancing the variety of personalities which are found among humankind. Rather than relying upon the repression of any particular traits, the well-ordered society would be organized so that all of the people's passions would contribute towards the general good. According to Fourier, all people shared twelve basic desires. Yet, inasmuch as they were shared in different proportions and in ways, it was possible to specify a total of 810 distinct human personalities. The ideal community would include at least twice this number and would be arranged so that the various types would mesh into an organic whole. Select individuals would initially come together because of their shared preferences and in order to contribute towards a common project. Once united, they would naturally be attracted to all the various tasks and duties which were required for the efficient functioning of their specific community. The name which Fourier gave to this basic social unit was "phalanx."

Life in the phalanx reflected Fourier's understanding of utopian existence. Each phalanx would be a self-sufficient agricultural and industrial unit in which production was the responsibility of economic cooperatives. Individuals, in turn, would work in several cooperatives and be paid according to their abilities. As a consequence, all individuals would work only in those jobs for which each was suited by his or her personality. Accordingly there would be no forced division of labor; one could change employment whenever one desired and would receive a minimum subsistence even if one chose not to work at all. The undesirable jobs would be given to children, for they were often able to make a game out of what appeared to be work to the adults. Inasmuch as one was paid according to one's abilities, private property and economic inequality would not disappear. Yet, inasmuch as there was neither a forced division of labor nor the threat of impoverishment, such institutions would no longer be exploitative in nature. The three

---

[6] Poster, *Harmonian Man: Selected Writings of Charles Fourier*, p. 90.

classes of labor, talent, and capital would thus exist harmoniously in mutual attraction.

Socially the phalanx was constructed in such a way as to promote a fundamental sense of equality and liberty. Women were to be the complete equals of men and, as a consequence, the institution of the family would have to be abolished. Children would be raised communally and receive a free public education. Everyone could live as they wished and there would be no restrictions governing sexual conduct. In such an environment of egalitarian liberty Fourier believed that the traditional political institutions would no longer be necessary. Government would be reduced to the administration of economic affairs, and a commitment to democratic principles would inform all decision making. Eventually all phalanxes would combine to form a world confederation characterized by the rule of all (*omnarchy*) and charged primarily with the development of public works.

The romantic quality of Fourier's writings sometimes assumed a rather bizarre form. His picture of a reconstructed world included such features as the melting of glaciers, the taming of the deserts, and the domestication of wild animals. At one point he argued that, as humanity extended its dominion over nature, the seas would become lemonade and the air would smell of perfume. These visions, in turn, were part of an overall cosmology which spoke of copulating planets, antilions, and a woman named Phoebe who had been transformed into the moon. Indeed it was as if the cosmos were a living organism evolving through a cycle of 80,000 years and mankind was but a part of this all-encompassing evolutionary development.

Because of such eccentricity Fourier was often dismissed as a crank. Yet it was precisely this grand historical scheme which ultimately supported his critique of bourgeois society, and it was this critique of bourgeois society which Engels praised during his discussion of the origins of Marxism. Like Saint-Simon, Fourier based his political speculation upon a general theory of history. For Fourier history was not simply a random collection of events. Rather it was an evolutionary cycle within which each phase developed those forces which eventually brought about its own passing and, thereby, moved life to a higher form.

The 80,000-year natural cycle was divided into two periods of 40,000 years each; one period was that of "ascending vibrations"; the other of "descending vibrations." The period of ascending vibration was further divided into a 5000-year era of chaos and a 35,000-year age of harmony. Fourier placed the bourgeois civilization of his day at the end of but included within the period of chaos. Accordingly, bourgeois society was understood as being akin to such other chaotic periods as savagery, patriarchy, and barbarism. This interpretation, in turn, obviously challenged the self-understanding of bourgeois culture. In the eyes of its apologists bourgeois society appeared to be a truly liberating force which had succeeded in freeing humanity from the superstitions and limitations of its past. According to Fourier, however, bourgeois civilization simply represented a more sophisticated form of repression which ". . . succeeded only in establishing Relative Poverty, Individual Anxiety, The Reign of All Vices, [and] Duplicity of Action."[7] Thus, as Engels wrote:

> Fourier takes the bourgeoisie, their inspired prophets before the Revolution, and their interested eulogists after it, at their own word. He lays bare remorselessly the material and moral misery of the bourgeois world. He confronts it with the earlier philosophers' dazzling promises of a society in which reason alone should reign . . . and with the rose-coloured phraseology of the bourgeois ideologists of his time. He points out how everywhere the most pitiful reality corresponds with the most high-sounding phrases, and he overwhelms this hopeless fiasco of phrases with his mordant sarcasm.[8]

In addition to exposing the oppression which lies behind the appearance of freedom within liberalism, Fourier also called attention to its transitory nature. Accordingly, bourgeois capitalism was not based upon the immutable truths of eternal reason as Locke had argued. Rather it was but a moment within the larger dialectic of historical progress, "in which the human race gropes its way by instinct towards its destiny."[9]

Although one can find a number of particular themes in Fourier which appear once again in Marx, it is, perhaps, Fourier's vision of the harmonious person which was most influential. Indeed it appears that Fourier's harmonious person possessed many of the characteristics which will later be attributed to Marx's nonalienated worker. For example, both offer us a picture of the fully developed human who is capable of excelling in a number of tasks and finding, thereby, creative joy in labor. Both foresee a transformed humankind living within a society which will govern itself without relying upon traditional political structures, and both project a view of the postcommercial individual who is at once truly harmonious and fully social.

Robert Owen

The last utopian socialist on Engels' list was England's Robert Owen (1771–1858). As the sixth of seven children Owen left his impoverished home at the age of ten. He apprenticed as a draper and in 1785 moved to Manchester as an assistant within a textile firm. At this time En-

---

[7] Poster, *Harmonian Man: Selected Writings of Charles Fourier*, p. 56.

[8] Tucker, *The Marx-Engels Reader*, p. 611.

[9] Poster, *Harmonian Man: Selected Writings of Charles Fourier*, p. 56.

gland was in the midst of an unprecedented industrial expansion. Due primarily to a series of technological developments, the traditional techniques of production were rapidly changing. For example, in the textile industry the invention of the steam-driven spinning mill and the development of the power loom enabled manufacturers to take advantage of a relatively abundant supply of cheap raw cotton. Soon cotton goods would replace woolens as Britain's leading export. Owen, sensing this, formed a partnership to take advantage of the opportunities to be found in the growing market. By the age of twenty he was the manager of a firm which employed over five hundred workers, and in 1800 he and his partners succeeded in buying a huge spinning mill in New Lanark, Scotland. Not only did this acquisition enable Owen to amass a private fortune, it also provided him with the opportunity he needed to undertake his experiments in social engineering.

According to Owen's own account, New Lanark was a typically impoverished textile town. The people were poor and almost totally dependent upon the mill for their livelihood. The working conditions were bad, and the village suffered from crime, illness, and illiteracy. Given this situation Owen resolved to transform New Lanark into a model working community. He reduced the working hours to under eleven per day (low for the period) and, at the same time, maintained the wages of his employees. Whereas the common practice was for children of six to be working up to sixteen hours a day, Owen prohibited labor by children under ten and introduced a system of free public schooling. In addition he established relatively hygienic working conditions, put in a drainage system, and built housing for the townspeople.

To the amazement of many observers, Owen's reforms not only improved the life of the workers but, at the same time, they actually led to an increase in the mill's productivity and profits. Thus as New Lanark entered into a period of relative prosperity Owen attempted to use its success as an example of what could be achieved by the humanitarian reform of industrial capitalism. Accordingly, he argued that a series of reforms in the monetary, wage, and educational systems would produce benefits for both worker and owner alike.

In 1816 a meeting was called in London to discuss the problem of England's rising unemployment and to reconsider the system of public welfare which was at that time administered at the local level on a parish-by-parish basis. Owen, renowned for his philanthropic success at New Lanark, was invited to prepare a written statement for the commission, and in 1817 he published his famous *Report to the Committee for the Relief of the Manufacturing Poor*. (To many, Owen's recommendations appeared too radical, and thus his report was officially forgotten.) Rather than spending public funds for unproductive welfare relief, Owen suggested that the government should invest its money in the formation of agricultural and industrial communes. Up to 1200 of the urban unemployed should be resettled in these "villages of industry." There, sharing certain public buildings and enjoying reforms similar to those at New Lanark, the formerly unemployed could work to support themselves and, thereby, eventually pay back the initial investment required to establish the village project. Ideally an entire network of such cooperatives would cover all of England and, as their success became apparent, they could expand to form a worldwide federation.

Although Owen's villages represented an alternative form of society, based as they were on cooperation rather than competition, they were not strictly speaking socialist. Rather than being self-governing, they would be administered by an officer appointed by those who provided the original capital necessary for their formation. As such, they would "be subject to the rules and regulations laid down by their founders."

Between 1817 and 1824 Owen spent most of his time trying to win public support for his village project. Consequently he slowly withdrew from any involvement in New Lanark, and in 1825 he stepped down as its manager. In the meantime, however, he had met with little success in his effort to gain official backing for his various reforms. The one important exception was the passage of the Factory Act of 1819 which regulated child labor within the textile industry. Facing increasing opposition at home Owen decided to set up his own model village in America.

Arriving in America in 1824 Owen invested his entire fortune in the purchase of New Harmony, Indiana. Unfortunately the community was marked by disagreement among its internal factions from the very beginning. Over a period of two years its constitution had to be changed seven times. Yet even those maneuvers were unable to solve the deeper problem, and the experiment came to an end in 1827.

Returning to England in 1829 Owen developed a new strategy for the actualization of his plan. The repeal of the Combination Act in 1824 had legalized labor unions. Owen hoped to use the now-growing trade-union movement as a vehicle for the realization of his own worker's commonwealth. Accordingly he set about organizing that movement. At one time, Owen had shared his generation's optimism in science and the persuasive power of reason. He had hoped that the industrial middle class would ultimately recognize the merits of his arguments and adopt his plan, and he had supported the bourgeoisie's efforts to acquire political power. Now, however, Owen placed his hopes in the political and economic power of organized labor. His goal was to establish a socialist commonwealth wherein the trade unions would assume the control of industry and eventually replace the state with a federation of worker's cooperatives. In 1834 Owen formed the Grand National Consolidated Trade Union.

While leading the Union Owen faced both internal and external resistance. Internally certain members of the Union were not entirely convinced that Owen's nonrevolutionary strategy was in their best interest. As an alternative they advocated a more radical version of class warfare. Externally the Union was confronted by the antagonistic forces of both government and business. Eventually, the Grand Union dissolved, and with its disappearance Owenism moved outside of the main stream of the trade-union movement. In his final years, Owen devoted himself to writing propagandistic tracts and traveling to deliver lectures wherever he could find an audience. It was during one such lecture tour that he died in 1858.

In spite of the variety of strategies which Owen adopted during his long life, the underlying theoretical principles which informed his vision remained remarkably consistent. They were expressed best in his *A New View of Society or Essays on the Principle of the Formation of the Human Character* (1813–1814). Central among these principles was Owen's belief in the malleability of human nature. Given the plasticity of human nature Owen believed that it was possible to construct a community according to whatever principles one desired simply by manipulating the social environment:

> . . . any community may be arranged, on a due combination of the foregoing principles, in such a manner, as not only to withdraw vice, poverty, and, in a great degree, misery, from the world, but also to place *every* individual under such circumstances in which he shall enjoy more permanent happiness than can be given to *any* individual under the principles which have hitherto regulated society.[10]

According to Owen, the great error of the past had been the mistaken belief that it was the individual who is ultimately responsible for the development of his or her own personality. This belief, as promulgated in religious teachings, blinded individuals to the fact that their character was formed for them and not by them. On the contrary, it was obvious to Owen that an individual's personality was primarily the result of the community's influence, and that the community's own character can be changed at will. Given such malleability, it would be possible to mold human beings in such a way that a practical social harmony would emerge. Two reforms, in particular, would be necessary to accomplish this feat.

The first would require a transformation of the educational system. In this respect, Owen was in agreement with the fundamental principles of the Enlightenment. Thus for him, the primary purpose of education was

---

[10] A. L. Morton, ed., *The Life and Ideas of Robert Owen* (New York: International Publisher, 1969), p. 75.

that of forming the character of children in preparation for life, not imparting information simply for the sake of knowledge. Consequently, according to Owen major attention should be given to the construction of a loving and supporting environment which would evoke students' curiosity and bolster their confidence.

The second major reform would be concerned with the improvement of working conditions. The competitive character of commercial society would have to be minimized. This could be done, in part, by substituting labor certificates for money as the medium of exchange. As a developer of the labor theory of value Owen believed that economic value should be measured in terms of the amount of labor required to produce a particular item. By introducing labor certificates the circulating "currency" would always correspond to the amount of goods produced, and consequently the wild fluctuations of the market system could be avoided. Indeed, Owen himself actually looked forward to the day when cooperatives would directly exchange their goods with one another and thus bypass the market system altogether.

In the history of socialism Owen is noted more for his practical achievements than for his theoretical ingenuity. He was praised by Engels both for moving beyond philanthropy and for initiating a powerful movement on behalf of political and social reform. Unlike Marx, however, Owen did not foresee the necessity of a proletarian revolution. On the contrary, he continued to argue by an appeal to universal human needs and, as a consequence, paid little attention to the formation of a proletarian-class consciousness. Thus, according to Engels, Owen never succeeded in escaping from the limitations of the utopian attitude.

From the Marxist perspective the utopian socialists are to be praised for the righteousness of their moral indignation. Yet, unless such a moral fervor can be guided by a correct comprehension of the history and structure of capitalism, it must necessarily remain politically ineffective. Summarizing his criticism, Engels wrote:

> The socialism of earlier days certainly criticized the existing capitalistic mode of production and its consequences. But it could not explain them, and, therefore, could not get the mastery of them. It could only simply reject them as bad. The more strongly this earlier socialism denounced the exploitation of the working class, inevitable under capitalism, the less able was it clearly to show in what this exploitation consisted and how it arose. But for this it was necessary—(1) to present the capitalistic method of production in its historical connection and its inevitableness during a particular historical period, and therefore, also, to present its inevitable downfall; and (2) to lay bare its essential character, which was still a secret. This was done by the discovery of *surplus value* . . . . These

two great discoveries, the materialistic conception of history and the revelation of the secret of capitalistic production through surplus value, we owe to Marx. With these discoveries socialism became a science.[11]

However before it is possible to examine the materialist conception of history, it is first necessary to review its idealistic alternative. Thus a true appreciation of Marx requires a brief examination of the writings of Georg Hegel and Ludwig Feuerbach.

GERMAN IDEALISM

Georg Hegel

Hegel was born in Stuttgart in 1770 and originally intended a career in the Lutheran ministry. However, his growing discontent with certain orthodox Christian dogmas eventually forced him to abandon his original plans, and he turned towards the academy instead. After several interruptions and various appointments at Jena and Heidelberg, Hegel was called to the chair of philosophy at the University of Berlin in 1818. There he reigned as the dominant voice in German philosophy until his death in 1831. The four major works published during his lifetime were *Phenomenology of Mind* (1807), *Science of Logic* (1816), *Encyclopedia of the Philosophical Sciences* (1817), and *Philosophy of Right* (1821). After his death Hegel's students collected their lecture notes and published an additional ten volumes of papers which included materials on such topics as art, history, religion, and the history of philosophy. For the political theorist, however, the most important of these posthumous publications is *Philosophy of History* (1837).

In a letter written to his father in 1837, Marx spoke of his discovery of Hegel in quasi-religious terms, "A curtain had fallen, my holy of holies had been shattered, and new gods had to be found."[12] The crisis to which this passage referred was Marx's discovery of the inadequacies of German Idealist philosophy as developed by Immanuel Kant (1724–1804) and Johann Fichte (1762–1814). In its Kantian form, Idealism had insisted upon a sharp distinction between reality as it appeared to the human mind and reality as it really was. Such a position, in turn, implied a rigorous ethical distinction between what is and what ought to be. Given this distinction, the human being appeared obligated to actualize what ought to be and thus

[11] Tucker, *The Marx-Engels Reader*, p. 622.

[12] Loyd D. Easton and Kurt H. Guddat, eds., *Writings of the Young Marx on Philosophy and Society* (Garden City: Doubleday, 1967), p. 46.

was involved in an eternal conflict between the dictates of reason (what ought to be) and the structures of worldly existence (what is). In time Marx rejected this dichotomous view of reality and, in so doing, followed the example of Hegel. This was so because it was Hegel who first attempted to construct a philosophy of reality which would overcome the Idealist distinction between the apparent and the real or the factual and the ideal. For Hegel, Kant's dichotomy between the actual (is) and the rational (ought) could be resolved once one understood that, "What is rational is actual; and what is actual is rational."

The problem which Hegel faced was not simply an academic one. Rather the issues involved were ones rooted directly in human experience. For example, from the human perspective reality does not immediately appear as an ordered whole. Rather it seems to contain rifts which are experienced as tension. For example, individuals are caught in a tension between freedom and obligation. At the same time they are aware of the gap between being and nonbeing, and they are also sensitive to the differences between the absolute and the contingent. Given such experiences it would seem unlikely that these dichotomies can ever be resolved. Why is there anything rather than nothing? And why does history move the way it does? Is there a meaning to its development which we can decipher and use as our guide? For Hegel, the key to answering these questions could only be found if one was willing to reconsider the context out of which they first emerged. Specifically the tensions and dichotomies in reality appeared from within the human perspective. The solution, therefore, was to adopt a perspective which was superior to that of the human, that is, that of the divine. In doing so, according to Hegel the individual would eventually discover that what originally appeared to the self as evil or as contingent or as meaningless did so only because of the limitations which are inherent within the human perspective. However, as the individual expanded this perspective in a divine-like fashion, so as to include a comprehensive view of the whole, the meaning of reality would become apparent once and for all. To comprehend the whole of reality is, however, to achieve an absolute knowledge, and the possibility of absolute knowledge, in turn, implies the existence of an absolute knower. For Hegel, therefore, the only appropriate perspective from which to view reality was that which is achieved by absolute consciousness as such. The fact that Hegel described the condition of absolute consciousness as an achievement rather than as a given implies that it has a history. For Hegel, humankind had not begun with a comprehension of the whole; rather, such an understanding had emerged only slowly over time. History, accordingly, could be interpreted as the story of the mind's progression towards its absolute perfection in consciousness. From this perspective, then, the apparent accidents of history, such as the rise and fall of civilizations, now appeared essentially to be necessary moments within the dramatic development of absolute knowledge. Indeed Hegel attempted to trace this drama in his *Phenomenology of the Mind.*

Following a tradition that goes as far back as Plato and Parmenides, Hegel began with the assumption that the spiritual is the primary mode of being. Given this presumption he then argued that material reality could be explained strictly in spiritual terms. This could be done, in turn, if it could be shown that the material realm is, in fact, only a manifestation of that which is essentially spiritual in nature. Indeed, it was this task which Hegel set for himself, and in accomplishing it he hoped to overcome the perceived rift in reality which supported such Idealistic dichotomies as "is" and "ought" or "rational" and "actual." Within the Hegelian perspective the rational "ought" is revealed as the actual "is." The history of this insight, in turn, begins with an act of divine revelation.

Breaking from the orthodox Judeo-Christian tradition that understood God as an absolute being and, thus, as one who is in no need of perfection, Hegel argued that God as a spirit lacked true self-awareness and, therefore, was in need of that knowledge which could only be gained through an act of self-revelation. In short, for Hegel this god was not yet fully god because it lacked knowledge of itself as god. As pure consciousness god could not know itself because it could not be an object for its own investigation. Consciousness is always consciousness of something; as such, it requires an object upon which to focus its attention. Yet, being pure consciousness, god was also pure subject; it could not know itself because it could not serve as the focus for its own awareness. Given this restriction, therefore, god was not yet absolute. Lacking self-awareness, it was in need of perfection, which in turn could only be satisfied through the creation of the world.

According to Hegel, god created the world by an act of self-externalization. It extended itself into time and space so as to appear as an object over and before its own consciousness. In doing so, it became both subject and object and thus entered into a state of alienation. In achieving alienation, god was able to take an aspect of itself and objectify it in such a way that it stood over and against god as an "other," or alien. In this situation, then, the material world appeared as alien or foreign to the spiritual, and as a consequence objective reality seemed to be a limitation and restriction upon spiritual consciousness. In truth, however, the material realm was simply the alienated form of the spiritual. Thus, for Hegel, god was the All.

Having alienated itself so as to contemplate itself as object, god then began a process of self-realization which was intended to lead to its absolute perfection. Originally it lacked self-awareness; now, however, confronting its own alienated manifestation god comes to see that creation for what it truly is, that is, god's own self. Thus as divine self-consciousness develops the alien character of the natural world slowly disappears. As the divine quality of the natural world emerges its alien character is eventually transcended altogether. Consequently, at this moment, god achieves its perfection in absolute self-awareness. The rifts and gaps in being have disappeared. Reality is one; god is All; and the actual and the rational are the same. For Hegel, then, divine consciousness had finally reached its absolute perfection through the dialectical process of alienation and its eventual transcendence. Summarizing this process, the political scientist Robert Tucker writes:

> Thus, Hegelian knowing means self-discovery, whereby spirit in a given conscious subject comes to recognize itself in what had appeared to be a world apart from it. Knowing is the de-alienation of the external world which (by Hegel's definition) is a product of spirit's own activity of self-externalization . . . . The act of knowing is the piercing of the illusion of otherness. It strips the object of its alien objectivity, and the false consciousness of the object as "other" gives way to a true consciousness of it as "self-ish."[13]

Central to Hegel's metaphysical system is his insistence that this divine movement towards absolute consciousness is an historical event. God's effort to achieve self-perfection does not take place on a level which is removed from that of everyday reality. Indeed Hegel was anxious to overcome the traditional distinction between the level of the sacred and that of the profane. As a consequence, the divine effort of self-perfection includes both human beings and their society as necessary actors within this historical drama. Specifically, the human being is involved inasmuch as the human mind is consciousness's location in the world. Thus the activities of human reason actually constitute that process through which divine consciousness is perfected, and the history of human thought is, in fact, equivalent to the self-realization of god. Indeed being more than simply the means for god's self-development, the person actually comes to know himself/herself as god. Thus, as Leszek Kolakowski writes, "Hegel is not writing about the Mind; he is writing the Mind's autobiography."[14]

Prior to this realization, humanity participated in the historical process without actually being aware of its true function. Following what it perceived to be its own subjective interests, humanity contributed, in fact, to the dialectical unfolding of the meaning of history itself. It was as if there were a higher logic which assimilated the particular achievements of the

[13] Robert Tucker, *Philosophy and Myth in Karl Marx* (Cambridge: Cambridge University Press, 1961), p. 51.

[14] Kolakowski, *Main Currents of Marxism*, p. 60.

human being and through this assimilation revealed their real, though perhaps unintended, meaning. Thus Hegel wrote:

> The History of the World begins with its general aim—the realization of the Idea of Spirit—only in an *implicit* form . . . that is, as Nature; a hidden, most profoundly hidden, unconscious instinct; and the whole process of History . . . is directed to rendering this unconscious impulse a conscious one. Thus appearing in the form of merely natural existence, natural will—that which has been called the subjective side—physical craving, instinct, passion, private interest, as also opinion and subjective conception—spontaneously present themselves at the very commencement. This vast congeries of volitions, interests and activities, constitute the instruments and means of the World-Spirit for attaining its object; bringing it to consciousness, and realizing it. And this aim is none other than finding itself—coming to itself—and contemplating itself in concrete actuality.[15]

According to Hegel, however, now that history, operating according to the "cunning of reason," had achieved this moment of self-awareness, it was presently possible for humanity to consciously appropriate the principles of reality and thereby understand the meaning of its historical past. At this moment of insight the unity of history became apparent. It was a unity derived from the existence of a single historical purpose. For Hegel, this purpose was the realization of freedom:

> The History of the World travels from East to West, for Europe is absolutely the end of History, Asia the beginning . . . . The History of the World is the discipline of the uncontrolled natural will, bringing it into obedience to a Universal principle and conferring subjective freedom. The East knew and to the present day knows only that *One* is Free; the Greek and Roman world, that *some* are free; the German World knows that *All* are free.[16]

Thus just as history is the movement of god towards its perfection, history is, at the same time, the actualization of freedom. For Hegel freedom entailed the overcoming of alienated objectivity. An alienated object confronts its subject as a limit; something the subject is not. As such, it establishes a boundary which limits the subject's reality. However, as consciousness develops in history, it eventually realizes that the object is not truly other. Losing its alien character, the object also loses its power to bind

[15] Georg Hegel, *The Philosophy of History*, trans. J. Sibree (New York: Dover Publications, 1956), p. 25.
[16] Hegel, *The Philosophy of History*, pp. 103–04.

the subject. Consequently, as history moves towards its perfection in self-consciousness, it becomes intelligible as the realization of the consciousness of freedom. For Hegel, therefore, freedom was reconciled with necessity; the necessity of god's self-perfection demanded the realization of history as freedom. As a consequence the tension between freedom and obligation had been resolved. Humanity was obligated to obey reason; yet, according to Hegel, the triumph of reason appeared as the victory of freedom. Thus true freedom is achieved only when the subjective individual is reconciled with the objective universal, or as Hegel referred to it, the "ethical idea." However, for Hegel, the "ethical idea" existed as the state. Thus in his system true individual freedom was equivalent to obedience to the state:

> The state is the actuality of concrete freedom. But concrete freedom consists in this, that personal individuality and its particular interests not only achieve their complete development and gain explicit recognition for their right (as they do in the sphere of the family and civil society) but, for one thing, they also pass over of their own accord into the interest of the universal, and, for another thing, they know and will the universal; they even recognize it as their own substantive mind; they take it as their end and aim and are active in its pursuit. The result is that the universal does not prevail or achieve completion except along with particular interests and through the co-operation of particular knowing and willing; and individuals likewise do not live as private persons for their own ends alone, but in the very act of willing these they will the universal in the light of the universal, and their activity is consciously aimed at none but the universal end.[17]

Hegel's attempt to reconcile the citizen with the political community was based upon his rejection of the liberal understanding of the human being as an autonomous individual. For Hegel humans were social and political beings. Consequently human development and happiness depended upon their involvement with others. The family, the society, and the state served, therefore, as the means for human self-realization and shared, thereby, the individual's goal of freedom.

In *Philosophy of Right*, Hegel developed his understanding of the modern political order. As such, it was Hegel's attempt to specify the true essence of political life. Inasmuch as every existing state was a state, each, more or less, embodied the principles which defined the essence of statehood. None, however, did so perfectly. Thus rather than looking at particular states, Hegel attempted to comprehend the rational essence of the

---

[17] Georg Hegel, *Philosophy of Right*, trans. T. M. Knox (Oxford: Oxford University Press, 1967), pp. 160–61.

state as such. His analysis, therefore, focused upon the ideal or rational state.

At the outset, Hegel attempted to distinguish between "civil society" and the "state." According to Hegel the civil society was that arena of social interaction wherein individuals confront one another in competition for scarce resources. As such it is a battlefield upon which isolated individuals pursue their own selfish interests. Such competition necessarily encourages a sense of individuality and, in doing so, promotes economic development. Yet, at the same time, such economic warfare produces a situation in which there is wealth for the relatively few and poverty for the many. If this situation were left unchecked, the competition within civil society would soon lead to chaos and, as a consequence, destroy the very basis for social existence.

To prevent this, Hegel argued that a certain amount of control and direction was necessary. On one hand, society's anarchistic competition was rationalized and channeled by the formation of economic corporations. According to Hegel, corporations were self-governing associations whose members came together to pursue their common economic interests. As such, they provided a certain discipline and cooperation to the otherwise individualistic tendencies of civil society. Yet, left alone, corporations were not capable of monitoring the clash of subjective selfish desire which defined the social arena. Thus, according to Hegel, the state became necessary. As a representative of the universal ethical idea, the state oversaw the competition which was characteristic of the social struggle and governed its result in the light of universal reason. In essence, then, the state attempted to achieve a universal harmony among its citizens by reconciling the particular interests of its social actors.

According to Hegel the ideal constitution for such a state would be that of a limited monarchy based upon a three-way division of power. The legislature would determine the fundamental laws of society and, therefore, serve as the representative of universal reason. It would be composed of two houses. The upper house would represent the landed aristocracy, and the lower house would be elected by the common people acting through their corporations. This arrangement, in turn, would insure that the legislature would act as the representative of the major socioeconomic groups within society rather than as the spokesperson for the interests of individual citizens. According to Hegel, the representatives were to be more than simply the agents of those who selected them. Rather, as true legislators, they were to be concerned with the universal interests of society and, in doing so, had to be willing to transcend the particular interests of their individual constituencies.

The ideal executive branch would be primarily concerned with enforcing and administering the decisions of the legislature. As such it would have to apply the legislature's universal intent within the context of particular decisions for specific cases. Hegel, therefore, envisioned a vast bureaucracy which would extend throughout the civil society. As such, it would serve as the state's primary means for regulating the competitive activities of social humanity.

The final branch of government would be the office of the constitutional monarch. As head of state the monarch would act in those situations where a formal expression of political sovereignty was necessary. Rather than being a despot ruling on his or her own behalf, Hegel's monarch was intended to serve as a symbol of political legitimacy. Accordingly the monarch's seal would establish an act as an official one and represent, thereby, the sovereignty of the state as a whole.

As interesting as Hegel's analysis of the bureaucracy and its role within the modern nation-state may be, the most important argument in his discussion of the ideal state centered upon the actual character or nature of the state itself. According to Hegel, the state was "the universal spiritual life." Consequently, as the carrier of the world-spirit, the state is absolutely necessary for the realization of god's perfection. Indeed, it is god's will that the state exist. As a result, in those instances where the continued existence of the state is in doubt, the citizen's obligation to defend it is almost absolute. Yet, according to Hegel, inasmuch as individuals are dependent upon the state for their very spirituality, they were, in fact, actually serving themselves when they joined in the defense of their country. Thus, although Hegel did speak of such concepts as "human rights," "individuality," and "legality," it would appear that in moments of crisis, the individual exists primarily in order to serve the state.

In his reaction against Kantian Idealism Hegel repeatedly argued against a dichotomous view of reality. Accordingly he rejected any philosophy which described reality as if it were composed of two separate and irreducible dimensions. Indeed, for Hegel, it was a mistake to contrast the realm of the rational and ideal with that of the actual and existing. Thus for him a correct understanding of reality necessarily posited its unitary nature. For example, in Hegel's own metaphysical system the poles of transcendence and immanence were effectively collapsed into the single dimension of history. Or, put in other terms, for Hegel the historical dimension expanded in such a way as to absorb the transcendent. In the process of this expansion profane existence unavoidably assumed a sacred character and, as a consequence, it was no longer possible to speak of a "merely historical development." Rather, for Hegel, history assumed exactly those qualities which formerly had been understood to be uniquely characteristic of the transcendent or divine. History, in effect, had become sacred, and as a result historical events assumed an absolute importance.

An example of this tendency can be found in Hegel's theory of war.

The state, for Hegel, was the carrier of the world-spirit. Inasmuch as the world-spirit is evolving, its most advanced form resides only in the most developed state of any particular epoch. Given this, the other states of that period assume a certain insignificance. As Hegel wrote in his *Philosophy of Right:*

> This nation is dominant in world history during this one epoch, and it is only once . . . that it can make its hour strike. In contrast with this its absolute right of being the vehicle of this present stage in the world mind's development, the minds of the other nations are without rights, and they, along with those whose hour has struck already, count no longer in world history.[18]

According to Hegel, then, the epoch-making state enjoys an absolute right, and in its wars with other states it is promoting, thereby, the development of the world-spirit. As a result, for Hegel, wars are not evil. Rather they are the necessary means by which the world-spirit evolves, and thus they insure the dominance of reason in history. For Hegel, the victors are always right because in His wisdom God so constructed history that the powerful and the righteous are always one and the same.

The Young Hegelians and Ludwig Feuerbach

Although Hegel spent his life as an academic, the influence of his writings extended far beyond the confines of the university. His writing not only encouraged other philosophers to devote their energies to the study of art, religion, and history but, at the same time, succeeded in influencing the political discussion of his day. At first, apologists for the Prussian state borrowed from Hegel's work to justify the existence and practices of the Prussian monarchy. To do this, they emphasized the antiutopian spirit of Hegelian thought. Accepting Hegel's denial of the distinction between the actual and the rational, the Prussian apologists argued for an acceptance of the status quo as being an historically necessary and entirely reasonable manifestation of reality's unfolding. This argument was ultimately based upon the assumption that, inasmuch as the actual was rational, the factual situation within Prussia was, by definition, ideal.

Within a few years of Hegel's death, however, the official and conservative interpretation of his work became increasingly unpopular. A group, referred to as the "Young Hegelians," attempted to radicalize the teachings of their mentor by arguing that the slogan, "the actual is the rational," meant, in fact, that only the rational was truly actual. Thus in reversing the conservative interpretation the Young Hegelians attempted to

---

[18] Hegel, *Philosophy of Right*, pp. 217–218.

distinguish between the factual conditions of the moment and the compelling demands of universal reason. If only the rational were truly actual, then those elements of historical existence which appeared to be irrational were, in fact, unreal and should, as a consequence, be destroyed. Given this perspective, then, the Young Hegelians set for themselves the task of exposing those irrationalities which existed within Prussian society in particular and Western culture in general. Through a program of criticism they hoped to expose the irrationality of the status quo and promote, thereby, the development of the world-spirit. Politically this critical attitude implied a rejection of the Prussian monarchy and favored the establishment of a republican, bourgeois, and democratic order which was to be modeled after that of France.

At its beginning, the Young Hegelian movement was based at the University of Berlin, and it was there during his student days that Marx would be exposed to its program. Among its most important representatives were David Strauss (1808–1874), Count Anton Cieszkowski (1814–1894), Bruno Bauer (1809–1882), and Arnold Ruge (1802–1880).

Generally, the Young Hegelians's efforts at radicalization included three distinct arguments. First, the Young Hegelians reintroduced the traditional tension between the realms of the factual and the rational. In Hegel's system the dichotomy between "is" and "ought" had theoretically been absorbed into a higher dialectical unity. For the Young Hegelians, however, normative reason once again stood over and against empirical history as its judge. Second, the Young Hegelians rejected Hegel's accommodation with Protestant Christianity. Rather than seeing philosophy and religion as allies, they rejected Christianity in favor of a thorough-going atheism. Finally, the Young Hegelians broke with Hegel's loyalty to the nation-state. Whereas Hegel accepted the permanent division between the state and society and acknowledged the priority of the former, the Young Hegelians envisioned a future society in which such a division would no longer exist and, as a consequence, in which the common good would no longer appear as superior to the individual's private interests. Rejecting reformism they looked forward to a political revolution that would usher in an age of peace, consensus, and liberty.

Of all the Young Hegelians, it was Ludwig Feuerbach (1804–1872) who exerted the greatest influence upon Marxist socialism. Born in Landshut, Germany, Feuerbach went to Berlin to study under Hegel in 1824. By 1828 he had received an appointment to teach philosophy at Erlangen but after a short time retired from the academy in pursuit of a private life devoted solely to scholarship. Included among his most important works are *The Essence of Christianity* (1841), *The Philosophy of the Future* (1843), and *The Essence of Religion* (1851).

In his early years, Feuerbach was an ardent disciple of Hegel and spent most of his time defending the doctrines of his former teacher. However by 1839 a series of disagreements had developed which eventually forced Feuerbach to reconsider his previous loyalties. In general, these disagreements centered around the issue of religion. For Hegel, the contents of religion and philosophy were essentially the same, and thus the two traditions differed from one another only in form. On one hand, philosophy expressed its content through ideas; on the other hand, religion relied upon the use of sensuous symbols. Yet, according to Hegel, each was saying fundamentally the same thing in spite of their different forms. For Feuerbach, however, religion and philosophy were not, in fact, equivalent. Philosophy belonged to the realm of thought; religion, however, was a product of emotion and feeling. As such religious beliefs were outside the realm of reason and constituted, thereby, an autonomous and essentially illegitimate domain.

By removing religion from the domain of reason Feuerbach had implicitly attacked a fundamental presupposition of the Hegelian system. For Hegel reason was absolute; it therefore applied universally to everything. For Feuerbach, however, reason was limited precisely because it was circumscribed by the realm of emotion, feeling, and passion which found expression in religious belief. As such, the absolutistic claim of Hegel's speculative idealism could no longer be honored. Thus beginning from a critique of religion, Feuerbach ultimately arrived at a rejection of idealistic philosophy itself.

Feuerbach's critique of religion made two fundamental charges. First, according to Feuerbach, religion had historically functioned as a reactionary social force which typically supported the status quo. By emphasizing the hereafter religion served to reconcile humanity with an earthly existence of poverty, misery, and injustice. As such it purposively worked against the forces of progress and development. Second, religious consciousness, according to Feuerbach, represented an alienated form of human existence. For the religious person, God exists as an independent being; in reality, however, according to Feuerbach, there can be no direct human experience of the divine. Thus, for Feuerbach, God was an illusion. He was simply the result of a psychological projection in which humanity confused its own imaginary creation with objective reality. The challenge, accordingly, was to expose religion for what it really was—"a dream of the mind."

The urgency with which Feuerbach undertook this challenge can be explained in terms of his understanding of human nature and its potential for self-realization. Human beings, for Feuerbach, had impoverished themselves by sumbitting to their own religious illusions. In creating their divinities they infinitized their own limited qualities, objectified them, and then worshipped them in the form of a god. Humanity was, as a consequence, alienating itself by removing from itself those properties which were truly its own and projecting them onto another. Thus such finite human qualities as goodness, justice, and love were infinitized and then projected as the absolute goodness, perfect justice, and total love of a god. The motive for doing this can be traced to the human need for an experience of the absolute. As creatures limited by their very condition, human beings desire to escape the finite order. Thus through an act of imagination they create the realm of the infinite and seek to console themselves by submitting to its principles. Yet, in doing this, the human race is at the same time depriving itself of those opportunities for true self-realization which are concretely at hand. In effect, by enriching god, humanity impoverishes itself.

Given this analysis, Feuerbach believed that the solution to this problem was essentially one of enlightenment. Humankind must come to realize that the so-called divine attributes are really only the alienated expressions of what are fundamentally human characteristics. The task, then, is to reappropriate these features by an overt act of consciousness. Having relocated these qualities within the sphere of the human, humanity can then proceed to structure its existence so as to reflect their presence. In effect, then, Feuerbach's conclusion is that god must be destroyed so that humanity can be realized. It is, as the philosopher Henri de Lubac has suggested, an example of atheist humanism:

> But if we look down the course of the ages to the dawn of modern times we make a strange discovery. That same Christian idea of man which had been welcomed as a deliverance was now beginning to be felt as a yoke. And that same God in whom man had learnt to see the seal of his own greatness began to seem to him like an antagonist, the enemy of his dignity . . . . This atheist humanism is not to be confused with a hedonist and coarsely materialist atheism—a commonplace phenomenon to be found in many periods of history. It is also quite contrary in principle—if not in its results—to an atheism of despair . . . . The problem posed was a human problem—it was *the* human problem—and the solution which is being given to it is one that claims to be positive. Man is getting rid of God in order to regain possession of the human greatness which, it seems to him, is being unwarrantably withheld by another. In God he is overthrowing an obstacle in order to gain his freedom.[19]

Having broken with Hegel on the issue of religion, Feuerbach proceeded with an attack on Hegelian idealistic philosophy proper. At the

---

[19] Henri de Lubac, S. J., *The Drama of Atheist Humanism*, trans. Edith M. Riley (Cleveland: World Publishing Co., 1963), pp. 5–6.

center of this critique was Feuerbach's perception that idealistic philosophy, especially as developed by Hegel, was, in fact, nothing more than a rationalized form of religious consciousness. Referring to Hegel's thought as "speculative philosophy," Feuerbach wrote in 1842:

> The secret of *theology* is *anthropology* but *theology* itself is the secret of *speculative philosophy* which thus turns out to be *speculative* theology. As such, it distinguished itself from *ordinary* theology by the fact that it places the divine being back into this world—ordinary theology projects it into the beyond out of fear and ignorance; in contrast to ordinary theology, it [speculative theology] *actualizes, determines,* and *realizes* the Divine Being.[20]

According to Feuerbach Hegel's religious character was evident in his neo-Platonism. Similar to Plotinus Hegel had refused to accept the fact that matter existed as an independent reality. For Hegel the material realm was simply an alienated manifestation of the spiritual. Once this was understood, reality could be seen as singular, simple, and indistinct; everything was god or spirit. For Feuerbach, on the other hand, Hegel's monistic system was faulty because it ignored the fundamentally dichotomous nature of reality. According to him, the realm of the material and that of the spiritual existed independently of one another, and consequently neither could be adequately explained in terms of the other. Efforts to do so would necessarily lead to an unduly abstracted view of nature. For Feuerbach, an adequate understanding of humanity and nature had to remain at the level of the concrete and particular:

> Do not think as a thinker, that is, with a faculty torn from the totality of the real human being and isolated for itself; think as a living and real being, as one exposed to the vivifying and refreshing waves of the world's ocean. Think in existence, in the world as a member of it, not in the vacuum of abstraction as a solitary monad, as an absolute monarch, as an indifferent, superworldly god.[21]

Inasmuch as the concrete, sensuous particular can only be grasped by sense perception, ideas and abstract thought can never really capture the objects of reality in their individuality. Thus, according to Feuerbach, there will always be a necessary gap between reason and reality; just as there is always a separation between subject and object, and the spiritual and material. Indeed, it was precisely Hegel's failure to acknowledge these

---

[20] Zawar Hanli, ed., *The Fiery Brook: Selected Writings of Ludwig Feuerbach* (Garden City: Doubleday, 1972), p. 153.

[21] Ludwig Feuerbach, *Principles of the Philosophy of the Future*, trans. Manfred H. Vogel (Indianapolis: Bobbs-Merrill, 1966), p. 67.

irreducible dichotomies which finally convinced Feuerbach of the religious and unreal quality of Hegelian thought. For Feuerbach both religion and idealistic philosophy were exposed as creations of humanity's alienated consciousness. To overcome this, therefore, humanity had to turn its attention to the sphere of the human and the realm of the finite:

> Just as in theology, *man* is the *truth* and *reality* of God—for all predicates that realize God as God, or make God into a *real* being, predicates such as power, wisdom, goodness, love, even infinity and personality, which have as their condition the *distinction* from the finite, are posited first *in* and *with* man—likewise in speculative philosophy the *finite* is the *truth* of the infinite.[22]

In doing this humanity would have begun the process of human self-realization. Commenting on the importance of Feuerbach for Marx's development, Henri de Lubac has written:

> The combination of French socialism, English economics, and German metaphysics might have produced something quite different from Marxism, if Marx had not found a master in Feuerbach.[23]

In particular, Feuerbach led the way for Marx's adoption of a radical anthropocentrism. This is clear in three distinct cases. First, whereas Hegel had been correct in specifying that an analysis of alienation was the central task facing the philosopher, he had, nonetheless, mistakenly argued that it was God who was alienated. Feuerbach, on the other hand, treated alienation as a strictly human phenomenon. According to his analysis it was humanity, not God, who was alienated, and, indeed, a belief in God's existence actually served as proof of this fact. Second, whereas Hegel had interpreted history as the process by which alienation would be overcome and thus had read history as if it were a great spiritual drama, Feuerbach insisted upon history's human importance. Inasmuch as alienation was a human attribute, history became the story of humanity's self-realization. It was nothing less than humankind's movement towards an immanent perfection. Finally, Feuerbach had shown that Hegel had confused the subject and object of history. For Hegel, consciousness was the subject of history and humanity its object. For Feuerbach, the reverse was the case. Humanity was the true subject of history, and thought was its predicate. Thus philosophers who wanted to realize their theory in practice must begin with history's true subject—the concrete, natural human being.

By following Feuerbach's example, Marx was able to free himself

---

[22] Hanfi, *The Fiery Brook: Selected Writings of Ludwig Feuerbach*, p. 159.
[23] de Lubac, *The Drama of Atheist Humanism*, p. 17.

from the limitations of the idealist tradition. Yet, at the same time, because of Feuerbach, he could do so while still maintaining such important idealistic concepts as "alienation" and "history-as-drama."

BIBLIOGRAPHY

AVINERI, SHLOMO. *Hegel's Theory of the Modern State.* Cambridge: Cambridge University Press, 1972.

COLE, G.D.H. *The Life of Robert Owen.* London: Macmillan, 1930.

GRAY, ALEXANDER. *The Socialist Tradition: Moses to Lenin.* New York: Longmans, Green, & Co., 1946.

HOOK, SIDNEY. *From Hegel to Marx.* New York: Humanities Press, 1950.

LICHTHEIM, GEORGE. *The Origins of Socialism.* New York: Praeger, 1969.

LOEWITH, KARL. *From Hegel to Nietzsche.* Translated by David Green. Garden City: Doubleday, 1967.

MANUEL, FRANK. *The Prophets of Paris.* New York: Harper & Row, 1965.

MARCUSE, HERBERT. *Reason and Revolution: Hegel and the Rise of Social Theory.* Boston: Beacon Press, 1960.

MORTON, A. L. *The Life and Ideas of Robert Owen.* New York: International Publishing, 1969.

TALMON, J. L. *Romanticism and Revolt: Europe 1815–1848.* New York: Harcourt, Brace & World, 1967.

TAYLOR, CHARLES. *Hegel and Modern Society.* Cambridge: Cambridge University Press, 1979.

16

KARL MARX

LIFE AND WRITINGS

Karl Marx was born into a comfortable Jewish middle-class family in Trier, Germany, in 1818. As such he was exposed to both the anti-Prussian feelings of his native Rhineland and the tenets of liberal rationalism as preached by his father. After a year of semiserious study at the University of Bonn, Marx was transferred to the University of Berlin in 1836. There he met with members of the Young Hegelian movement, which at that time was organized under the leadership of Bruno Bauer. Following Bauer's example Marx decided to prepare himself for a career as a university instructor. He wrote a dissertation comparing the atomic theories of Democritus and Epicurus and eventually received his doctorate from the University of Jena. Upon completing his studies Marx looked forward to an academic appointment which he believed could be secured through Bauer's influence. Unfortunately, however, Bauer's own career was short-lived: he was dismissed in 1842 for publishing a work which challenged the historicity of Christ. Having lost all hope for an academic career Marx subsequently turned to political journalism.

In the spring of 1842 Marx began to write a series of articles and commentaries for the *Rheinische Zeitung*. But since, in general, the paper reflected the liberal political principles of the Rheinish business community, it was not long before it was suppressed by the censors of the Prussian monarchy. Following this setback Marx migrated to Paris. There he joined with Arnold Ruge to publish the *Deutsch-Franzoesische Jahrbuecher* (Yearbook) and in his spare time began reading extensively in the areas of modern French history and British economic theory. The notes he wrote during this period were discovered only much later; they were first published in 1927 as *The Economic and Philosophical Manuscripts*.

While serving as an editor of Ruge's yearbook, Marx received two articles for publication which were sent to him by a German industrialist who was living at that time in Manchester, England. The author of these articles was Friedrich Engels (1820–1895), and he wrote them after he had been sent to Manchester to apprentice in his father's factory. As a youth, Engels had been influenced by the philosophical writings of such Young Hegelians as David Strauss and Ludwig Feuerbach. At the same time he had come to accept the socialist vision of the communist rabbi Moses Hess. Thus while in Manchester, Engels resolved to take advantage of his location by studying firsthand the social effects of the industrial revolution. The eventual result of this investigation was his *The Conditions of the Working Class in England in 1844*.

Returning to Germany from Manchester in that same year, Engels decided to stop in Paris in order to meet with Marx. This meeting, which Engels later described as being extremely cordial, began one of the most important collaborations in the history of Western political theory. In addition to providing Marx with financial support, Engels joined him both in the pursuit of socialist scholarship and in the practical organization of the communist movement. With Marx's death in 1883, Engels became the major spokesman for Marxist socialism and wrote such important works as *Anti-Duehring* (1877–1878), *Ludwig Feuerbach and the Outcome of Classical German Philosophy* (1888), and the posthumously published *Dialectics of Nature*.

After their meeting in 1844, Marx and Engels resolved to work together in criticizing the idealism of the Young Hegelians. The results of this early collaboration included both *The Holy Family* (1844) and *The German Ideology* (1845). In addition to the *Communist Manifesto of 1848*, their most famous cooperative project was the massive *Das Kapital*. Marx lived only long enough to complete volume I. Consequently volume II (1885) and volume III (1895) were published only after Engels had worked through and edited Marx's unfinished manuscripts. The fourth and final volume was published by Karl Kautsky under the title *Theories of Surplus Value.*

Marx's work as a journalist in Paris soon led to his expulsion from France. Moving to Brussels, he quickly became involved with a group of German emigres who at that time were attempting to organize a clandestine communist movement throughout Germany, France, and England. This group, the League of the Just, approached Marx in 1847, requesting that he and Engels prepare a theoretical statement which would summarize the philosophy of the working-class movement. The result of this effort was the *Communist Manifesto of 1848.* This attempt to summarize the philosophy of the movement was necessitated in part by the doctrinal differences which separated the major socialist theorists of Marx's time. Given this division Marx and Engels found themselves continually defending their own preferred position against the alternatives of such theorists as German evangelical communist Wilhelm Weitling (1808–1871) and French anarchist Pierre Joseph Proudhon (1809–1865).

Weakened by its internal theoretical disagreements, the international working-class movement was further damaged by the events of 1848. Throughout France, Germany, and Austria the bourgeoisie were successfully demanding a liberal reform of the traditional aristocratic political order. Unlike other socialists Marx originally supported the aspirations of the middle class in the hope that its liberal reforms would eventually lead to socialist goals. In time, however, a conservative reaction set in, and it soon became apparent that the political events of 1848 would not serve as a vehicle for proletarian liberation. Indeed, by 1849 the European monarchies were restored and the reform movement was effectively ended. In that same year Marx moved with his family to London, England.

Once settled, Marx began his visits to the reading room of the British Museum. There he engaged in the study and research which would eventually culminate in his most important works. After publishing his analysis of the events of 1848, which he entitled *The Class Struggle in France*, Marx focused almost exclusively on the study of political economy and its relationship to humanity's historical condition. The program for these studies was outlined in an 800-page manuscript known as the *Grundrisse.* There Marx indicated his intention to publish his *magnum opus* which would contain six major sections. Although he collected notes and materials for the entire project, as we know, Marx actually succeeded in publishing only the first of four volumes, which together constituted only the first section of the entire study. That first section became his *Das Kapital.*

The immense scope of Marx's total project explains in part his difficulty in finishing the work. There are, however, other facts to be considered. First, Marx did not manage his personal finances carefully. Consequently his family was often impoverished. Although Engels helped to support him, Marx finally sought a regular income by working as a foreign correspondent for the *New York Daily Tribune*. His articles covered all aspects of contemporary politics, and so they required a fair amount of research. As a consequence, Marx's newspaper work often distracted him from his larger project outlined in the *Grundrisse*. Second, Marx's theoretical work was restricted by his practical political involvements. In 1864 he joined in forming the International Workingmen's Association and served on its general council for eight years. During that period he was concerned with formulating the International's position vis-à-vis such political questions as Polish independence, Irish home rule, and, most importantly, the Franco-Prussian War and the Paris Commune. In addition to facing the expected external pressures, the First International, as it would later be called, was also threatened by internal dissent. In particular, the followers of the Russian anarchist Mikhail Bakunin (1814–1876) resisted Marx's efforts to centralize the administration of the International and to promote, thereby, his own theoretical preferences. As Bakunin's influence grew, Marx decided to relocate the headquarters of the International in New York and thus succeeded in destroying the organization.

Because of Engels, Marx was able to spend the last years of his life in relative luxury. His work, however, was hampered by his ill-health and subsequent loss of energy. He suffered terribly from boils and had a stroke in 1873. It was during this period, however, that he wrote his famous analysis of the German socialist party, published as *Critique of the Gotha Program*. Having lost both his wife and daughter, Marx died peacefully in 1883.

THE THEORY OF ALIENATION

The fact that Marx moved several times before finally settling in London has had an interesting effect upon the history of Marxist scholarship. His sudden departure from Paris meant that many of his earliest writings remained unpublished during his own lifetime. Indeed, it was only in the third decade of this century that writings such as *The Economic and Philosophical Manuscripts*, *German Ideology*, and *Grundrisse* were finally published. Consequently, prior to their appearance an interpretation of Marx's ideas depended entirely upon a reading of his later works in general and of *Das Kapital* in particular. Hence, Marx at one time was often understood to be preoccupied with the technical analysis of complex economic structures. With the publication of his earlier writings, however, it soon became apparent that Marx was seriously concerned with an entire set of humanistic and philosophical issues. Among these, the most important was that of alienation.

According to Marx, every natural species is characterized by its own unique activity. Thus humankind can be differentiated from the other animal species because the human being alone is capable of performing certain defining tasks. Specifically, humanity's uniqueness is established by the fact that it alone is capable of creative labor. Animals may work within their environment but only humanity is able to transform it. Thus the essence of our humanness is to be found in our ability to freely and creatively work. To be fully human means to be freely engaged in creative labor. And being engaged in such labor allows individuals to experience the fullness of their human potential. For Marx, then, the rewards of work cannot be reduced to the immediate material benefits that are derived from its completion. On the contrary, for Marx work is the essential means by which people both express and enjoy their individual lives. In describing the joy of creative and therefore human labor, Marx wrote:

> Supposing that we had produced in a human manner; each of us would in his production have doubly affirmed himself and his fellow men. I would have: (1) objectified in my production my individuality and its peculiarity and thus both in my activity enjoyed an individual expression of my life and also in looking at the object have had the individual pleasure of realizing that my personality was objective, visible to the senses and thus a power raised beyond all doubt. (2) In your enjoyment or use of my product I would have had the direct enjoyment of realizing that I had both satisfied a human need by my work and also objectified the human essence and therefore fashioned for another human being the object that met his need. (3) I would have been for you the mediator between you and the species and thus been acknowledged and felt by you as a completion of your own essence and a necessary part of yourself and have thus realized that I am confirmed both in your thought and in your love. (4) In my expression of my life I would have fashioned your expression of your life, and thus in my own activity have realized my own essence, my human, my communal essence. In that case our products would be like so many mirrors, out of which our essence shone.[1]

Central to Marx's analysis is the argument that humans have never actually enjoyed the benefits of creative labor precisely because they have never been allowed to labor freely. Indeed Marx began the above quotation

---

[1] David McLellan, ed., *Karl Marx: Selected Writings* (Oxford: Oxford University Press, 1977), pp. 121–122.

with a presupposition—one which he felt was necessary because humanity, according to Marx, has never in fact "produced in a human manner." For Marx historical humankind has never realized its true humanness. Rather it has been and continues to live as an animal, and thus the human being is alienated.

Alienation results from those distortions in the human condition which are introduced by the division of labor. The division of labor, whereby specific tasks are assigned to specific individuals, developed as a response to a growing population, the historical development of human needs, and increased productivity. As the division of labor increased, people were compelled to specialize in a given trade and, in so doing, ultimately became nothing more than mere tradespeople. Rather than living full, well-rounded lives, they became specialists who adjusted their lives according to the narrow demands of their profession:

> For as soon as the distribution of labour comes into being, each man has a particular, exclusive sphere of activity which is forced upon him and from which he cannot escape. He is a hunter, a fisherman, a shepherd, or a critical critic, and must remain so if he does not want to lose his means of livelihood. . . . [2]

Several consequences followed immediately from this introduction of the division of labor. First, in the same manner that the tasks of labor were being assigned, so, too, were its products being distributed. Thus the division of labor implied the creation of private property and established, thereby, the reign of inequality. Second, by enforcing narrow specialization, the division of labor created a distinction between the interest of the individual specialist and the interest of the community at large. Soon the state emerged as the embodiment of the community's interest and placed itself in opposition to the legitimate needs of the individual. Finally, the division of labor destroyed the real meaning of human work. Labor no longer appeared as a mode of self-expression but rather simply became a means to material life.

According to Marx's analysis, humans introduced the division of labor early in their history. At first, it was simply an extension of the natural division of labor found within the sex act. Yet as the means of material production developed, the division of labor evolved so as to accommodate the improving forces of technology. This occurred because a fundamental change in the dominant techniques of production necessarily required a corresponding adjustment in the division of labor. Yet, inasmuch as each of the various stages in the development of the division of labor required its own particular form of property and ownership, the history of tech-

---

[2] McLellan, *Karl Marx: Selected Writings*, p. 169.

nological development was, in effect, the history of property. Indeed for Marx, an examination of the various property systems was the only "natural base" for the writing of history. Accordingly, in analyzing humanity's history, Marx focused upon five fundamental forms of ownership:

TRIBAL OWNERSHIP.   Tribal society corresponded to the most primitive stage of productive techniques. Hunting, fishing, and some forms of agriculture were the main economic occupations. Accordingly, the division of labor was quite elementary, and society was composed of three basic classes: the chieftains, the tribespeople, and slaves.

ANCIENT COMMUNAL OWNERSHIP.   When several tribes came together to form a city, the community, as a whole, joined in the ownership of certain goods. In addition, there were some forms of private property, but these were always subordinated to the requirements of communal ownership. Slavery continued, but the division of labor became more complex. As the techniques of production developed tensions arose among the several groups associated with the various forms of production. For example, conflicts occurred between the commercial interests of the town and the agricultural interests of the country. In addition, within the towns themselves maritime and industrial interests began to clash. As these groups struggled with one another, the victors acquired the property of the losers, and more and more wealth began to concentrate in fewer and fewer hands.

FEUDAL OWNERSHIP.   With the destruction of the Roman Empire by the barbarians both agricultural and industrial production fell sharply. Trade was almost nonexistent, and the population of Europe began to decline. Out of these conditions the semimilitary feudal order emerged. On the land the nobility owned the property and thereby exploited the enserfed peasantry. In the cities the manufacturing classes commanded the labor of the guildmembers. In both cases, however, the scale of production was small, and initially the division of labor was limited. Soon, however, with the discovery of America and the extension of markets into China and East India, trade, navigation, and industry began to develop rapidly. The traditional industrial system of feudalism was too limited to take full advantage of these opportunities and was, therefore, replaced by the manufacturing order of capitalism.

CAPITALIST OWNERSHIP.   In capitalism the division of labor reached its most extreme state. Industrialization, world trade, and the demands of a constantly expanding market required increased mechanization within the production process. Consequently work became simplified and repetitious. Politically, the bourgeoisie replaced the landed aristocracy as the ruling class, and the nation-state emerged as the structure for social order. Most importantly, however, capitalism produced the proletariat, and with its emergence the solution to "the riddles of history" was at hand.

COMMUNISM.   The final social form would be that of communism. Although it was the product of the history of the division of labor, communism would be unlike all previous forms of ownership precisely because it would overcome the division of labor. Recalling his earlier statement about humanity as condemned to being "a hunter, a fisherman, [or] a shepherd," Marx wrote:

> . . . in communist society, where nobody was one exclusive sphere of activity but each can become accomplished in any branch he wishes, society regulates the general production and thus makes it possible for me to do one thing today and another tomorrow, to hunt in the morning, fish in the afternoon, rear cattle in the evening, criticize after dinner, just as I have in mind, without ever becoming hunter, fisherman, cowherd, or critic.[3]

From this analysis of the stages of ownership, it is obvious that Marx believed that humankind had been alienated throughout all of its previous history. Yet, like Hegel, Marx's theory of history was an essentially dramatic one. Thus for him alienation was a condition to be overcome and the moment was finally at hand. The means for this transformation would be the revolutionary activity of the proletariat.

THE REVOLUTIONARY PROLETARIAT

For Marx the proletariat was capable of completing history by overcoming alienation because of its unique condition. Although all people had suffered from some form of alienation, only the proletariat had experienced its total effect. Thus, inasmuch as the proletariat was totally alienated, it was at the same time capable of being totally revolutionary. According to Marx, all previous revolutionary classes had only accomplished partial revolutions. They had succeeded in overthrowing one form of class rule only to replace it with another. For example, the bourgeoisie defeated the landed aristocracy only to replace monarchy with democracy. Liberal democracy, however, was still a form of class rule and, as such, represented the preferred status of the commercial interests. With the total revolution of the proletariat, however, class rule as such would be destroyed. In destroying the state the pro-

---

[3] McLellan, *Karl Marx: Selected Writings*, p. 169.

letarian revolution would actually abolish the political sphere itself. The proletariat's ability to accomplish this world historical event was due to its total alienation—an alienation, in turn, which was made possible by capitalism. Unlike all previous social orders, only capitalism has succeeded in producing the totally dehumanized person. Thus, as Marx wrote in his *Communist Manifesto:*

> The bourgeoisie, wherever it has got the upper hand, has put an end to all feudal, patriarchal, idyllic relations. It has pitilessly torn asunder the motley feudal ties that bound man to his "natural superiors," and has left remaining no other nexus between man and man than naked self-interest, than callous "cash payment." It has drowned the most heavenly ecstasies of religious fervour, of chivalrous enthusiasm, of philistine sentimentalism, in the icy water of egotistical calculation. It has resolved personal worth into exchange value, and in place of the numberless indefeasible chartered freedoms, has set up that single, unconscionable freedom—Free Trade. In one word, for exploitation, veiled by religious and political illusions, it has substituted naked, shameless, direct, brutal exploitation.
>
> The bourgeoisie has stripped of its halo every occupation hitherto honoured and looked up to with reverent awe. It has converted the physician, the lawyer, the priest, the poet, the man of science into its paid wage labourers.
>
> The bourgeoisie has torn away from the family its sentimental veil, and has reduced the family relation to a mere money relation.[4]

According to Marx, the proletarian class is defined by two characteristics. First, it is characterized by its unique relationship to the means of production. Although it works with the tools of industrial production, it does not own them. Thus it possesses nothing but its own labor power and consequently sells that power to the capitalist in an exchange for wages. Second, the proletariat is defined by its own unique consciousness. Its situation within the capitalist system has provided it with an important insight into the working structures of bourgeois society. Accordingly, proletarian consciousness is revolutionary consciousness. The working class realizes that it can end its own suffering only by destroying the capitalist system as such. General improvements in working conditions and the specific reforms sought by the trade-union movement are not sufficient. Rather capitalism itself and the division of labor as such must be overcome. This insight, in turn, develops as a spontaneous achievement brought about by the very conditions of proletarian existence. The most important feature of this existence is the fact of alienation.

[4] McLellan, *Karl Marx: Selected Writings,* p. 223–24.

All individuals within capitalism are alienated. Yet the bourgeoisie is unaware of its condition because capitalists both enjoy the benefits of wealth and are immune to the frustration of alienated labor because they do not, in fact, work. The working class, on the other hand, has no such protection. Indeed, its alienation is experienced in four distinct ways. First, the product of the workers' labor appears to them as an alien object. Although it is their power which has produced it, the object, itself, belongs to the capitalists. Thus, as Marx wrote:

> . . . it exists outside him [the workers], independent and alien, and becomes a self-sufficient power opposite him . . . the life that he has lent to the object affronts him, hostile and alien.[5]

Second, inasmuch as the products of labor appear alienated, so, too, does the laboring process itself. The proletariat works not because it wants to but because it is forced to. Thus rather than experiencing labor as the free expression of their creative talents, the workers learn to tolerate it for the sake of their wages. In such a situation, labor becomes a means to an end, and the end is simply basic material existence. Ideally, nonalienated labor would be that activity which distinguishes humanity from the lower animal species. Yet, in capitalism, it is distorted and thus reduced simply to being the means by which humanity services its lower animal needs:

> The result we arrive at then is that man [the worker] only feels himself freely active in his animal functions of eating, drinking, and procreating, at most also in his dwelling and dress, and feels himself an animal in his human functions.[6]

Third, inasmuch as creative labor is the characteristic function of the human species, its alienation inevitably produces a distortion in humanity's species awareness. While on one hand, true labor allows individuals to express their own unique personalities, on the other, it is the means by which the species articulates its own essential character. Thus free labor allows human beings to develop both as individuals and members of the human species. Specifically, it provides the only opportunity for individuals to participate in and identify with their species-life. Its alienation, in turn, denies humans such a possibility:

> Therefore when alienated labour tears from man the object of his production, it also tears from him his species-life . . . . Similarly, in that alienated labour degrades man's own activity to a means, it

[5] McLellan, *Karl Marx: Selected Writings*, p. 79.
[6] McLellan, *Karl Marx: Selected Writings*, p. 80–81.

turns the species-life of man into a means for his physical existence. Thus consciousness, which man derives from his species, changes itself through alienation so that species-life becomes a means for him.[7]

Finally, the members of the proletariat experience their alienation even in their relationship with one another. Having lost an appreciation of their species-relatedness, each individual comes to understand himself/herself primarily as a solitary, egoistical being. Given this, one's fellow humans necessarily appear as competitors rather than as compatriots. The result is a society wherein people are estranged from one another and thereby deprived of any meaningful social relationships. Ironically, therefore, the highly organized and complex relations of capitalistic production have had the effect of producing a society of isolated individuals.

THE CRISIS OF CAPITALISM

The plight of the proletarian class is not, however, a sufficient condition for a successful revolution from the Marxist perspective. Human alienation cannot be overcome by simply wishing to do so. Rather the successful abolition of alienation requires a concrete, practical opportunity. Specifically, before the proletariat can revolt, capitalism must be in a crisis situation. Accordingly, much of Marx's economic analysis was designed to demonstrate the reality of such a crisis. Indeed his examinations concluded that capitalism had finally reached a point in its development in which it was threatened by internal contradictions. At the most general level, these contradictions arose from a conflict between the forces and forms of production.

According to Marx, at each level of technological development, certain institutions are created to organize and administer the available instruments of production. For example, the private property system originally provided an efficient and supportive environment for the forces of production employed in both agriculture and small industry during the sixteenth and seventeenth centuries. However, as science and technology develop new instruments of production, the productive forces soon expand beyond their original limits. In doing so, they outgrow those institutions which were originally created to administer the more primitive instruments. Thus a contradiction develops. The outdated institutions no longer support the expansion of production. On the contrary, they tend to

[7] McLellan, *Karl Marx: Selected Writings*, p. 82–83.

thwart further development and, thereby, interfere with the necessary growth of productive ability.

As an example, one can consider the situation in manufacturing during feudalism. Under feudalism manufacturing was administered from within the guild system. The guilds, however, were not only bound by tradition but were fundamentally uninterested in technological development. As such, they discouraged the creation of new instruments for production and limited the opportunities for commercial investment. If the newly available instruments of production were to be employed in an efficient manner, the restraints of the feudal order had to be removed. This, in turn, was precisely what was accomplished by the introduction of the free market and its appropriate capitalistic institutions. Accordingly, capitalism created an economic, political, and social environment which encouraged the full use of the available forces of production. In doing so, it revolutionized the industrial system, created a world market, and established the ascendancy of the big city.

According to Marx's analysis, however, contemporary capitalism, like feudalism in its day, has now reached a point where it can no longer sustain significant productive growth. Its institutions, in turn, have become fetters to further expansion. And, thus, its history has become one of contradiction and conflict:

> The history of industry and commerce for many a decade past is but the history of the revolt of modern productive forces against modern conditions of production, against the property relations that are the conditions for the existence of the bourgeoisie and of its rule.[8]

For Marx, the proof of this argument was provided by the recurring crises within capitalism itself. As a system, it had exhausted its potential and was currently plagued by internal contradictions which were endemic to its very principles. As such, it could not correct its problems without destroying itself.

According to Marx, then, capitalism had finally evolved to that point where its forms of production actually contradicted its developed forces of production. Specifically, the capitalist system is based upon an antagonism between the effective socialization of production and its private capitalistic form of appropriation. With the development of mechanized industry and its subsequent need for specialized labor, no one individual produces all that he or she needs. Rather the work of each has become indispensable for the survival of all, and production, therefore, has assumed a cooperative character. Modern industry requires the careful organization

[8] McLellan, *Karl Marx: Selected Writings*, p. 226.

or coordination of thousands of particular operations. Its high productivity, in turn, is the result of precisely such an effort. Yet, even though the forces of industrialized production have, in fact, been "socialized," their direction and control are not the result of any conscious plan. On the contrary, in capitalism it is the blind forces of the market which determine the eventual decisions of those who own the means of production. Having appropriated the results of production, the individual capitalist is motivated solely by a consideration of private interest. Thus private profit becomes the driving force of production, and the satisfaction of enduring social needs is achieved only indirectly, if at all. For Marx, this fundamental contradiction between the socialized forces and the private forms of production had finally reached a critical stage. In demonstrating this, he pointed to several specific problems.

First, inasmuch as there is no binding social regulation of production, capitalists cannot be assured of a constant demand for their product. In a competitive market, success today may not be followed by success tomorrow. Thus the capitalists are under constant pressure to acquire more profit as the sole means by which they can develop their competitive advantage. This thirst for profit, in turn, compels capitalists to undertake certain adventures. Specifically, they must invest their available resources in those enterprises which promise the most return. Accordingly, in the free-market system, money tends to flow and ebb. It flows into those areas where profits are large and ebbs from those where they are small. This feature of capitalism, however, has several disturbing consequences. First, those areas of production which are relatively unprofitable may, nevertheless, be essential for the satisfaction of society's legitimate needs. Consequently, it is possible that at a given time, such important social goods as medical care or educational services may be in short supply. Likewise, high profits may be available in areas which are relatively frivolous or only of a secondary importance, that is, luxury items. Yet, as long as the profits remain high, there will be an overproduction of such items. Given this pattern, the production of goods within capitalism appears uncontrolled. Capital is transferred from project to project with little consideration of this action's effect upon the common good. As a result, society, as a whole, is deprived of all direct control over its economic processes. Marx referred to this feature of capitalism as *anarchy*.

As more and more capital flows into a certain area of production, the number of goods produced increases. Yet, as the overall supply increases, the price per item will necessarily decline. Given this, the level of profit will eventually fall below that of other areas, and capital will be withdrawn as a result. This withdrawal of capital causes a decline in productivity, and the market adjusts by raising the price of each item. As this occurs, the level of profit rises once again and in time capital will return.

Thus the cycle of overproduction and underproduction is completed only to begin once again. As it does, each industry moves from a crisis of overproduction to one of underproduction, and the economy, as a whole, alternates between periods of deflation and inflation. Thus rather than being an efficient and rational system of production, capitalism operates in fits and starts. If it is to survive, it must rely upon the exploitation of the worker.

According to Marx, the exploitation of the worker is a necessary feature of the capitalistic system. Workers, owning nothing, must sell their labor power in order to receive those wages necessary to support themselves and their families. Thus in exchange for a certain amount of capital they offer a certain amount of labor power. Capitalists are interested in such an exchange because, according to Marx's labor theory of value, labor power is the source of all value. Any item is only as valuable as that amount of socially necessary labor which is required for its production. Thus in the capitalists' effort to produce valuable goods which they can sell, they must purchase that labor power which will be invested in the production of their commodities. If the values exchanged between capitalists and workers were equivalent, there would be no exploitation. According to Marx, however, such an equivalency does not exist in capitalism. Workers are paid a given wage but in return are required to contribute more labor power than is represented by the capital which they receive in exchange. For example, it may be that a worker could produce enough value in four hours to fully repay the capitalist for the wage he or she has received. However, typically in capitalism the laborer may be required to work an additional four to six hours a day. The additional value created during that period belongs to the capitalist as surplus value and represents the source of his or her profits. According to Marx, therefore, capitalism exploits workers, not the consumers. Profits are extracted during the process of production by appropriating excess labor power rather than during the process of exchange by overcharging customers.

In view of this theory, it is obvious that capitalists' search for profits is simultaneously a search for surplus labor power. As their need for profit increases, so, too, does their need to extract additional labor power beyond that of the value represented in the wages paid out. The most obvious means of doing so is to extend the working day. Rather than requiring an additional four to six hours beyond that necessary to cover the cost of wages, some may demand instead eight or ten. There is, however, an obvious natural limit to such a strategy, and that limit is approached as overworked laborers become less and less efficient. The second and superior alternative, therefore, is to increase the productivity of laborers during their actual hours of working, and this, in turn, can best be achieved through the introduction of machinery. The mechanization of the manufacturing process, therefore, appears as the immediate solution to the dilemma of capitalists.

Thus, it is not surprising that the history of capitalism reflects a fundamental commitment to technological progress. Unlike the guild system, capitalism attempts to rationalize every aspect of the production process and, in doing so, subjects every tradition and technique to the test of efficiency.

Capitalism's commitment to technological progress has produced a marked increase in the level of profits. Yet, according to Marx, there are other, unintended long-range consequences which will eventually dictate the destruction of the very system which first produced them. First, although mechanization may appear to ease the plight of the proletariat, it eventually intensifies the suffering of workers and thereby radicalizes their political consciousness. For example, Marx saw the large-scale introduction of machinery as the primary cause of massive unemployment. In addition, by simplifying the tasks to be performed, technology denies the value of skilled labor. And finally, by intensifying the division of labor, industrial production increases the experience of alienation. One long-term effect of this process, then, is the creation of a revolutionary class.

The second unintended consequence of capitalist mechanization concerns its very strategy for development. Originally, the capitalists had introduced machinery in order to secure a higher level of profit. According to Marx, however, industrial technology eventually must lead to an unavoidable decline in the rate of profit itself. The capitalists, therefore, are caught in a dilemma. In order to survive the present, they must initiate a process which will necessarily destroy them in the future. To explain the inevitability of this decline in the rate of profit, Marx employed an analysis which was based upon the labor theory of value. As has been shown, this theory argues that the value of any commodity is essentially the sum total of three factors. The price which the capitalists charge must include: (1) their investment in the machinery (C); (2) the wages they pay to the workers (V); and (3) the surplus value or profit (S) which they need to derive from the transaction. The rate of profit, therefore, is a function of the relationship between the capitalists' costs and their surplus value. More precisely, it may be expressed by the formula $S/C + V$. Inasmuch as labor power (V) is the source of new value, its increase will, nonetheless, produce an additional increase in the amount of surplus value (S) and thereby improve the rate of profit overall. However, an increase in the value of the machinery (C) does not produce a corresponding increase in surplus value (S) because surplus value is created only by appropriating living labor power. Thus as the capitalists invest greater and greater amounts of their available capital into machinery they are, at the same time, reducing that portion of their wealth which can be used to purchase surplus labor power. As a result, the capitalists' rate of profit declines precisely as their investment in machinery (C) increases. Thus, assuming Marx's labor theory of value, the very process of mechanization, itself, implies an eventual decline in profit. Although each individual capitalist is required by his or her own subjective interests to modernize, the capitalistic system as a whole faces an inevitable decline in its rate of profit. With this decline, its growth ceases and its contribution to history ends. According to Marx, the increasingly radicalized proletariat and the correspondingly exhausted capitalistic system were two factors which converged to produce a truly revolutionary situation.

THE COMMUNIST SOCIETY

In his writings, Marx refused to predict the exact details of the future communist society. Nonetheless, he did suggest certain general characteristics by which his new age could be identified. For example, the movement into communism would require two distinct phases. First, following the proletarian revolution, a transition stage of relatively short duration would be necessary. This period, called "crude communism," would cleanse society from any remaining capitalistic attributes. Accordingly, it would bring about the destruction of the private-property system by ruthlessly fulfilling the contradictory logic of its development. As such, it would be an unpleasant and painful experience characterized by the division of labor, the distribution of wealth according to work, and social inequality. Politically crude communism would be organized as a dictatorship of the proletariat. In his *Paris Manuscripts of 1844* Marx described this period in the following terms:

> In its original form [crude communism is] only a generalization and completion of private property. As such it appears in a dual form: firstly, it is faced with such a great domination of material property that it wishes to destroy everything that cannot be possessed by everybody as private property; it wishes to abstract forcibly from talent, etc. It considers immediate physical ownership as the sole aim of life and being. The category of worker is not abolished but extended to all men. The relationship of the community to the world of things remains that of private property. Finally, this process of opposing general private property to private property is expressed in the animal form of opposing to marriage (which is of course a form of exclusive private property) the community of women where the woman becomes the common property of the community. One might say that the idea of the community of women reveals the open secret of this completely crude and unthinking type of communism. Just as women pass from marriage to universal prostitution, so the whole world of wealth, that is the ob-

jective essence of man, passes from the relationship of exclusive marriage to the private property owner to the relationship of universal prostitution with the community. By systematically denying the personality of man this communism is merely the consistent expression of private property which is just this negation. Universal envy setting itself up as a power is the concealed form of greed which merely asserts itself and satisfies itself in another way. The thoughts of every private property owner as such are at least turned against those richer than they as an envious desire to level down. This envious desire is precisely the essence of competition. Crude communism is only the completion of this envy and levelling down to a preconceived minimum. It has a particular and limited standard. How little this abolition of private property constitutes a real appropriation is proved by the abstract negation of the whole world of culture and civilization, a regression to the unnatural simplicity of the poor man without any needs who has not even arrived at the stage of private property, let alone got beyond it.[9]

Although Marx does not specify how long this period of crude communism would last, there is little doubt that he considered it to be a relatively short-lived necessity. With its disappearance he envisioned the development of mature communism, and it is the latter stage which represents for Marx the culmination of humanity's historical development. In mature communism each person would work according to individual ability. In return, each would be assured of receiving all that he or she needed. Thus freed from the demands of wage labor, the workers could devote themselves to those tasks which they individually found most rewarding. Society, on the other hand, would plan and organize its economic activities so as to assume control of its own fate. Inasmuch as for Marx this task resembled more "the administration of things" than the "governing of men," mature communism could be characterized as an anarchy. Society would be centrally organized, but it would require neither the services of a state nor the political domination that such services seemed to imply in the past. Most importantly, mature communism would be characterized by the absence of alienation. Because the material conditions of production would be the cooperative property of all, there would be no class divisions. With the destruction of the class system and the overcoming of the division of labor, individuals would labor for the first time as total human beings. Freed from alienation, they would consequently each realize their true species-potential. Aware of their species-being, workers would, in turn, transcend the selfish egoism of the bourgeois age and, thereby, find their individual perfection to be a function of their social nature. In short, mature com-

[9] McLellan, *Karl Marx: Selected Writings*, p. 87–88.

munism promises the development of a new and perfected form of human nature. Describing this, Marx wrote:

> ... there is communism as the positive abolition of private property and thus of human self-alienation and therefore the real appropriation of the human essence by and for man . . . . It is the genuine solution of the antagonism between man and nature and between man and man. It is the true solution of the struggle between existence and essence, between objectification and self-affirmation, between freedom and necessity, between individual and species. It is the solution to the riddle of history and knows itself to be this solution.[10]

This statement not only represents Marx's vision of the future but also reveals an essential characteristic of his thinking. In spite of his apparent preoccupation with the science of economics, Marx's thinking is fundamentally a form of radical humanism. For him, history is a drama within which human nature is achieving its own immanent perfection. As such, his writings exhibit an intense moral passion, and it is precisely this quality which accounts for much of their enduring appeal. Marx does not simply promise to improve humanity's material well-being. Rather his is an appeal on behalf of a higher form of human existence and, as such, relegates the mere enjoyment of material possessions to a secondary level:

> Private property has made us so stupid and narrow-minded that an object is only ours when we have it, when it exists as capital for us or when we directly possess, eat, drink, wear, inhabit it, etc., in short, when we use it . . . . Thus all physical and intellectual senses have been replaced by the simple alienation of all these senses, the sense of having . . . . The supersession of private property is therefore the complete emancipation of all human senses and qualities. . . . [11]

Perhaps it was the Russian revolutionary Leon Trotsky who best expressed this theme in Marx when he wrote:

> Man will become immeasurably stronger, wiser, and subtler; his body will become more harmonized, his movements more rhythmic, his voice more musical. The forms of life will become dynamically dramatic. The average human type will rise to the heights of an Aristotle, a Goethe, or a Marx. And above this ridge new peaks will rise.[12]

---

[10] McLellan, *Karl Marx: Selected Writings*, p. 89.

[11] McLellan, *Karl Marx: Selected Writings*, p. 91–92.

[12] Leon Trotsky, *Literature and Revolution*, trans. Rose Strunsky (Ann Arbor: University of Michigan Press, 1960), p. 256.

However, this suggestion that Marx focuses upon a vision of the truly emancipated human being does not go far enough in explaining the total character of his work. This larger quality becomes evident once it is realized that Marx was not simply arguing for an improvement within the human condition. On the contrary, his theory represents an effort to abolish that very condition as it has been experienced throughout human history. Earlier Marx had referred to such traditional dichotomies as those between humanity and nature, existence and essence, and freedom and necessity. He suggested that communism would overcome such antagonisms and solve, thereby, the riddle of history. Yet these terms are not merely logically distinct categories. They are, at the same time, symbols created by humans to express their experience of a tension or rift within being itself. Indeed, humanity has acknowledged a tension within the human condition because its experience of reality has forced it to accept the fact that both freedom and necessity exist together. Neither can be reduced to the other because each is real. Similarly humanity has traditionally felt itself to be both a part of and apart from nature. To deny either experience would be to deny an aspect of our humanity.

These conceptual dichotomies, along with such others as existence–essence, individual–species, and objectification–self-affirmation, are, in part, expressions of humanity's awareness that reality is not a single, organized whole. Thus this clash of concepts is not simply a matter of logical inconsistency. Rather it reflects humanity's awareness of a real tension or rift within reality itself. If this is true, no single, self-consistent intellectual system can possibly account for the full range of human experience. Reality, therefore, must appear as essentially mysterious, and humankind, as part of this reality, shares in this fundamental mystery.

Given this perspective, Marx's promise to overcome such antagonisms and consequently to solve the riddle of history appears to have been an effort to overcome the human condition itself. Communism represents, then, a new era which will be free from those limitations which have typified the human condition throughout history. Marx's awareness of this is indicated by the fact that he referred to all precommunist human history as the history of our "animal" existence. Thus the movement into communism represents a qualitative leap in being, a human self-transformation.

Given the scope of Marx's promise, it is necessary to question whether humankind is capable of such a fundamental self-transformation. Does the human being possess the power and independence which is necessary for such an accomplishment? Or are we limited by our very nature and dependencies so that such a mastery of reality is beyond our grasp? To state this question in other terms, are we our own creators, or are we a part of a larger creation? Marx's answer to this question is straight-forward:

But since for socialist man what is called world history is nothing but the creation of man by human labour and the development of nature for man, he has the observable and irrefutable proof of his self-creation and the process of his origin. Once the essential reality of man in nature . . . has become evident in practical life and sense experience, then the question of an alien being, of a being above nature and man . . . has become impossible in practice.[13]

It would appear then that at the root of Marx's system is a fundamental faith in the sovereignty of humankind. Like Feuerbach, Marx rejects God because of his overriding faith in humanity. Yet, unlike Feuerbach, Marx's "man" does not yet exist. According to Marx, the person for whom self-creation will become apparent is the man or woman who will first emerge in the socialist future. Thus the real possibility of an emancipated humanity appears to depend upon the possible reality of a future age. A belief in such a reality, however, is akin to an act of faith, and thus in this sense Marxism would appear to be a form of religious consciousness. However, as a form of religion, Marxism must be differentiated from the more traditional types. Although it is based on an act of faith and is characterized by an eschatological expectation, Marxism lacks, nonetheless, a spiritual or transcendental reference. It is a religion without a theological basis and, as such, can appeal to humanity's religious needs without at the same time acknowledging its finite limitations.

MARXISM AFTER MARX

As with any theoretical system which becomes involved in the complexities of practice, Marxism has assumed a certain dynamic of its own. As Marx's ideas became indices for action, it was inevitable that they would be adjusted to fit the changing needs of his followers. Like Christianity, therefore, Marxism has produced a number of sects—each, in turn, claiming its own favored interpretation. In a recent study of Marxist thought, Leszek Kolakowski identified the two parties that have come to form the basic polarity within the Marxist tradition since the beginning of this century:

> . . . on one hand, reformist socialism bearing only a tenuous relation to Marxism and, on the other hand, the monopolization of Marxism by Leninism and its derivates.[14]

It may be helpful to look briefly at each of these alternatives.

[13] McLellan, *Karl Marx: Selected Writings*, p. 95.
[14] Leszek Kolakowski, *Main Currents of Marxism*, trans. P. S. Falla (Oxford: Oxford University Press, 1978), II, p. 30.

In 1889, and thus when Engels was still alive, the Second International was formed out of a loose confederation of national socialist parties and local trade-union organizations. Common to all the members was the general belief that socialism was the way of the future. Yet, in spite of this consensus, there was a notable lack of agreement both on the precise nature of the future socialist age and on the best tactics to realize that new tomorrow. Throughout its relatively short history, the Second International was characterized by a series of lively debates and serious disagreements. These disputes tended to cluster around three issues.

The first of these concerned the question of anarchism. The followers of such thinkers as Kropotkin, Malatesta, and Reclus argued that if human beings were only left alone they would naturally and spontaneously form their own harmonious communities. Skeptical of Marx's call for a dictatorship of the proletariat, which they considered a new form of tyranny, the anarchists thus urged that the Second International refrain from organized political agitation and that it refuse to support bourgeois economic reforms. With the growing influence of the Marxists, however, the Second International eventually expelled the anarchists in 1896.

The second major issue facing the new International was the gathering inevitability of the First World War. The orthodox Marxists argued that all socialists should adopt policies which would be designed to prevent the war. Thus by threatening widespread general strikes and by posing the possibility of a massive popular resistance, these socialists hoped to undermine any attempt to mobilize for the war effort. Opposing the orthodox strategy were such leaders of the Marxist left-wing as Lenin, Rosa Luxemburg, and Karl Liebknecht. They argued, on the contrary, that socialists should not attempt to postpone the outbreak of the war. Rather the Second International should exploit the occasion of the war in order to trigger the revolutionary overthrow of capitalism itself. However, in 1914 this entire question became moot. During that year the various independent socialist parties joined with their national bourgeois counterparts in supporting those policies which eventually culminated in World War I. On this occasion, then, proletarian solidarity appeared to fall victim to the passions of a militaristic nationalism.

The third and most enduring issue facing the Second International was that of reformism. Indeed, it was this dispute which eventually led to the polarized condition characteristic of the present socialist situation. Typically, the issue of reformism arose as a response to certain developments within twentieth-century European capitalism. For example, by the turn of the century the working class was able to take advantage of the widespread economic growth and development which had occurred within almost all of Europe. With the improvement of manufacturing techniques and its expansion into colonial markets, Europe was enjoying a period of marked economic prosperity. Thus rather than realizing Marx's prediction of growing worker misery, the proletariat was actually experiencing a steady improvement in its economic condition. Likewise, the working-class movement had made significant political progress. By this century the voting franchise was almost universal. Thus the proletariat was now able to elect its own representatives to the various national parliaments. This—coupled with the fact that the national governments were increasingly involved in overseeing and controlling the economy—brought about a significant increase in labor-reform legislation. Such developments, and the promise of future gains, forced the socialist parties to rethink their revolutionary strategies. By cooperating with capitalism, the socialists appeared capable of securing real benefits for the workers. Yet, at the same time, such cooperation might imply that capitalism was remediable. And if it were, then it might appear that the goals of a Marxist revolution could be accomplished through a series of pivotal parliamentary reforms.

The general position of such revisionists as Jean Jaures, Eduard Bernstein, and Filippo Turati was that the recent developments within parliamentary democracy allowed for a gradual reformist approach towards the goals of socialism. On the whole, they did not share Marx's contempt for liberal democracy and thus refused to accept his revolutionary radicalism. According to the revisionists, as labor became more productive, and as the laboring classes developed both intellectually and morally, socialism could be achieved gradually through a process of democratic and economic reforms. However, under the influence of the more radical Marxists, the Second International met in Amsterdam in 1904 and voted to condemn "the revisionist efforts to change the victorious tactics we have hitherto followed based on the class struggle."[15] On one hand this resolution symbolized the personal political defeat of such socialists as Bernstein and Jaures. Yet on the other it could do nothing to prevent the growing acceptance of the various revisionist doctrines among the masses which actually made up the national socialist parties. Indeed, such recent phenomena as the separation of Socialist Democratic parties from Communist parties and the emergence of Eurocommunism in Italy, France, and Spain in fact suggest that the revisionist position has survived to become a vital element within the contemporary socialist tradition.

Lenin and the Russian Revolution

After reformism (though hardly second in significance), the other major form of contemporary Marxism is Marxism-Leninism. Indeed it is

---

[15] As quoted in James Joll, *The Second International, 1889–1914* (New York: Harper & Row Publishers, 1966), p. 100.

only in this particular form that Marxism has actually succeeded in becoming an operative ideology for a specific government. As its title suggests, Marxism-Leninism is formed, in part, by the particular contributions of Lenin (1870–1924). Born Vladimir Ulianov, Lenin was introduced to Marxism by George Plekhanov (1856–1918) and eventually joined the latter's party-in-exile while in Geneva, Switzerland. Even as an exile, Lenin was allowed to participate as a delegate to several of the Second International's congresses. At the Brussel-London Congress of 1903 the Russian Social Democrats split into two factions—the Mensheviks and the Bolsheviks. This split developed because of a disagreement concerning the principles of party organization. Exploiting this situation, Lenin assumed command of the party's Bolshevik wing and directed its deputies in the Russian parliament of 1912. With the outbreak of the revolution in 1917, Lenin returned to Russia to assume control of the state—a position which he maintained until his death in 1924.

The difficulties facing Lenin and the other Marxists of his day can be traced back to the peculiar features of the Russian situation. The most striking fact was that twentieth-century Russia did not resemble the industrial England upon which Marx had originally based his revolutionary analysis. Indeed, rather than being a mature capitalist society, Russia was in fact a feudal order. Its emperor claimed absolute authority and based his rule upon a civil and military bureaucracy whose officers were primarily members of the landed aristocracy. Although the Russian serfs had been set free in the second half of the nineteenth century, their actual poverty forced them to maintain a *de facto* economic bondage to the landowners. Thus, although a modest level of industrialization had been introduced, a full nine-tenths of the Russian population consisted of those who remained in the peasant classes.

Given this condition, it seemed apparent that Marxism provided no immediate remedy for the Russian situation. Indeed, Marx's vision of a large and spontaneously revolutionary working class seemed altogether out of place within the Russian setting. Yet, at the same time, Lenin was convinced that Russia was ripe for revolution, and consequently he attempted to modify Marx's teachings so they might apply to the Russian situation. Generally speaking, his revision contained four distinct elements.

First, Lenin argued that the party should be considered the vanguard of the proletariat and, as a consequence, should be organized accordingly. Although Marx, himself, had not developed a complete theory of the party's proper relationship to the masses, the Second International consistently rejected the idea that a mass socialist revolution could be achieved through a *coup d'etat*. Indeed, according to the Menshevik wing of the Russian Social Democrats, the party should be a broad-based and democratically organized element within the proletariat. Decisions were to be reached according to an egalitarian procedure in which each vote would receive equal weight. Lenin's Bolsheviks, on the other hand, conceived of the party as an elitist cadre composed of those few who correctly perceived the demands of the future age. According to Lenin, history had clearly demonstrated that, on its own, the working class was incapable of achieving a truly revolutionary consciousness. On the contrary, the workers tended to be satisfied with any improvement in either their economic status or working conditions. Thus, rather than seeking political changes, the proletariat was content to support those objectives pursued by the trade-union movement. Given this situation, Lenin understood the party to be a vanguard which would impose its own proper form of radical consciousness upon the working masses. Thus, rather than representing the actual proletariat, the party was to transform it. As a group of professional revolutionaries, the Bolsheviks were to bring about a revolution from above. In doing so, it was necessary that the party be organized in a paramilitary fashion. It was to be closed, elitist, and authoritarian. Once a decision had been made, the members were no longer at liberty to question its validity or to criticize its merit. Through a program of propaganda, agitation, and infiltration, the party was to move into mass society and thereby prepare it for the revolution at hand.

The second major revision associated with Lenin's reworking of Marxism concerns the class composition of the revolution. In Marx's original scenario capitalism would eventually produce a society in which only the proletariat and the bourgeoisie would survive as distinct classes. According to this scheme, the peasantry and the landed aristocracy would, in time, collapse into the proletariat. Yet, in Russia, the peasants were still the largest single class and therefore posed a real problem for the socialists. Traditionally, Russian peasants had not opposed the private-property system. Moreover, they were generally conservative, nationalistic, anticosmopolitan, and religious. There was, therefore, a long-standing debate among Russian revolutionaries over the proper role and place of the peasants. Should the proletarian revolution incorporate the goals and demands of the peasantry, or should it retain its strict class character? In 1917, the debate ended with Lenin's adoption of the slogan, "land to the peasants." As such, this slogan became a signal that Lenin had decided to include the peasants and petite bourgeoisie in the coming revolution. For strategic reasons, Lenin had decided that the proletarian movement was to exploit agrarian unrest for its own purposes.

The third major element of Leninism is the concept of "permanent revolution." For those schooled in Marx's writings, it was assumed that a socialist revolution would be possible only after a capitalist revolution had been completed and its effects realized. Applying this assumption to the Russian situation most Marxists, including at one time Lenin himself, believed that the bourgeoisie would have to make its own democratic revolution against the Tsar before any further action was possible. Central to Marx's theory was the argument that the proletariat would achieve its necessary strength and commitment only after capitalism had played out its own contradictory logic. This, in turn, would happen only after the bourgeoisie succeeded in destroying the feudal order. Thus the first priority for the Russian socialists appeared to be encouraging and supporting the political and economic aspirations of the emerging middle class. This view, similar to Marx's attitude toward the revolutions of 1848, was resisted by Leon Trotsky (1877–1940). Trotsky not only doubted the ability of the Russian capitalists to make their own revolution, but he also feared that they would compromise the movement by accepting, in part, the demands of the former ruling class. Describing his alternative concept of permanent revolution, Trotsky wrote:

> [it] demonstrated that the democratic tasks of backward bourgeois nations in our epoch lead to the dictatorship of the proletariat and, that the dictatorship of the proletariat places socialist tasks upon the agenda . . . . If the traditional view held that the road to proletarian dictatorship ran through a lengthy democratic period, the doctrine of permanent revolution asserted that for the backward countries the road to democracy leads through the dictatorship of the proletariat.[16]

By 1917 Lenin himself had come to accept Trotsky's position. The proletarian party would not wait for the capitalist revolution; instead it would make the next revolution its own. This could be done first by organizing large-scale production on the basis of what capitalism had already accomplished and secondly by bringing about the inevitable transition to socialism proper. Historically this doctrine encouraged Lenin's Marxists to assume immediate political control. Rather than waiting for the emergence, development, and demise of capitalism, Lenin's party would seek political power directly and use its position to guide Russia through capitalism and beyond towards socialism. Oriented this way, the idea of permanent revolution gave a certain priority to the realm of the political. Rather than being simply a by-product of economic development, the state appeared to have acquired a certain independence from and superiority to the economic sphere. In Marxist terms, the doctrine of permanent revolution implied that the political superstructure was in some way capable of leading and determining developments within the economic substructure. As such, it represented a fundamental revision of Marxist theory.

The last major theme of Leninism is contained in his analysis of im-

---

[16] As quoted in George Lichtheim, *Marxism: An Historical and Critical Study*, 2nd ed., rev. (New York: Praeger Publishers, 1965), pp. 342–43.

perialism. Although Marx avoided specifying the precise moment of capitalism's collapse, there is little doubt that he believed it would be in the relatively near future and that it would occur first in an advanced industrialized nation. Yet, by the twentieth century, the conditions of Western Europe seemed to reflect less and less Marx's original model. There was a decline in proletarian misery, a growth in productivity, and a waning of revolutionary spirit among the workers. The question arose, therefore, whether Marxism had been disproven by the recent events. Although some suggested that this was indeed the case, Lenin attempted to account for these apparent contradictions by his analysis of imperialism. According to Lenin, as monopolies developed within capitalism there arose a need to find markets for the excess capital which was being generated by monopolistic practices. If it were invested within the domestic market, productivity would increase and subsequently prices would fall. In view of this, then, foreign markets had to be found; and Lenin saw imperialism as the best hope capitalism had for doing so. Thus, the advanced capitalist nations of Europe began to create large colonial empires in Africa and the Far East. Spurred on by the needs of large industry, the various national governments entered into a fierce competition for new investment opportunities. At first, this technique appeared to work. The growth of monopolies and the involvement of national governments in economic matters helped to reduce the anarchy which was characteristic of traditional capitalism. In addition, by exploiting the backward nations of the world monopolistic capitalism enjoyed unprecedented profits. These profits were so large that they enabled the owners of industry to grant concessions to the working class without at the same time limiting their own wealth. Thus the proletariat could enjoy a rising standard of living at the same time that the capitalists were earning greater profits. These economic improvements tended to dampen any revolutionary enthusiasm and this, in turn, was reflected in the popularity of socialist revisionism during the Second International. Finally, the competition among imperial powers for scarce foreign markets engendered a heightened sense of nationalistic pride among European workers. As nationalistic passions were inflamed, international proletarian solidarity began to dissolve.

Central to Lenin's analysis of imperialism, however, was his argument that its benefits were only temporary at best. Imperialism had not prevented but only postponed the downfall of capitalism inasmuch as the contradictions of the system continued to exist. According to Lenin, the contradictions within capitalism which Marx had analyzed on the national level had, in fact, been internationalized by imperialistic expansion. For example, Marx wrote of the anarchistic character of capitalistic production. And, although the development of national monopolies had succeeded in imposing a certain order on domestic production, Lenin argued that the condition of anarchism still characterized the international realm. Thus capitalistic anarchism was preserved in the form of the fierce competition among nations for foreign markets which, according to Lenin, could only lead to an eventual international war. Similarly, Marx's understanding of history had emphasized the importance of class struggle. Lenin argued, however, that imperialism had the effect of transforming the class struggle into an international conflict. Whereas earlier Marx had distinguished between the oppressing and the oppressed classes, it was now necessary to analyze the relationship between the exploiting and the exploited nations. In either case, however, a revolution of the oppressed would determine the issue. By exporting capitalism, imperialism had in fact only exported its revolutionary potential. Finally, Lenin argued that the economic prosperity of imperialist capitalism would be relatively short-lived. In its hunger for profits, imperialism was inevitably eating up the resources and markets which capitalism required. Once further expansion became impossible, the Marxist law of the declining rate of profits would once again become operative. Therefore capitalism as a worldwide system was destined to collapse in a worldwide revolution. This revolution, in turn, could best be realized if it were aimed at the weakest link in the capitalist chain. For Lenin, Russia provided the obvious opportunity. It was to be the first step in a European and world revolution.

BIBLIOGRAPHY

ALTHUSSER, LOUIS. *For Marx.* Translated by Ben Brewster. New York: Random House, 1970.

AVINERI, SHLOMO. *The Social & Political Thought of Karl Marx.* Cambridge: Cambridge University Press, 1970.

BERLIN, ISAIAH. *Karl Marx: His Life and Environment.* Oxford: Oxford University Press, 1963.

HEILBRONER, ROBERT. *Marxism: For and Against.* New York: W. W. Norton & Co. 1980.

JOLL, JAMES. *The Second International: 1889–1914.* New York: Harper & Row, 1966.

KOLAKOWSKI, LESZEK. *Main Currents of Marxism.* 3 vols. Translated by P. S. Falla. Oxford: Oxford University Press, 1978.

LICHTHEIM, GEORGE. *Marxism: An Historical and Critical Study.* New York: Praeger, 1965.

LOBKOWICZ, NICHOLAS, ed. *Marx and the Western World.* Notre Dame: University of Notre Dame Press, 1967.

MANDEL, ERNEST.   *Marxist Economic Theory*. 2 vols, Translated by Brian Pearce. New York: Monthly Review Press, 1970.

MARCUSE, HERBERT.   *Soviet Marxism: A Critical Analysis*. New York: Random House, 1961.

McLELLAN, DAVID.   *Karl Marx: His Life and Thought*. New York: Harper & Row, 1973.

MEYER, ALFRED G.   *Leninism*. New York: Praeger, 1972.

TUCKER, ROBERT C.   *Philosophy and Myth in Karl Marx*. Cambridge: Cambridge University Press, 1961.

PART

V

Modernity Questioned

17

TWENTIETH-
CENTURY
DEVELOPMENTS

INTRODUCTION

The Tradition of the Political Philosophers

As the previous chapters have gone about discussing the particular teachings of individual thinkers, they have also revealed something about a vastly larger subject: the nature of political theory itself. Indeed, the history of political philosophy seems to indicate that the writing of political theory is, in part, the way philosophers have of responding to an experience of critical disorder. Like all citizens, political philosophers begin as members of particular societies. As such they find themselves sharing in those particular social beliefs and mutual expectations which constitute the reality of their social and political world. As Eric Voegelin has written:

> Human society is not merely a fact, or an event, in the external world . . . it is as a whole a little world, a cosmion, illuminated with

meaning from within by the human beings who continuously create and bear it as the mode and condition of their self-realization.[1]

As social creatures, each of us necessarily assumes those particular traditions that are embodied in the laws and institutions of our society and that provide, thereby, the standards according to which we construct our understanding of the order and meaning of life.

Most of the time the particular assumptions and beliefs of a society appear to its citizens to be commonsensical; thus they are often easily, if not blindly, followed. However, during times of great upheaval, severe political crisis, or serious personal dislocation, the adequacy of a particular social order or of the life style which it recommends may become questionable. In short, serious crises tend to undermine the authority of those traditions and beliefs which may have worked in the past but which appear to be failing in the present. As disorder threatens to replace order, the very principles of order itself come under attack. And what at one time may have appeared to be only commonsensical now may appear both arbitrary and capricious. As a social order collapses, its members are necessarily deprived of those meanings and standards by which they had previously ordered their lives. And the threat of meaninglessness and a lack of personal orientation erode the very basis of what was formerly perceived as the necessary conditions for human self-realization.

One possible response to such a social disintegration is that of the nihilist. With the collapse of order, all is permitted; and when all is permitted, nothing is forbidden. Another possible response, however, is that of the political philosophers. Beginning with an experience of disorder they attempt first to analyze its causes and then to attend to its treatment. Thus for political theorists disorder implies diagnosis, and diagnosis leads to therapy. As a form of therapy, however, political philosophy is of a particular type. As a response to crisis it is first of all a creative effort to discover a new source of order. To do so, political philosophers must move beyond the limits of their immediate experience. As Sheldon Wolin has written of this need for a leap of imagination:

> . . . to act intelligently and nobly demanded a perspective wider than the immediate situation for which the action was intended; intelligence and nobility were not *ad hoc* qualities, but aspects of a more comprehensive vision of things. This more comprehensive vision was provided by thinking about the political society in its corrected fullness, not as it is but as it might be.[2]

[1] Eric Voegelin, *The New Science of Politics* (Chicago: University of Chicago Press, 1952), p. 27.

[2] Sheldon Wolin, *Politics and Vision: Continuity and Innovation in Western Political Thought* (Boston: Little, Brown, 1960), p. 20

Looking beyond the traditions, practices, and institutions of the immediate environment, political philosophers typically locate those principles which will structure their vision within a more comprehensive understanding of God, humanity, and nature. As such, political philosophy is creative but not necessarily aribitrary. It would be arbitrary if the principles of the philosophers' therapeutic visions were merely the products of their idle wishing. It is creative, however, if those principles are grounded upon a larger vision of reality which is derived from an open investigation of the structure of being itself. Indeed it is precisely such a grounding which is attempted by serious political philosophers, and it is specifically this attempt which justifies their claim to our attention.

The Dominance of Scientific and Secular Civilization

As we have seen, political philosophy begins as a response to a particular situation. The contemporary political thinker must therefore begin by acknowledging the success with which modernity has replaced earlier forms of civilizational order. Ever since the Enlightenment it is clear that critical rationalism has succeeded in its attempt to replace religious faith as the fundamental ground for one's personal and social existence. Thus during the twentieth century a new scientific and secular civilization has achieved dominance in the West. Politically this new order exhibits several important characteristics. First, the nation-state, with its reliance upon a bureaucratic administration, has become the most important form of political organization. Second, a thoroughly secular democratic ideology has become the most widely accepted political belief, and this, in turn, has committed the modern nation-state to such values as mass suffrage and human equality. Finally, with the removal of the traditional moral and political restrictions upon economic activity, the modern nation-state is committed to the pursuit of both technological excellence and productive efficiency. However, inasmuch as a concern for scientific achievement and efficiency seems to contradict the democratic commitment to equality, the modern project exhibits its own particular form of tension. Indeed, whether this contradiction will prove to be a creative or a destructive one is one of the important questions facing the contemporary age.

In general, twentieth-century political philosophy has been concerned with diagnosing the major elements of disorder that threaten the modern project. Thus it continues to raise a critical mirror before the age. Yet, at the same time, it seems fair to suggest that no twentieth-century political philosopher has succeeded in creating a therapeutic vision with either the force or impact of those which have already been discussed in earlier chapters.

This lack of a distinctively contemporary therapeutic vision does not imply, however, that twentieth-century political philosophers have accepted uncritically all the features of contemporary political reality. Indeed, since the First World War a number of theorists have written important critiques of the present age. For some, the very achievement of modernity itself threatens to destroy many of the most important elements of the good life. For them, then, the crisis of the age is to be found in its very success.

EXISTENTIALISM

Probably the most widely employed definition of contemporary existentialism is that philosophy whose first principle holds that existence is prior to essence. Accordingly, the French existentialist Jean-Paul Sartre (1905–1980) has written:

> In philosophical terminology, every object has an essence and an existence. An essence is an intelligible and unchanging unity of properties; an existence is a certain actual presence in the world. Many people think that the essence comes first and then the existence . . . . Existentialism, on the contrary, maintains that in man—and in man alone—existence precedes essence. This simply means that man first *is*, and only subsequently is this or that. In a word, man must create his own essence: it is in throwing himself into the world, suffering there, struggling there, that he gradually defines himself.[3]

Although this formula is useful for some purposes, it is, nonetheless, misleading if it is taken to suggest that existentialism is a uniform body of thought whose teachings can be summarized in a simple fashion. Indeed, although it is true that certain authors tend to appear in all the standard studies of existentialism, they, themselves, have made repeated efforts to avoid being classified together. For example, the German philosopher Karl Jaspers (1883–1969) was extremely critical of the work of his fellow existentialist Martin Heidegger (1889–1976), while at the same time the writings of the Christian existentialist Gabriel Marcel (1889–1973) show little sympathy for the openly professed atheism of Jean-Paul Sartre. Given this situation, it is appropriate to suggest that any degree of unity that does exist among the existentialists is more properly attributed to a similarity of influences and concerns than to any agreement about doctrines and principles. For example, historically all the existentialists appear to have been influenced by the writings of Soren Kierkegaard (1813–1855) and Friedrich

---

[3] Jean-Paul Sartre, "A More Precise Characterization of Existentialism," in Michel Contat & Michel Rybalka, eds., *The Writings of Jean-Paul Sartre*, Volume 2: *Selected Prose*, trans. Richard McCleary (Evanston: Northwestern University Press, 1974), p. 157.

Nietzsche (1844–1900). In the case of both writers, the existentialists claim to have found thinkers who were concerned with the subjective and individual struggle for human self-realization. In addition, many existentialists were influenced by the literary and artistic works of such men as Fydor Dostoyevski (1821–1881), Franz Kafka (1883–1924) and Paul Cezanne (1839–1906).

As important as such common intellectual influences were, however, they do not provide a sufficient account of the existentialist movement. Equally important in any depiction is the fact that each of these existentialists was reacting, in his own way, to certain features of modern Western civilization which were perceived as threatening the very meaningfulness of human life itself. Thus, as the influence and vitality of organized religion declined and as science and technology proceeded to despiritualize humanity's experience of nature, the existentialists found themselves within a modern era in which the very meaning of life was no longer clear to those who must live it. In describing this experience, Karl Loewith has stated:

> The world which is concretely analyzed by contemporary existentialism is neither a living *cosmos*, seen with Greek eyes, nor an order of creation, as understood by Christian faith; nor is it the world of mathematical physics. It is only our historical world without nature . . . . And, indeed, how can one feel at home in a universe which is conceived as the chance result of statistical probabilities and which is said to have come into existence through an explosion? Such a universe cannot inspire confidence or sympathy nor can it give orientation and meaning to man's existence in it.[4]

As Loewith's statement indicates, existentialism began as a reaction to a loss of meaning and the rise of alienation. The problem of finding meaning in one's life is not a particularly modern concern. Indeed in traditional philosophy the discussion of the relationship of being to nonbeing centered upon this issue. Yet, for the existentialists, this perennial problem assumed a thoroughly modern form. With the growth of the modern scientific spirit the traditional metaphysical and religious systems of the West became increasingly unacceptable. At the same time, however, science itself appeared to be incapable of successfully filling the very void which it had created. First, humanity's faith in scientific reasoning was severely shaken by the events of the First World War. At one time it was believed that wars arose out of ignorance, prejudice, and an uninformed understanding of

---

[4] Karl Loewith, "Nature, History, & Existentialism," in Arnold Levison, ed., *Karl Loewith: Nature, History, and Existentialism and Other Essays in the Philosophy of History* (Evanston: Northwestern University Press, 1966), p. 28.

one's own self-interest. Scientific reason, therefore, seemed to provide an alternative which promised perpetual peace. The First World War, however, served as a brutal denial of that aspiration. Not only was it one of the most ferocious wars in history, but it also broke out in a Europe which at that time prided itself on being the most scientifically advanced civilization in the world. Second, science's objectivist understanding of humanity and nature failed to provide a sufficiently full account of the human being as both a subject and an actor. Although rationalism claimed to explain humanity in general terms, it seemed incapable of appreciating the individual's radically unique and truly personal qualities. As a result, the objectivist world-view seemed oblivious to those very realities which mattered most to the human individual. Given both the collapse of traditional religion and a heightened appreciation of the limits of scientific reason, it is not surprising that the perennial problem of humanity's being and nonbeing became an urgent issue for the contemporary existentialist. As William Barrett wrote:

> Indeed the whole problematic of Existentialism unfolds from this historical situation. Alienation and estrangement; a sense of the basic fragility and contingency of human life; the impotence of reason confronted with the depths of existence; the threat of Nothingness, and the solitary and unsheltered condition of the individual before this threat . . . . A single atmosphere pervades them all like a chilly wind: the radical feeling of human finitude.[5]

Karl Jaspers and Man in the Modern Age

It is possible to illustrate the existentialist reaction to the modern age by examining the work of Karl Jaspers in general and his *Man in the Modern Age* in particular.

Born in Oldenburg, Germany, on February 23, 1883, Karl Jaspers originally intended a career in psychiatric medicine. Upon completing his research assistantship at a hospital, Jaspers received a teaching appointment as a psychologist at Heidelberg University. During this time, however, his interests began to change, and his research increasingly carried him beyond the field of medicine and toward that of philosophy. This movement culminated in 1919 when Jaspers published what some consider to be the first book of existentialism, his *Psychologie der Weltanschauungen*. Based upon this work Jaspers was offered the Heidelberg chair in philosophy in 1921.

When Hitler came to power in Germany in 1933, his followers attempted to force the German universities into supporting the new regime.

---

[5] William Barrett, *Irrational Man: A Study in Existential Philosophy* (Garden City: Doubleday, Inc.), p. 36.

Those who refused were punished. Accordingly, in 1937 Jaspers was forbidden to teach, and by 1943 his books had been banned throughout the country. In 1945 both he and his wife, a Jewess, were scheduled to be transported to an extermination camp. The allied armies fortunately occupied Heidelberg before that particular order could be carried out, and Jaspers, as a consequence, was able to return to the university later that year.

In 1948 Jaspers decided to leave Heidelberg and accept an appointment in philosophy at the University of Basel in Switzerland. His decision to depart Germany was primarily due to his belief that the German nation had failed to fully comprehend the horror of its Nazi past and thus had not made a sufficient effort to rededicate itself to the principles of political democracy. While in Basel, Jaspers not only continued his philosophical work but at the same time attempted to use the popular mass media in an effort to promulgate his belief that humankind would perish unless it could discover the moral and political will to join together by forming a responsible world community.

On February 26, 1969, Karl Jaspers died of a stroke. Among his most important philosophical and political writings are *Philosophy* (1931), *Man in the Modern Age* (1931), *On Truth* (1947), *Great Philosophers* (1957), *The Future of Mankind* (1958), and *Philosophical Faith and Revelation* (1962).

A key to understanding Jaspers's writings is found in his early decision to leave science for philosophy. For Jaspers, philosophy was not simply a more abstract and generalized approach toward the same material that science encountered in a specific and concrete way. Rather, according to Jaspers, philosophy is concerned with an altogether different reality than is science, and, as such, it operates according to its own distinct method and logic. Writing in his memoirs, he said:

> Thus I developed an idea of philosophy as something altogether different from science: the satisfaction of a need for truth unknown to science, the discharge of a responsibility alien to science, the achievement of something unattainable to any science.[6]

This distinction between science and philosophy was central to Jaspers's thinking because it formed the basis for his understanding of human nature. According to Jaspers, science necessarily assumes a particular sense of what is true, a particular view of what is real, and a particular image of human nature. Specifically, for modern science objective truth is characterized by the fact that it is universally valid, demonstrable, self-evident, and value-free. The reality which science investigates, on the

[6] Karl Jaspers, *Philosophy and the World*, trans. E. B. Ashton (Chicago: Henry Regnery, 1963), p. 225.

other hand, is the immanent and objective world as it appears to our human consciousness. The human being, finally, is understood by modern science to be an instance of consciousness-at-large. This being achieves its condition when it is able to suppress all the subjective and personal elements which might distract its thinking or interfere with its dispassionate investigation of nature.

As a scientist, Jaspers accepted the validity of those assumptions that actually make the practice of science possible. Yet, while accepting these assumptions as valid for the sake of science, he rejected the modern tendency to impose them on every other area of human endeavor. Indeed, according to Jaspers, rationalism in general and Descartes in particular had attempted to reduce reality to those specific forms which were the most appropriate for the needs of science. Thus the rationalist assumed that the world was the only reality capable of being known; that only scientific truth could qualify as real knowledge; and, most importantly, that the human being was nothing but consciousness-at-large. As an existentialist, Jaspers refused to accept such reductions. Indeed, according to him, human experience itself suggested that the rationalist project was unfeasible. Humanity's awareness of certain "ultimate situations" forces it to realize that the world alone is not enough. Such "ultimate situations" as the experience of death, suffering, struggle, and guilt force the human race to acknowledge the essentially antinomian character of its existence. Because of this, reality cannot be reduced to an ordered whole and, it follows, can never be known in the systematic way that science intends. The world is part of reality; because its objective structure lends itself to scientific investigation, it can be known by the mind as consciousness-at-large. But the experience of ultimate situations reminds one that there is a part of reality which is beyond the world and, as such, which escapes the intellectual categories of the scientist.

Jaspers referred to this reality beyond objective existence as transcendence (*Transcendenz*), and he understood philosophy as humanity's attempt to elucidate its experiences of this transcendental realm. As such, philosophy is fundamentally different than science. Whereas science investigates the world, philosophy illuminates the transcendent. Whereas science seeks universal, conditional, and methodic truth, philosophy seeks a personal, nonuniversal, and absolute awareness. And finally, whereas science assumes that human beings are consciousness-at-large, philosophy believes them to be existential, that is, individuals as *Existenz*.

Jaspers's view of the human being as an *Existenz* is at the heart of his philosophical work. For Jaspers, humans as *Existenz* are humans as they encounter the transcendent. This encounter, in turn, transforms human beings themselves. In touch with the transcendent, the existential beings are no longer simply worldly creatures. Although the world is an aspect of reality, it no longer appears to be all of reality. The existential human is thus freed from the limits of his or her objective existence and thereby achieves a level of personal authenticity which gives a new meaning to the individual's life and inspires within the desire to communicate that meaning to others. In short, the individual-as-*Existenz* achieves a level of fulfillment and development which serves as the goal for all human existence. For Jaspers humans are intended to achieve the condition of *Existenz*, and, with such an achievement, they thereby realize the highest possibilities of their being. To *do* philosophy is to encounter transcendence; to encounter transcendence is to become an *Existenz;* and to be an *Existenz* is to fulfill the purpose of human existence. In describing *Existenz*, Jaspers compares it to mere human existence as follows:

> Existence is either there or not. *Existenz*, however, because it is possible, approaches its being or recedes from it into nothingness through the faculty of choice and decision. My existence has a distinct perimeter in comparison to that of other existences. *Existenz*, however, is essentially distinct from other *Existenzen* due to its base in freedom. Existence as being lives and dies; *Existenz* knows of no death but rather stands to its being through rise and fall. Existence is empirically present; *Existenz* is only as freedom. Existence is absolutely temporal; *Existenz* is more than time in time. My existence is finite in so far as it is not all of existence and closed for itself around itself; *Existenz* is not for itself alone nor is it everything because it is only when it is related to other *Existenzen* and to Transcendence, the absolutely other in whose presence it becomes aware of itself as not yet being its own cause. While existence can be infinitely named because it is the relative closure of the finite, the infinity of *Existenz* as open possibility is without closure.[7]

Jaspers's understanding of the human being as potentially both consciousness-at-large and *Existenz* is central to his criticism of the modern order. Originally published in Germany in 1931, his *Man in the Modern Age* was intended as a companion piece to his major work, *Philosophy*, which was published the same year. In his three-volume *Philosophy* Jaspers attempted to develop his understanding of both the nature of philosophy in general and the universal potential for human *Existenz*. In his *Man in the Modern Age*, on the other hand, he was interested in documenting the particular impediments to the practice of philosophy and the achievement of transcendence that are operative within contemporary Western civilization. According to Jaspers the philosophical enterprise presupposes the absolute value of the individual. Given this, philosophy requires two condi-

---

[7] Karl Jaspers, *Philosophie* (Berlin: Springer Verlag, 1956), II, p. 2. My Translation.

tions for its continued practice. First, it requires an awareness of the integrity of the individual; second, it postulates an appreciation of the transcendental source of human order. According to Jaspers, however, both of these conditions face critical challenges in a modern age during which Western society is increasingly becoming a mass order.

With the despiritualization of nature and the concomitant growth of industry, modern life is increasingly ruled by the needs of technology as interpreted by an impersonal bureaucracy. According to Jaspers the resulting mass order values mere preservation over excellence, pleasure over fulfillment, and functionalism over authenticity. This, in turn, has resulted in the collapse of the family, a loss of joy in one's work, and the spread of nihilism throughout the formal cultures of the West. Just as importantly, however, Jaspers sees life in a mass society as undermining that very sense of individuality which true *Existenz* necessarily presupposes. Thus he wrote:

> When the average functional capacity has become the standard of achievement, the individual is regarded with indifference. No one is indispensable. He is not himself, having no more genuine individuality than one pin in a row, a mere object of general utility. Those most effectively predestined to such a life are persons without any serious desire to be themselves. Such have the preference.
>
> It seems as if the world must be given over to mediocrities, to persons without a destiny, without a rank or difference, without genuinely human attributes.
>
> It is as if the man thus deracinated and reduced to the level of a thing, had lost the essence of humanity. Nothing appeals to him with the verity of substantial being.[8]

With the collapse of human individuality life as *Existenz* becomes an impossibility. As a consequence, individuals are deprived of their participation within the transcendent ground of order. Lacking this basis, they inevitably seek to find order among the objects of immanence. Thus philosophy is replaced by sophistry, and the radical freedom of humanity's openness unto transcendence is replaced by the rendering of a particular life style as absolute. In their need for order, the masses either blindly obey individual heroes who promise to deliver them from their condition or erect pseudo-religions which worship science as the source of all knowledge. In either case, however, the general possibility of an authentic, meaningful, and free human existence has been destroyed.

The destruction of philosophical *Existenz* is, for Jaspers, an important political event inasmuch as a true political order can only be based

---

[8] Karl Jaspers, *Man In the Modern Age*, trans. Eden and Cedar Paul (Garden City: Doubleday, Inc., 1957), p. 51.

upon a faith which desires freedom. Without such a faith political decisions involving spiritual and cultural goods are replaced by an automatic submission to the laws of a technical mass order. In such instances, societies cease to function as true political communities; and failing to be such, they become incapable of contributing to the effort to realize full human potential.

Published in 1931, Jaspers's *Man in the Modern Age* was primarily a study of Germany. Yet, at the same time he recognized that the very forces which were at work in Germany were also operative throughout the entire Western world. Jaspers's hope was that once citizens became aware of the serious threat posed by mass society they would resist its full development. Indeed he ended his argument on a somewhat hopeful note:

> The contemplation of a world of complete unfaith, a world in which men have been degraded to the level of machines and have lost their own selves and their Godhead, a world in which human nobility will have been scattered and dispersed and in the end utterly ruined is possible to us only in the formal sense, and for a fleeting moment. Just as it conflicts with the inward, unfathomable dignity of man to think that he must die, must become as if he had never been, so likewise does he find it impossible to accept for more than a moment the conviction that his freedom, his faith, his self-hood will cease to be, and that he will be degraded to become a mere cog-wheel in a technical apparatus. Man is something more than he can vision in such perspectives.[9]

Jaspers's concern for the individual within mass society is a theme which runs throughout all of his philosophical and political writings. It is, however, at the same time a topic developed by many other existentialists as well. Some of the more important examples include Gabriel Marcel, *Man Against Mass Society;* Ortega y Gasset, *The Revolt of the Masses;* Nicolas Berdyaev, *The Fate of Man in the Modern World;* and Martin Heidegger, *Being and Time.* Together such writings represent a sustained and significant appeal on behalf of human dignity and freedom.

TWENTIETH–CENTURY CONSERVATISM

Historical Background

The term "conservative" first acquired its modern political meaning after the French Revolution; it was then that Francois Rene de Chateaubriand (1768–1848) founded the journal *Le Conservateur* in an effort to

---

[9] Jaspers, *Man In the Modern Age*, pp. 227–28.

support the clerical and political restoration of France. The timing of this founding is significant because it clearly indicates the concrete political event which provoked the rise of the conservative movement. Specifically, conservatism was a reaction to the principles of the French Revolution. As early as 1790 such conservatives as Edmund Burke had accounted for the Revolution's continual violence by calling attention to the unrealistic nature of its engendering philosophy. From this perspective the revolutionaries' inability to implement their programs was due, in part, to the fact that their guiding ideals were somehow unreal and thus incapable of being translated into practice. For Burke politics was always concerned with acting according to real possibilities. The French Revolution, however, was an attempt to create a *possible* reality. In particular, the French revolutionaries were attempting to regenerate human nature by creating a social order to be based upon the ideals of liberty, equality, and fraternity. Underlying this program was the belief that such an order was not only possible but, once achieved, would solve many of the traditional problems of political existence. In short, for many, the French Revolution promised a form of perfection. The Enlightenment *philosophes* had taught the French that human reason was capable of both understanding and manipulating human nature. Rousseau, in turn, had shown that human evil and malice were primarily the result of inappropriate social and historical organization and thus not rooted in human nature as such. Together these teachings combined to form the idea of an immanent human self-perfection. It was this idea, in turn, which the conservatives rejected. N. K. O'Sullivan has summarized this rejection succinctly:

> They [conservatives] had to show, in other words, that the world imposes limitations upon what either the individual or the state can hope to achieve without destroying the stability of society. Conservative ideology, accordingly, may be defined as a philosophy of imperfection, committed to the idea of limits, and directed towards the defense of a limited style of politics.[10]

Throughout the nineteenth century, the theory of perfectionism found its most important expression within the teachings of political liberalism. Accordingly, most conservatives followed the lead of Edmund Burke and opposed both liberalism's political doctrines and its emphasis upon the individual. At the heart of the conservative critique, however, was its insistence upon the unavoidable nature of human imperfection and limitation. Indeed, during the nineteenth century this theme was the common issue which united the two distinct schools of conservative thought.

In France, the reactions to the French Revolution of such conserva-

---

[10] N. K. O'Sullivan, *Conservatism* (New York: St. Martin's Press, 1976), pp. 11–12.

tive thinkers as Joseph de Maistre (1754–1821) and Louis de Bonald (1754–1840) were based upon a particular theological and moral understanding of the universe. Like Burke, de Maistre and de Bonald viewed the world as an ordered and hierarchical whole created by God. Everything within it was assigned its proper function and place, and humanity, as a part of this creation, was to conduct itself in a fitting and appropriate manner. Thus for de Maistre, for example, the revolutionary expectation of a perfected human and social order was ultimately based upon a fundamental denial of humanity's creaturely nature. He held that the essence of the French Revolution could be found in its misconceived theology. A proper theological understanding of humanity and nature, on the contrary, dictated a politics of moderation and prudence. Thus, in his *Considerations on France*, he wrote:

> In the works of man, everything is as poor as its author; vision is confused, means are limited, scope is restricted, movements are labored and results are humdrum. In divine works boundless riches reveal themselves even in the smallest components; its power operates effortlessly: in its hands everything is pliant, nothing can resist it; everything is a means, nothing an obstacle: and the irregularities produced by the work of free agents [human beings] come to fall into place in the general order.[11]

In addition to the French reactionaries, the other major nineteenth-century school of conservatism was the German romantics. Again following certain themes in Burke, such German romantics as Adam Mueller (1779–1829), Friedrich Schlegal (1772–1829), and the poet Novalis (1772–1801) turned to the realm of history and nature in their quest for human meaning. Unlike the Enlightenment *philosophes*, the German romantics distrusted the power of abstract reason. Thus they looked to the traditions and practices of existing nations rather than to the teachings of dogmatic reason in their efforts to create a meaningful political order. For the romantics a sympathetic appreciation of nature and history was a better guide to human order than were the artificial schemes of Enlightenment logic. Consequently they rejected the revolutionary attempt to construct a universal and abstract theory of natural rights. Instead each romantic wished to experience reality in that individual's own unique way, and this, in turn, could best be done through the instrumentalities of feeling, sentiment, and passion, rather than through an exercise of systematic reasoning and logical calculation.

In turning from the realm of abstract ideas the romantic conservatives turned towards the realm of the historical and contingent. Thus his-

---

[11] Jack Lively, ed., *The Works of Joseph de Maistre* (New York: Schocken, 1971), p. 47.

tory not only provided the standards for human happiness but, at the same time, set the limits for any effort to actualize human potential. As thoroughly historical beings, the nature of human beings unfolds slowly in time. Thus for the romantics it was outside of humanity's power to will its own perfection at any given moment. Inasmuch as history becomes both the condition for and limitation upon human development, the revolutionary hope for immanent perfection becomes a never-ending quest. In other words, for the German romantic, the human being would always remain an imperfect creature. Summarizing this theme within romanticism, the historian J. L. Talmon wrote:

> Philosophical knowledge, ethical perfection, and scientific truth were . . . beginning to be seen not as something to be acquired once and for all, but as objects of Romantic striving which could have no end, an aspiration approaching its never attainable goal only through the substitution, or indeed negation, of one achieved stage by a higher one.[12]

Thus, by its own method, German romanticism reached the same essential conclusion as did its French conservative counterpart, that is, as a fundamentally imperfectable species humanity is always better served by a politics of limitation, moderation, and continuity.

Shift in the Modern Conservative Critique

During the nineteenth century the belief in social progress and human perfectability was primarily associated with the teachings of political liberalism. Accordingly, in their efforts to reject such a faith, conservatives attempted to offset liberalism's emphasis upon the autonomous individual by stressing the essential contributions of society to human well-being. During the present century, however, an important change occurred. Even though liberalism retained its tendency towards perfectionism, for many conservatives the most radical form of perfectionist philosophy now began to be found in the doctrines of modern socialism. Whereas the horror of the First World War had called into question the progressivist assumptions of nineteenth-century European liberalism, the success of the Russian Revolution, to the contrary, inspired similar if not more radical aspirations among those with socialist sympathies. The Soviet evocation of the "New Socialist Man" provided the conservatives with an even more explicit example of perfectionist philosophy. Thus, in time, con-

---

[12] J. L. Talmon, *Romanticism and Revolt: Europe 1815–1848* (New York: Harcourt, Brace, & World, 1967), p. 153.

servatives began to move from a critique of liberalism to a confrontation with socialism. Referring to this tactical shift, N. K. O'Sullivan writes:

> In that early period the main danger seemed to be that all authority would be destroyed as a result of individualistic doctrines which tended to present all moral, social, and political arrangements as a matter of personal taste or fancy. Confronted by the prospect of the destruction, in the name of liberty, of all authority, of law, of property, of personal security, and of liberty itself, conservatives followed Burke and threw their weight behind the defence of the state. In the present century, however, the situation has now changed dramatically, for liberalism has now been replaced by socialism as the principal threat to conservative values. The danger, as a result, no longer comes from an excess of individual liberty but from an excess of state power, for socialism has meant the constant encroachment of governments upon the lives of their subjects.[13]

The conservative response to this situation has taken at least two distinct forms. First, some conservative thinkers, like Leo Strauss (1899–1973), George Grant (1918–), and T. S. Eliot (1888–1965), have attempted to find an alternative to the modern order by appealing to an essentially spiritual set of values.

Eric Voegelin and The New Science of Politics

An example of such an approach can be found in Eric Voegelin's *The New Science of Politics*, first published in 1952. Written as an analysis of modernity in general, Voegelin's *The New Science of Politics* was, nonetheless, provoked by the phenomenon of twentieth-century totalitarianism in particular. In short, Voegelin's pressing question was, how can one explain the fact that modern Europe produced two totalitarian regimes within twenty years of one another? Voegelin felt the answer would not be found through a simple analysis of election techniques or constitutional mechanics. Indeed for him totalitarianism in both its German and Russian forms was symptomatic of a deeper spiritual crisis which pervaded much of modern Western civilization. Voegelin called this spiritual crisis "gnosticism."

Although certain gnostic doctrines can be traced back throughout and even before Christianity, Voegelin is not concerned with particular gnostic teachings or principles *per se*. Rather the problem is with that specific form of consciousness which, in an effort to express its own self-

---

[13] O'Sullivan, *Conservatism*, p. 30.

understanding, typically constructs a gnostic system. For Voegelin, therefore, the spiritual crisis of the modern age is fundamentally a crisis in consciousness. Failing to understand their own human nature, modern individuals have, as a consequence, attempted to construct an essentially inhuman environment.

In his four-volume study *Order and History* Voegelin analyzed the development of Western self-understanding. Beginning with an examination of Homeric mythology and proceeding to an analysis of Jewish theology and Greek philosophy, Voegelin traced Western humanity's increasing awareness of its fundamental relationship to a transcendental source of order. It was as if Western thinkers discovered that their human nature existed only in its relationship to the divine. Thus, for example, in Christianity humanity saw itself as both proceeding from and ultimately returning to a transcendent god. Yet, inasmuch as the Christian God was a truly transcendent one, humans could never possess it fully in the here and now. Given this, Voegelin argued that the human experience of transcendence is essentially a faith encounter and, as such, is both insecure and uncertain.

According to Voegelin's reading of Greek philosophy and the Judeo-Christian tradition, this insight that humanity both yearns for and yet cannot possess the divine is the very realization which constitutes the correctly ordered form of human consciousness. Accordingly, the human being understands itself as both a material and a spiritual being. Yearning for the spiritually transcendent, it cannot, as a consequence, be totally satisfied with the goods of the material world. Yet, at the same time, being a material creature the human being is also incapable of fully participating in that transcendent good toward which it is drawn. In truth, then, to be fully human is to live an existence which is, in fact, between the spheres of material and spiritual being. As such, humanity is fundamentally estranged. It belongs neither simply to the world nor simply to the transcendent. It is neither animal nor god.

For the correctly ordered consciousness this realization of estrangement constitutes the unique and therefore definitive quality of our human nature. Yet, for those who cannot tolerate the uncertainty and tension which such an estrangement implies, this situation must be overcome. For Voegelin the inability to live within the limits of the human situation characterizes the gnostic mentality, and as such it is a sign of spiritual weakness. The gnostic rebels against the essential structure of human nature itself, and does so in an effort to escape the very tensions and strains which define our humanity. The essential technique for such a rebellion is to invest mundane reality with a divine or absolute quality. By acting as if the world had become sacred gnostics are able to acquire once and for all the source of order which they previously lacked. In effect, according to Voegelin, security and certitude are gained at the cost of our humanity:

On this point there is no doubt. They achieved a certainty about the meaning of history, and about their own place in it, which otherwise they would not have had. Certainties, now, are in demand for the purpose of overcoming uncertainties with their accompaniment of anxiety, and the next question then would be: What specific uncertainty was so disturbing that it had to be overcome by the dubious means of fallacious immanentization? One does not have to look far afield for an answer. Uncertainty is the very essence of Christianity. The feeling of security in a "world full of gods" is lost with the gods themselves; when the world is dedivinized, communication with the world-transcendent God is reduced to the tenuous bond of faith, in the sense of Heb. 11:1; as the substance of things hoped for and the proof of things unseen. Ontologically, the substance of things hoped for is nowhere to be found but in faith itself; and epistemologically, there is no proof for things unseen but again this very faith.[14]

The immediate consequences of treating the world as an absolute is to divinize the doing of politics. Inasmuch as mundane reality is treated as if it were the only sphere of being, politics, as that activity by which the world is organized, assumes a paramount importance. With the collapse of the transcendent into the world there is no longer a higher order to which one can appeal in an effort to resist the claims of the state. As a result, politics assumes a "totalistic" character. Loyalty to the state replaces fealty to God, and the obligations of citizenship become the highest demands facing the state's members. From within their perspective, then, the gnostics are charged with remaking the world so that it eventually exhibits that true and final order which is its appropriate form. According to Voegelin, therefore, the gnostics actually are seeking a form of heaven on earth by attempting to achieve salvation within history. The tensions, uncertainty, and anxiety which arise from the in-between quality of natural human existence are to be resolved once and for all through political and historical action. The fact that such a "resolution" is contrary to human nature and thus impossible to achieve establishes for Voegelin both the irony and ultimate tragedy of the gnostic experiment.

Central to Voegelin's analysis is his insistence that the gnostic mentality is operative within many of the major political movements of the day. Thus he finds evidence of gnosticism within totalitarianism, fascism, Marxism, liberalism, progressivism, and scientism. In each case, according to Voegelin, there is a tendency to absolutize that which is truly immanent and thereby detract from the bipolar quality of human nature. The only effective response in such a situation is essentially a spiritual one. Inasmuch as

[14] Voegelin, *The New Science of Politics*, p. 122.

gnosticism arises because of human beings' inability to maintain a position of openness towards the divine, the task is essentially one of acquiring that spiritual strength which is necessary if one is to accept the anxiety and tensions of human existence. For Voegelin, such a task is precisely the goal of philosophy, and the political future of humanity depends upon whether the life of philosophy can actually become a dominant force within the contemporary world.

Milton Friedman and Capitalism and Freedom

The second form of conservative response to the rise of the modern order is much less ambitious and perhaps also less consistent. Rather than attempting to provoke a form of spiritual renewal throughout the West, such conservative thinkers as Milton Friedman (1912–), Wilhelm Roepke (1899–1966), and F. A. Hayek (1899–) seek to restrict unwanted state influence by adopting certain techniques which were originally proposed by nineteenth-century *laissez-faire* liberals. For example, this school of twentieth-century conservatism favors the relatively unrestricted operation of the free market. Thus it opposes many of the practices of the modern welfare state and seeks to reduce government planning to an essential minimum.

An example of this approach is found in Milton Friedman's *Capitalism and Freedom*, published in 1962. Friedman's argument is essentially a defense of the private-enterprise/free-market system. According to Friedman such a system (or as he terms it "competitive capitalism") not only establishes a realm of economic freedom but at the same time serves as the necessary condition for political liberty. In effect, then, Friedman justifies the operations of the capitalist system in strictly instrumental terms. Capitalism is a necessary means for securing the ultimate political value of freedom:

> The fact that . . . arguments against the so-called capitalist ethic are invalid does not of course demonstrate that the capitalist ethic is an acceptable one. I find it difficult to justify either accepting or rejecting it, or to justify any alternative principle. I am led to the view that it cannot in and of itself be regarded as an ethical principle; that it must be regarded as instrumental or a corollary of some other principle such as freedom.[15]

Friedman's advocacy of freedom as the ultimate political goal and of the individual as the ultimate entity in society follows from his rejection of such alternative political goals as the pursuit of the common good or the

---

[15] Milton Friedman, *Capitalism & Freedom* (Chicago: University of Chicago Press, 1962), pp. 164–65.

search for equality. Thus for Friedman while each person has an equal right to be free, those policies which attempt to promote either material equality or an equality of outcome as distinct from an equality of opportunity inevitably come into conflict with individual freedom and thus must be opposed. Similarly, although there may be a consensus among the various purposes which the citizens of a society severally serve, there can be no independent national purpose or common good, other than freedom itself, which would demand the subordination of individuals to the interest of the state. In short, the common good of society is simply the sum of the individual goods of its citizens. The idea that there may be a common good which transcends the wishes of a society's constituent members is, for Friedman, a direct threat to individual liberty.

In his analysis of the U.S. political tradition Friedman claims to have discovered the two essential principles by which a society dedicated to freedom must be structured. First, the scope of government must be limited; second, governmental power must be dispersed. To a certain extent these goals can be achieved by the design of a society's political constitution. Yet the best (and for Friedman, the indispensable) means for achieving the desired order is the establishment of a free economic market. Ideally in capitalism economic coordination is achieved through the voluntary cooperation of individuals. Thus by allowing the market to operate extensively capitalism not only separates economic from political power but at the same time limits the scope within which political coercion is permissible. According to Friedman the government still must set and enforce the rules, but it no longer needs to actively serve as an agent of social cooperation:

> The existence of a free market does not of course eliminate the need for government. On the contrary, government is essential both as a forum for determining the "rules of the game" and as an umpire to interpret and enforce the rules decided on. What the market does is to reduce greatly the range of issues that must be decided through political means, and thereby to minimize the extent to which government need participate directly in the game.[16]

It is apparent that the school of modern conservatism represented by such thinkers as Milton Friedman shares many of the essential elements of classical *laissez-faire* liberalism. Its emphasis upon freedom, its concern for the individual, and its distrust of state power are features which many classical liberals placed at the center of their teachings. There is, however, one important difference which should not be overlooked. Classical liberalism was often based upon the progressivist assumption of human per-

[16] Friedman, *Capitalism & Freedom*, p. 15.

fectability, but twentieth-century conservatives such as Friedman take as a given the fact of human imperfection. Thus rather than advocating a policy of individualism as the necessary means for unleashing the creative powers which will move humankind ahead, modern conservatism uses it as a tool for minimizing the negative effects of human error. It remains, therefore, essentially a philosophy of limitation and restraint.

WESTERN MARXISM

Central to all of Marx's writings was his insistence upon the necessary and insoluble relationship between theory and practice. As a consequence, he not only argued that the purpose of philosophy was to change the world but also that its very ability to do so actually constituted the proof of its theoretical worth. For example, in 1845 he wrote:

> The question whether human thinking can reach objective truth— is not a question of theory but a practical question. In practice man must prove the truth, that is, actuality and power, this-sidedness of his thinking. The dispute about the actuality or nonactuality of thinking—thinking isolated from practice—is a purely *scholastic* question.[17]

Given this argument, it is not surprising that many of the early Marxists were essentially political activists. Although such individuals as Lenin (1870–1923), Rosa Luxemburg (1871–1919), Leon Trotsky (1879–1940), and Otto Bauer (1881–1938) wrote important theoretical works, all understood themselves primarily in political and practical terms. As Marxists, they were essentially revolutionaries; they wrote to develop strategic and tactical policies which were suitable for their specific situations. In particular, the Marxist writers of this period were interested in analyzing the development of both monopoly capitalism and international imperialism. For many, it appeared as if capitalism were moving into a new stage of historical development and, as activists, it was essential for them to comprehend those laws which would determine the character of the emerging order. Similarly, as capitalism evolved, it also became apparent to this generation of Marxists that their movement was in need of a systematic political theory. The future proletarian revolution would require an explicit strategy, and neither Marx nor Engels had developed one. Thus as intellectuals they discovered that their agenda was already set by the revolutionary possibilities of the day, and they responded accordingly.

[17] Loyd Easton & Kurt Guddat, eds., *Writings of the Young Marx on Philosophy and Society* (Garden City: Doubleday, Inc., 1967), p. 401.

With the advent of the Second World War and the subsequent dissolution of the Third International, or the Comintern, in 1943, and with the
emergence of Stalin in the Soviet Union and his attempt to force a concern
for Russian national interests upon all Marxist movements, the situation
confronting European Marxists changed dramatically. On one hand, the
major Western parliamentary democracies had entered into a period of
relative stability and growth. Yet on the other, it appeared as if the oppres-
sive bureaucracies of the Soviet Union and Eastern Europe were incapable
of initiating the necessary structural changes that the new times required.
The result was a new political and economic environment, which, in turn,
produced a new type of Marxist theory. Observing this change, the historian Perry Anderson has written:

> It was in this altered universe that revolutionary theory completed
> the mutation which produced what can today retrospectively be
> called "Western Marxism." For the body of work . . . constituted
> an entirely new intellectual configuration within the development
> of historical materialism. In their hands Marxism became a type of
> theory in certain respects quite distinct from anything that had pre-
> ceded it. In particular the characteristic themes and concerns of the
> whole ensemble of theorists who came to political maturity before
> the First World War were drastically displaced, in a shift that was
> at once generational and geographical.[18]

Among the thematic shifts which Anderson notes are the following.
First and most important was the fact that contemporary Western Marxist
theory has become increasingly divorced from the concerns and issues of
political practice. In many cases Western Communist parties have adopted
a rigid and dogmatic orthodoxy which has tended to discourage theoretical
experimentation among their members. In addition, the Soviet Union in its
effort to export the "Russian model" of communism has imposed an external
discipline upon internal party developments. Indeed, recent efforts by the
European Communist parties to work out their own form of Eurocommunism as an alternative to traditional Marxism-Leninism have been carefully watched and resisted by the Soviet authorities. At the same time, many
of the European intellectuals on the Left have become affiliated with
academic or other nonpolitical institutions. As professional philosophers
rather than activists, their theoretical work has evolved essentially outside
of the structures of the organized party and reflects, therefore, a wider
range of interests. This separation of theory and practice parallels Western
Marxism's increasing interest in cultural themes. Whereas earlier Marxists

---

[18] Perry Anderson, *Considerations on Western Marxism* (London: New Left Books, 1976),
p. 25.

tended to disregard cultural issues in order to concentrate upon the development of political and economic strategies, today they are paying increasing attention to what was at one time regarded as mere superstructure. With this shift there has emerged a concern for themes which are only peripherally related to the original Marxist program. For example, aesthetic theory and literary criticism became significant issues in the work of such Marxists as Georg Lukacs (1885–1971), Theodor Adorno (1903–1969), and Lucien Goldman (1913–1970). Similarly, other Marxists such as Herbert Marcuse (1898–1979) and Louis Althusser (1918–) attempted to incorporate some of the teachings of Freudian psychoanalysis in an effort to supplement Marx's somewhat mechanistic view of human nature. Finally, the theme of humanity's relationship to nature—and thus the related issue of modern science and technology—assumed major importance in the works of such writers as Max Horkheimer (1895–1973) and Jurgen Habermas (1929–).

Herbert Marcuse and One-Dimensional Man

A specific example of the new directions in which contemporary Marxism has moved may be found through an examination of Herbert Marcuse's *One-Dimensional Man*, which was first published in 1964. Marcuse's work, in general, is considered to fall within what is known as "critical theory." That term was first applied to the work of a group of theorists who were associated with the Institute of Social Research, which was founded at Frankfurt, Germany, in 1923. Among its most widely known members were Max Horkheimer, Theodor Adorno, and Herbert Marcuse. As diverse as they were, the members of the "Frankfurt School" nonetheless were motivated by their common abhorrence of totalitarianism, especially in its German fascist form, and by their fear that the cult of technology was producing a form of society that was essentially indifferent to human values and needs. Although the institute's program did not explicitly identify with any particular political movement, its members did adopt Marxism as a starting-point for much of their analysis. Their form of Marxism, however, was not of the strictly orthodox type. On the contrary, the critical theorists were particularly influenced by the work of Georg Lukacs and Karl Korsch (1889–1961). These writers both had been critical of the official determinist, or positivist, interpretation of historical materialism, and they had emphasized as a corrective the importance of human subjectivity and consciousness. In addition to Lukacs and Korsch, the critical theorists also borrowed freely from such non-Marxist sources as Hegel, Kant, Nietzsche, and Freud.

Although the Frankfurt school admitted that it had no particular utopia to offer, it did, nonetheless, insist upon the total and revolutionary transformation of society. Yet, unlike traditional Marxists, it did not look to the proletariat in order to accomplish this aim. Not only did the proletariat appear to lack the necessary revolutionary consciousness, but, more importantly, the fundamental problem of alienation affected all groups within society and thus required a truly universal solution. In part, such a solution would entail an effort to save culture, and especially art, from the degrading influences generated by a mass society under the control of an irresponsive bureaucracy.

Born in Berlin in 1898, Marcuse received his doctorate under Martin Heidegger at Freiburg after submitting his dissertation on Hegel. He joined the Institute of Social Research in the early 1930s but emigrated first to Switzerland and then to the United States when Hitler came to power. After serving with the U.S. Office of Strategic Services during World War II, Marcuse returned to full-time teaching and spent the rest of his life as an American academic. Among his most important books are *Reason and Revolution* (1941), *Eros and Civilization* (1955), *Soviet Marxism* (1958), and *One-Dimensional Man* (1964).

Marcuse is perhaps best known for his effort to blend the teachings of Marx and Freud into a coherent political doctrine. Borrowing from Marx the Hegelian argument that history is the story of humanity's progress to freedom, Marcuse added what he believed to be the Freudian suggestion that a complete understanding of the human good also includes an appreciation of the role of pleasure. Thus, for Marcuse, full human liberation requires, not ony that humanity be freed from the impersonal control of the market, but also that human sexuality be freed from the psychological domination of false renunciation and unnecessary repression. In his *An Essay on Liberation*, Marcuse wrote:

> The construction of a free society would create new incentives for work. In the exploitive societies, the so-called work instinct is mainly the (more or less effectively) introjected necessity to perform productively in order to earn a living. But the life instincts themselves strive for the unification and enhancement of life; in nonrepressive sublimation they would provide the libidinal energy for work on the development of a reality which no longer demands the exploitive repression of the Pleasure Principle . . . Freud's last theoretical conception recognizes the erotic instincts as work instincts—work for the creation of a sensuous environment.[19]

Marcuse's most widely read book, *One-Dimensional Man*, was at the same time the one which was the least explicitly Marxist in tone. Reverting to his earlier studies in Hegel, Marcuse adopted an essentially Idealistic understanding of reason which pictured philosophy as providing those transcendental norms of rationality against which the actual world is to be

---

[19] Herbert Marcuse, *An Essay on Liberation* (Boston: Beacon Press, 1969), p. 91.

judged. In short, reason is to provide a negative or critical principle which would allow us to distinguish between the essence of such things as justice, beauty, or goodness and those particulars in which they are actualized at a given moment. If such a critical principle is absent, humanity is threatened with becoming totally absorbed into the status quo and thus eventually becoming incapable of either resisting its demands or improving its arrangements. For Marcuse, then, negative or critical thinking is the source of social creativity, and with its disappearance the possibility of human liberation and individual development is destroyed. This, in turn, is precisely the situation he claimed to have discovered within modern technological society in both its capitalist and communist forms:

> And yet this society is irrational as a whole. Its productivity is destructive of the free development of human needs and faculties, its peace maintained by the constant threat of war, its growth dependent upon the repression of the real possibilities for pacifying the struggle for existence—individual, national, and international . . . . The capabilities (intellectual and material) of contemporary society are immeasurably greater than ever before—which means that the scope of society's domination over the individual is immeasurably greater than ever before. Our society distinguishes itself by conquering the centrifugal social forces with technology rather than Terror, on the dual basis of an overwhelming efficiency and an increasing standard of living.[20]

According to Marcuse's analysis, modern industrial society is characterized by its unique ability to resist change. Locked into the status quo, the political order is capable of thwarting all efforts to bring about fundamental improvements. Thus, rather than being attracted to the opportunities which are represented by a second dimension of alternative possibilities, contemporary society, according to Marcuse, is purely one-dimensional. It has, as a result, lost that fundamental ability to contrast the world as it is with the true world as it is revealed in the normative concepts of critical theory. Without such a contrast there is no reason to change, and without the possibility of change humanity is trapped within the present structures of domination and repression.

Marcuse attempted to illustrate this point by examining the realms of art, language, philosophy, logic, and science. In each case, he found a similar situation. For example, whereas at one time art functioned essentially as an expression of artists' alienation from and dissatisfaction with their world, today, according to Marcuse, it has become a form of enter-

---

[20] Herbert Marcuse, *One-Dimensional Man: Studies in the Ideology of Advanced Industrial Society* (Boston: Beacon Press, 1964), pp. ix–x.

tainment and thus actually reflects and reinforces rather than questions the present situation. In Marcuse's own words:

> Now this essential gap between the arts and the order of the day, kept open in artistic alienation, is progressively closed by the advancing technological society. And with its closing . . . the "other dimension" is absorbed into the prevailing state of affairs. . . . The intent and function of these works have thus fundamentally changed. If they once stood in contradiction to the status quo, this contradiction is now flattened out.[21]

According to Marcuse, this one-dimensional quality pervades all of contemporary culture. It is, therefore, as if the status quo has become capable of absorbing and, thereby, perverting all attempts to maintain some degree of critical distance from the present. This situation finds its purest political expression in the present-day condition of the workers. Typically, Marxists have argued that the disenfranchised proletarian class is the inevitable source for radical political change. Today, however, according to Marcuse, the workers have been absorbed into the status quo and, therefore, can no longer be expected to play a radical role. For example, in the West industrial technology and the high productivity which it has made possible have fundamentally transformed the work situation. Mechanization has removed many of the most repulsive features of manual labor; structural mobility has broken down the traditionally sharp class divisions; and the mass media have succeeded in destroying the remains of a thriving workers' culture. Indeed, according to Marcuse, in both the Western and Eastern blocs the workers have actually become a conservative force, while those in the Third World are moving in a similar direction.

The overall tone of Marcuse's assessment is strikingly pessimistic. Yet, if a revolution were to occur, what would be his preferred outcome? Although vague, several features are apparent. First, the postrevolutionary society would be more than simply a new type of institutional organization. It would instead produce nothing less than a new form of human individual, or in Marcuse's terms "a new historical subject." This new historical subject would be freed from want by the power of a reformed technology and thus, most importantly, would be free for meaningful self-determination. Second, with the dismantling of the market system this new historical subject would be released from previous enslavement to false needs and thereby allowed to pursue the true and vital needs. Finally, the new historical subject would be truly autonomous. Freed from both indoctrination and manipulation, Marcuse's new individual would be first and most of all true to himself/herself.

[21] Marcuse, *One-Dimensional Man*, p. 64.

The vision which Marcuse has offered has enjoyed a certain influence in America, France, and Germany throughout the 1960s and 1970s. Yet, as with other examples of contemporary Western Marxist theory, one may question its relationship to the tradition of orthodox Marxism itself. Is it a further development or a fundamental denial of the spirit of Marx's original work? On this point, Leszek Kolakowski writes:

> What he offers is Marxism without the proletariat (irrevocably corrupted by the welfare state), without history (as the vision of the future is not derived from a study of historical changes but from an intuition of true human nature), and without the cult of science; a Marxism, furthermore, in which the value of liberated society resides in pleasure and not in creative work. All this is a pale and distorted reflection of the original Marxist message.[22]

BIBLIOGRAPHY

ANDERSON, PERRY. *Considerations on Western Marxism.* London: New Left Books, 1976.

BARRETT, WILLIAM. *Irrational Man: A Study in Existential Philosophy.* Garden City: Doubleday, 1962.

BREINES, PAUL, ed. *Critical Interruptions: New Left Perspectives on Herbert Marcuse.* New York: Herder & Herder, 1972.

GOLDWIN, ROBERT A., ed. *Left, Right and Center.* Chicago: Rand McNally, 1963.

GRENE, MARJORIE. *Introduction to Existentialism.* Chicago: University of Chicago Press, 1959.

HEINEMANN, F. H. *Existentialism and the Modern Predicament.* Second edition. New York: Harper & Row, 1958.

HELD, DAVID. *Introduction to Critical Theory: Horkheimer to Habermas.* Berkeley: University of California Press, 1980.

HOWARD, DICK, and KARL KLARE, eds. *The Unknown Dimension: European Marxism Since Lenin.* New York: Basic Books, 1972.

MACINTYRE, ALASDAIR. *Herbert Marcuse: An Exposition and A Polemic.* New York: Viking Press, 1970.

MACQUARRIE, JOHN. *Existentialism.* Baltimore: Penguin Books, 1973.

NISBET, ROBERT A. *The Quest for Community.* New York: Oxford University Press, 1953.

OAKESHOTT, MICHAEL. *Rationalism in Politics and Other Essays.* New York: Basic Books, 1962.

O'SULLIVAN, NÖEL K. *Conservatism.* New York: St. Martin's Press, 1976.

WALLRAFF, CHARLES F. *Karl Jaspers: An Introduction to His Philosophy.* Princeton: Princeton University Press, 1970.

---

[22] Leszek Kolakowski, *Main Currents of Marxism: The Breakdown,* trans. P. S. Falla (New York: Oxford University Press, 1978), p. 415.

INDEX